THE EATINGWELL™ DIABETES COOKBOOK

© Copyright 2005 by Eating Well, Inc., publisher of
EATINGWELL, The Magazine of Food & Health™
823A Ferry Road, P.O. Box 1010, Charlotte, VT 05445
www.eatingwell.com

First paperback edition, 2007
ISBN 978-0-88150-778-2

The Library of Congress has cataloged the hardcover edition as follows:

The EatingWell diabetes cookbook : 275 delicious recipes and 100+ tips
for simple, everyday carbohydrate control / Joyce Hendley & the editors
of EatingWell; foreword by Marion J. Franz.
   p. cm.
  Includes index.
  ISBN 0-88150-633-8 (alk. paper)
  1. Diabetes—Diet therapy—Recipes.
  I. Title: EatingWell diabetes cookbook. II. Hendley, Joyce, 1960–
  RC662.E256 2005
  641.5'6314—dc22
                   2005042003

Editorial Director: James M. Lawrence
Writer & Editor: Joyce Hendley **Recipe Editor:** Patsy Jamieson

Nutrition Consultants: Marion Franz, M.S, R.D, C.D.E; Sylvia Geiger, M.S., R.D.
Production Director: Alice Z. Lawrence **Managing Editor:** Wendy S. Ruopp
Recipe Analysis & Editorial Support: Alesia Depot
Contributing Editors: The EATINGWELL Staff **Contributing Writer & Editor:** Lee Ann Cox
Test Kitchen: Jim Romanoff, Stacy Fraser, Jessica Price, Katie Webster
Research Editor: Anne C. Treadwell **Proofreader:** David Grist

Designer: Susan McClellan **Photographer:** Ken Burris

Published by
The Countryman Press, P.O. Box 748, Woodstock, Vermont 05091

Distributed by
W.W. Norton & Company, Inc., 500 Fifth Avenue, New York, New York 10110

PRINTED IN THE UNITED STATES OF AMERICA

10 9 8 7 6 5 4 3

The EatingWell™ DIABETES COOKBOOK

275 DELICIOUS RECIPES AND 100+ TIPS FOR SIMPLE, EVERYDAY CARBOHYDRATE CONTROL

Joyce Hendley & the Editors of EatingWell

Foreword by Marion J. Franz, M.S., R.D., C.D.E.

THE COUNTRYMAN PRESS

WOODSTOCK, VERMONT

Dedicated to the memory of Elizabeth Hiser, M.S., R.D.,
Founding Nutrition Editor of EATINGWELL MAGAZINE,
and this book's guiding light.
—J.H.

Joyce Hendley, M.S., is EATINGWELL's nutrition editor and co-author of *The EatingWell Diet* (2007). A former food editor at *Weight Watchers* magazine, she wrote Sarah Ferguson's best-selling *Win the Weight Game* (2000). Joyce also co-wrote *Forbidden Foods Diabetic Cooking* (2000, with Maggie Powers, R.D.), which won the National Health Information Award (Silver).

Marion J. Franz, M.S., R.D., C.D.E., former director of Nutrition and Health Professional Education at the International Diabetes Center in Minneapolis, Minnesota, is a nutrition/health consultant with Nutrition Concepts by Franz, Inc. Her books include *Exchanges for All Occasions* (2000) and *The ADA Guide to Medical Nutrition Therapy for Diabetics* (2003).

RECIPE GUIDELINES & NUTRIENT ANALYSES

Notes from the EATINGWELL *Editors*

The **PREP TIME** for each recipe is the amount of time it takes to prepare the ingredients before you start to cook; **START TO FINISH** includes the prep time plus any marinating, baking, chilling and so on that may be involved from when you start cooking to when you serve, unless otherwise noted.

PER SERVING: Each recipe is analyzed for calories, total fat, saturated (SAT) and monounsaturated (MONO) fat, cholesterol, carbohydrate, protein, fiber and sodium. We used Food Processor software (ESHA Research), version 8.4, for analyses.

When a recipe states a measure of salt "or to taste," we analyze the measured quantity. (Readers on sodium-restricted diets can reduce or eliminate the salt.) Butter is analyzed as unsalted. We do not include trimmings or marinade that is not absorbed. When alternative ingredients are listed, we analyze for the first one suggested. Optional ingredients and garnishes are not analyzed. Portion sizes noted are consistent with healthy-eating guidelines.

CARBOHYDRATE SERVINGS:
Each recipe is given a Carbohydrate Servings value based on the Carbohydrate-Servings Calculator method explained on page 15. These values are based on the given recipe's carbohydrate analysis, without the use of alternative low- or no-calorie sweeteners. If a sweetener alternative is suggested, a second analysis of calories and carbohydrate is given below the main analysis.

EXCHANGES:
Diabetic exchanges, calculated by a Registered Dietitian, are based on the current Diabetic Exchanges of the American Diabetes Association. For more information on diabetic exchanges, consult the Resources listed on page 321.

ICONS:
This icon highlights quick & easy recipes that are ready to eat in 45 minutes or less.

High ⬆ Fiber This icon indicates that the recipe provides 5 grams or more of fiber per serving. As explained on page 15, the carbohydrate count for such recipes can be reduced by the grams of fiber to yield the carbohydrate number that is used to determine Carbohydrate Servings.

OTHER EATINGWELL BOOKS (AVAILABLE AT EATINGWELL.COM):

The Essential EatingWell Cookbook (The Countryman Press, 2004)
ISBN-13: 978-0-88150-701-0 (softcover)

The EatingWell Healthy in a Hurry Cookbook (The Countryman Press, 2006)
ISBN-13: 978-0-88150-687-7 (hardcover)

EatingWell Serves 2 (The Countryman Press, 2006)
ISBN-13: 978-0-88150-723-2 (hardcover)

The EatingWell Diet (The Countryman Press, 2007)
ISBN-13: 978-0-88150-722-5 (hardcover)

Contents

The Power of Knowledge

If you, a family member or a friend has diabetes, you know there is a lot to learn about how to manage it successfully. You also know that lifestyle is important. Of course making healthy food choices and being physically active is a goal for everyone, but this is especially true for individuals who have diabetes. But sometimes you read and receive conflicting advice about where and how to start making changes. As a decades-long Certified Diabetes Educator and Registered Dietitian, I have found there are three major questions that people with diabetes want answered:

> **"** Enjoy the recipes and tips in this book and use them as the basis for a healthy lifestyle and successful diabetes management or prevention. This is the way *everyone* should be eating! **"**

> ➤ What is healthy eating for people with diabetes?
> ➤ How does healthy eating integrate into diabetes management?
> ➤ How do I know if the lifestyle changes I make are helpful?

Healthy Eating for Diabetes

Basic to either the management or prevention of diabetes is optimal nutrition through healthy food choices and an active lifestyle. Although studies often focus on the role of a single nutrient, such as carbohydrate or fat, emerging research shows that no one nutrient, food or food group by itself has priority over any other. Instead it is *the pattern of eating* that is important. This means that a healthy diet includes a mixture of foods containing multiple nutrients. Although a low-carbohydrate diet is often promoted as a popular approach to managing diabetes, research actually supports the importance of eating healthy carbohydrate-containing foods, such as whole grains, fruits, vegetables and low-fat milk. A healthy diet also includes low-fat protein sources, such as fish, poultry, lean meats or vegetable proteins. Healthy fats are also advised: monounsaturated and polyunsaturated fats, such as olive or canola oil, and nuts, such as walnuts or almonds, are good sources. A low-to moderate-fat diet, but low in saturated fats and food cholesterol, is recommended.

In general, a healthy diet includes five servings of fruits and vegetables, three servings of whole grains, two to four servings from the low-fat milk group, four to six ounces of lean meat or a meat substitute, and three to five servings of a healthy fat per day. The recipes in this book are based on a healthy eating pattern. Besides tasting delicious, they are the foundation for a lifetime of healthy eating for the entire family.

Integrating Healthy Eating into Diabetes Management

The two major types of diabetes, type 1 and type 2, have different priorities for nutrition therapy. In people with type 1 diabetes, the beta cells of the pancreas no longer produce insulin, so these people must take insulin by injection or insulin pump for survival. An insulin program can usually be developed that will match an individual's preferred food choices and meal routine. By learning carbohydrate counting (explained on pages 14-16), individuals can learn to adjust their insulin doses based on what they plan to eat.

The majority of people with diabetes, however, have type 2 diabetes. There are two problems in type 2 diabetes: insulin resistance and insulin deficiency as a result of beta-cell failure. As long as the beta cells can release enough insulin to overcome insulin resistance, blood-glucose levels remain normal. But over time there is a progressive decline in beta-cell function, resulting in above-normal blood-glucose levels. Because of this natural failure of beta cells, therapy must change also. While many individuals can initially manage their diabetes well with a food and activity program, eventually they will need to combine their program with oral medications and insulin. This does *not* mean that they or the "diet" has failed. Rather it means the beta cells of the pancreas are failing.

The first nutrition priority for either type of diabetes is to normalize glucose levels, but of equal concern are optimal lipid (cholesterol and triglyceride) levels and blood pressure goals (*see box*).

Making appropriate food choices contributes to meeting these goals. The recipes in this book are an excellent starting point. Physical activity is also of importance. The goal is to achieve 30 minutes a day of added physical activity or 150 minutes a week. Many individuals start with 5 to 10 minutes at one time and gradually increase to the goal.

Measuring Success

Blood-glucose monitoring is used to evaluate the effectiveness of lifestyle changes. People with type 1 diabetes may check their blood glucose four to eight times a day, usually before meals and at bedtime. People with type 2 diabetes may check their blood glucose less often. Good times to check are first thing in the morning and before and after the largest meal of the day. Hemoglobin A1c—a measure of long-term glucose control—should also be checked on a regular basis. Your health-care provider will generally do this at every office visit.

AMERICAN DIABETES ASSOCIATION GOALS FOR ADULTS WITH DIABETES

GLYCEMIC CONTROL	
Hemoglobin A1c	<7%
Glucose before meals	90-130 mg/dl
Glucose after meals	<180 mg/dl
Blood pressure	<130/80 mmHg

LIPIDS	
Total cholesterol	<200 mg/dl
LDL cholesterol	<100 mg/dl
Triglycerides	<150 mg/dl
HDL cholesterol	
women	>50 mg/dl
men	>40 mg/dl

Preventing Diabetes

The good news is that diabetes can be prevented or delayed. Research studies have shown clearly that sustained, moderate weight losses of 5 to 7 percent of an individual's starting weight and accumulating 150 minutes per week of physical activity reduce risk. However, increased use of whole grains and reducing fat, especially saturated fat, may also improve insulin sensitivity and reduce the risk of diabetes, even without weight loss.

Bottom Line

Knowledge is important, but knowledge is not enough. It must lead to action. This book will help you translate knowledge into action. A lifetime of health is yours for the taking. Enjoy the recipes and tips in this book and use them as the basis for a healthy lifestyle and successful diabetes management or prevention. This is the way *everyone* should be eating!

—*Marion J. Franz, M.S., R.D., C.D.E*

EatingWell: It's Not Dieting

It's time to debunk, once and for all, the myth of the "diabetic diet." If you have diabetes, you don't have to eat special foods, and you don't have to be excluded from what "everyone else" is eating. The truth is, everyone else should be taking their cue from what's on *your* plate.

If you look at the most current and widely accepted eating guidelines, what's recommended for people with diabetes is virtually the same as what's recommended for the population at large. And, despite the sometimes cacophonous debate among nutrition experts about what constitutes a "healthy" diet, there are some core principles that just about everyone agrees on. Those principles apply just as much, if not more, in diabetes.

What do we know for sure? We know that eating well means:

- selecting a variety of foods in sensible portions
- considering no food either a magic bullet or a forbidden fruit
- choosing whole foods over processed ones as much as possible
- embracing plant foods like vegetables, fruits, beans and whole grains
- including low-fat dairy products, fish and shellfish, lean meats and poultry, with optional lean red meat and sweet treats in moderation
- relying on seasoning and cooking dishes with olive oil and the other "good fats" that make food tastier and more satisfying, while

> **"**Eating wisely and well can help you bring your diabetes under control, even as effectively as drugs.**"**

at the same time keeping a watchful eye on saturated fat and trans fat.

But most of all, eating well means eating with pleasure—in a relaxed and friendly environment whenever possible. As delicious as that way of eating sounds, it is also one of the most powerful weapons in our diabetes-fighting arsenal. Eating wisely and well can help you bring your diabetes under control, even as effectively as diabetes drugs. That's why eating guidelines are an essential part—and occasionally, the only part—of any initial diabetes treatment plan.

This book is your ally in that healthy journey. In the first few pages, you'll find the essential information anyone involved with diabetes needs to know, including a few fundamentals about the disease and how it develops. There's an overview of how food choices can help manage diabetes, culling from the latest and most influential research findings. From understanding portion sizes to mastering the Carbohydrate Counting method, you'll have the foundation on which to build your own healthy eating strategy. Sample menu plans, starting on page 36, will help you get started.

Included in this book are tips and wisdom from people across the nation who are living with diabetes every day. Some have kindly shared their inspiring personal stories as well. And of course, at the heart of the book, there are delicious and satisfying recipes that answer the all-important question: "What can we eat?" Each one reflects the passion and expertise of the inventive team of cooks at EATINGWELL, the leading consumer magazine devoted to both cooking and nutrition. From hearty breakfasts and satisfying snacks to family dinners, portable lunches and glorious "no-deprivation" desserts, you'll find easy inspiration to take into the kitchen. Complete nutrition information accompanies each recipe so that it can easily fit into any eating plan, including carbohydrate and fiber counts, Carbohydrate Servings and Diabetes Exchanges.

None of the recipes are intended solely for the diabetes-conscious, however. These are dishes you can enjoy wholeheartedly with your friends and family, bring to potluck dinners and serve with confidence at holiday celebrations. These are the trustworthy recipes you'll turn to, time and again, with gusto. If you're a reader of EATINGWELL, you've always known you can expect nothing less from our kitchens.

So if you came to these pages expecting rules and special meals for a "diabetic diet," we're sorry—and delighted—to disappoint you. Enjoy every bite!

—*Joyce Hendley*

PROFILES IN REAL LIFE

COOKING UP A HEALTHIER LIFESTYLE

Dan M., New York

In his 17-year career as a professional chef, Dan was used to high pressure. Working seven-day weeks, and even 22-hour days, was par for the course—and he was known for his speedy knife skills. But when he was sidelined in 2000 with a workplace injury, the stresses began to mount. Unable to use his right arm (the one that had always held his knife), he wondered how he would provide for his wife and 1-year-old son; a year later, another son was born. In the meantime, he was diagnosed with Regional Stress Disorder, requiring several surgeries, including the insertion of a titanium rod in his right arm. "I was in a lot of pain and taking all kinds of medications," he remembers.

Throughout this stressful period, Dan turned to his one reliable source for comfort: food, in ample portions. "Fried foods, fast foods, and just big amounts of everything," he recalls. "I'd go to a restaurant and have three slices of pizza, then an order of wings." Soon, his weight rose to 235 pounds, on a 5-foot-8-inch frame.

Then, on New Year's Day 2002, Dan's wife announced she was filing for divorce. In February, he found out he had type 2 diabetes. That double-punch, however, turned out to be a turning point.

"It was my wake-up call," says Dan. "My diabetes was definitely triggered by the stress in my life, but I couldn't turn to food to help me anymore, because it was the problem. I had to embrace a healthier way of eating." Working with a dietitian, he began what he calls a "relearning" process. "I had to learn how to eat just until I was comfortable and satisfied, but not full. I learned I could eat things in moderation." And, though limited by his injuries in his ability to exercise, Dan also began regular workouts with an occupational therapist to restore his muscular and cardiovascular fitness. Today, he is closing in on his weight goal of 180 pounds and, at least for now, has been able to stop taking metformin.

Dan's outlook has changed, too. Instead of feeling frustrated that he can no longer do the lightning-fast slicing and dicing that used to be his trademark, he has refocused his creative energies on advising other chefs. "I help them create the highest-quality, healthier versions of their recipes," he explains. Whether he's grinding portobello mushrooms to give "meaty" richness to marinara sauce, or pureeing a microwaved apple to moisten a peerless banana bread, he summons his many years in restaurant kitchens as well as his experience as someone with diabetes.

Dan also relishes his role as custodial parent of his two young boys, who benefit from their dad's nutrition and culinary expertise. They're also learning a powerful life lesson from someone who didn't let diabetes stop him from doing the work he loves. "With diabetes, you're only limited by your imagination," says Dan. "You don't have to give up on your goals, you just have to take charge."

Diabetes 101: Essential Facts

To get an understanding of diabetes, it's helpful to know what happens when you eat, say, an apple. Through digestion, your body breaks down the apple into usable components that travel in your blood. One of these components is **glucose**, a form of sugar your body's cells need for fuel. But to get into most of your cells, glucose requires an escort: insulin, a hormone made in the pancreas. Think of insulin as the "key" that unlocks the door to your cells to allow glucose inside.

When all is well, beta cells in your pancreas make the correct amount of insulin whenever your blood-glucose level rises—usually after a meal—so that the glucose can get to where it's needed. But with diabetes, your body can't make enough insulin, or becomes less able to use the insulin you do make. The result? Glucose stays in the bloodstream rather than getting into the cells where it belongs, and the glucose level builds up in your blood. This condition is known as **hyperglycemia**, or high blood glucose.

> **"** Think of insulin as the 'key' that unlocks the door to your cells to allow glucose inside. **"**

A DIABETES GLOSSARY can be found on page 318.

The Immediate Effects

When there's too much glucose in your blood, your body tries to compensate by drawing fluid into the blood from the tissues to dilute the concentration. This loss of fluid can cause you to become dehydrated and to feel extremely thirsty—one of the hallmark symptoms of diabetes. You might also feel terribly hungry, as your body isn't able to get enough fuel from what it eats; unplanned weight loss is a frequent result.

The problems multiply when the glucose-rich blood reaches your kidneys, whose job it is to filter out waste products and produce urine. With a higher volume of blood—and so much glucose to process—the kidneys become overwhelmed and the excess glucose "spills out" into your urine. This series of events explains why diabetes can cause you to urinate more often, and why your urine will contain excess sugar. (The phenomenon of sweet urine, in fact, is what gives diabetes its full name, diabetes *mellitus*—Latin for "honey.")

All these symptoms are more pronounced if you have type 1 diabetes (often called "juvenile diabetes"), since the beta cells in your pancreas make little or no insulin. If you have type 2 diabetes (often called "adult-onset diabetes"), the symptoms may be more subtle, since you still have some insulin available—but that means diabetes is more likely to be causing problems without you being aware of them. That's why as many as one-third of people with diabetes may not even know they have it.

Longer-Term Effects

If diabetes isn't diagnosed and treated to bring blood-glucose levels under control, the long-term consequences can be serious indeed. Many of these problems are related to the body's circulation system, as glucose-heavy blood moves through blood vessels, damaging them. Most troubling is a significant increase in the risk of heart disease—already the country's number one killer—as well as a higher chance of developing high blood pressure or strokes. Other eventualities of uncontrolled diabetes include blindness, kidney disease, nerve damage and such poor circulation that limb amputation may be necessary.

These possibilities are frightening, but there are positive actions you can take. If you stay on top of your diabetes treatment plan to manage your blood glucose as well as your blood fat and blood-pressure levels, you can cut your risks of many complications—or even avoid them altogether. And, with today's many treatment options, that's a reasonable goal.

If you are following a weight-loss program, a small amount of ketones (*see box, above*) in your blood or urine might be okay, since your body is burning up some of its fat stores. Slightly elevated ketones may simply mean you've gone too long without eating something. But high blood glucose and high ketones are a warning sign that your diabetes isn't under good control. If not treated immediately with insulin, the ketone buildup can progress to a dangerous condition called **diabetic ketoacidosis**, and even diabetic coma. Your diabetes care plan should include guidelines for monitoring your ketones—either by testing your blood for ketones or by dipping a test strip into your urine.

What Causes Diabetes?

It's certainly true that you can inherit a tendency toward developing diabetes—that's one reason why it tends to run in families. Type 2 diabetes is also more common in people who belong to certain ethnic groups (*see "5 Risk Factors for Diabetes," page 12*). But genetics apparently aren't

> **TIPS FOR REAL LIFE**
>
> **ACETONE BREATH: A WARNING SIGN**
>
> Another problem that diabetes can cause comes from your body's inability to get glucose to the cells that need it. If it is deprived of its main fuel source, your body will launch into a backup plan: burning fat for energy. The breakdown products of the process, called ketones, can accumulate in your blood, and eventually in your urine. One type of ketone, called acetone, has a fruity smell; if you're making ketones, you'll likely have fruity "acetone breath." (Since acetone is a key ingredient in nail-polish remover, it might better be called "nail-polish-remover breath.")

the whole story, since many people who are predisposed to developing diabetes never do. And the incidence of type 2 diabetes, once considered a disease of adults, has climbed dramatically in the last 30 years among adults *and* children, even though our collective gene pool hasn't changed. Clearly, the environment in which we live plays a critical role—and that environment, experts say, has made it much easier to develop diabetes by making it all too easy to become overweight.

Call it the flip side of affluence: in recent decades food has become cheaper, more abundant and always within reach, while at the same time, computerization of our work and leisure time gives us fewer reasons to move our bodies. As a result, we're eating more, and moving less, than ever: at last count, Americans' average food intake had increased by about 150 calories per day, and around one in five adults reported getting little or no physical activity. At 3,500 calories per pound, these extra daily calories can result in a gain of 15 pounds per year! Many experts fault this so-called "obesigenic" environment for the finding that nearly two-thirds of American adults are now classified as overweight or obese.

Since both overweight and lack of exercise are

> **"Too much food and too little activity are pushing more and more people with the underlying tendency for type 2 diabetes over the edge."**
>
> —*EATING WELL Founding Nutrition Editor Elizabeth Hiser, M.S., R.D., in* The Other Diabetes, *2002*

Types of Diabetes

Type 1

Five to 10 percent of people with diabetes fall into this category, which used to be called "juvenile diabetes" because it is most often diagnosed before age 30. However, type 1 diabetes can occur at any age, even in the elderly. People with type 1 diabetes are unable to produce their own insulin, so they must take insulin daily in order to survive. Given in injections or through a pump, the insulin doses are timed to correspond with food intake, so an eating plan is an essential part of treatment.

Type 2

Type 2 diabetes—by far the most common kind, accounting for nine out of ten American cases—is caused by a combination of problems. It usually begins as body cells become **insulin resistant**— less able to process insulin's signals. But as long as the body can make enough insulin to overcome the resistance, blood-glucose levels remain normal. Eventually, however, the pancreas can't produce enough insulin to overcome this resistance, and the problem becomes a deficiency in insulin. Even though insulin levels may still be higher than normal, the amount just isn't enough to keep blood-glucose levels within a normal range. The longer a person has diabetes, the more likely it is that insufficient insulin is the cause of high blood-glucose levels.

When type 2 diabetes is first diagnosed, many people can control their glucose by making and maintaining changes in their eating and physical activity. But diabetes is a progressive disease; over time, lifestyle changes need to be combined with medications, such as diabetes pills—and, eventually for many, insulin. When some people with diabetes reach this point, they may blame themselves, or feel as if they've "failed." In fact, diabetes progression isn't anyone's fault, but rather the result of inheriting beta cells that fail over time. To keep the beta cells working longer, it's important to keep blood-glucose levels as normal as possible by whatever means necessary.

Gestational Diabetes

This form of diabetes affects about 7 percent of all pregnant women in the U.S. It usually develops during the last part of a pregnancy, when hormonal changes can increase the body's demand for insulin. It is generally treated with an eating plan and careful blood-glucose monitoring, to make sure both mother and infant are getting the nutrients they need. Most cases resolve once the baby is born, but women who have had gestational diabetes are at an increased risk of developing type 2 diabetes. Close to 40 percent of women who have had gestational diabetes eventually develop type 2 diabetes.

Prediabetes

Before people develop type 2 diabetes, they often have higher-than-normal blood-glucose levels, but not high enough for a diagnosis of diabetes. An estimated 41 million people fit this "prediabetes" category. They have attracted lots of attention from diabetes researchers, and not just because of their numbers. Studies show that people with prediabetes can cut their risk of progressing to full-blown diabetes by at least half. How? By making small lifestyle changes, such as exercising regularly and losing just 5 to 10 percent of their body weight (for a 150-pound person, that's 7½ to 15 pounds). In one study, such changes were more powerful in lowering diabetes risk than a widely used diabetes drug!

key risk factors for developing diabetes, it's not surprising that the prevalence of diabetes has grown alarmingly, along with the obesity rate. Both have become epidemics.

Bottom Line: It's a Way of Life

If lifestyles can pave the way to developing diabetes, they are also some of our best means for fighting back. For many people with diabetes, lifestyle changes make all the difference. Eating better and being more physically active can have major effects on your blood-glucose levels. The recipes and tips in this book will be invaluable supports in carrying out your plan. Staying on top of diabetes, then, is all about living well. By following healthy eating guidelines and making regular activity a part of your life, by taking medications or insulin as prescribed and by staying in touch with your diabetes care team, you are taking an active role in managing your diabetes, rather than letting it manage you.

PROFILES IN REAL LIFE

STAYING HEALTHY IS A FAMILY AFFAIR

Sharlyn and Dan P., Texas

When Dan was diagnosed three years ago with type 2 diabetes, he didn't need to be educated much about the disease. He was already something of an expert, since both parents and a sister also had type 2. More important, he'd long had an ideal role model of how to live with diabetes—his wife, Sharlyn, who has had type 1 since she was 18 years old. "Following Sharlyn's excellent lead makes it easier for me to follow my doctor's suggestions," says Dan.

While others might have felt as if lightning had struck twice, Dan and Sharlyn, who are both 51, have chosen to look at their dual diagnosis as a blessing of sorts—one that has made their relationship stronger. "We're using a team approach now to ensure we're taking good care of each other," says Dan.

Although they each take a different approach to diabetes management—Sharlyn uses an insulin pump and tracks her blood glucose several times daily with finger sticks, while Dan takes rosiglitazone—both keep a close eye on what they eat. "We eat 'normal' main dishes, casseroles, vegetables... anything that doesn't have a high concentration of sugar or fat," says Sharlyn. "We don't fry foods." And because Sharlyn needs to eat a consistent amount of calories each day to match her insulin, she avoids eating too much of anything. "We don't keep temptation foods like chocolate or French fries in the house," she explains. "That way, if we get the urge, we'll have to get in the car to get them." They've also made a commitment to regular exercise. Sharlyn walks in the mornings, and Dan at his lunch hour—then, after dinner, they take a walk together.

Having diabetes in their lives has had an impact on their two sons, now in their twenties. "I've had a few incidents when I've had to rely on others—usually Dan or the boys—to take care of me," Sharlyn recalls. "One Christmas Eve, they had to carry me downstairs in my pajamas and load me in the back of Dan's car to drive me to the hospital, because my blood sugar was too low to wake me up."

On the other hand, their kids have grown up with good eating and exercise habits that they might not have acquired had their household not been affected by diabetes. "Our boys will hopefully be able to take good care of themselves, so they can possibly avoid being diagnosed themselves," says Dan.

Looking back at her 30-plus years of living with diabetes, Sharlyn is philosophical. "No matter what advances in treatment have been made, some days are good, and some days aren't as good.... I have to pay attention to my treatment 24 hours a day. Sometimes I just want a vacation." She adds, "As strange as it may sound, I consider myself fortunate to have diabetes. It has forced me to eat well, exercise, and take responsibility for my health. I've learned that I'm a fighter. I've also learned that my family—especially Dan—will be right beside me every step of the way."

Food Matters: Eating to Manage Diabetes

We all eat to live (and, indeed, live to eat), but for someone with diabetes, that adage isn't just academic. It's a matter of staying well and living longer. Because diabetes is a disorder in how your body processes foods, every choice you make to eat or drink is important. The benefits of eating well are powerful, helping to keep your blood glucose, blood fats and blood-pressure levels under control and helping prevent complications of diabetes. Most of all, eating right helps you feel in control.

But that doesn't mean eating has to be like taking medicine. Eating is one of life's most fundamental pleasures, and it's part of our social fabric. Food plays a central role in family celebrations, holidays and business deals; special foods are part of the traditions that define us. Food shouldn't lose all that importance just because you have diabetes.

For the most part, eating to manage diabetes means eating with your eyes open—knowing what's going into your body and when. That means planning for, and keeping track of, your meals. Ideally, you'll work with a dietitian or diabetes educator to determine an eating plan that works with your schedule and your needs. You'll likely use one of two methods: Carbohydrate Counting or the Exchange System. The recipes in this cookbook

> **"**No matter which system you use to plan and track your eating, you'll be staying on top of the amount of carbohydrate you take in at each meal, trying to keep the amount consistent throughout the day, and from one day to the next.**"**

provide nutrition information that works with either system.

The Exchange System

Used in diabetes management for over 50 years, this method groups together foods that have roughly the same amounts of calories, carbohydrate, fat and protein into "Exchange" groups, so that one may be exchanged for another. One exchange in the "Starch" group, for instance, could be a 6-inch corn tortilla or ½ cup of green peas or ⅓ cup of pasta; an exchange in the "Lean Meats" group could be an ounce of tuna or lean pork. If you're following the Exchange System, you'll work with a dietitian to plan out your daily meal pattern: which exchanges to include in each meal and how many.

Carbohydrate Counting

For most people with diabetes, Carbohydrate Counting is a more flexible and simple alternative to the Exchange System. It centers on keeping a count of the carbohydrate you take in at each meal, aiming to stay within a predetermined daily range. Carbohydrate is measured in terms of Carbohydrate Servings (*see page 15*), or in grams.

No matter which system you use to plan and track your eating, you'll be staying on top of the amount of carbohydrate you consume, trying to keep it consistent throughout the day, and from one day to the next. That's because of all the nutrients we eat—protein, carbohydrate and fat—carbohydrate affects blood-glucose levels the most.

But that doesn't mean you must avoid carbohydrate altogether. That's nearly impossible—and dangerous. Even with diabetes, some carbohydrate is vital to maintain a steady supply of glucose to cells in the body, particularly to the brain, for fuel. The brain needs about 130 grams of glucose from carbohydrate each day (about 9 Carbohydrate Servings) to function well. And carbohydrate-containing foods are important sources of vitamins, minerals and fiber. Today's nutrition guidelines recognize that people with diabetes need a wide variety of foods to stay healthy, and most recommend that people get about half their daily calories from carbohydrate.

There are two different forms of carbohydrate—sugars and starches—but both are made up of the same building blocks: sugar molecules. What we call "sugars" are simply short chains of sugar molecules, while "starches" are longer chains of sugar molecules. When you eat a carbohydrate-containing food, no matter where it comes from, the process of digestion breaks down those sugar molecules into glucose—the form your body can use.

Carbohydrate is found chiefly in plant-based foods, such as grains, fruits and vegetables, and in sweets, as well as in dairy foods like milk and yogurt. These are the kinds of foods you'll be monitoring closely if you are Carbohydrate Counting.

Basics of Carbohydrate Counting

The goal of Carbohydrate Counting is to make sure you're eating a fairly consistent amount of carbohydrate each day, in a similar pattern. You can do this

TIPS FOR REAL LIFE
WHAT ABOUT SUGAR?

Not so long ago, people with diabetes were told they had to avoid eating sugar altogether. If they wanted treats, they could only have artificially sweetened "diet" foods that often didn't taste very good. Today's guidelines let sugar be counted just like any other carbohydrate, acknowledging that it is the total carbohydrate that usually matters most in a meal plan, not the source.

Keep in mind, though, that most foods containing sugar are usually low in other nutrients, so getting all your daily carbohydrate from, say, a can of regular soda or a brownie would be self-defeating. Moreover, most people with diabetes are watching their calories, and don't have many to squander on something that isn't going to give them any other nutritional "bang for the buck." Better to consider sweets an occasional treat rather than a daily staple—and that goes for everyone, whether or not they have diabetes.

(For information on low- and no-calorie sweeteners, see pages 18-19.)

CARBOHYDRATE-SERVINGS CALCULATOR

Use the ranges given below to convert a food's carbohydrate content to its equivalent in Carbohydrate Servings.

GRAMS (G) CARBOHYDRATE	CARBOHYDRATE SERVINGS
0-5	0
6-10	½
11-20	1
21-25	1½
26-35	2
36-40	2½
41-50	3
51-55	3½
56-65	4

NOTE: If a food contains 5 or more grams of dietary fiber per serving, subtract that number from the Total Carbohydrate grams. For example, a 38-gram carbohydrate portion with 5 grams of fiber would count as 38-5=33 grams. This would make it equivalent to 2 Carbohydrate Servings instead of 2½.

For the recipes in this cookbook, we have made these calculations for you.

WHAT ABOUT THE GLYCEMIC INDEX?

All the carbohydrate foods we eat cause a release of glucose into the bloodstream—and a corresponding rise in insulin—but some raise glucose more than others. The glycemic index is a system of ranking foods containing equal amounts of carbohydrate according to how much they raise blood-glucose levels. It can help you, at least theoretically, to choose foods that have a gentler effect on blood-glucose levels.

How? The glycemic index (GI) categorizes carbohydrate foods based on how much a food containing 50 grams of carbohydrate raises blood-glucose levels after eating. A food with a GI under 55 is considered low, while anything more than 70 is high. A similar tool is the glycemic load (GL), which considers both a food's GI and how much carbohydrate the food contains in a standard portion.

In general, most vegetables, whole grains, beans and other high-fiber foods are lower on the glycemic scale, while refined starches rank higher. But individual responses of blood glucose can vary, particularly in people with diabetes, and most of us don't eat foods in isolation, we eat combinations of different foods—and the other parts of a meal also influence the glycemic value.

Does paying attention to the glycemic scale help treat diabetes? The results from clinical studies haven't been consistent—some have shown modest benefits, others have shown no effect.

Bottom line? You don't need a number to tell you that whole grains, vegetables, beans and other high-fiber foods are great choices—and that processed and refined foods and sweets should be on the back burner.

hydrate Servings will be about 12 (for a 1,500 calorie/day plan) or 16 (for a 2,000 calorie/day plan).

With either system, you'll need to know the carbohydrate content of a food first. Your diabetes specialist can provide you with food lists to get you started. As you become more familiar with standard portions, you'll be able to estimate the carbohydrate of more complex foods, like pizza. Recipes with nutrition information, like those in this book, are a good source of carbohydrate amounts. On packaged foods, such information is on the nutrition label: First, check the food's "Serving Size," then look for the "Total Carbohydrate" value in grams. The "Dietary Fiber" listing is also important. The higher the better, as explained in the Carbohydrate-Servings Calculator box (*page 15*).

in either of the following ways:

Count Carbohydrate Grams. You aim for a specific amount of carbohydrate grams at each meal—say, 30 grams at breakfast, 45 grams at lunch and 60 grams at dinner. You track your carbohydrate through the day by keeping a running total.

Count Carbohydrate Servings. You track carbohydrate by thinking of it in terms of portions of foods. One Carbohydrate Serving, sometimes called a "Carbohydrate Choice," is a **portion of food that contains 15 grams of carbohydrate**—about the amount in a small potato, a slice of bread or a medium apple. You aim for a predetermined amount of Carbohydrate Servings at each meal, typically, 3 to 5 Carbohydrate Servings at main meals and 1 to 2 Carbohydrate Servings for snacks. For most people, the daily total number of Carbo-

Carbohydrate Bargains

Since you are following a carbohydrate "budget" of sorts, it makes sense to opt for the best quality you can get. **That means the bulk of your carbohydrates should come from so-called "good carbohydrates": fiber-rich and whole-grain foods.**

Whole-grain foods are made with all the original parts of the grain: the **bran** (the fiber-rich, protective outer coating), the **endosperm** (the starchy center, containing mostly carbohydrate and a little protein) and the **germ** (the vitamin- and mineral-rich seed core). That means they contain all the original nutrients, including fiber, B vitamins, vitamin E, zinc, iron and other protective phytochemicals. Good examples of whole-grain foods are whole-wheat flour, whole cornmeal, barley, whole-grain oats and brown rice.

But when these grains are processed, such as when wheat is ground and the bran is removed to make white flour, or when brown rice is hulled to make white rice, the result is pure endosperm—basically, just starch. Some of these so-called "refined" grains are enriched to add back some of their nutrients—white flour and white rice are enriched with B vitamins—but some nutrients, notably fiber, are not restored. And the phytochemicals are lost.

Studies show that people who eat more whole grains and fewer refined grains have lower risks of diabetes and heart disease; whole grains may even help people maintain a healthy weight. That's why in the latest edition of the Dietary Guidelines for Americans, the U.S. Department of Agriculture recommends all Americans get at least three daily servings of whole grains—preferably replacing the refined-grain foods they'd normally eat.

Trading Up to Whole Grains

- Seek out whole-grain versions of your favorite foods, such as whole-wheat pasta, whole-wheat bread, brown rice and whole-grain crackers. If you don't like one brand, experiment with another.
- Phase in a whole grain by mixing it half-and-half with a refined one—for example, a blend of whole-wheat and regular pasta, or brown and white rice. Gradually increase the proportions until your palate—and digestive tract—have adjusted.

- Expand your whole-grain pantry—how about bulgur (cracked, steamed and dried wheat kernels), whole-wheat couscous, quinoa or millet? A trip to a natural-foods store will inspire you.
- Start your day with whole-grain breakfast cereal or old-fashioned (not instant) oatmeal.

The Fiber Plus

Fiber is the part of plant foods that the body can't digest, and it's chiefly found in carbohydrate foods: whole grains, vegetables, beans, peas and whole fruits (rather than fruit juice).

Fiber, especially fiber from whole-grain cereals and bread, bran and the skins of fruits and vegetables, helps add bulk to digestive waste and keeps you "regular." Though it doesn't dissolve in water, fiber absorbs water as it moves through the digestive system, helping to push other substances along.

Fiber also has proven cholesterol-lowering benefits. Some fiber, especially fiber from oats, barley, fruits, vegetables, beans, seeds, nuts and brown rice,

Low- and No-Calorie Sweeteners:
An EATINGWELL Guide

The debates in the nutrition world about the value of low- and no-calorie sweeteners are often loud and raucous, but when the discussion turns to their role in diabetes, the conversations become much more harmonious. Let's face it, the availability of something that makes food taste sweet, without contributing carbohydrate grams, can sometimes make life with diabetes a little easier. That said, there are still some important issues to keep in mind.

Safety

Currently, the U.S. Food and Drug Administration (FDA) has approved four low- or no-calorie sweeteners as safe for use: aspartame (NutraSweet, Equal), acesulfame potassium (Sunett, Sweet One), saccharin (Sweet'n Low, SugarTwin and other brands) and sucralose (Splenda). To earn FDA approval, these sweeteners had to undergo rigorous testing and be shown safe when consumed by the general public—including people with diabetes. However, some organizations—notably, the nonprofit consumer-advocacy group Center for Science in the Public Interest (CSPI)—remain skeptical. Of the currently approved sweeteners, only sucralose earns CSPI's vote as safe.

Taste

Low-calorie sweeteners have no problem in the sweetness department; most are hundreds of times sweeter than regular sugar. But some people find they have an aftertaste, or that the foods prepared with them "just don't taste right." It's a matter of personal preference, of course; some people claim saccharin has a bitter aftertaste, for example, while others appreciate that it isn't tooth-achingly sweet. And low-calorie sweeteners tend to be an acquired taste; people who regularly use a particular sweetener sometimes become loyal to its flavor profile. In our own Test Kitchen, we found sucralose, which is derived from cane sugar, came closest to the taste of regular sugar, but still had its own aftertaste.

Performance

If you use a low-calorie sweetener just to perk up your iced tea, just about any one will do. But when you want to use it for something more complex, like a batch of muffins, performance can be a problem. Aspartame, for instance, breaks down when heated, so it's a no-go in baking. Other problems result from the one-dimensionality of low-calorie sweeteners compared to sugar: while they contribute only sweetness, sugar adds volume and texture, and, when heated, it caramelizes, adding complex toasty flavors as well as an appealing browned look. Recreating those properties without using sugar can be tricky.

Substituting with Splenda

In the EATINGWELL Test Kitchen, sucralose is the only alternative sweetener we test with when we feel the option is appropriate. For nonbaking recipes, we use Splenda Granular (boxed, not in a packet). For baking, we use Splenda Sugar Blend for Baking, a mix of sugar and sucralose. It can be substituted in recipes (½ cup of the blend for each 1 cup of sugar) to reduce sugar calories by half while maintaining some of the baking properties of sugar. If you make a similar blend with half sugar and half Splenda Granular, substitute this homemade mixture cup for cup.

When choosing any low- or no-calorie sweetener, be sure to check the label to make sure it is suitable for your intended use.

What About Stevia?

While stevia (stevioside), a natural sweetener extracted from the leaves of the stevia plant, has not been

> ### SUBSTITUTING?
> ### IT'S YOUR CHOICE
>
> The recipes for desserts and baked goods in this cookbook all have 3 carbohydrate servings or fewer when made with sugar. The nutrient analysis also provides revised totals for carbohydrate and calories, if you choose the suggested sweetener option.

approved by the FDA for use as a sweetener, it's widely available as a "dietary supplement" that makes no sweetening claims on its labels. Stevia is about 300 times sweeter than sugar, with a slight licorice flavor; some health-food aficionados seek it out as a "natural" alternative to manmade sweeteners.

The FDA hasn't given stevia the green light because of questions about its safety. There's a reason for setting the bar high: while the herb has been used safely for centuries in Paraguay, and since the 1970s in Japan, it's likely to be used much more liberally in the soft-drink-and-sweet-treat-loving United States. If you choose to use stevia, use it the way the Japanese and Paraguayans do, only in small amounts—say, to sweeten your coffee.

What About Fructose?

Fructose (sometimes called "levulose" on food labels) is a simple sugar that occurs naturally in foods, including fruits and honey; it's also a key component in table sugar (which is sucrose, a blend of half fructose and half glucose). While it has the same amount of calories and carbohydrate as sugar, fructose produces a lower and slower rise in blood glucose, and requires less insulin for the body to process. For that reason, some "health" or so-called "diabetic" foods are sweetened with fructose, and pure fructose is sold in the alternative sweetener section in supermarkets.

Should you buy fructose-sweetened foods? Most experts don't feel it's necessary or desirable. For one, foods sweetened with added fructose may contain other carbohydrates that can also affect your blood-glucose levels. And they cost more than traditionally sweetened foods. But perhaps the most important concern is that fructose can raise triglycerides and LDL cholesterol, potentially raising heart-disease risks. The American Diabetes Association recommends people with diabetes avoid fructose, other than that naturally occurring in foods.

You're most likely to encounter fructose in the form of high-fructose corn syrup (HFCS), a manmade sweetener that has steadily been replacing sugar in many foods and beverages, including soda, juice drinks, baked goods, breakfast cereals, desserts and condiments (ketchup, for example). Don't consider it equivalent to fructose, however, because it doesn't have fructose's gentler effects on blood-sugar levels. In fact, despite its name, HFCS only contains 50 to 55 percent fructose—so chemically, it's virtually identical to table sugar (sucrose). Metabolic studies suggest our bodies break down HFCS and sucrose the same way. So when you see HFCS on a food label, think "added sugar," and look for a brand that contains less, or better yet, none at all.

What About Sugar Alcohols?

While their names sound less than appetizing, and sometimes like a boozy dessert sauce, sweetening agents like sorbitol, mannitol, xylitol, maltitol, lactitol and hydrogenated starch hydrolysates (HSH) are familiar to many people with diabetes. These so-called sugar alcohols are often added to food products such as "sugar-free" candy or gum, cookies or certain medications. They are listed on food labels under the Total Carbohydrate heading. Because these sweeteners are only partially digested compared to other sugars, they cause a lower rise in blood glucose. They also don't cause tooth decay. But their lack of digestibility can be a problem, causing stomach upset, gas or diarrhea in some people, especially if eaten in large amounts. The most important fact about sugar alcohols is that they still contribute some carbohydrate (about half is digested). To calculate how much, note the grams of carbohydrate contributed by any sugar alcohol listed on the food label, then subtract half that number from the Total Carbohydrate count.

forms a gel in the digestive tract, which binds with cholesterol particles and removes them from the body unabsorbed.

Focus on getting at least 25 grams of fiber daily. That's about twice as much as most Americans now eat, so you'll probably have to make a conscious decision to include more fiber-rich plant foods, and to get at least half of your grain-based foods each day from whole-grain sources (*see "5 Simple Ways to Get More Fiber," page 17*).

Another benefit to put you in the pro-fiber camp: fiber can help you control your weight. Although it contains nary a calorie, fiber adds bulk to foods—so you'll feel fuller after eating. And since fiber-rich foods take longer to digest, they can help you stay satisfied longer. **Recipes containing 5 grams or more of fiber per serving are marked with this icon: High ⬆ Fiber.**

Beyond Carbohydrate: Other Essentials for Healthy Eating

❥ **PROTEIN** is used by the body to build tissues, as well as to repair and replace body cells. Found in both plants and animal-based foods, it's especially high in fish, poultry, meat, dairy products, eggs, beans, soy foods and nuts. Because it's so widely available, getting enough protein is rarely a problem. In fact, most Americans eat at least 50 percent more protein than they need. The recent popularity of high-protein diets for weight loss has made that issue all the more acute.

Does having diabetes mean you need more protein than the rest of the population? On the surface, it might seem to be a helpful ally, since protein produces no rise in glucose levels. Not long ago people with diabetes were encouraged to eat a little protein at every meal and snack with the belief that

> **PROTEIN: THE TAKE-HOME**
>
> Aim for 2 to 3 servings of protein foods per day. The best choices come from sources that are low in saturated fat and cholesterol.

adding protein would slow the rise in glucose from carbohydrate foods. But when this theory was put to the test, it didn't hold water. Studies showed that blood glucose rises were the same following a meal whether it contained carbohydrate alone or in combination with protein. Furthermore, even if protein does not affect blood-glucose levels, it still stimulates insulin.

More reasons to avoid protein overload: when you eat more protein than you need, your body will store the excess the way it stores any other caloric substance—as fat. And favorite protein sources like meats and cheeses can also be sources of heart-threatening saturated fat.

The protein recommendations for people with diabetes, then, are similar to what's recommended for all Americans: aim to get between five and seven ounces of protein foods each day, or about two to three servings. Be picky about your protein sources, favoring types that are lowest in saturated fat and cholesterol, such as beans and tofu, lean meats, skinless poultry and reduced-fat dairy products.

❥ **FAT** is our body's storage form of energy, supplying essential fatty acids and fat-soluble vitamins. It's important to the functioning of the immune and nervous systems and in maintaining the integrity of the body's cells. It also makes food more delicious and satisfying—we couldn't live, physically or spiritually, without it.

Like protein, though, getting enough fat isn't a problem in the American diet. It's easy to find, in oils, butter, meats, cheeses and full-fat dairy products, nuts, fried foods and sweet treats. On average, the fat we eat accounts for about a third or more of the calories we consume each day.

While most nutrition experts no longer routinely recommend a low-fat diet for everyone, there's no denying that fat is—well, fattening. At 9 calories per gram, it contains more than twice the amount of calories as protein and carbohydrate (both 4 calories per gram). So if you're trying to lose weight, as are many people with diabetes, keeping your fat intake moderate is a good goal. Just as important, if not more, is to be vigilant about the *kinds* of fats you eat. There are several different types, and each has different actions in the body.

The Right Fats

Nutrition experts recommend that most of the fat you eat come from the following sources:

❧ **MONOUNSATURATED FATS** are favored by cardiologists and nutritionists alike. "Mono" fats are found in plant-based oils like olive, canola and high-oleic varieties of safflower and sunflower oil, as well as in nuts and avocados. They tend to raise heart-healthy HDL cholesterol, while lowering "bad" LDL cholesterol—an undeniable win-win combination, especially for people with diabetes who are at increased risk of heart problems. Mono fats play an important role in the cuisines of countries around the Mediterranean Sea, one of the world's healthiest eating patterns (*see "Eating Like a Mediterranean," page 23*).

❧ **POLYUNSATURATED FATS** also come from plant sources, including corn oil, soybean oil and other salad oils. These "poly" fats also tend to lower LDLs, but can lower heart-protective HDLs at the same time. The negatives on HDL seem to be modest, though, and mostly outweighed by the heart-healthy positives. In the huge Nurses' Health Study at Boston's Harvard School of Public Health, for example, women who used the most salad dressings (including poly-fat-rich mayonnaise-based types) had half the risk of fatal heart disease as those who rarely used dressings.

FAT: THE TAKE-HOME

Aim for 25 to 35 percent of your daily calories to come from fat, staying on the lower end of the range if you need to lose weight.

If your eating plan averages 2,000 calories per day, that's 56 to 78 grams of fat. If your plan averages 1,500 calories per day, that's 42 to 58 grams of fat.

Fats to Limit

The following fats fall squarely into the "eat less" category, whether or not you have diabetes.

❧ **SATURATED FATS** are easy to spot because they're solid at room temperature—like the marbling in a steak, or a pat of butter. Saturated fats come mostly from animal sources, like meats, poultry skin and dairy products, such as cheese, butter and whole milk, as well as from palm and coconut oils. Saturated fats hinder LDLs, or "bad" cholesterol particles, from getting into cells where they belong. As a result, cholesterol stays in the blood longer, and can become a part of the blood-vessel plaques that build up and cause heart disease. So decreasing saturated fat intake is the most important dietary step you can take to lower your blood cholesterol. Because of an increased heart-disease risk, people with diabetes need to be vigilant about limiting saturated fats.

SATURATED FATS: THE TAKE-HOME

Limit saturated fat to 7 to 10 percent of your daily calories, staying on the low end of that range or below if you have high blood cholesterol.

If you get about 2,000 calories per day, that means no more than 15 to 22 grams of saturated fat daily—about the amount in two to three (3½-ounce) hamburgers.

If you eat about 1,500 calories per day, that means no more than 12 to 17 grams of saturated fat daily. That's two to three (1-inch) Cheddar cheese cubes.

❧ **TRANS FATTY ACIDS** are a product of modern technology that, like Frankenstein, haven't quite turned out as hoped. Trans fats are formed by a chemical process called *hydrogenation* that enables unsaturated fats (usually vegetable oils) to resemble saturated ones, giving them a solid texture and a longer shelf life. From your heart's point of view, trans fats are even

TRANS FATS: THE TAKE-HOME

There is currently no "safe" daily amount of trans fats, so avoid them as much as possible.

worse than saturated fats. Not only do they raise harmful LDLs, they reduce heart-protective HDLs.

Solid vegetable shortenings and margarines are our main sources of trans fats, especially the crackers, chips, cookies, cake mixes, bakery goods and other foods made with them. Federal regulations were recently updated to require food manufacturers to list trans fats on their nutrition labels. To detect trans fats on older labels, look for the words "partially hydrogenated" or "hydrogenated." Thankfully trans fats are becoming scarcer as many manufacturers are reformulating their products to be "trans-fat-free." Seek out those choices.

CHOLESTEROL: THE TAKE-HOME

Keep your intake of cholesterol to 300 milligrams (mg) per day—under 200 mg if you have an LDL cholesterol reading of over 100. For comparison, a large egg yolk contains 218 mg cholesterol.

CHOLESTEROL is a fatlike substance that's an essential component in the walls of all our cells; we also need it to make hormones and bile acids. Technically, there's no need to get any cholesterol in the foods we eat, because our bodies manufacture all the cholesterol we need. But we take in cholesterol every time we eat foods from other animals that make their own cholesterol too: meat and poultry, eggs and full-fat dairy products.

Compared with saturated fat and trans fat, dietary cholesterol isn't as powerful an influence on our blood-cholesterol levels. Usually, our bodies compensate for the cholesterol we eat by manufacturing less. But it's still important to limit—possibly more so with diabetes. **Compared with the general public, people with diabetes appear to be more sensitive to dietary cholesterol**. Not to mention the fact that the foods that supply cholesterol frequently deliver a hefty dose of saturated fat too.

What About Sodium?

Since many people with diabetes have high blood pressure, chances are you've been asked by your

TIPS FOR REAL LIFE

5 WAYS TO LOWER SODIUM INTAKE

- Read nutrition labels and scout out lower-sodium versions of your favorite foods.

- Don't cook foods with salt; add it at the table instead, after you've tasted a bite. Chances are, it doesn't need salt.

- Shake salt into your hand before sprinkling it on your food so you see exactly how much you're adding.

- Experiment with sodium-free ways to boost flavors in foods. Acidic flavorings, such as lemon juice and vinegar, impart a sensation similar to salt. Be creative with herbs and sodium-free spices too.

- Give it time. It might take a while for your palate to adjust to the taste of less-salty foods, but eventually you'll probably prefer them.

health-care team to limit your sodium (the main ingredient in table salt). Studies show that, on average, as sodium intake rises, so does the incidence of high blood pressure—and, when people make a conscious effort to reduce their salt intake, their blood pressure tends to drop.

The Institute of Medicine of the National Academies (IOM) recently revised its guidelines for sodium, recommending that adults get no more than 2,300 milligrams (mg) of sodium daily—and that people with diabetes try to stay under that amount. That's slightly less than the amount in a teaspoon of salt (2,400 mg). Since most Americans regularly take in much more sodium than current recommendations, you'll probably have to make a concerted effort to cut salt intake if that's your goal.

Most of the sodium in our daily eating— approximately 77 percent, according to the IOM report—comes from prepared or processed foods. So one of the best ways to limit sodium is to cook and eat more meals made "from scratch." Our recipes, while not strictly low-sodium, are developed with the goal of keeping added salt to a minimum.

What About Supplements?

Some nutrients your body needs only in trace amounts. These micronutrients include vitamins and minerals, some of which are involved in the process of blood-glucose control. Does that mean you need to take special supplements? You might be hearing from well-meaning friends or on the Internet that taking chromium picolinate or magnesium is advised. But scientific studies have not really supported their efficacy. Unless there's a proven deficiency, say experts, there's little evidence that taking specific micronutrient supplements can help. But **a daily multivitamin/multimineral supplement is a good dietary "insurance policy."** Choose one with *no more than 100 percent of the daily value* (DV) of the listed nutrients.

Eating Like a Mediterranean

What is the world's healthiest way to eat? Back in the 1960s, researcher Ancel Keys organized an effort to find out, gathering data on diet and disease patterns throughout the world. The Seven Countries Study that resulted was nothing short of a watershed. It established the connection between saturated fat and heart disease, just for starters. But it also identified one of the world's healthiest eating patterns.

The study reported one of the lowest rates of heart disease, and some of the longest lifespans, in the people of Crete, an island in the Mediterranean. Later work confirmed that Cretans had much lower rates of cancer and type 2 diabetes, as well.

What was it about their lifestyle that was so protective? Lots of physical activity, for one; most of the men made their living as farmers. And Cretans ate in a way that hadn't much changed since ancient times. Their meals were full of vegetables and fruits, abundant in beans and fish, and almost devoid of red meat and processed foods. They regularly took in high amounts of fat—40 percent of daily calories—but most of it came from olive oil; their average saturated-fat intake was among the world's lowest. This eating pattern was soon christened the "Mediterranean Diet," and it still stands as one of the world's healthiest, tastiest ways to eat.

The Mediterranean pattern has stood up to clinical scrutiny as well; large-scale studies have shown that when people are put on a Mediter-ranean eating program, they tend to live longer and have lower rates of heart disease and some cancers, when compared with other groups following conventional eating plans.

Bottom Line: EATINGWELL recipes readily satisfy the guidelines of the Mediterranean Diet, emphasizing whole grains, vegetables, beans, legumes, nuts and unsaturated fats.

TIPS FOR REAL LIFE

7 GUIDELINES FOR EATING THE MEDITERRANEAN WAY

❧ Eat more **whole foods** and fewer processed foods.

❧ Use **unsaturated fats**, particularly monounsaturated fats like olive oil, for cooking and flavoring foods, and for salad dressings.

❧ Eat an abundance of **vegetables**, especially leafy greens, every day.

❧ Eat more servings of **fruits, grains and legumes** than animal-based foods, and include low-fat or fat-free **dairy products**.

❧ Serve **beans and fish** as your main protein sources.

❧ Make **small amounts of meat** an occasional treat, rather than a daily staple.

❧ Enjoy **nuts,** such as almonds, peanuts and walnuts, regularly, in moderate amounts.

What Healthy Eating Looks Like

No matter how clear the principles of healthy eating may be, putting them into practice can be downright confusing. How does "30 percent of calories from fat" or "2 Carbohydrate Servings" translate to what's on your plate? And where does your eating plan come in when your only choice for a meal is a convenience store? In this section, we'll address many of the issues that may come up in everyday eating.

Circular diagram text: DIVIDE YOUR PLATE DIVIDE YOUR PLATE DIVIDE YOUR PLATE DIVIDE YOUR PLATE DIVIDE YOUR PLATE DIVIDE YOUR PLATE

¼ = WHOLE GRAINS

¼ = LEAN PROTEIN

½ = VEGETABLES

Start with Your Team

Many resources can point you toward good eating, including guidelines from the American Diabetes Association and the International Diabetes Center (*see Resources, page 321, for suggestions*). But for the most practical advice that applies to your own health situation and lifestyle, start with a diabetes specialist. This person is likely to be a Registered Dietitian (RD) and/or a Certified Diabetes Educator (CDE)—both are experts in translating the abstract principles of nutrition into real-life eating.

Divide and Conquer

Getting started on eating better would be much easier if there were a simple, "big picture" image of what a sensible eating pattern looks like. The current debate about the relevance of the U.S. Department of Agriculture's Food Guide Pyramid, as well as the many competing pyramids produced by others, is a case in point. But one method is winning converts and praise across the board—perhaps because of its utter simplicity. **Call it the "Divide Your Plate" strategy.**

❧ Imagine a plate and divide it in half. Fill one half with vegetables, and divide the other half into two quarters.

❧ Fill one quarter with a lean protein, such as fish, skinless poultry, beans or tofu.

❧ Fill the other quarter with a grain-based or starchy side dish, preferably whole grains, like brown rice, whole-wheat pasta or a slice of whole-grain bread.

What this method lacks in precision it more than makes up for in good sense. If you focus on making most of your meals look this way, you'll automatically be following sound nutrition guidelines and choosing appropriate portions—without having to pull out a nutrition guide or a measuring cup every time.

A Primer on Portion Size

A key first step in building sound eating habits is to understand what reasonable portions of foods look like. For most of us, that requires a bit of re-education—and downscaling.

Many nutrition authorities believe our ability to estimate correct portions is deteriorating—

largely because we are becoming used to the ever-bigger food helpings served up to us in restaurants and other venues. From soft drinks to muffins, the foods we buy in the marketplace are almost always larger than standard portion sizes—sometimes two to eight times bigger. Consider "standard"-size bagels: not long ago, they averaged 2 to 3 ounces; today, they can weigh in at up to 7 ounces. That's equivalent to seven slices of bread, and that's just at breakfast! Restaurant-size helpings of pasta, too, can be big enough to feed a family of six. Imagine what your blood-glucose levels would look like if you considered either of these carbohydrate bonanzas as a "single serving."

The insidious effect of these overblown portions is that larger helpings almost always encourage us to eat more. Several studies have shown that when adults and children are repeatedly served bigger-than-normal portions of food, they tend to eat more—regardless of how hungry they were when they sat down. This is standard procedure in restaurants, where we almost always feel compelled to clean our plates, but it also happens at home, when we serve ourselves the supersized portions we've come to perceive as "normal." No wonder our nation's obesity rate has risen in parallel with rising average portion sizes.

The best way to reclaim normal portion sizes, say experts, is by measuring them out repeatedly until it becomes instinctive. To begin, ask your diabetes-care team to provide a food list or a standard food guide that includes portion sizes. The American Diabetes Association is another good information source (*see Resources, page 321*).

Use measuring cups and spoons and, if needed, a kitchen scale to portion out your foods. Don't

> **"**I put everything in a measuring cup. I don't assume I know what a correct portion looks like, even though I've been doing this for months.**"**
> —*Jan M., Florida*

TIPS FOR REAL LIFE

WHAT DOES A PORTION LOOK LIKE?

1 teaspoon oil	The tip of your thumb
1 tablespoon salad dressing	Your whole thumb
2 tablespoons peanut butter	A Ping-Pong ball
1 to 2 ounces nuts	Your cupped hand
1½ ounces cheese	A 9-volt battery
½ cup cottage cheese	A tennis ball
1 cup cereal	A baseball
1 small baked potato	A computer mouse
3-ounce serving of meat, fish or poultry	A cassette tape
1 standard pancake or waffle	A 4-inch DVD

---

forget to measure the serving utensils you use, so you'll know how "one ladleful" of soup or stew measures up. Take note of how the food looks on a plate—and try to use the same plate each time you eat that item, so you'll have a second visual reference. Continue practicing and measuring until the portions become second nature to you. This can take a few days or a few weeks; some people might opt for always measuring rather than eyeballing. It's a good idea to recheck your portion-size skills every so often, as they tend to creep up with time.

Eating on Schedule, and When Life Gets in the Way

Eating at regular intervals helps ensure that your blood-glucose levels are fairly constant, so your diabetes food plan likely includes designated times for eating breakfast, lunch, dinner and, if appropriate, snacks. If you're taking insulin or other glucose-lowering medications, it's even more important to stay within those time ranges. But disruptions can throw off the best-laid plans, particularly when you're eating away from home: planes get delayed, dinner takes longer than anticipated to cook, food deliveries arrive late.

If you are within 30 minutes to an hour of your designated mealtime, there's probably no need for

TIPS FOR REAL LIFE

10 PACKABLE SNACKS

Each of the following provides 1 Carbohydrate Serving (15 grams carbohydrate):

- ¾ cup to 1 cup unsweet-ened whole-grain cereal

- 3 graham cracker squares

- 2 tablespoons raisins or other dried fruit (a mini, Halloween-size box)

- 1 small can water-packed peaches, pears or fruit cocktail

- 5 mini rice cakes

- 7 animal crackers

- 6 saltines

- Small juice box

- 4 peanut-butter-filled cheese-cracker snacks

- 1 cereal or granola bar

concern. But what should you do if a mealtime gets delayed, or moved up, significantly? Most people with diabetes carry a supply of emergency snacks or glucose to help them handle these situations (*see 10 possibilities at left*); your diabetes-care team can help you create your own contingency plan. Some general rules:

- If you have to eat earlier than planned, save one Carbohydrate Serving for your regular mealtime.

- If you have to wait to eat a meal, have one Carbohydrate Serving at your usual mealtime, then eat the rest of the meal later. Or, if you usually have a snack later on, have the snack at your mealtime and eat the meal during your snack time.

Snacking—Green Light or Red?

It wasn't so long ago that people with diabetes were told they needed snacks to help them manage their diabetes—timing snacks to offset drops in their blood glucose caused by insulin and other diabetes medications. But today's diabetes medication choices are much more flexible, so snacks aren't strictly necessary; the decision to snack, or not, is up to you. If you manage your glucose better by eating more frequent, smaller meals, you'll want to include some planned-for snacks in your daily routine. If there's a time of day when your blood-glucose levels tend to drop regularly, a small snack can help tide you over.

That said, a go-ahead on snacking isn't a green light to nosh uncontrollably. The keys are to consider snacks as mini-meals, and to make room for them in the rest of your day's eating. Ideally, they can complement your other meals, supplying nutrients rather than just empty calories. Get in the habit of snacking on vegetables (especially nonstarchy ones like cucumbers and cut-up bell peppers), and you'll painlessly boost your vegetable intake.

You don't have to include protein, carbohydrate and fat at every snack, but it helps make them more balanced, substantial and satisfying. A good guide to aim for is 1 or 2 Carbohydrate Servings in your snack. Check the "Snacks & Appetizers" chapter, starting on page 78, for some delicious inspirations.

Eating on the Road

Having diabetes shouldn't keep you from traveling, but it does require you to plan ahead. Be sure your diabetes supplies and medications are up to date, and carry them with you rather than in checked luggage, so you don't risk losing them. It's a good idea to include a copy of your prescriptions plus a letter from your doctor identifying you as a person with diabetes. Pack some nonperishable snacks to keep

TIPS FOR REAL LIFE

9 SNACKS TO STASH IN YOUR DESK DRAWER

- Whole-wheat crispbreads (>3 grams fiber/serving)

- 3-ounce pouches water-packed tuna

- Natural peanut or other nut butter

- 1-ounce bags of peanuts or almonds

- Small (8-ounce) cans low-sodium mixed-vegetable juice

- Single-serving packets of trail mix

- Reduced-fat string cheese sticks

- Apples, oranges, pears, bananas, kiwis or "single-serving" fruits

- Single-serving boxes of unsweetened whole-grain cereals

you going if your meals are delayed, such as the suggestions on page 26. And, if you'll be crossing time zones, check with your diabetes specialist about adjusting your mealtimes and medications.

The biggest challenge, though, is finding something to eat in new territory. Again, planning ahead is the answer. Call a hotel before your visit and ask about area restaurants; pack a portable meal with you on the train or plane—or, if a meal will be served en route, ask if you can pre-order a "diabetes" or "heart-healthy" meal instead. If you're driving, use travel guides to plot a route where you'll have access to accommodating restaurants, farmers' markets, grocery stores and other easy venues for nutritious food. And even if your only choice is a fast-food rest stop, you still have plenty of options (see 10 possibilities at right). You can ask for nutrition information if you're not sure about how an item adds up in your food plan; most fast-food restaurants have this information available.

Skip the Soft Drinks

Enticing, big-bucks ad campaigns make soft drinks look like a fabulous way to quench thirst—but the reality is anything but refreshing. The average 12-ounce can of regular soda supplies about 150 calories and 38 grams of carbohydrate—the equivalent of more than 9 teaspoons of sugar. And most of us drink all those calories and carbohydrate without noticing: studies show that when people have soft drinks with meals, they don't compensate for the extra, liquid calories by eating less solid food. So drinking soda regularly is a prescription for overconsumption.

Another reason to avoid soda: it may raise the risk of developing diabetes. A recent report from the Nurses' Health Study, which surveyed the health behaviors of over 51,000 women, found that those who drank one or more regular sodas a day were twice as likely to develop diabetes during the study period as women who drank less than one can a month. Even when the researchers took such factors

---

TIPS FOR REAL LIFE

5 AIRPORT OR TRAIN STATION STANDBYS

Each of the following provides 1 Carbohydrate Serving (15 grams carbohydrate):

- 1 slice plain or vegetable-topped pizza

- ½ roast turkey or lean roast beef sandwich, hold the mayo

- Small low-fat, sugar-free frozen yogurt with a sprinkle of nuts

- Soft pretzel, 1 small

- A single-serving packet of nuts

10 FAST-FOOD FALLBACKS

Fight back against fast-food supersizing! Mini-size by ordering a kids' meal instead. You don't have to show proof of age—and really, who's going to stop you?

- Kids'-meal-size burger (toss the fries and opt for low-fat milk over soda)

- Grilled chicken sandwich with lettuce and tomato

- Garden or side salad with low-fat dressing

- Grilled chicken salad with low-fat dressing (hold the croutons and bacon bits)

- Soft chicken taco

- Mexican rice

- Southwest chicken wrap

- Baked potato with broccoli and cheese

- Chili

- Fruit and yogurt parfait (or low-fat frozen yogurt)

as weight, diet and lifestyle differences into account, they still found that the soda drinkers were 1.3 times more likely to develop diabetes.

If you have a regular soft drink habit, switching to diet soda is a start. It makes sense to also focus on finding calorie-free ways to quench thirst or wash down your meals—like sparkling water or plain water, nature's best refresher.

Alcohol and Diabetes

In your diabetes treatment counseling, you were probably warned to limit your intake of alcohol, because when consumed without food, alcohol can cause low-blood-glucose episodes and, in large amounts, raise blood pressure. At the same time, you've no doubt seen reports that a daily drink can help reduce the risk of heart disease and stroke—two diseases that pose more problems for people with diabetes. Moderate drinking is even associated with lower risk of type 2 diabetes. What can you conclude from this conflicting advice?

According to the American Diabetes Association, recommendations for people who have their diabetes under control are no different from those aimed at the general population: If you choose to drink, limit it to two drinks a day for men and one daily drink for women. If you're pregnant, have high blood triglycerides (over 500 mg/deciliter) or a history of alcohol problems in your family, it makes sense to stay away from alcohol altogether.

The limits are there for a reason; for people with diabetes, there are real risks associated with going beyond them. The first is low blood glucose. When your liver is processing alcohol, it can't make new glucose. This can cause your blood-glucose levels to drop, sometimes sharply—if you're drinking on an empty stomach and are taking insulin or diabetes drugs. Worse, this effect can last for as long as 12 to 16 hours after you drink, depending on how long it takes your body to process the alcohol. And low blood glucose can make you feel and act tipsy, so you could be doubly impaired.

So, make sure to eat something whenever you decide to drink—and take it slow. For a good model, think of the healthy way many Mediterraneans enjoy alcohol: slowly sipped throughout a meal, rather than served alone in cocktails. It's a good idea to check your blood glucose regularly after you've had a drink too.

Another issue to consider is alcohol's effects on your heart, which can be a double-edged sword. When alcohol is enjoyed in small amounts, like the ones defined as "one drink" (*see box*), it doesn't affect blood pressure, and in fact might reduce heart problems by boosting heart-healthy IIDL cholesterol and by improving sensitivity to insulin. But increase the amount of daily alcohol, and the risk of high blood pressure rises sharply—on a graph, it follows a J-shaped curve. (*For several fabulous alcohol-free drink suggestions, see page 90.*)

(For several fabulous alcohol-free drink suggestions, see page 90.)

WHAT IS "ONE DRINK"?

"One drink" is 15 grams of alcohol, or:

12	ounces	beer
5	ounces	wine
1½	ounces	spirits

ALCOHOL: THE TAKE-HOME:

Alcohol in moderation, enjoyed with food to decrease the risk of low blood glucose, might help your heart, but talk with your health-care providers to determine the best strategy for you. If you're not a drinker now, there's no reason to start. If it's heart disease or diabetes risk you want to avoid, there are plenty of nonalcoholic ways to do it.

Changing for Good

Many people with diabetes talk about how they've had to "reinvent themselves," and with good reason. Having diabetes makes you reconsider almost everything you do, from the foods you choose and the activities in your day, to the way you interact with others. Sometimes the thought of making all those changes can be overwhelming. That goes for anyone contemplating a healthier lifestyle, diabetes or not.

But the good news is that there are many, many ways to succeed at life change—and millions of people do it every day. The trick is to find what works for you. Luckily, scientific literature documents many successful ways to make that journey, and we've collected some of the best in these pages.

Take Small Steps

When you have a big goal ahead of you—say, losing 20 pounds or bringing your blood glucose down to normal levels—it's easy to feel defeated right from the start. With such a big target to aim for, it will be a long time before you feel you've made any progress. After a while, that lack of rewarding feedback can make it easier to give up altogether.

A better strategy, say experts, is to break down your goal into smaller, more achievable goals you have control over—such as finding time to take a 10-minute walk each day for a week, eating breakfast every day, or not eating after dinner. Or, if you're trying to count your Carbohydrate Servings and cut saturated fat from your eating plan, try

> **"**Habit is habit and not to be flung out of the window… but coaxed downstairs a step at a time.**"**
> *—Mark Twain*

working on just the carbohydrate component until you feel you've mastered it, then move on to watching saturated fat. Goals like these are challenging enough to keep you motivated, but not so challenging that they're out of reasonable reach.

If you think this approach sounds halfhearted, think again. Small changes are often the most powerful of all, because they're the ones we're most likely to stick with. And small changes can produce big results: Just adding a little more activity to your day, for example, might be all you need to bring your blood glucose down to a manageable level. Just losing 10 percent of your body weight can reduce your risk for heart problems as well as improve your diabetes.

Once you reach a goal, you can set another if you like—but be sure to mark the achievement first, with a reward. Taking the time to acknowledge your success makes your achievement all the more real, and motivating. If weight loss is your goal, try rewarding yourself with things other than food—say, a trip to the movies, some clothing you've been coveting or a massage.

Write It Down

One of the most potent weapons for making change can be a pencil—the pencil you use to keep a journal. Studies show that people who keep track of their health behaviors — whether it's tallying the foods they eat each day in a food diary, plotting their blood-glucose levels on a chart or keeping an exercise log—are more likely to reach their goals, even if that's the only thing they do. So, even if you don't feel up to making a big change right now, you're probably able to take this simple and powerful step.

Why are these diaries and journals so effective? Just keeping track of something helps you feel more in control over it, and that can be empowering. Seeing your activities tallied up on a page also helps you identify problem areas and where you need to focus your efforts most effectively. And, if you're making progress, documenting it will give you proof positive that you're making a difference, helping you to stay on track. For all these reasons, food diaries are often the first step in a diabetes-treatment program, as well as in most doctor-recommended weight-loss programs.

Your health-care advisor can get you started on

PROFILES IN REAL LIFE

DENYING DENIAL

Jan M., Florida

Even though her blood test (hemoglobin A1c) came back at a high of 8.6 percent, Jan M. didn't think she had diabetes. "It was a term that didn't exist in my vocabulary," she remembers. At the age of 44, she seemed too young for such a serious-sounding diagnosis—and she didn't feel particularly unwell, despite being overweight most of her adult life. Even though her father had died of heart disease years earlier, and her grandmother had had type 2 diabetes, it just didn't seem possible. "I was scared and in denial," she admits.

So when she was advised to attend a Diabetes Education Class at the Joslin Diabetes Center in Clearwater, Florida, Jan did so "reluctantly." The sessions, led by Certified Diabetes Educators Cindy Bray and Anne Schreiner, turned out to be a revelation.

"They told me that I'm 90 percent responsible for my own health, and that they could only help me with the remaining 10 percent," she remembers. "It was the kick in the pants I needed to jump-start my life on the road to better health."

Working with Schreiner, Jan developed a meal plan she could live with—one that "didn't make anything forbidden." Unlike the many weight-loss diets she'd tried unsuccessfully in the past, it gave her the flexibility to include the foods she loved, such as pasta and chocolate. Her care team at Joslin also focused on tackling one issue at a time, rather than overwhelming Jan with too many changes at once. "First, I worked on limiting the carbs I ate, then we worked on cutting down on saturated fat." And she acquired the habit of measuring all her portions, rather than resorting to "eyeballing" them.

Jan's options for exercise were limited by injury; a former Recreation Therapist, she'd been sidelined by knee replacement surgery, spinal fusion and a fused left foot. So she started from ground zero. "The first evening it was a matter of just putting on my sneakers and walking to the end of the driveway and back." With her mother along for support, she increased her walking by small, realistic increments. "The next day, we walked to the end of the street and back; the day after, to the next telephone pole and back," and so on, until she reached her goal of a 2.2-mile daily loop.

The pounds started melting off, gradually but persistently. A year and a half later, she had dropped 101 pounds and six dress sizes—and had greatly reduced her daily dose of metformin. Now, within a few pounds of her weight-loss goal, Jan is a committed daily exerciser who aerobic water-walks in a swimming pool for an hour every day and does a cardio/strength workout three times a week (30 minutes on an exercise bike and 30 minutes on cardio and strength machines). Support from family and friends has been vital throughout her journey, and she's especially grateful to her diabetes-education team. "I always know they're just a phone call away."

Today, Jan feels like a new person, "with more life and more energy"—and looks like one too. "When I run into people I haven't seen in a few years, they don't recognize me. Some of them figure I must have had gastric-bypass surgery!" she laughs.

creating your own health journal, but you don't have to have an official document. A simple page-a-day calendar or a small notebook is all you need. Take time each day to write in it—it will soon become a daily habit. (*See pages 42-43 for diary models.*)

Get the Right Support

The more help you get in your effort to make a change, the better. Such is the foundation of every support group. Knowing who your own supporters are, and how to call on them, can go a long way toward helping you succeed.

Your family is usually your first tier of support, since they are the ones who will be most directly affected by a change in your life. Because of this, they need to be informed of your commitment to becoming healthier, right from the start. Let them know what you plan to do, and that you'll need their encouragement along the way. They'll probably have some concerns and may not always agree with everything you're doing—but they deserve to know what's coming. If there are issues, work on them together to find common ground. If your kids resent you taking time out to go to a health club, for example, they might be appeased if you promise a weekly family bike ride or outing to a roller rink.

Your friends and peers are also an important source of support, especially if there are some "kindred spirits" who are also pursuing similar goals. Just finding a walking buddy you don't want to disappoint by not showing up—or someone to call at 3 p.m. when you're dying for a soft drink—can be tremendously motivating. Perhaps there are people you know who have already achieved some of the goals you're aiming for; consider them role models,

> ### TIPS FOR REAL LIFE
>
> ### HOW TO SPOT—AND DEAL WITH—SABOTEURS
>
> Sometimes the people around you might act to undermine your resolve, whether they're aware of it or not. That aunt who brings you her famous banana bread when she visits, for example, or the spouse who resents when you'd rather walk than watch TV after dinner. Another type of saboteur might act like the food police, commenting on every bite you take and pointing out when you "trip up." None are doing your health commitment any favors.
>
> The best way to handle people like these is to make them aware of what they're doing, by talking about it in a nonconfrontational way. Many times, their behavior isn't intentional; it simply may not have occurred to your aunt that banana bread isn't appropriate for someone who's watching his or her blood glucose. Bringing it out into the open may be all that's needed.
>
> But some people in your life may not truly support your efforts. Perhaps the thought of you succeeding at your goals makes them feel threatened or inadequate. Or, they might miss an activity you're no longer able to share with them—say, the daily doughnut break at work. Talking about it can help, especially if you can come up with alternatives that accommodate you both—for instance, meeting your doughnut-break buddy for a daily walk instead of pastries. But if you're unable to resolve the problem, don't let it hold you back. Focus instead on seeking the support you need from other sources.

with life lessons you can learn from. Another plus: every healthy get-together is another opportunity to build on your friendship, or to just have fun.

If there's no one in your inner circle who shares your get-healthy goals, expand your social horizons. Look in your community directory for health-focused or fitness programs and classes or local walking clubs. To reach other people with diabetes, check with your local hospital or diabetes-education center for support groups.

Overcoming the Obstacles

What's stopping you from getting to your goal of a healthier life? For many of us, it's the same litany of reasons. If you've found yourself saying any of these phrases, here are some helpful ways to answer back.

"I don't have time to eat healthy." The food and restaurant industries, ever responsive to the public, have heard you. Today, it's easier than ever to put a nutritious meal on the table in minutes, with ever-expanding choices now in most supermarkets and take-out counters—from freshly cooked rotisserie chickens to whole-grain-and-vegetable salads. Thanks to today's packaged salad kits and prewashed, precut vegetables, fresh produce is close to becoming convenience food too.

There's no getting around the fact, though, that it's much easier to eat nutritiously if most of your meals are home-cooked. After all, cooking from scratch puts you most in control of what goes into your food. But homemade meals don't have to be time-consuming or difficult, as the recipes and tips in this book attest. And, with planning ahead—say, cooking big batches of vegetables and beans, roasting poultry or meats, and preparing salad greens on weekends—your weekday meals can be a simple matter of assembly.

"I don't have time to exercise." In truth, if something is important enough to you, you will find a way to make it work with your life. Often that means cutting out other activities that aren't so crucial to you, and it might take some soul-searching to make those decisions. Perhaps you'll need to get up a half-hour earlier in the morning to fit in a walk, or spend your lunch hour at the gym instead of the cafeteria.

If the thought of "exercise" scares you, keep in mind that just about anything that gets you moving counts, whether it's raking leaves, washing the car or walking from the far end of the parking lot to the store. The American Diabetes Association suggests aiming to be active for a total of about 30 minutes a day, at least five days a week—more, if you're trying to lose weight. If that seems like a lot, start modestly. Try just 5 or 10 minutes a day, and work up to more time each week. Or take it in small bits: say, a 10-minute walk after breakfast and lunch, and 10 minutes of housecleaning after dinner.

Finding activities you can do in your home, like lifting weights, jumping rope or moving to exercise videos, might also do the trick. If you have the means and space, a home-exercise machine could

---

TIPS FOR REAL LIFE

HOW TO SAY NO (POLITELY) TO FOOD PUSHERS

"Have more—it's delicious!"
"Why won't you even try it?"
"Come on, lighten up—one bite won't kill you!"

Phrases like these are usually meant in the kindest way, but if you're trying to watch what you eat, they can trigger a tremendous emotional charge. After all, when people offer us food, they are often offering us love; they may feel that if you reject a food, you're rejecting them too. These emotions can be especially raw during the holidays, when cooks tend to invest more time and effort into making special dishes.

How do you stick to your resolve when you're offered something you're not comfortable eating?

Choose phrases that acknowledge the person's feelings, but still make your point: "That looks amazing, and I wish I had room, but I'm really enjoying the [insert other food here]." If the server persists, take a little of the food and give it a try, if you like; there's no law that says you have to clean your plate. If you're offered a second helping you don't need, keeping your reply in the past tense gives your words a sense of finality: "It sure was delicious, but I've had enough." "I couldn't eat another bite, but it was fantastic."

If you have trouble saying no, take a tip from trained speakers and practice, practice, practice. Take some time ahead of the event to imagine what it will be like, being as specific as possible. Who will be there? What will be served? How will you act, and what will you say? Rehearse as much as you need to, until you feel you can head into the festivities with confidence.

---

be worth the investment. One study of women in a weight-loss program found that those who had exercise equipment in their homes were better able to stick with a regular exercise routine, and maintained weight loss longer, than those who didn't. The trick is to choose machines you already have a history with and can see yourself using for a lifetime—otherwise, you might end up with an exercise bike that doubles as a coat rack.

"What problem? I don't have a problem." For most people with diabetes, some denial is almost inevitable—especially when they're first told they have the disease. It's a natural instinct to want to shield yourself from being too overwhelmed by bad news, and many doctors feel it's a first step toward accepting the diagnosis. But when denial persists, it can keep you from the day-to-day care that's essential in managing diabetes, and that can be life-threatening.

The key to managing denial, then, is to expect it, and know when it's coming. Usually, denial follows a typical script, with recognizable catch phrases like "I'll do it tomorrow, I don't have the time today," or "One bite won't hurt." If you hear yourself talking like this, or if you seem to be "forgetting" to follow your meal plan or missing medical appointments, you're probably in some stage of denial. Learn to recognize these signs in yourself— and make sure your family and friends know them too. Ask your diabetes-care team for help.

"Why bother?" This hopeless-sounding phrase can be a warning sign of depression. Studies show that depression is more common in people with diabetes than in the rest of the population. If you find yourself feeling "down" most of the time for more than two weeks, you may be depressed; talk to your health-care provider right away and get help. Other warning signs you should heed:

- Loss of pleasure; nothing seems to make you happy anymore.
- Loss of appetite.
- Feeling tired all the time.

- Changes in sleep patterns: difficulty getting to sleep, waking up too early or wanting to sleep all day.
- Trouble concentrating or remembering.
- Feeling like you can't do anything right.
- Suicidal thoughts, or thinking about ways to hurt yourself.

It's easy to see that these feelings can have a major impact on the all-important work of caring for yourself each day. How can you stick with your eating plan if you have no appetite or remember to take your medication when you're too tired to get out of bed? Depression can create a vicious cycle of feeling hopeless and overwhelmed, letting self-care slide and worsening diabetes symptoms. Don't keep your feelings to yourself.

Another important reason to see your health-care provider right away: Your depression may have a physical cause. Sometimes, if your blood glucose isn't under good control, it can produce depression-like symptoms; getting your levels back on track may clear up the problem. Depression can also signal thyroid problems or side effects of diabetes medications— all fully treatable.

"Why me? It's not fair!" It's easy to feel angry about having diabetes. After all, it's an illness that has life-threatening complications, and has to be dealt with every day. A little anger might even be a good thing, if it summons your energies to fight back against your diabetes by taking care of yourself. But sometimes anger can have just the opposite effect; you might be so angry at having diabetes that you refuse to deal with it. That can make you sicker—and angrier.

If you think anger is getting in your way, you

> **"**The most important thing to remember is moderation, not denial. People with diabetes just need to eat sensibly and get exercise… sounds like a diet for everyone!**"**
> —*Toni B., Florida*

8 TRADE-PROOF GOODIES FOR LUNCHBOXES

When your child has diabetes, a homemade lunch is your safest bet. A few items any kid would enjoy:

➧ **Fruity Kebabs:** Spear chunks of pineapple, cucumber, orange and/or grapes on toothpicks; include a small cup of sugar-free yogurt for dipping.

➧ **Happy Trails Mix:** Combine equal parts popcorn and whole-grain unsweetened cereal; add a small handful of orange-flavored dried cranberries.

➧ **Chips & Dip:** Pack up a small bag of baked tortilla chips; include a separate container of salsa you've spiked with shredded Cheddar cheese for dipping.

➧ **Do-It-Yourself Mini Stackers:** Provide whole-grain crackers, 1-inch squares of sliced roast turkey breast and cucumber rounds in separate containers. Let your child stack her own "sandwiches."

➧ **Mini Rice-Cake Sandwiches:** Spread peanut butter between mini rice cakes.

➧ **Taco Bites:** Provide separate containers of mini-taco shells (preferably trans-fat-free), low-fat bean dip, shredded part-skim mozzarella cheese and salsa.

➧ **Ham "Sushi":** Spread turkey ham lunchmeat with a thin layer of reduced-fat cream cheese. Sprinkle with shredded carrot and roll into a cylinder; slice crosswise into "sushi."

➧ **Petite Pitas:** Fill mini whole-wheat pitas with hummus, shredded lettuce and chopped tomato. Drizzle with Italian dressing; wrap tightly in plastic wrap.

Kids and Diabetes

If you have a child with diabetes, the only thing you can count on is change. It might seem as if you're dealing with an entirely different person each year or even every few months. Although most of these kids have type 1 diabetes, a growing number are facing type 2 at earlier ages. Wherever your child falls on the spectrum, it's important to get support. Other families going through similar experiences are a great resource, as is your diabetes specialist. A few considerations:

Toddlers and preschoolers. This is an age when kids are notoriously picky about their food; adding an eating plan to the picture makes it all the more challenging. The best approach is to try not to make food an issue. Make a variety of foods available so she'll have some choices, and don't urge her to eat if she's not hungry. If she needs to get something down to keep her blood sugar steady, offer some fruit juice or milk instead.

Children at this age also might not be able to understand symptoms of low blood glucose or be able to communicate them well—so you'll probably need to do blood-glucose checks more frequently. No child likes fingersticks or having insulin injections, but you can make them easier to administer by linking them with a reward, such as a sticker after each "poke" that can be collected and redeemed for nonfood treats.

School-age kids. Once a child with diabetes enters school, the teachers, school nurses, coaches and other support staff become partners in his care. Inform them on a need-to-know basis. Your child might not want anyone to know about his diabetes, because he wants to "fit in"; use your best judgment.

Many food-centered activities are part and parcel of American childhood, including birthday parties, Halloween, and holiday events. Your child shouldn't have to be excluded because he has diabetes. Often it's just a matter of planning ahead—calling the host to find out what will be served and deciding which to eat and which to skip. Your child could also bring some of his own treats to share. You and your child could adjust his eating plan and insulin schedule that day to accommodate some extra treats; he might skip his usual snack of pretzels so he can have a slice of birthday cake or some pieces of Halloween candy, for instance.

Tweens and Teens. In these years, kids' bodies are growing at differing rates, and they're usually dealing with the hormonal changes of puberty. All this can make their blood-glucose levels unpredictable and their diabetes harder to manage. Couple that with the emotional challenges of being a teen and you have a recipe for a bumpy ride. The biggest challenge for parents is allowing tweens and teens to earn the privilege of more freedom, while helping them understand their responsibilities. It means moving from a relationship where the parent is in control to more of a partnership. If your teen is slacking from her usual diabetes care, it's time to come up with a new plan—together. Set goals you can both agree on; praise her when she meets them, and refrain from criticizing her when she doesn't.

need to get to the bottom of it. What is it you're really mad about—and why? To find answers, experts recommend keeping an "anger diary": Before you go to bed, review the day you've had and write down the situations in which you found yourself angry at something or someone. After a while, you'll probably be able to see a pattern that can help you understand where your anger comes from and how to manage it. Maybe, like many people, you still haven't accepted that you have diabetes—or you feel as if you're battling something all alone. Talk with your health-care specialist about ways to help you deal with your angry feelings.

The Momentum of Healthy Change

Eating better, staying on top of your blood glucose, getting more activity each day — does it sound like a lot of work? Actually, the hardest work is just getting started. Once you've made the decision to take charge of your health, you'll find that other changes will be much easier to make. Each step you take will have a trickle-down effect on the rest of your health, boosting your feelings of well-being and your sense of being in charge. You'll carry that positive momentum into the next healthy decision, and the next, and the next. It all begins here, and now. Here's wishing you a wonderful journey!

PROFILES IN REAL LIFE

A NEW LIFE AND AN OLD LOVE

Margaret N., Ohio

Margaret N. is living proof that one good thing can lead to another. Within a year of being diagnosed with prediabetes, she had a stronger, healthier body—and had rekindled an old romance. "It's been quite a year," she admits.

The process began with the news at age 74 that she had "borderline" type 2 diabetes. "I wanted to do everything I could to stay on the right side of the border," Margaret recalls. Her first step was to meet with dietitians at the Westlake Family Health Center at the Cleveland Clinic Foundation to come up with an eating plan. She also took up walking. That's when the good things began: she started feeling stronger and more energetic, gradually losing 30 pounds—and, most important, her blood-glucose levels returned to the normal range.

Then, on the day she turned 75, she got a "Happy Birthday" e-mail from a man she'd reluctantly turned down when he asked her to marry him 32 years earlier. "Javier still remembered my birthday, after all those years!" she remarks. Though their lives' paths had diverged—he was now divorced and retired, living in Mexico City, and she was a widow—they still had strong feelings for each other. Now, their rekindled romance is back in full swing, albeit in long-distance form. "I love when he comes to visit because I have someone to walk with," laughs Margaret.

For Margaret, staying on top of her diabetes is largely a matter of portion control. Because she lives alone, she avoids bringing home large-quantity foods, especially of the fruits and breads she loves. "Instead of buying a whole watermelon, I'll get a smaller package of cut-up pieces and have just a little." She doesn't deny herself treats; rather, she enjoys them at restaurants instead of keeping them around the house. "I rarely have ice cream, but when I do, I'll get a single-serving ice cream bar."

Margaret also balances her meals throughout the day, eating just a cup of cottage cheese or sugar-free yogurt for dinner if she's had a big lunch. "I like to make lunch the biggest meal, because I've got most of the day still ahead of me to move around and work it off." And chances are, she'll be doing that with Javier, her favorite walking partner: "We both go at about the same pace—we're pretty compatible."

A Week of Menus
1,500 calories/day

Mix and match any breakfast with any lunch and any dinner to total about 11 Carbohydrate Servings with an average of 1,460 calories/day. This leaves you with the flexibility for 1 added Carbohydrate Serving snack per day (15 grams carbohydrate) whenever you would like to have it. A few snack suggestions that qualify:

1 small fresh fruit
1 cup fresh berries
2½ cups microwave popcorn
1½ cups raw vegetables
1 cup nonfat *or* low-fat milk *or* yogurt
¾ ounce pretzels (about 15 small)
More snack suggestions can be found on page 26.

Breakfast Menus

Each breakfast is 2 to 3 Carbohydrate Servings with an average of 369 calories.

	CARBOHYDRATE SERVINGS	CALORIES
Wake-Up Smoothie (*page 55*)	2	157
Whole-wheat toast, 1 slice	1	70
Natural peanut butter, 1 Tbsp.		94
Low-Sugar Plum Spread (*page 60*)		14
TOTAL	**3**	**335**
Scrambled Egg with Tofu (*page 46*)	0	140
Salsa Cornbread (*page 64*)	1	138
Milk, 1%, 8 oz.	1	102
TOTAL	**2**	**380**
Ingrid's Muesli (*page 58*)	2	190
Yogurt, nonfat, 6 oz., no-cal. sweetener	1	90
Soft-boiled egg	0	75
TOTAL	**3**	**355**

	CARBOHYDRATE SERVINGS	CALORIES
Zucchini Frittata (*page 48*)	1	376
⅓ cantaloupe	1	56
TOTAL	**2**	**432**
Berry Rich Muffin (*page 67*)	2	196
Yogurt, nonfat, 6 oz., no-cal. sweetener	1	90
Poached egg or Turkey, 1 oz. slice	0	75
TOTAL	**3**	**361**
Baked Asparagus & Cheese Frittata (*page 47*)	½	195
Milk, 1%, 8 oz.	1	102
Grapefruit half	1	51
TOTAL	**2½**	**348**
Crustless Crab Quiche (*page 50*)	1	225
Fresh strawberries, 1¼ cups	1	56
Yogurt, nonfat, 6 oz., no-cal. sweetener	1	90
TOTAL	**3**	**371**

Lunch Menus

Each lunch is 3 to 3½ Carbohydrate Servings with an average of 435 calories.

	CARBOHYDRATE SERVINGS	CALORIES
Shrimp Bisque (*page 96*)	1	184
Mixed Greens with Grapes & Feta		
(*page 111*)	½	135
Tropical Fruit Ice (*page 313*)	1	84
TOTAL	3½	403
Red Lentil Soup with a Spicy Sizzle		
(*page 100*)	1½	218
Spinach Salad with Goat Cheese &		
Pine Nuts (*page 112*)	½	194
Mandarin orange, ¾ cup	1	69
TOTAL	3	481
Lettuce Wraps with Spiced Pork		
(*page 215*)	1	331
Green Mango Salad (*page 115*)	1	64
Berry Frozen Yogurt (*page 315*)	1½	106
TOTAL	3½	501

	CARBOHYDRATE SERVINGS	CALORIES
Pasta & Bean Soup (*page 97*)	1	133
Spinach, Avocado & Mango Salad		
(*page 117*)	1	210
Yogurt, nonfat, 6 oz., no-cal. sweetener	1	90
TOTAL	3	433
Broccoli Chowder (*page 101*)	1½	180
Chicken Tabbouleh (*page 177*)	1½	260
Ginger-Orange Biscotti (*page 302*)	½	34
TOTAL	3½	474
Black Bean Burrito (*page 134*)	2	235
Southwestern Corn & Zucchini		
Sauté (*page 243*)	1	76
Strawberries with Vinegar (*page 280*)	½	31
TOTAL	3½	342
Curried Corn Bisque (*page 102*)	1½	138
Asian Slaw with Tofu & Shiitake		
Mushrooms (*page 108*)	½	178
Yogurt, nonfat, 6 oz., no-cal. sweetener	1	90
TOTAL	3	406

Supper Menus

Each supper is 3½ to 4 Carbohydrate Servings with an average of 571 calories.

	CARBOHYDRATE SERVINGS	CALORIES
Halibut Picante (*page 186*)	0	188
Bulgur-Chickpea Pilaf (*page 251*)	2	201
Green Beans with Toasted Nuts (*page 230*)	0	104
Roasted Mango Sorbet (*page 317*)	2	108
TOTAL	**4**	**601**
Curry-Roasted Shrimp with Oranges (*page 202*)	1	253
Brown rice, ½ cup	1	80
Roasted Green Beans with Sesame Seeds (*page 233*)	½	54
Mesclun greens (1½ cups) with	½	25
Orange-Ginger Vinaigrette (*page 121*)	0	39
Chocolate Cappuccino Wafers (2 wafers) (*page 300*)	1	84
TOTAL	**4**	**535**
Turkey Cutlets with Sage & Lemon (*page 147*)	0	205
Glazed Mini Carrots (*page 239*)	1	74
Mashed potatoes, ½ cup	1	125
Mixed greens (1½ cups) with	½	25
Light Ranch Dressing, 2 Tbsp. (*page 120*)	0	24
Plum Fool (*page 283*)	1½	156
TOTAL	**4**	**609**

	CARBOHYDRATE SERVINGS	CALORIES
Chicken Breast with Roasted Lemons (*page 148*)	½	219
Mediterranean Lima Beans (*page 245*)	1½	190
Arugula-Mushroom Salad (*page 106*)	0	62
One-Bowl Chocolate Cake (*page 288*)	1½	134
TOTAL	**3½**	**605**
Grilled Pork Tenderloin with Mustard, Rosemary & Apple Marinade (*page212*)	½	214
Sweet Potato Casserole (*page 254*)	2	223
Salad of Boston Lettuce with Creamy Orange-Shallot Dressing (*page 116*)	1	64
Rolled Sugar Cookie (*page 301*)	½	53
TOTAL	**4**	**554**
Southwestern Steak & Peppers (*page 222*)	1	226
Tex-Mex Summer Squash Casserole (*page 235*)	½	101
Roasted Corn, Black Bean & Mango Salad (*page 118*)	2	125
Ginger-Orange Biscotti (*page 302*)	½	34
TOTAL	**4**	**486**
Tofu with Peanut-Ginger Sauce (*page 126*)	1	225
Wild Rice with Shiitakes & Toasted Almonds (*page 248*)	1½	159
Spinach Salad with Black Olive Vinaigrette (*page 107*)	0	128
Apricot-Almond Bar with Chocolate (*page 306*)	1	96
TOTAL	**3½**	**608**

A Week of Menus
2,000 calories/day

Mix and match any breakfast with any lunch and any dinner to total about 13 to 14 Carbohydrate Servings with an average of 1,750 calories /day. This leaves you with the flexibility for 2 to 3 added Carbohydrate Serving snacks per day (15 grams carbohydrate each) whenever you would like to have them. A few snack suggestions that qualify:

1 small fresh fruit
1 cup fresh berries
½ cup ice cream
1½ cups cooked vegetables
1 cup nonfat *or* low-fat milk
1 cup nonfat *or* low-fat yogurt
More snack suggestions can be found on page 26.

Breakfast Menus

Each breakfast is 3 to 4½ Carbohydrate Servings with an average of 435 calories.

	CARBOHYDRATE SERVINGS	CALORIES
Eggs Baked over a Spicy Vegetable Ragout (*page 51*)	1	201
Zucchini-Walnut Loaf (*page 66*)	1½	118
Milk, 1%, 8 oz.	1	102
TOTAL	3½	421
Greek Potato & Feta Omelet (*page 49*)	1	298
Grapefruit half	1	51
Milk, 1%, 8 oz.	1	102
TOTAL	3	451
Spiced Apple Butter Bran Muffin (*page 69*)	2	197
Milk, 1%, 8 oz.	1	102
Sliced kiwi, 1 medium	1	56
Cottage cheese, ½ cup, fat-free	0	70
TOTAL	4	425

	CARBOHYDRATE SERVINGS	CALORIES
Scrambled Egg Burrito (*page 59*)	2	328
Milk, 1%, 8 oz.	1	102
TOTAL	3	430
Maple-Nut & Pear Scone (*page 71*)	2	233
Yogurt, nonfat, 6 oz., no-cal. sweetener	1	90
Cantaloupe, ⅓ melon	1	56
Poached egg	0	75
TOTAL	4	454
Tropical Fruit Smoothie (*page 55*)	1½	109
Orange-Date Pumpkin Muffin (*page 77*)	3	223
Cottage cheese, ½ cup, fat-free	0	70
TOTAL	4½	402
Healthy Pancakes, 2 each (*page 53*)	1½	272
Syrup, regular, 1 Tbsp., or light, 2 Tbsp.	1	80
Yogurt nonfat, 3 oz., no-cal. sweetener	½	45
Blueberries, ¾ cup	1	61
TOTAL	4	458

Lunch Menus

Each lunch is 4 to 5 Carbohydrate Servings with an average of 603 calories.

	CARBOHYDRATE SERVINGS	CALORIES
Spicy Mushroom & Rice Soup (*page 103*)	2	208
Tuna & White Bean Salad (*page 198*)	1	226
Milk, 1%, 8 oz.	1	102
Chewy Chocolate Brownie (*page 307*)	1	93
TOTAL	**5**	**629**
Lentil & Escarole Soup (*page 98*)	1	181
Spinach, Avocado & Mango Salad		
(*page 117*)	1	210
Milk, 1%, 8 oz.	1	102
Strawberry Frozen Yogurt (*page 312*)	1	82
TOTAL	**4**	**575**
Roasted Tomato Soup (*page 95*)	1	95
Asian Chicken Salad (*page 153*)	1	289
Milk, 1%, 8 oz.	1	102
Plum & Apple Compote with		
Vanilla Custard (*page 270*)	1½	119
TOTAL	**4½**	**605**

	CARBOHYDRATE SERVINGS	CALORIES
Tuscan Chicken & White Bean Soup		
(*page 94*)	½	164
Pasta, Tuna & Roasted Pepper Salad		
(*page 207*)	2	270
Milk, 1%, 8 oz.	1	102
Spiced Pumpkin Cookie (*page 305*)	1	68
TOTAL	**4½**	**604**
Honey Mustard Turkey Burger		
(*page 179*)	2	313
Broccoli Slaw (*page 109*)	½	80
Yogurt, nonfat, 6 oz., no-cal. sweetener	1	90
Grapes, 1 bunch, approx. 17	1	60
TOTAL	**4½**	**543**
Romaine Salad with Chicken,		
Apricots & Mint (*page 180*)	2	456
Milk, 1%, 8 oz.	1	102
Nectarine, small	1	67
TOTAL	**4**	**625**
Easy Chicken Burrito (*page 183*)	2½	371
Milk, 1%, 8 oz.	1	102
Frozen Raspberry Mousse (*page 316*)	2	168
TOTAL	**4½**	**641**

Supper Menus

Each supper is 5 to 6 Carbohydrate Servings with an average of 721 calories.

	CARBOHYDRATE SERVINGS	CALORIES
Salt & Pepper Sirloin (*page 221*)	1	294
Peppers Stuffed with Zucchini &		
Corn (*page 246*)	1½	198
Medium baked potato	2	160
with 1½ Tbsp. reduced-fat sour cream	0	23
Honeydew melon, 1 cup	1	59
TOTAL	**5½**	**734**
Grilled Lamb with		
Fresh Mint Chutney (*page 211*)	½	296
Green Beans with Poppy Seed		
Dressing (*page 241*)	1	113
Bulgur-Chickpea Pilaf (*page 251*)	2	201
Orange Slices with Warm		
Raspberries (*page 282*)	1½	122
TOTAL	**5**	**732**
Herbed Scallop Kebabs (*page 188*)	0	152
Citrusy Couscous Salad with Olives		
(*page 252*)	2	206
Roasted Green Beans with		
Sesame Seeds (*page 233*)	½	54
Lemony Carrot Salad with Dill		
(*page 109*)	½	90
Marmalade-Glazed Orange		
Cheesecake (*page 292*)	2	199
TOTAL	**5**	**701**

	CARBOHYDRATE SERVINGS	CALORIES
Oven-Fried Fish Fillet (*page 199*)	1	229
Tangy Tartar Sauce (*page 196*)	0	29
Roasted Asparagus with		
Pine Nuts (*page 244*)	1	112
Brown rice, ½ cup	1	80
Sugar Snap Salad (*page 113*)	½	104
Frozen Raspberry Mousse (*page 316*)	2	168
TOTAL	**5½**	**722**
Pampered Chicken (*page 151*)	½	258
Carrot Sauté with		
Ginger & Orange (*page 239*)	1	69
Fragrant Bulgur Pilaf (*page 236*)	1	176
Sliced Fennel Salad (*page 107*)	0	51
Strawberry-Rhubarb Tart (*page 294*)	2½	185
TOTAL	**5**	**739**
Spinach Salad with		
Black Olive Vinaigrette (*page 107*)	0	128
Chicken Paprikash (*page 155*)	1	234
Wide noodles, 1 cup	2	160
Rustic Berry Tart (*page 290*)	2	200
TOTAL	**5**	**722**
Whole-Wheat Spaghetti with Roasted		
Onions & Chard (*page 143*)	3	291
Chickpea-Spinach Salad with	1	119
Spiced Yogurt Dressing (*page 114*)		
Milk, 1%, 8 oz.	1	102
Almond Cream with		
Strawberries (*page 280*)	1	189
TOTAL	**6**	**701**

Model for a Food Diary

Make copies of this page and use one each day to keep track of your intake.

TIME	FOOD	PORTION	CALORIES	CARB GRAMS	CARB SERVINGS	NOTES

Model for an Exercise Log

Write down your time spent exercising or being active and add up the totals for each day.

DAY OF WEEK	ACTIVITY OR EXERCISE	MINUTES SPENT	NOTES/GOALS

CHAPTER ONE

Healthy Starts

Scrambled Egg with Tofu

Quick ☼ Easy

Even when you are cooking for one, it's worth taking a few minutes to make a hot, protein-rich breakfast. By stretching an egg with a little tofu, you reduce the cholesterol and saturated fat. Try tucking it into a whole-wheat pita pocket for a simple and satisfying breakfast sandwich—and a healthful alternative to fast-food fare.

O

CARBOHYDRATE
SERVINGS

MAKES 1 SERVING

PREP TIME: 5 MINUTES
START TO FINISH: 5 MINUTES

PER SERVING

140 CALORIES
11 G FAT (2 G SAT, 6 G MONO)
212 MG CHOLESTEROL
2 G CARBOHYDRATE
9 G PROTEIN
1 G FIBER
230 MG SODIUM

NUTRITION BONUS: Selenium
(23% DAILY VALUE).

EXCHANGES

1 MEDIUM-FAT MEAT
1 FAT (MONO)

1	large egg
½	teaspoon dried tarragon
	Dash of hot sauce, such as Tabasco
	Pinch of salt
	Freshly ground pepper to taste
1	teaspoon extra-virgin olive oil *or* canola oil
2	tablespoons crumbled tofu (silken *or* regular)

Blend egg, tarragon, hot sauce, salt and pepper in a small bowl with a fork. Heat oil in a small nonstick skillet over medium-low heat. Add tofu and cook, stirring, until warmed through, 20 to 30 seconds. Add egg mixture and stir until the egg is set, but still creamy, 20 to 30 seconds. Serve immediately.

TIPS FOR REAL LIFE

9 "GRAB-AND-GO" BREAKFASTS

No time to eat breakfast? Think again, because it's the most important meal of the day. These nine breakfasts will fit into the busiest schedule.

BREAKFAST CHOICE	CARBOHYDRATE SERVING(S)
➤ Whole-wheat English muffin half with 1 tablespoon peanut or almond butter	1
➤ 4-ounce container low-fat cottage cheese with 2 tablespoons raisins or dried cranberries	1
➤ Hard-cooked large egg with 2 brown-rice cakes	1
➤ 1 medium apple or orange with 1 ounce (small handful) almonds	1½
➤ 1 slice cold (leftover) cheese pizza	2
➤ ½ small whole-wheat pita with 3 tablespoons low-fat black-bean dip	2
➤ ½ small whole-wheat bagel with 2 tablespoons part-skim ricotta	2
➤ Whole-grain toaster waffle with 6-ounce container light fruit-flavored yogurt	2
➤ ¾ cup mixed unsweetened whole-grain cereal with 1 ounce (small handful) mixed nuts	2

Baked Asparagus & Cheese Frittata

Perfect for a spring brunch or light supper, this Italian omelet is baked so it is easy to serve to a group.

1/2

CARBOHYDRATE
SERVING

2	tablespoons fine dry breadcrumbs
1	pound thin asparagus
1½	teaspoons extra-virgin olive oil
2	onions, chopped
1	red bell pepper, chopped
2	cloves garlic, minced
½	teaspoon salt, divided
½	cup water
	Freshly ground pepper to taste
4	large eggs
2	large egg whites
1	cup part-skim ricotta cheese
1	tablespoon chopped fresh parsley
½	cup shredded Gruyère cheese

1. Preheat oven to 325°F. Coat a 10-inch pie pan or ceramic quiche dish with cooking spray. Sprinkle with breadcrumbs, tapping out the excess.
2. Snap tough ends off asparagus. Slice off the top 2 inches of the tips and reserve. Cut the stalks into ½-inch-long slices.
3. Heat oil in a large nonstick skillet over medium-high heat. Add onions, bell pepper, garlic and ¼ teaspoon salt; cook, stirring, until softened, 5 to 7 minutes.
4. Add water and the asparagus stalks to the skillet. Cook, stirring, until the asparagus is tender and the liquid has evaporated, about 7 minutes (the mixture should be very dry). Season with salt and pepper. Arrange the vegetables in an even layer in the prepared pan.
5. Whisk eggs and egg whites in a large bowl. Add ricotta, parsley, the remaining ¼ teaspoon salt and pepper; whisk to blend. Pour the egg mixture over the vegetables, gently shaking the pan to distribute. Scatter the reserved asparagus tips over the top and sprinkle with Gruyère.
6. Bake the frittata until a knife inserted in the center comes out clean, about 35 minutes. Let stand for 5 minutes before serving.

MAKES 6 SERVINGS

PREP TIME: 20 MINUTES
START TO FINISH: 1 HOUR

PER SERVING

195	CALORIES
11	G FAT (5 G SAT, 4 G MONO)
164	MG CHOLESTEROL
10	G CARBOHYDRATE
14	G PROTEIN
2	G FIBER
356	MG SODIUM

NUTRITION BONUS: Vitamin C (70% DAILY VALUE), Vitamin A (30% DV).

EXCHANGES

2	VEGETABLE
1	MEDIUM-FAT MEAT
½	HIGH-FAT MEAT

1

CARBOHYDRATE
SERVING

MAKES **2** SERVINGS

PREP TIME: 20 MINUTES

START TO FINISH: 35 MINUTES

PER SERVING

376 CALORIES

28 G FAT (10 G SAT, 13 G MONO)

445 MG CHOLESTEROL

11 G CARBOHYDRATE

21 G PROTEIN

3 G FIBER

591 MG SODIUM

NUTRITION BONUS: Vitamin A (40% DAILY VALUE), Vitamin C (40% DV), Iron (25% DV), Folate (22% DV), Calcium (20% DV).

EXCHANGES

2 VEGETABLE

2 MEDIUM-FAT MEAT

1 HIGH-FAT MEAT

2 FAT

Zucchini Frittata

Quick ☼ Easy

A frittata, as a flat omelet is known in Italy, can be filled with a variety of vegetables and cheeses and makes a great impromptu brunch dish or supper. In this version, fresh mint and basil brighten the mild taste of zucchini. If you prefer, use feta or ricotta salata in place of goat cheese. (*Photograph: page 169.*)

4	teaspoons extra-virgin olive oil, divided
1	cup diced zucchini (1 small)
½	cup chopped onion
½	cup grape tomatoes *or* cherry tomatoes, halved
¼	cup slivered fresh mint leaves
¼	cup slivered fresh basil leaves
¼	teaspoon salt, divided
	Freshly ground pepper to taste
4	large eggs
⅓	cup crumbled goat cheese (2 ounces)

1. Heat 2 teaspoons oil in a 10-inch nonstick skillet over medium heat. Add zucchini and onion; cook, stirring often, for 1 minute. Cover and reduce heat to medium-low; cook, stirring occasionally, until the zucchini is tender, but not mushy, 3 to 5 minutes. Add tomatoes, mint, basil, ⅛ teaspoon salt and a grinding of pepper; increase heat to medium-high and cook, stirring, until the moisture has evaporated, 30 to 60 seconds.

2. Whisk eggs, the remaining ⅛ teaspoon salt and a grinding of pepper in a large bowl until blended. Add the zucchini mixture and cheese; stir to combine.

3. Preheat the broiler.

4. Wipe out the pan and brush it with the remaining 2 teaspoons oil; place over medium-low heat. Add the frittata mixture and cook, without stirring, until the bottom is light golden, 2 to 4 minutes. As it cooks, lift the edges and tilt the pan so uncooked egg will flow to the edges.

5. Place the skillet under the broiler and broil until the frittata is set and the top is golden, 1½ to 2½ minutes. Loosen the edges and slide onto a plate. Cut into wedges and serve.

Greek Potato & Feta Omelet

Quick ☼ Easy

Potatoes have a special affinity with eggs. If you keep frozen hash browns on hand (check the label and choose hash browns with less than 1 gram of fat per serving), you can whip up a simple, satisfying omelet like this one at a moment's notice. To cut back on saturated fat, use 2 whole eggs and 2 egg whites.

2	teaspoons extra-virgin olive oil, divided
1	cup frozen hash brown potatoes *or* cooked potatoes cut into ½-inch cubes
⅓	cup chopped scallions
4	large eggs
⅛	teaspoon salt
	Freshly ground pepper to taste
¼	cup crumbled feta cheese

1. Heat 1 teaspoon oil in a 10-inch nonstick skillet over medium-high heat. Add potatoes and cook, shaking the pan and tossing the potatoes, until golden brown, 4 to 5 minutes. Add scallions and cook for 1 minute longer. Transfer to a plate. Wipe out the pan.
2. Blend eggs, salt and pepper in a medium bowl. Stir in feta and the potato mixture.
3. Preheat broiler. Brush the pan with the remaining 1 teaspoon oil; heat over medium heat. Add the egg mixture and tilt to distribute evenly. Reduce heat to medium-low and cook until the bottom is light golden, lifting the the edges to allow uncooked egg to flow underneath, 3 to 4 minutes. Place the pan under the broiler and cook until the top is set, 1½ to 2½ minutes. Slide the omelet onto a plate and cut into wedges.

1

CARBOHYDRATE
SERVING

MAKES 2 SERVINGS

PREP TIME: 10 MINUTES
START TO FINISH: 20 MINUTES

PER SERVING

298 CALORIES
17 G FAT (5 G SAT, 7 G MONO)
431 MG CHOLESTEROL
18 G CARBOHYDRATE
16 G PROTEIN
3 G FIBER
428 MG SODIUM

NUTRITION BONUS: Vitamin A (15% DAILY VALUE), Vitamin C (15% DV).

EXCHANGES

1 STARCH
2 MEDIUM-FAT MEAT
1½ FAT (MONO)

1

CARBOHYDRATE

SERVING

Crustless Crab Quiche

Here is an EATINGWELL take on a favorite seafood brunch dish that's usually dripping with saturated fat. Our version gets its richness from cottage cheese and yogurt, with a small amount of real Parmesan and Cheddar. We find that using just a little of a great-tasting cheese goes a long way in creating a full flavor.

MAKES 6 SERVINGS

PREP TIME: 20 MINUTES
START TO FINISH: 1¼ HOURS

PER SERVING

225 CALORIES

9 G FAT (4 G SAT, 3 G MONO)

112 MG CHOLESTEROL

14 G CARBOHYDRATE

22 G PROTEIN

2 G FIBER

558 MG SODIUM

NUTRITION BONUS: Vitamin C (70% DAILY VALUE), Calcium (25% DV), Vitamin A (20% DV).

EXCHANGES

2½ VEGETABLE

1½ VERY LEAN MEAT

1 HIGH-FAT MEAT

2	teaspoons extra-virgin olive oil, divided
1	onion, chopped
1	red bell pepper, chopped
12	ounces mushrooms, wiped clean and sliced (about 4½ cups)
2	large eggs
2	large egg whites
1½	cups low-fat cottage cheese
½	cup low-fat plain yogurt
¼	cup all-purpose flour
¼	cup freshly grated Parmesan cheese
¼	teaspoon cayenne pepper
¼	teaspoon salt, or to taste
¼	teaspoon freshly ground pepper
8	ounces cooked lump crabmeat (fresh *or* frozen and thawed), drained and picked over (about 1 cup)
½	cup grated sharp Cheddar cheese (2 ounces)
¼	cup chopped scallions

1. Preheat oven to 350°F. Coat a 10-inch pie pan or ceramic quiche dish with cooking spray.

2. Heat 1 teaspoon oil in large nonstick skillet over medium-high heat. Add onion and bell pepper; cook, stirring, until softened, about 5 minutes; transfer to a large bowl. Add the remaining 1 teaspoon oil to the skillet and heat over high heat. Add mushrooms and cook, stirring, until they have softened and most of their liquid has evaporated, 5 to 7 minutes. Add to the bowl with the onion mixture.

3. Place eggs, egg whites, cottage cheese, yogurt, flour, Parmesan, cayenne, salt and pepper in a food processor or blender; blend until smooth. Add to the vegetable mixture, along with crab, Cheddar and scallions; mix with a rubber spatula. Pour into the prepared baking dish.

4. Bake the quiche until a knife inserted in the center comes out clean, 40 to 50 minutes. Let stand for 5 minutes before serving.

Eggs Baked Over a Spicy Vegetable Ragout

High ⬆ Fiber

This rustic dish typifies Mediterranean home cooking at its best: a full-flavored vegetable stew is topped with eggs to become a main dish. Any hot sauce you have on hand will add a nice jolt of heat, but for a complex, authentic flavor, try harissa, a chile paste from North Africa.

3	teaspoons extra-virgin olive oil, divided
1	small eggplant, cut into ½-inch cubes
1	medium onion, chopped
1	large red bell pepper, diced
6	cloves garlic, minced
2	teaspoons ground cumin
⅛-¼	teaspoon hot sauce, such as Tabasco
1	medium summer squash, halved lengthwise and thinly sliced
1	14½-ounce can diced tomatoes
¼	cup water
3	tablespoons chopped fresh parsley, divided
⅛	teaspoon salt, or to taste
	Freshly ground pepper to taste
4	large eggs

1. Preheat oven to 400°F. Coat a shallow 2-quart baking dish with cooking spray.
2. Heat 2 teaspoons oil in a large nonstick skillet over medium-high heat. Add eggplant and cook, stirring frequently, until browned and softened, 5 to 7 minutes. Transfer to a plate.
3. Heat the remaining 1 teaspoon oil in a Dutch oven or large deep sauté pan over medium heat. Add onion and cook, stirring occasionally, until softened, 3 to 5 minutes. Add bell pepper and cook, stirring occasionally, until softened, 3 to 5 minutes. Add garlic, cumin and hot sauce and cook until fragrant, 15 to 30 seconds. Stir in squash, tomatoes, water and the eggplant. Cover and simmer for 10 minutes. Stir in 2 tablespoons parsley, salt and pepper.
4. Spread the vegetable ragout in the prepared baking dish. Make 4 shallow wells in the ragout and gently crack 1 egg into each well, being careful not to break yolks.
5. Bake, uncovered, until the eggs are barely set, 10 to 12 minutes. (Caution: Eggs can overcook very quickly. Check them often and remove from the oven when they still look a little underdone; they will continue to cook in the hot ragout. If the baking dish is ceramic, the cooking time will be closer to 12 minutes. A glass dish will cook eggs much faster.) Sprinkle with the remaining 1 tablespoon parsley. Serve immediately.

MAKES 4 SERVINGS

PREP TIME: 30 MINUTES
START TO FINISH: 1 HOUR 10 MINUTES

TO MAKE AHEAD: Prepare through Step 3, cover and refrigerate for up to 2 days. Reheat before continuing.

PER SERVING
201 CALORIES
9 G FAT (2 G SAT, 5 G MONO)
212 MG CHOLESTEROL
23 G CARBOHYDRATE
10 G PROTEIN
6 G FIBER
282 MG SODIUM

NUTRITION BONUS: Vitamin C (170% DAILY VALUE), Vitamin A (45% DV), Fiber (24% DV), Folate (17% DV), Iron (15% DV).

EXCHANGES
4 VEGETABLE
1 MEDIUM-FAT MEAT
½ FAT (MONO)

Swiss Fondue Strata

You can't beat strata for a convenient make-ahead breakfast or brunch dish. Assemble it the night before, take it out of the refrigerator when you get up and just pop it in the oven about 1½ hours before you need it. In this version, a splash of white wine complements the Gruyère, giving the strata a flavor that is reminiscent of a rich cheese fondue.

MAKES 8 SERVINGS

PREP TIME: 20 MINUTES

START TO FINISH: 2 HOURS
(plus 8 hours in the refrigerator)

PER SERVING

276	CALORIES
12	G FAT (5 G SAT, 4 G MONO)
135	MG CHOLESTEROL
19	G CARBOHYDRATE
21	G PROTEIN
2	G FIBER
783	MG SODIUM

NUTRITION BONUS: Calcium
(30% DAILY VALUE).

EXCHANGES

1	STARCH
½	MILK
2	MEDIUM-FAT MEAT

4	cups cubed whole-wheat country bread (8 ounces)
1	cup grated Gruyère cheese
⅓	cup coarsely chopped ham (2 ounces)
4	large eggs
4	large egg whites
1	tablespoon Dijon mustard
1¾	cups 1% milk
1	cup low-fat cottage cheese
½	cup dry white wine
½	cup chopped scallions
½	teaspoon salt, or to taste
¼	teaspoon freshly ground pepper
⅛	teaspoon cayenne pepper
½	cup freshly grated Parmesan *or* Asiago cheese

1. Coat a 9-by-13-inch or similar baking dish with cooking spray. Arrange bread evenly in the baking dish. Sprinkle Gruyère and ham over the bread.
2. Whisk eggs, egg whites and mustard in a large bowl until smooth. Whisk in milk, cottage cheese, wine, scallions, salt, pepper and cayenne. Pour the egg mixture over the cheese, ham and bread.
3. Cover the baking dish with foil and refrigerate overnight or up to 24 hours.
4. About 30 minutes before baking, remove the strata from the refrigerator. Preheat oven to 325°F.
5. Bake the strata, covered, until set, about 1 hour 10 minutes. Uncover and sprinkle Parmesan (or Asiago) over the top. Bake, uncovered, until the top is lightly browned and crusted, about 10 minutes more. Let stand for 10 minutes before serving.

Healthy Pancakes

High ↑ Fiber   Quick ☼ Easy

EatingWell reader Kathy Moseler of Barrington Hills, Illinois, contributed this convenient recipe to our *Kitchen to Kitchen* department. The pancakes are made with 100 percent whole-wheat flour and get an additional fiber boost from flaxseed meal.

1½ **cups skim *or* 1% milk**
¼ **cup canola oil**
1 **teaspoon vanilla extract**
2 **cups Healthy Pancake Mix (*recipe follows*)**

1. Combine milk, oil and vanilla in a glass measuring cup. Place Healthy Pancake Mix in a large bowl and make a well in the center. Whisk in the milk mixture until just blended; do not overmix. (The batter will seem quite thin, but will thicken up as it stands.) Let stand for 5 minutes.

2. Coat a nonstick skillet or griddle with cooking spray and place over medium heat. Whisk the batter. Using ¼ cup batter for each pancake, cook pancakes until the edges are dry and bubbles begin to form, about 2 minutes. Turn over and cook until golden brown, about 2 minutes longer. Adjust heat as necessary for even browning.

Healthy Pancake Mix

Quick ☼ Easy

With this mix on hand, you can enjoy homemade pancakes on busy weekday mornings. This is also a great item to pack on camping trips. Be sure to refrigerate or freeze the mix as flaxseed meal is highly perishable.

2½ **cups whole-wheat flour**
1 **cup buttermilk powder (*see Note*)**
5 **tablespoons dried egg whites, such as Just Whites (*see Ingredient Note, page 323*)**
¼ **cup sugar**
1½ **tablespoons baking powder**
2 **teaspoons baking soda**
1 **teaspoon salt**
1 **cup flaxseed meal (*see Note*)**
1 **cup nonfat dry milk**
½ **cup wheat bran *or* oat bran**

Whisk flour, buttermilk powder, dried egg whites, sugar, baking powder, baking soda and salt in a large bowl. Stir in flaxseed meal, dry milk and bran. Store in an airtight container.

VARIATIONS

❧ **CHOCOLATE-CHOCOLATE CHIP PANCAKES:** Fold ½ cup cocoa powder and 3 ounces chocolate chips into the batter.

❧ **BLUEBERRY:** Fold 1 cup frozen blueberries into the batter.

❧ **BANANA-NUT:** Fold 1 cup thinly sliced bananas and 4 tablespoons finely chopped toasted pecans into the batter.

1½

CARBOHYDRATE
SERVINGS

MAKES 6 SERVINGS, 2 PANCAKES EACH

PREP TIME: 5 MINUTES
START TO FINISH: 10 MINUTES

PER SERVING
272 CALORIES
13 G FAT (2 G SAT, 6 G MONO)
8 MG CHOLESTEROL
27 G CARBOHYDRATE
12 G PROTEIN
5 G FIBER
471 MG SODIUM

NUTRITION BONUS: Calcium (24% DAILY VALUE), Fiber (20% DV).

EXCHANGES
2 STARCH
1 VERY LEAN MEAT
2 FAT (MONO)

For Healthy Pancake Mix:

MAKES 6 CUPS, ENOUGH FOR 3 BATCHES OF PANCAKES

PREP TIME: 20 MINUTES
START TO FINISH: 20 MINUTES

TO MAKE AHEAD: Refrigerate the dry mix in an airtight container or ziplock bag for up to 1 month or freeze for up to 3 months.

INGREDIENT NOTES
Buttermilk powder, such as Saco Buttermilk Blend, is a useful substitute for fresh buttermilk. Look in the baking section or with the powdered milk in most markets.

You can find flaxseed meal in the natural-foods section of large supermarkets. You can also start with whole flaxseeds: Grind ⅔ cup whole flaxseeds to yield 1 cup. (*Sources: page 324.*)

Southwestern Omelet Wrap

Quick ☼ Easy

Folding a flat omelet in a whole-wheat wrapper makes a high-protein breakfast (or lunch) that is totable and fun. If you want to start the day with a hot egg breakfast, but don't want to fuss with cooking in the morning, you can make this wrap the night before. In the morning, just microwave and go.

- 1 **large egg**
- 1 **large egg white**
- ½ **teaspoon hot sauce, such as Tabasco**
  Freshly ground pepper to taste
- 1 **tablespoon chopped scallions**
- 1 **tablespoon chopped fresh cilantro *or* parsley (optional)**
- 2 **tablespoons prepared black bean dip**
- 1 **9-inch whole-wheat wrap (*see Note*)**
- 1 **teaspoon canola oil**
- 2 **tablespoons grated pepper Jack *or* Cheddar cheese**
- 1 **tablespoon prepared green *or* red salsa (optional)**

1. Set oven rack 6 inches from the heat source; preheat broiler. Stir eggs, hot sauce and pepper briskly with a fork in a medium bowl. Stir in scallions and cilantro (or parsley), if using.
2. If black bean dip is cold, warm it in the microwave on High for 10 to 20 seconds. Place wrap between paper towels and warm in the microwave on High for about 10 seconds. Spread bean dip over the wrap, leaving a 1-inch border all around.
3. Brush oil over a 10-inch nonstick skillet; heat over medium heat. Add the egg mixture and cook, lifting the edges with a heat-resistant rubber spatula so uncooked egg will flow underneath, until the bottom is light golden, 20 to 30 seconds. Place the skillet under the broiler and broil just until the top is set, 20 to 30 seconds. Immediately slide the omelet onto the wrap. Sprinkle with cheese. Fold the edges over the omelet on two sides, then roll the wrap up and around the omelet. Serve immediately, with salsa, if desired.

1½

CARBOHYDRATE

SERVINGS

MAKES 1 SERVING

PREP TIME: 15 MINUTES

START TO FINISH: 20 MINUTES

TO MAKE AHEAD: Wrap in plastic and refrigerate, overnight. To reheat, remove plastic wrap and rewrap in paper towel. Microwave at High for 1 to 2 minutes.

INGREDIENT NOTE
You can find wraps for roll-up sandwiches in the deli section of large supermarkets. Cedar's Foods (www.cedarsfoods.com) makes a good whole-wheat one.

PER SERVING

- 321 CALORIES
- 17 G FAT (5 G SAT, 5 G MONO)
- 227 MG CHOLESTEROL
- 24 G CARBOHYDRATE
- 18 G PROTEIN
- 2 G FIBER
- 677 MG SODIUM

NUTRITION BONUS: Calcium (25% DAILY VALUE), Vitamin A (15% DV).

EXCHANGES
- 1½ STARCH
- 1 MEDIUM-FAT MEAT
- 1 HIGH-FAT MEAT
- 1 FAT (MONO)

Tropical Fruit Smoothie

Quick Easy

A blend of tropical fruits makes a refreshing breakfast smoothie. You can boost the fiber content by adding a sprinkling of oat or wheat bran, if you like.

- 1 cup cubed fresh *or* canned pineapple
- 1 banana, sliced
- ½ cup silken tofu *or* low-fat plain yogurt
- ⅓ cup frozen passion fruit concentrate
- ½ cup water
- 2 ice cubes
- 1 tablespoon wheat bran *or* oat bran (optional)

Combine all ingredients in a blender; cover and blend until creamy. Serve immediately.

Wake-Up Smoothie

Quick Easy

With a stash of berries in your freezer, you can jump-start your day with this nutritious, tasty smoothie in just minutes. It provides vitamin C, fiber, potassium and soy protein.

- 1¼ cups orange juice, preferably calcium-fortified
- 1 banana
- 1¼ cups frozen berries, such as raspberries, blackberries, blueberries *and/or* strawberries
- ½ cup low-fat silken tofu *or* low-fat plain yogurt
- 1 tablespoon sugar *or* Splenda Granular (optional)

Combine all ingredients in a blender; cover and blend until creamy. Serve immediately.

1½

CARBOHYDRATE
SERVINGS

MAKES 3 SERVINGS, ¾ CUP EACH

PREP TIME: 5 MINUTES
START TO FINISH: 5 MINUTES

PER SERVING

109 CALORIES
2 G FAT (0 G SAT, 0 G MONO)
0 MG CHOLESTEROL
21 G CARBOHYDRATE
4 G PROTEIN
2 G FIBER
26 MG SODIUM

NUTRITION BONUS: Vitamin C (40% DAILY VALUE).

EXCHANGES

1 FRUIT
½ LOW-FAT MILK

For Wake-Up Smoothie:

2

CARBOHYDRATE
SERVINGS

MAKES 3 SERVINGS, 1 CUP EACH

PREP TIME: 5 MINUTES
START TO FINISH: 5 MINUTES

PER SERVING

157 CALORIES
2 G FAT (0 G SAT, 0 G MONO)
0 MG CHOLESTEROL
33 G CARBOHYDRATE
4 G PROTEIN
4 G FIBER
19 MG SODIUM

NUTRITION BONUS: Vitamin C (110% DAILY VALUE), Fiber (16% DV).

EXCHANGES

2 FRUIT
½ LOW-FAT MILK

MAKES **4** SERVINGS, ½ CUP EACH

PREP TIME: 5 MINUTES

START TO FINISH: 15 MINUTES

NOTE: The cooking times will vary considerably depending on the power of your microwave. New microwaves tend to cook much faster than older models.

PER SERVING

142 CALORIES

2 G FAT (0 G SAT, 1 G MONO)

0 MG CHOLESTEROL

30 G CARBOHYDRATE

4 G PROTEIN

4 G FIBER

40 MG SODIUM

NUTRITION BONUS: Fiber (16% DAILY VALUE).

EXCHANGES

1½ STARCH

½ FRUIT

Cocoa-Date Oatmeal

Quick ☼ Easy

"I was inspired by the news that chocolate can be good for you," wrote reader Jennifer Sanders of Cambridge, Ontario. "Why not eat it for breakfast?" She shared her recipe for this heart-warming chocolaty hot cereal. If you are looking for a way to get your kids to start their day with a bowl of oatmeal, this is it. The microwave is convenient, but you can also cook the oatmeal on the stovetop following package directions. Top the cereal with milk or soymilk and sweeten with brown sugar or no-calorie sweetener, if desired.

¼ **cup chopped pitted dates (10-12 dates)**
1 **cup old-fashioned rolled oats**
2 **tablespoons cocoa**
  Pinch of salt
2 **cups water**

Combine dates, oats, cocoa and salt in a 1-quart microwavable container. Slowly stir in the water. Partially cover with plastic wrap. Microwave on Medium for 4 or 5 minutes, then stir. Microwave on Medium again for 3 or 4 minutes, then stir. Continue cooking and stirring until the cereal is creamy.

NUTRITION NOTE

CHOCOLATE & HEALTH—REALLY

Chocolate contains compounds called flavonoids, which can function as antioxidants and also seem to keep blood from clotting. Cocoa is unusually rich in two kinds of flavonoids, flavonols and proanthocyanidins, which appear to be especially potent. To get the most health-promoting flavonols, choose dark chocolate that contains 70 percent cocoa or higher. Milk chocolate is not a smart choice because it has considerably less cocoa and more sugar and dairy fat.

Overnight Oatmeal

High ⬆ Fiber

Here is an easy way to serve a crowd a hearty breakfast before facing the elements for a day of winter sports. You can assemble it in the slow cooker in the evening and wake up to a bowl of hot, nourishing oatmeal. The slow cooker eliminates the need for constant stirring and ensures an exceptionally creamy consistency. It is important to use steel-cut oats; old-fashioned oats become too soft during slow-cooking. (*Photograph: page 161.*)

8	cups water
2	cups steel-cut oats (*see Note*)
⅓	cup dried cranberries
⅓	cup dried apricots, chopped
¼	teaspoon salt, or to taste

Combine water, oats, dried cranberries, dried apricots and salt in a 5- or 6-quart slow cooker. Turn heat to low. Put the lid on and cook until the oats are tender and the porridge is creamy, 7 to 8 hours.

Stovetop Variation

Halve the above recipe to accommodate the size of most double boilers: Combine 4 cups water, 1 cup steel-cut oats, 3 tablespoons dried cranberries, 3 tablespoons dried apricots and ⅛ teaspoon salt in the top of a double boiler. Cover and cook over boiling water for about 1½ hours, checking the water level in the bottom of the double boiler from time to time.

2

CARBOHYDRATE
SERVINGS

MAKES 8 SERVINGS, 1 CUP EACH

PREP TIME: 5 MINUTES
SLOW-COOKER TIME: 7-8 HOURS
STOVETOP TIME: 1 HOUR 35 MINUTES

INGREDIENT NOTE
Steel-cut oats, sometimes labeled "Irish oatmeal," look like small pebbles. They are toasted oat groats—the oat kernel that has been removed from the husk—that have been cut in two or three pieces.

PER SERVING

193	CALORIES
3	G FAT (0 G SAT, 1 G MONO)
0	MG CHOLESTEROL
35	G CARBOHYDRATE
6	G PROTEIN
9	G FIBER
78	MG SODIUM

NUTRITION BONUS: Fiber (36% DAILY VALUE).

EXCHANGES

2	STARCH
½	FRUIT

2

CARBOHYDRATE
SERVINGS

**MAKES 8 SERVINGS,
ABOUT ½ CUP EACH**

PREP TIME: 20 MINUTES

START TO FINISH: 2½ HOURS
(including cooling time)

TO MAKE AHEAD: Refrigerate the
muesli in an airtight container for
up to 2 weeks.

INGREDIENT NOTE
Rye or wheat flakes are simply rye
or wheat kernels that have been
steamed and rolled, oatmeal-style.
Look for them in natural-foods
stores.

TIP
Grind flaxseeds in a clean coffee
grinder or dry blender just before
using.

PER SERVING

190 CALORIES

5 G FAT (1 G SAT,
2 G MONO)

0 MG CHOLESTEROL

33 G CARBOHYDRATE

6 G PROTEIN

4 G FIBER

5 MG SODIUM

NUTRITION BONUS: Iron (40%
DAILY VALUE), Fiber (16% DV).

EXCHANGES

1½ STARCH

½ FRUIT

1 FAT

Ingrid's Muesli

In Scandinavian homes, breakfast typically consists of a bowl of yogurt with some muesli stirred in. Editor Joyce Hendley learned the tricks for making a delicious, healthful muesli from her friend Ingrid Persson, a Stockholm-based food writer. You can substitute any combination of chopped dried fruit for the raisins—think about apricots, apples, figs, cherries or cranberries—and walnuts or hazelnuts for the almonds. If you don't have rye or wheat flakes, compensate by using more rolled oats.

2	cups old-fashioned *or* quick-cooking (*not* instant) rolled oats
⅔	cup rye flakes *or* wheat flakes (*see Note*)
⅓	cup coarsely chopped almonds (1¾ ounces)
2	tablespoons flaked coconut (sweetened *or* unsweetened)
½	cup raisins
2	tablespoons honey
½	teaspoon vanilla extract
	Pinch of cinnamon
¼	cup flaxseeds, ground (optional; *see Tip*)

1. Preheat oven to 350°F. Coat a baking sheet with cooking spray. Spread oats and rye (or wheat) flakes on the baking sheet. Bake for 10 minutes. Stir in almonds and coconut; bake until the oats are fragrant, about 8 minutes. Turn off the oven. Stir raisins into the muesli.

2. Microwave honey for 10 seconds in a glass measuring cup. Stir in vanilla and cinnamon; drizzle over the muesli and stir to coat. Return the muesli to the turned-off warm oven and let cool completely, about 2 hours. Stir in flaxseeds, if using.

> **"**Breakfast is my favorite meal. My wife has located a protein cereal (high-protein, low-carbohydrate) that we make into a granola. Mixed with a cup of yogurt it is delectable. That and a cup of good coffee and I'm a happy man.**"**
>
> — *Les B.,*
> *Washington*

Scrambled Egg Burritos

High ⬆ Fiber   **Quick ☼ Easy**

These zesty Southwestern egg burritos are always a hit whether you serve them for breakfast, brunch, lunch or a casual dinner. The homemade black bean salsa adds a special touch, but these are extra-quick if you use your favorite jarred salsa. (*Photograph: page 165.*)

4	9-inch whole-wheat flour tortillas
4	large eggs
⅛	teaspoon salt, or to taste
	Freshly ground pepper to taste
1	teaspoon extra-virgin olive oil
1	4-ounce can chopped green chiles
½	cup grated Cheddar *or* pepper Jack cheese
2	cups Black Bean & Tomato Salsa (*page 267*) *or* prepared salsa
¼	cup reduced-fat sour cream

1. Preheat oven to 350°F. Wrap tortillas in foil and heat in the oven for 5 to 10 minutes.
2. Blend eggs, salt and pepper in a medium bowl with a fork until blended. Heat oil in a 10-inch nonstick skillet over medium-low heat. Add chiles and cook, stirring, for 1 minute. Add eggs and cook, stirring slowly with a wooden spoon or heatproof rubber spatula, until soft, fluffy curds form, 1½ to 2½ minutes.
3. To serve, divide eggs evenly among the tortillas. Sprinkle each with about 2 tablespoons cheese and roll up. Serve with salsa and sour cream.

2

CARBOHYDRATE
SERVINGS

MAKES 4 SERVINGS

PREP TIME: 15 MINUTES
START TO FINISH: 30 MINUTES

PER SERVING

328 CALORIES
15 G FAT (6 G SAT, 5 G MONO)
232 MG CHOLESTEROL
35 G CARBOHYDRATE
18 G PROTEIN
7 G FIBER
719 MG SODIUM

NUTRITION BONUS: Fiber (29% DAILY VALUE), Vitamin C (25% DV), Calcium (20% DV), Vitamin A (20% DV).

EXCHANGES

2 STARCH
1 VEGETABLE
1 MEDIUM-FAT MEAT
½ HIGH-FAT MEAT
½ FAT

Toast Toppers

Low-Sugar Plum Spread

This simple homemade fruit spread has less than one-fourth the calories and one-third the carbohydrate grams of a common commercial variety (you can trim those numbers even further by opting for no-calorie sweetener). Cooking the plums in fruit juice with apples allows you to sweeten the spread without an excessive amount of sugar and take advantage of the natural pectin in the fruit. This method also works well with strawberries, blackberries or peaches.

5	pounds plums, pitted and sliced (14-15 cups)
3	Granny Smith apples, washed and quartered (*not* cored)
¼	cup white grape juice *or* other fruit juice
2	tablespoons lemon juice
¾	cup sugar *or* Splenda Granular (*see page 18*)
¼	teaspoon ground cinnamon *or* ginger (optional)

1. Place a plate in the freezer for testing consistency later.
2. Combine plums, apples, grape juice (or fruit juice) and lemon juice in a large, heavy-bottomed, nonreactive Dutch oven. Bring to a boil over medium-high heat, stirring. Cover and boil gently, stirring occasionally, until the fruit is softened and juicy, 15 to 20 minutes. Uncover and boil gently, stirring occasionally, until the fruit is completely soft, about 20 minutes. (Adjust heat as necessary to maintain a gentle boil.)
3. Pass the fruit through a food mill to remove the skins and apple seeds.
4. Return the strained fruit to the pot. Add sugar (or Splenda) and cinnamon (or ginger), if using. Cook over medium heat, stirring frequently, until a spoonful of jam dropped onto the chilled plate holds its shape, about 15 minutes longer. (*See Tip.*) Remove from heat and skim off any foam.

TIP

YOU'RE JAMMIN'

To test the consistency of the spread: Drop a dollop of cooked spread onto a chilled plate. Carefully run your finger through the dollop. If the track remains unfilled, the jam is done.

O

CARBOHYDRATE
SERVINGS

MAKES 8 CUPS

PREP TIME: 20 MINUTES
START TO FINISH: 1¾ HOURS

TO MAKE AHEAD: Store in an airtight container in the refrigerator for up to 2 months. For longer storage, process in a boiling-water bath (for detailed instructions, refer to www.homecanning.com or call the Home Canner's Hotline at 800-240-3340).

PER TABLESPOON WITH SUGAR

14 CALORIES
0 G FAT (0 G SAT, 0 G MONO)
0 MG CHOLESTEROL
4 G CARBOHYDRATE
0 G PROTEIN
0 G FIBER
0 MG SODIUM

EXCHANGES
FREE FOOD

PER TABLESPOON WITH SPLENDA
0 CARBOHYDRATE SERVINGS
12 CALORIES, 3 G CARBOHYDRATE

Roasted Apple Butter

Making apple butter in the oven, rather than on the stovetop, produces a delectable spread with a distinctive caramelized flavor. This is a healthful alternative to commercial varieties, which usually contain added sugars.

> 8   medium McIntosh apples (2¾ pounds), peeled, cored and quartered
> 2   cups unsweetened apple juice

1. Preheat oven to 450°F. Arrange apples in a large roasting pan. Pour apple juice over the apples. Bake until tender and lightly browned, about 30 minutes. Using a fork or potato masher, thoroughly mash the apples in the roasting pan.
2. Reduce oven temperature to 350°. Bake the apple puree, stirring occasionally, until very thick and deeply browned, 1½ to 1¾ hours. Scrape into a bowl and let cool.

Pear Butter

Simmering pears in pear nectar (available in the natural-foods section of supermarkets) and then reducing the puree until thickened produces an exceptionally rich-tasting spread that contains no added fat or sugar. It is a great item to have on hand; spread it on toast or layer it with vanilla yogurt and top with nuts for a quick dessert or snack. If you have a good supply of pears, feel free to double the recipe, using a large saucepan.

> 4   ripe but firm Bartlett pears (1-1¼ pounds), peeled, cored and cut into 1-inch
>   chunks
> ¾   cup pear nectar

1. Place pears and pear nectar in a heavy medium saucepan; bring to a simmer. Cover and simmer over medium-low heat, stirring occasionally, until the pears are very tender, 30 to 35 minutes. Cooking time will vary depending on the ripeness of the pears.
2. Mash the pears with a potato masher. Cook, uncovered, over medium-low heat, stirring often, until the puree has cooked down to a thick mass (somewhat thicker than applesauce), 20 to 30 minutes. Stir almost constantly toward the end of cooking. Scrape the pear butter into a bowl or storage container and let cool.

CARBOHYDRATE
SERVING

MAKES 2 CUPS

PREP TIME: 10 MINUTES
START TO FINISH: 2½ HOURS

TO MAKE AHEAD: Store in an airtight container in the refrigerator for up to 2 weeks or freeze for up to 6 months.

PER TABLESPOON

27 CALORIES
0 G FAT (0 G SAT, 0 G MONO)
0 MG CHOLESTEROL
7 G CARBOHYDRATE
0 G PROTEIN
1 G FIBER
0 MG SODIUM

EXCHANGES
½ FRUIT

For Pear Butter:

CARBOHYDRATE
SERVING

MAKES ABOUT 1 CUP

PREP TIME: 10 MINUTES
START TO FINISH: 1 HOUR

TO MAKE AHEAD: Store in an airtight container in the refrigerator for up to 2 weeks or freeze for up to 6 months.

PER TABLESPOON

22 CALORIES
0 G FAT (0 G SAT, 0 G MONO)
0 MG CHOLESTEROL
6 G CARBOHYDRATE
0 G PROTEIN
1 G FIBER
1 MG SODIUM

EXCHANGES
½ FRUIT

Muffins &
Breads

> **❝**I don't have a lot of time to cook…but I do make my own almond granola, and whole-grain bread with seeds to satisfy my need for one piece of bread per day. I also make a 'fauxtato' soup with cauliflower, chicken broth, low-fat white cheddar cheese, butter and cream cheese, and an artichoke soup with chicken broth, artichoke hearts and cream of chicken soup.**❞**
>
> —*Whitney B.,*
> *Texas*

Salsa Cornbread

EatingWell reader Chuck Allen of Dana Point, California, contributed this moist vegetable-studded cornbread. It makes a fine accompaniment to stews, chilis and breakfast eggs.

1 CARBOHYDRATE SERVING

MAKES **10** SERVINGS

PREP TIME: 25 MINUTES
START TO FINISH: 55 MINUTES

TIP
If you do not have an ovenproof skillet of the correct size, use an 8-inch-square glass baking dish. Do not preheat the empty baking dish in the oven before filling it.

PER SERVING
138 CALORIES
4 G FAT (2 G SAT, 1 G MONO)
70 MG CHOLESTEROL
20 G CARBOHYDRATE
6 G PROTEIN
1 G FIBER
319 MG SODIUM

EXCHANGES
1 STARCH
1 FAT

- 1 cup all-purpose flour
- ½ cup whole-wheat flour
- ½ cup cornmeal
- 2 teaspoons baking powder
- ½ teaspoon salt
  - Freshly ground pepper to taste
- 3 large eggs, lightly beaten
- ½ cup buttermilk *or* equivalent buttermilk powder (*see page 323*)
- 1 tablespoon butter, melted
- 1 tablespoon honey
- ½ cup drained canned corn kernels
- 1 small onion, diced
- ½ cup chopped tomato
- 1 clove garlic, minced
- 1 jalapeño pepper, seeded and minced
- ½ cup grated Cheddar cheese

1. Preheat oven to 425°F. Place a 9-inch cast-iron skillet (or similar ovenproof skillet) in the oven to heat.
2. Whisk all-purpose flour, whole-wheat flour, cornmeal, baking powder, salt and pepper in a large mixing bowl.
3. Whisk eggs, buttermilk, butter and honey in a medium bowl. Add the egg mixture to the dry ingredients; mix with a rubber spatula. Stir in corn, onion, tomato, garlic and jalapeño.
4. Remove the skillet from the oven and coat it with cooking spray. Pour in the batter, spreading evenly. Sprinkle cheese over the top. Bake the cornbread until golden brown and a knife inserted into the center comes out clean, 20 to 25 minutes. Serve warm.

Savory Breakfast Muffins

Quick ☼ Easy

With the smoky flavor of Canadian bacon, Cheddar and a healthy hit of protein, these hearty scallion- and pepper-flecked muffins are like eating a pretty, portable omelet.

- 2 cups whole-wheat flour
- 1 cup all-purpose flour
- 1 tablespoon baking powder
- ½ teaspoon baking soda
- ½ teaspoon freshly ground pepper
- ¼ teaspoon salt
- 2 large eggs
- 1⅓ cups buttermilk *or* equivalent buttermilk powder (*see page 323*)
- 3 tablespoons extra-virgin olive oil
- 2 tablespoons butter, melted
- 1 cup thinly sliced scallions (about 1 bunch)
- ¾ cup diced Canadian bacon (3 ounces)
- ½ cup grated Cheddar cheese
- ½ cup finely diced red bell pepper

1. Preheat oven to 400°F. Coat 12 standard 2½-inch muffin cups with cooking spray.
2. Combine whole-wheat flour, all-purpose flour, baking powder, baking soda, pepper and salt in a large bowl.
3. Whisk eggs, buttermilk, oil and butter in a medium bowl. Fold in scallions, bacon, cheese and bell pepper. Make a well in the center of the dry ingredients. Add the wet ingredients and mix with a rubber spatula until just moistened. Scoop the batter into the prepared pan (the cups will be very full).
4. Bake the muffins until the tops are golden brown, 20 to 22 minutes. Let cool in the pan for 5 minutes. Loosen the edges and turn the muffins out onto a wire rack to cool slightly before serving.

> ### TIP
>
> ### REHEAT & RUN
>
> Bake muffins on weekends and enjoy the leftovers for grab-and-go weekday breakfasts. Wrap leftover muffins individually in plastic wrap, place in a plastic storage container or ziplock bag and freeze for up to 1 month. To thaw, remove plastic wrap, wrap in a paper towel and microwave on High for 30 to 60 seconds.

1½
CARBOHYDRATE
SERVINGS

MAKES 1 DOZEN MUFFINS

PREP TIME: 20 MINUTES
START TO FINISH: 45 MINUTES

PER SERVING

- 217 CALORIES
- 9 G FAT (3 G SAT, 4 G MONO)
- 50 MG CHOLESTEROL
- 24 G CARBOHYDRATE
- 9 G PROTEIN
- 3 G FIBER
- 339 MG SODIUM

NUTRITION BONUS: Vitamin C (25% DAILY VALUE), Fiber (13% DV).

EXCHANGES

- 1½ STARCH
- ½ MEDIUM-FAT MEAT
- 1 FAT

1¹/₂

CARBOHYDRATE

SERVINGS

Zucchini-Walnut Loaf

Lisa Asuncion Feliciano of Manila, Philippines, shared this recipe in our *Kitchen to Kitchen* department. She recommends making extra loaves when zucchini is abundant because they freeze well.

**MAKES 2 MINI LOAVES
(8 SLICES EACH)**

PREP TIME: 30 MINUTES
START TO FINISH: 1¹/₄ HOURS

PER SLICE
118 CALORIES
3 G FAT (0 G SAT, 1 G MONO)
0 MG CHOLESTEROL
22 G CARBOHYDRATE
2 G PROTEIN
1 G FIBER
88 MG SODIUM

EXCHANGES
1¹/₂ STARCH

PER SLICE WITH SPLENDA
1 CARBOHYDRATE SERVING
100 CALORIES, 15 G CARBOHYDRATE

¾	cup whole-wheat flour
¾	cup all-purpose flour
1	teaspoon baking powder
¼	teaspoon baking soda
¼	teaspoon salt
1	teaspoon ground cinnamon
¼	teaspoon ground nutmeg
2	large egg whites, at room temperature (*see Cooking Tip, page 324*)
1	cup sugar *or* ½ cup Splenda Sugar Blend for Baking (*see page 18*)
½	cup unsweetened applesauce
2	tablespoons canola oil
¼	teaspoon lemon extract (optional)
1	cup grated zucchini, lightly packed (about 8 ounces)
2	tablespoons chopped walnuts

1. Preheat oven to 350°F. Coat 2 mini 6-by-3-inch loaf pans with cooking spray.
2. Whisk whole-wheat flour, all-purpose flour, baking powder, baking soda, salt, cinnamon and nutmeg in a large bowl.
3. Whisk egg whites, sugar (or Splenda), applesauce, oil and lemon extract (if using) in a medium bowl. Stir in zucchini.
4. Make a well in the dry ingredients; slowly, mix in the zucchini mixture with a rubber spatula. Fold in walnuts. Do not overmix. Transfer the batter to the prepared pans.
5. Bake the loaves until a toothpick comes out almost clean, 40 to 45 minutes. Cool in the pan on a wire rack for about 5 minutes, then turn out onto the rack to cool completely.

Berry Rich Muffins

Quick ☼ Easy

Dried blueberries or cherries enhance the fruitiness of these wholesome berry muffins. If it is more convenient, use frozen berries instead of fresh (*see Tip, page 68*).

1	cup whole-wheat flour
1	cup all-purpose flour
1	teaspoon baking powder
½	teaspoon baking soda
¼	teaspoon salt
1	large egg
1	large egg white
⅔	cup packed light brown sugar *or* ⅓ cup Splenda Sugar Blend for Baking (*see page 18*)
1	cup buttermilk *or* equivalent buttermilk powder (*see page 323*)
¼	cup canola oil
1½	teaspoons grated lemon *or* orange zest, preferably organic
1	teaspoon vanilla extract
1½	cups mixed fresh berries, such as blueberries, raspberries *and/or* blackberries
¼	cup dried blueberries *or* dried cherries
1	tablespoon sugar

1. Preheat oven to 400°F. Coat 12 standard 2½-inch muffin cups with cooking spray.
2. Whisk whole-wheat flour, all-purpose flour, baking powder, baking soda and salt in a large bowl.
3. Whisk egg, egg white and brown sugar (or Splenda) in a medium bowl until smooth. Add buttermilk, oil, lemon (or orange) zest and vanilla; whisk until blended.
4. Make a well in the center of the dry ingredients. Add the wet ingredients; stir with a rubber spatula until just combined. Gently stir in mixed berries and dried fruit. Scoop the batter into the prepared pan and sprinkle sugar over the tops.
5. Bake the muffins until the tops spring back when touched lightly, 20 to 25 minutes. Let cool in the pan for 5 minutes. Loosen the edges and turn the muffins out onto a wire rack to cool slightly before serving.

2
CARBOHYDRATE SERVINGS

MAKES 1 DOZEN MUFFINS

PREP TIME: 20 MINUTES
START TO FINISH: 40 MINUTES

PER MUFFIN
- 196 CALORIES
- 6 G FAT (1 G SAT, 3 G MONO)
- 18 MG CHOLESTEROL
- 32 G CARBOHYDRATE
- 4 G PROTEIN
- 3 G FIBER
- 174 MG SODIUM

EXCHANGES
- 2 STARCH
- 1 FAT

PER MUFFIN WITH SPLENDA
2 CARBOHYDRATE SERVINGS
183 CALORIES, 27 G CARBOHYDRATE

Blueberry Corn Muffins

Quick ☼ Easy

Yellow cornmeal, preferably stone-ground, adds a delicious flavor and golden hue to these moist, honey-sweetened muffins.

MAKES 1 DOZEN MUFFINS

PREP TIME: 20 MINUTES
START TO FINISH: 40 MINUTES

PER MUFFIN

172 CALORIES
4 G FAT (0 G SAT, 2 G MONO)
18 MG CHOLESTEROL
30 G CARBOHYDRATE
4 G PROTEIN
2 G FIBER
157 MG SODIUM

EXCHANGES

2 STARCH

- ⅔ cup whole-wheat flour
- ⅔ cup all-purpose flour
- ⅔ cup cornmeal
- 1 tablespoon baking powder
- 1 teaspoon ground cinnamon
- ¼ teaspoon salt
- 1 cup blueberries
- 1 large egg
- ⅔ cup 1% milk
- ½ cup honey
- 3 tablespoons canola oil
- 1 teaspoon sugar

1. Preheat oven to 400°F. Coat 12 standard 2½-inch muffin cups with cooking spray.
2. Whisk whole-wheat flour, all-purpose flour, cornmeal, baking powder, cinnamon and salt in a large bowl. Add blueberries and toss to coat.
3. Whisk egg in a medium bowl. Add milk, honey and oil, whisking until well combined. Add the wet ingredients to the dry ingredients and stir until just combined. Do not over-mix. Scoop the batter into the prepared pan, filling each cup about two-thirds full. Sprinkle the tops with sugar.
4. Bake the muffins until the tops spring back when touched lightly, 18 to 22 minutes Let cool in the pan for 5 minutes. Loosen the edges and turn the muffins out onto a wire rack to cool slightly before serving.

TIP

BAKING WITH BERRIES

Berries are a high-fiber, low-carbohydrate fruit that provide a wealth of antioxidants. They are a great way to boost nutrition and flavor in baked goods. When fresh berries are not in season, frozen are a good alternative. If using frozen blueberries, do not thaw. Simply rinse off ice crystals, then pat dry completely on paper towels. Toss separately with about 3 tablespoons of the flour, then stir into the batter after the liquid has been added.

Spiced Apple Butter Bran Muffins

Quick ☼ Easy

These are dense, grainy, fruity and delicious. A double dose of apple—diced fresh apple and dark, spiced apple butter (Smucker's brand is good)—makes them extra moist and flavorful. (*Photograph: page 165.*)

½ cup raisins

¾ cup whole-wheat flour

¾ cup all-purpose flour

2½ teaspoons baking powder

¼ teaspoon salt

½ teaspoon ground cinnamon

¾ cup unprocessed wheat bran *or* oat bran

1 large egg, lightly beaten

½ cup 1% milk

½ cup spiced apple butter

½ cup packed light brown sugar *or* ¼ cup Splenda Sugar Blend for Baking
     (*see page 18*)

¼ cup canola oil

3 tablespoons molasses

1 cup finely diced peeled apple

MAKES 1 DOZEN MUFFINS

PREP TIME: 20 MINUTES
START TO FINISH: 40 MINUTES

PER MUFFIN

197 CALORIES

6 G FAT (1 G SAT, 3 G MONO)

18 MG CHOLESTEROL

35 G CARBOHYDRATE

4 G PROTEIN

4 G FIBER

144 MG SODIUM

NUTRITION BONUS: Fiber (16% DAILY VALUE).

EXCHANGES

2 STARCH

1 FAT

PER MUFFIN WITH SPLENDA

2 CARBOHYDRATE SERVINGS
187 CALORIES, 31 G CARBOHYDRATE

1. Preheat oven to 375°F. Coat 12 standard 2½-inch muffin cups with cooking spray. Put raisins in a small bowl and cover with hot water. Set aside.

2. Whisk whole-wheat flour, all-purpose flour, baking powder, salt and cinnamon in a large bowl. Stir in bran.

3. Whisk egg, milk, apple butter, brown sugar (or Splenda), oil and molasses in a large bowl until blended. Make a well in the dry ingredients and pour in the wet ingredients. Drain the raisins; add them and the diced apple to the bowl. Stir with as few, deft strokes as possible, until the batter is evenly moistened. Scoop the batter into the prepared pan (the cups will be very full).

4. Bake the muffins until the tops spring back when touched lightly, 18 to 22 minutes. Let cool in the pan for 5 minutes. Loosen the edges and turn the muffins out onto a wire rack to cool slightly before serving.

Dutch Apple Bread

With 500 calories and 27 grams of fat per slice, the original recipe for this bread was an ideal candidate for our *Rx for Recipes* column. We replaced butter and whole eggs with canola oil and egg whites, substituted buttermilk (or yogurt) for sour cream, and used half as many nuts. The result is delicious, with just 194 calories and 5 grams of fat per slice.

STREUSEL

1/3	cup whole-wheat flour
1/4	cup brown sugar
3/4	teaspoon ground cinnamon
	Pinch of salt
1/4	cup chopped walnuts
1	tablespoon frozen apple juice concentrate, thawed
1	tablespoon canola oil

BREAD

3	large egg whites
1/4	teaspoon cream of tartar
1	cup sugar *or* 1/2 cup Splenda Sugar Blend for Baking (*see page 18*), divided
1	cup buttermilk *or* nonfat plain yogurt
3	tablespoons canola oil
1	teaspoon vanilla extract
1 1/4	cups all-purpose flour
1	cup whole-wheat flour
2	teaspoons baking powder
1	teaspoon baking soda
1/2	teaspoon salt
1	teaspoon ground cinnamon
1 1/2	cups chopped peeled apples (2 medium)

1. **To prepare streusel:** Combine flour, brown sugar, cinnamon and salt in a small bowl. Stir in walnuts. Drizzle apple juice concentrate and oil over dry ingredients and rub in with your fingers until crumbly. Set aside.
2. Preheat oven to 350°F. Coat two 8½-by-4½-inch loaf pans with cooking spray.
3. **To prepare bread:** Beat egg whites in a large bowl with an electric mixer on low speed until foamy. Add cream of tartar, increase speed to medium-high and beat until soft peaks form. Gradually add ½ cup sugar (or ¼ cup Splenda), beating until stiff peaks form.
4. Combine buttermilk (or yogurt), oil and vanilla in a small bowl. Whisk the remaining ½ cup sugar (or ¼ cup Splenda), all-purpose flour, whole-wheat flour, baking powder, baking soda, salt and cinnamon in a large bowl. Make a well in the center of the dry ingredients; add wet ingredients and stir with a rubber spatula until just combined. Fold in apples, then beaten whites. Spoon the batter into the prepared pans, smoothing the tops. Sprinkle with the reserved streusel.
5. Bake the loaves until lightly browned and a skewer inserted in the center comes out clean, 35 to 45 minutes. Cool in the pans on a wire rack for 10 minutes. Remove from the pans and finish cooling on the rack.

2

CARBOHYDRATE SERVINGS

MAKES 2 LOAVES (8 SLICES EACH)

PREP TIME: 30 MINUTES
START TO FINISH: 1 HOUR 10 MINUTES

TO MAKE AHEAD: Wrap well and store at room temperature for 1 to 2 days or freeze for up to 1 month.

PER SLICE
194 CALORIES
5 G FAT (0 G SAT, 2 G MONO)
1 MG CHOLESTEROL
33 G CARBOHYDRATE
4 G PROTEIN
2 G FIBER
236 MG SODIUM

EXCHANGES
2 STARCH
1 FAT

PER SLICE WITH SPLENDA
2 CARBOHYDRATE SERVINGS
175 CALORIES, 26 G CARBOHYDRATE

Maple Nut & Pear Scones

Delicate pears, pecans and maple flavor make these scones really special. Our makeover of this tender, flaky breakfast pastry uses reduced-fat cream cheese, canola oil and just a touch of butter to replace 1½ sticks of butter. The addition of rolled oats and whole-wheat pastry flour boosts fiber and enhances the nutty flavor. For more fruit intensity, serve with Pear Butter (*page 61*).

2

CARBOHYDRATE
SERVINGS

MAKES 1 DOZEN SCONES

PREP TIME: 30 MINUTES
START TO FINISH: 1 HOUR

TO MAKE AHEAD: The scones are best served the day they are made. Wrap any leftovers individually, place in a plastic bag or container and freeze for up to 1 month. For a quick weekday breakfast, wrap a frozen scone in a paper towel and microwave on Defrost for 1 to 2 minutes.

INGREDIENT NOTE
Maple extract, which can be purchased in the spice section of the supermarket, contains the essential flavors of maple syrup, usually diluted with alcohol. Maple syrup cannot be used as a substitute. Products labeled "maple flavoring" usually contain imitation or artificial ingredients.

PER SERVING

233 CALORIES
12 G FAT (3 G SAT, 5 G MONO)
9 MG CHOLESTEROL
27 G CARBOHYDRATE
5 G PROTEIN
3 G FIBER
201 MG SODIUM

EXCHANGES
2 STARCH
2 FAT

1 cup whole-wheat pastry flour (*see Ingredient Note, page 324*)
1 cup all-purpose flour
1 cup old-fashioned rolled oats
¼ cup plus 1½ teaspoons sugar
2 teaspoons baking powder
½ teaspoon baking soda
¼ teaspoon salt
1 teaspoon ground cinnamon
4 tablespoons chilled reduced-fat cream cheese (Neufchâtel), cut into small pieces (2 ounces)
2 tablespoons chilled butter, cut into small pieces
¼ cup canola oil
1 cup diced peeled pear, preferably Bartlett (1 large)
½ cup chopped pecans *or* walnuts, divided
¾ cup low-fat buttermilk *or* equivalent buttermilk powder (*see page 323*)
1 teaspoon maple extract (*see Note*) *or* vanilla extract
1 egg lightly beaten with 1 tablespoon water for glaze

1. Preheat oven to 400°F. Line a large baking sheet with parchment paper or coat with cooking spray.
2. Combine whole-wheat flour, all-purpose flour, oats, ¼ cup sugar, baking powder, baking soda, salt and cinnamon in a large bowl; whisk to blend. Using a pastry blender or your fingertips, cut or rub cream cheese and butter into the dry ingredients. Add oil and toss with a fork to coat. Add pear and ¼ cup nuts; toss to coat. Mix buttermilk and maple (or vanilla) extract in a measuring cup and add just enough to the dry ingredients, stirring with a fork, until the dough clumps together. (It will be sticky.)
3. Turn the dough out onto a lightly floured surface and knead several times; do not overwork it. Divide the dough in half and pat each piece into a 7½-inch circle. Cut each circle into 6 wedges and transfer to the prepared baking sheet. Brush the tops with the egg glaze and sprinkle with the remaining ¼ cup nuts, pressing lightly. Sprinkle with the remaining 1½ teaspoons sugar.
4. Bake the scones until golden and firm to the touch, 20 to 30 minutes. Transfer to a wire rack to cool slightly before serving.

2

CARBOHYDRATE
SERVINGS

Whole-Wheat Irish Soda Bread

Irish soda bread offers all the pleasures of homemade bread in half the time. Because the loaf is leavened with baking soda instead of yeast, there is no rising time. Kneading is minimal as well. This recipe is from Darina Allen, owner of the Ballymaloe Cookery School in County Cork, Ireland.

**MAKES ONE 2-POUND LOAF
(12 SLICES)**

PREP TIME: 10 MINUTES
START TO FINISH: 1½ HOURS

PER SLICE

165 CALORIES
1 G FAT (0 G SAT, 0 G MONO)
2 MG CHOLESTEROL
31 G CARBOHYDRATE
7 G PROTEIN
3 G FIBER
347 MG SODIUM

EXCHANGES

2 STARCH

2 cups whole-wheat flour
2 cups all-purpose flour, plus more for dusting
1 teaspoon baking soda
1 teaspoon salt
2¼ cups buttermilk *or* equivalent buttermilk powder
  (*see page 323*)

1. Preheat oven to 450°F. Coat a baking sheet with cooking spray and sprinkle with a little flour.
2. Whisk whole-wheat flour, all-purpose flour, baking soda and salt in a large bowl. Make a well in the center and pour in buttermilk. Using one hand, stir in full circles (starting in the center of the bowl and working toward the outside) until all the flour is incorporated. The dough should be soft but not too wet and sticky. When it all comes together, in a matter of seconds, turn it out onto a well-floured surface. Clean dough off your hand.
3. Pat and roll the dough gently with floury hands, just enough to tidy it up and give it a round shape. Flip over and flatten slightly to about 2 inches. Transfer the loaf to the prepared baking sheet. Mark with a deep cross using a serrated knife, and prick each of the four quadrants.
4. Bake the bread for 20 minutes. Reduce oven temperature to 400° and continue to bake until the loaf is brown on top and sounds hollow when tapped, 30 to 35 minutes more. Transfer the loaf to a wire rack and let cool for about 30 minutes before serving.

VARIATION: SCONES
In Step 3, form the dough into a round and flatten to about 1½ inches thick. Stamp out into scones with a cutter or cut with a knife. Bake on a baking sheet at 450°F for about 30 minutes.

72

Anadama Bread

This updated Anadama is made quicker with the use of RapidRise yeast and a food processor. You can knead the dough by hand but the temperature of the cornmeal mixture should be a little hotter: 125 to 130°F.

¼   cup cornmeal, preferably stone-ground
1⅓ cups boiling water
¼   cup molasses
1½ cups whole-wheat flour
1½ cups bread flour (*see Ingredient Note, page 323*) *or* all-purpose flour
1   package RapidRise yeast
1½ teaspoons salt
1   egg white mixed with 2 teaspoons water for glaze

1. Combine cornmeal and boiling water in a large glass measuring cup. Add molasses and let stand for 5 minutes or longer to soften the cornmeal and to cool the liquid until it is the temperature of a baby's bottle (105 to 115°F).

2. Combine whole-wheat flour, bread (or all-purpose) flour, yeast and salt in a food processor. Pulse to mix. With the motor running, gradually pour the cornmeal mixture through the feed tube until a ball forms. Process for about 45 seconds to "knead" the dough (it will be sticky). Turn the dough out onto a floured surface. Cover with plastic wrap and let rest for 10 minutes.

3. Coat a baking sheet with cooking spray. Dust with cornmeal (or flour), shaking off excess. Punch down dough and form into a 7-inch-diameter round loaf. Place on the prepared baking sheet. Cover lightly with plastic wrap that has been sprayed with cooking spray and let rise until doubled in bulk, 40 to 45 minutes.

4. Set a rack in the center of the oven; preheat to 425°F. Just before baking, place a shallow pan of hot water on the lowest shelf in the oven.

5. Brush the risen loaf lightly with the egg-white mixture, taking care not to let it drip onto the pan. Use a sharp knife to make two slashes, ½ inch deep, in a crisscross pattern on top.

6. Bake the bread for 10 minutes. Brush again with the glaze and rotate pan 180° (from front to back). Lower oven temperature to 400° and bake for 10 to 15 minutes more, or until golden and the bottom sounds hollow when tapped. Transfer the bread to a wire rack to cool.

2

CARBOHYDRATE
SERVINGS

MAKES 1 LOAF (12 SLICES)

PREP TIME: 10 MINUTES
START TO FINISH: 2-2½ HOURS

PER SLICE
142 CALORIES
1 G FAT (0 G SAT, 0 G MONO)
0 MG CHOLESTEROL
29 G CARBOHYDRATE
5 G PROTEIN
3 G FIBER
299 MG SODIUM

EXCHANGES
2 STARCH

Triple-Rich Whole-Wheat Bread

In the 1930s, scientists at Cornell University developed a formula for improving the nutritive value of bread by adding soy flour for protein, dry milk powder to boost calcium, and wheat germ, a good source of vitamin E and folic acid. Devised for bread made with refined flour, Cornell Bread, or Triple-Rich Bread, makes a great whole-wheat loaf as well. We have adapted the concept to today's time-saving appliances. You can use a bread machine or your food processor to make this convenient, wholesome loaf.

2-CUP BREAD MACHINE (1-POUND LOAF)

- ¾ cup water, 75-80°F
- 1 tablespoon molasses
- 2 teaspoons canola oil
- ¾ teaspoon salt
- 1½ cups whole-wheat flour
- ¾ cup bread flour (*see page 323*)
  or all-purpose flour
- 2 tablespoons soy flour (*see page 324*)
- 2 tablespoons nonfat dry milk
- 2 teaspoons wheat germ
- 1½ teaspoons bread-machine yeast (*see Note*)

3-CUP BREAD MACHINE (1½-POUND LOAF)

- 1 cup plus 2 tablespoons water, 75-80°F
- 2 tablespoons molasses
- 1 tablespoon canola oil
- 1 teaspoon salt
- 2 cups whole-wheat flour
- 1 cup bread flour (*see page 323*)
  or all-purpose flour
- 3 tablespoons soy flour (*see page 324*)
- 3 tablespoons nonfat dry milk
- 1 tablespoon wheat germ
- 2 teaspoons bread-machine yeast (*see Note*)

BREAD-MACHINE METHOD:

Place all ingredients in the bread machine pan in the order recommended by the manufacturer. (Do not place the yeast in direct contact with liquids and salt.) Select Whole-Wheat or Basic cycle and Medium crust, then press Start. Once the dough is mixed, check consistency of dough: it should be smooth, yet soft to the touch. Adjust, if necessary, by adding flour, 1 tablespoon at a time, or water, 1 teaspoon at a time. When the loaf is ready, transfer it to a wire rack to cool.

FOOD-PROCESSOR METHOD (USING EITHER LIST OF INGREDIENTS):

1. Combine whole-wheat flour, bread (or all-purpose) flour, soy flour, dry milk, wheat germ, salt and yeast in a food processor; pulse several times to blend. Stir water, molasses and oil in a measuring cup until the molasses is fully dissolved. With the motor running, slowly pour enough of the liquid through the feed tube until the dough is smooth and pulls away from the sides. It should be smooth, yet soft to the touch. Adjust, if necessary, by adding flour, 1 tablespoon at a time, or water, 1 teaspoon at a time. Process for 1 minute to knead. Transfer the dough to a bowl coated with cooking spray. Cover with plastic wrap and let dough rise until doubled, 1 to 1½ hours.
2. Coat an 8½-by-4½-inch loaf pan with cooking spray. Turn the dough out onto a lightly floured surface. Punch down and shape into a loaf. Place the loaf seam-side down in the prepared pan. Cover with plastic wrap that has been sprayed with cooking spray and let rise until almost doubled, about 1 hour.
3. Preheat oven to 375°F. Bake the bread until golden brown and hollow-sounding when tapped, 25 to 35 minutes. Turn out onto a wire rack to cool.

2

CARBOHYDRATE
SERVINGS

MAKES 1 LOAF

PREP TIME: 15 MINUTES

START TO FINISH: 2½-3 HOURS

INGREDIENT NOTE
Bread-machine yeast is a finely granulated yeast specially formulated for use in bread machines. Ascorbic acid is added as a dough conditioner to promote volume. This yeast can also be used in the food-processor method. If it is not available, you can substitute active dry yeast; heat the water to 120-130°F.

1-POUND LOAF (8 SLICES),
PER SLICE

- 155 CALORIES
- 2 G FAT (0 G SAT, 1 G MONO)
- 0 MG CHOLESTEROL
- 29 G CARBOHYDRATE
- 6 G PROTEIN
- 4 G FIBER
- 227 MG SODIUM

1½-POUND LOAF (12 SLICES),
PER SLICE

- 143 CALORIES
- 2 G FAT (0 G SAT, 1 G MONO)
- 0 MG CHOLESTEROL
- 27 G CARBOHYDRATE
- 5 G PROTEIN
- 3 G FIBER
- 203 MG SODIUM

EXCHANGES

- 2 STARCH

Whole-Wheat Flax Bread

High ⬆ Fiber

The bakers at King Arthur Flour came up with this super-high-fiber bread. Its nutty whole-grain taste and texture make particularly great sandwiches and toast.

- ⅓ cup whole flaxseeds (*see Tip*)
- 1¾ cups lukewarm water
- 1 tablespoon honey
- 1 package active dry yeast (2¼ teaspoons)
- 1¼ cups bread flour (*see Ingredient Note, page 323*) *or* all-purpose flour, divided
- ½ cup pumpernickel *or* dark rye flour
- 1½ teaspoons salt
- 2 cups whole-wheat flour *or* white whole-wheat flour (*see Note*)
- 1 egg lightly beaten with 1 tablespoon water for glaze

1. Grind flaxseeds into a coarse meal in a spice mill (such as a clean coffee grinder) or dry blender. Set aside 2 teaspoons for topping.
2. Stir lukewarm water and honey in a large bowl until the honey is dissolved. Sprinkle in yeast and let stand until it bubbles, about 5 minutes.
3. Add 1 cup bread flour (or all-purpose flour), pumpernickel (or rye) flour, salt and the remaining ground flaxseeds. With a wooden spoon, stir vigorously in the same direction until the batter is smooth. Gradually stir in whole-wheat flour until it becomes too difficult to stir. (*Alternatively, mix dough in a stand-up mixer fitted with a paddle attachment.*)
4. Turn the dough out onto a lightly floured surface and knead, adding only enough of the remaining bread flour (or all-purpose flour) to keep it from sticking, until smooth and elastic, 10 to 12 minutes. (The dough will be slightly sticky.)
5. Place the dough in a large oiled bowl. Turn to coat and cover with plastic wrap. Let rise until doubled in bulk, about 1½ hours.
6. Coat a 9-by-5-inch loaf pan with cooking spray. Punch the dough down, flatten into a disk and tightly roll into a log. Place seam-side down in the prepared pan. Cover with plastic wrap that has been sprayed with cooking spray; let rise until the dough domes over the top of the pan, about 45 minutes.
7. Preheat oven to 400°F. Lightly brush the loaf with the egg mixture and sprinkle with the reserved 2 teaspoons ground flaxseed.
8. Bake the bread for 15 minutes. Reduce oven temperature to 350° and continue baking until the bread pulls away from the sides of the pan, 20 to 25 minutes. Turn out onto a wire rack and cool completely before slicing.

2

CARBOHYDRATE
SERVINGS

MAKES 1 LOAF (12 SLICES)

PREP TIME: 30 MINUTES
START TO FINISH: 3 HOURS 25 MINUTES

TEST KITCHEN TIP
Store flaxseeds in the refrigerator or freezer. Flaxseeds are available in health-food stores or from King Arthur Flour. (*Sources: page 323.*)

INGREDIENT NOTE
White whole-wheat flour, made from a special variety of white wheat, is light in color and flavor but has the same nutritional properties as regular whole-wheat flour.

PER SLICE
- 184 CALORIES
- 4 G FAT (0 G SAT, 1 G MONO)
- 18 MG CHOLESTEROL
- 32 G CARBOHYDRATE
- 8 G PROTEIN
- 6 G FIBER
- 300 MG SODIUM

NUTRITION BONUS: Fiber (23% DAILY VALUE), Folate (15% DV), Iron (15% DV).

EXCHANGES
- 2 STARCH
- ½ FAT

2½

CARBOHYDRATE

SERVINGS

MAKES 1½ DOZEN MUFFINS

PREP TIME: 20 MINUTES

START TO FINISH: 40 MINUTES

PER MUFFIN

199 CALORIES

6 G FAT (0 G SAT, 2 G MONO)

0 MG CHOLESTEROL

36 G CARBOHYDRATE

5 G PROTEIN

3 G FIBER

176 MG SODIUM

EXCHANGES

2½ STARCH

1 FAT

PER MUFFIN WITH SPLENDA

2 CARBOHYDRATE SERVINGS

180 CALORIES, 29 G CARBOHYDRATE

Carrot & Banana Muffins

Quick ☼ Easy

Packed with flavorful and wholesome ingredients, these muffins make a good snack or breakfast. Ann Arndt of Minneapolis, Minnesota, contributed the recipe.

1	cup raisins
¾	cup whole-wheat flour
¾	cup all-purpose flour
1	cup oat bran
½	cup toasted wheat germ
2	teaspoons baking powder
1	teaspoon baking soda
¼	teaspoon salt
2	teaspoons ground cinnamon
¼	teaspoon ground allspice
4	large egg whites
1	cup packed brown sugar *or* ½ cup Splenda Sugar Blend for Baking (*see page 18*)
1	cup mashed bananas (2 medium bananas)
½	cup 1% milk
¼	cup canola oil
1	teaspoon vanilla extract
2	cups grated carrots (4 medium carrots)
⅓	cup chopped walnuts

1. Preheat oven to 400°F. Coat 18 standard-size 2½-inch muffin cups with cooking spray.
2. Place raisins in a small bowl and cover with hot water; let soak for 5 minutes. Drain and set aside.
3. Whisk whole-wheat flour, all-purpose flour, oat bran, wheat germ, baking powder, baking soda, salt, cinnamon and allspice in a large mixing bowl.
4. Whisk egg whites in a medium bowl until frothy. Add brown sugar (or Splenda) and whisk until it has dissolved. Mix in bananas, milk, oil and vanilla.
5. Make a well in the center of the dry ingredients. Add the wet ingredients; stir with a rubber spatula until just combined. Gently stir in carrots and the drained raisins. Scoop the batter into the prepared pan and sprinkle with nuts.
6. Bake the muffins until the tops spring back when touched lightly, 15 to 20 minutes. Let cool in the pan for 5 minutes. Loosen the edges and turn the muffins out onto a wire rack to cool slightly before serving.

Orange-Date Pumpkin Muffins

Quick ☼ Easy

A whole orange pulverized in the food processor gives these nutrient-rich muffins a wonderful intense flavor.

3

CARBOHYDRATE
SERVINGS

- 1 cup whole-wheat flour
- 1 cup all-purpose flour
- 2 teaspoons baking powder
- 1 teaspoon baking soda
- ½ teaspoon salt
- ½ teaspoon ground cinnamon
- 1 large seedless orange, preferably organic, scrubbed and cut into 8 sections
- 1 large egg
- 1 large egg white
- ⅔ cup canned unseasoned pumpkin puree
- ½ cup packed brown sugar *or* ¼ cup Splenda Sugar Blend for Baking (*see page 18*)
- ¼ cup honey
- 3 tablespoons canola oil
- ¾ cup chopped pitted dates
- 3 tablespoons chopped walnuts *or* pecans

1. Preheat oven to 400°F. Coat 12 standard 2½-inch muffin cups with cooking spray.
2. Whisk whole-wheat flour, all-purpose flour, baking powder, baking soda, salt and cinnamon in a large bowl.
3. Place orange sections in a food processor and puree. Add egg, egg white, pumpkin, sugar (or Splenda), honey and oil; process until mixed. Make a well in the center of the dry ingredients; add the wet ingredients and dates, and stir with a rubber spatula until just combined. Scoop the batter into the prepared pan and sprinkle with nuts.
4. Bake the muffins until the tops spring back when touched lightly, 18 to 20 minutes. Let cool in the pan for 5 minutes. Loosen the edges and turn the muffins out onto a wire rack to cool slightly before serving.

MAKES 1 DOZEN MUFFINS

PREP TIME: 20 MINUTES
START TO FINISH: 40 MINUTES

PER MUFFIN

223	CALORIES
6	G FAT (0 G SAT, 3 G MONO)
18	MG CHOLESTEROL
41	G CARBOHYDRATE
5	G PROTEIN
3	G FIBER
280	MG SODIUM

EXCHANGES

3	STARCH
1	FAT

PER MUFFIN WITH SPLENDA

2½ CARBOHYDRATE SERVINGS
209 CALORIES, 36 G CARBOHYDRATE

CHAPTER THREE

Snacks & Appetizers

O
CARBOHYDRATE SERVINGS

1/2
CARBOHYDRATE SERVING

☼ DRINKS & NIBBLES   90–91

COLD DRINKS

HOT DRINKS

SNACKS

APPETIZERS

> "For an evening snack, combine 1/2 cup nonfat plain yogurt with 1/4 cup rolled oats, 1/4 cup blueberries or strawberries, or a combination, a few whole almonds and 1/4 teaspoon ground cinnamon."
> —Marilyn C., Minnesota

Asian Peanut Dip

Quick ☼ Easy

For a sure-hit hors d'oeuvre, serve this sauce with crudités and/or skewered grilled chicken, pork or beef. Or spread on whole-grain bread and top with grated carrot, sliced cucumber and lettuce for "grown-up" peanut butter sandwiches.

    ¼   cup natural peanut butter
    2   tablespoons hot black tea *or* boiling water
    1   tablespoon reduced-sodium soy sauce
    1   tablespoon lime juice
    1   teaspoon brown sugar
    1   clove garlic, minced
    ¼-½ teaspoon crushed red pepper

Combine peanut butter and tea (or water) in a small bowl; stir until smooth. Stir in soy sauce, lime juice, brown sugar, garlic and crushed red pepper. If the sauce seems too thick, add water.

Black-Eyed Pea Dip

Quick ☼ Easy

Need a little incentive to eat more vegetables? Keep this easy, healthful dip on hand— who knew that raw vegetables could be so addictive?

    1   15½-ounce can black-eyed peas, rinsed
    ¼   cup fresh parsley leaves
    2   tablespoons lemon juice
    2   tablespoons extra-virgin olive oil
    1½   teaspoons chopped garlic
    1½   teaspoons chopped fresh tarragon *or* ½ teaspoon dried
    ⅛   teaspoon salt, or to taste
         Freshly ground pepper to taste

Place peas, parsley, lemon juice, oil, garlic, tarragon, salt and pepper in a food processor; process until smooth. Transfer to a serving bowl.

CARBOHYDRATE
SERVINGS

MAKES ABOUT ½ CUP

PREP TIME: 10 MINUTES
START TO FINISH: 10 MINUTES

TO MAKE AHEAD: Cover and refrigerate for up to 4 days.

PER TABLESPOON

54 CALORIES
4   G FAT (1 G SAT, 0 G MONO)
0   MG CHOLESTEROL
3   G CARBOHYDRATE
2   G PROTEIN
1   G FIBER
67 MG SODIUM

EXCHANGES
1   FAT (MONO)

For Black-Eyed Pea Dip:

CARBOHYDRATE
SERVINGS

MAKES ABOUT 1¼ CUPS

PREP TIME: 10 MINUTES
START TO FINISH: 10 MINUTES

TO MAKE AHEAD: Cover and refrigerate for up to 2 days.

PER TABLESPOON

31 CALORIES
1   G FAT (0 G SAT, 1 G MONO)
0   MG CHOLESTEROL
3   G CARBOHYDRATE
1   G PROTEIN
1   G FIBER
70 MG SODIUM

EXCHANGES
FREE FOOD

Lima Bean Spread with Cumin & Herbs

Quick ☼ Easy

Humble limas are transformed into a sensational Mediterranean spread that is vibrant with a mix of fresh herbs and spices. You can substitute frozen edamame beans for the limas in Step 1; cook according to package directions.

> 1 10-ounce package frozen lima beans
> 4 cloves garlic, crushed and peeled
> ¼ teaspoon crushed red pepper
> 2 tablespoons extra-virgin olive oil
> 4 teaspoons lemon juice
> 1 teaspoon ground cumin
> ½ teaspoon salt, or to taste
>   Freshly ground pepper to taste
> 1 tablespoon chopped fresh mint
> 1 tablespoon chopped fresh cilantro
> 1 tablespoon chopped fresh dill

1. Bring a large saucepan of lightly salted water to a boil. Add lima beans, garlic and crushed red pepper; cook until the beans are tender, about 10 minutes. Remove from heat and let cool in the liquid.
2. Drain the beans and garlic. Transfer to a food processor. Add oil, lemon juice, cumin, salt and pepper; process until smooth. Scrape into a bowl, stir in mint, cilantro and dill.

White Bean Spread

High ⬆ Fiber   Quick ☼ Easy

You can't beat this easy spread, made with fiber-rich canned beans, for convenience and taste. Keep some on hand to layer with vegetables for sandwiches or spread over toasted country bread for a delicious bruschetta.

> 2 15½-ounce cans cannellini beans (white kidney beans), rinsed
> ¼ cup extra-virgin olive oil
> 2 tablespoons lemon juice
>   Pinch of cayenne pepper
> ⅛ teaspoon salt, or to taste
>   Freshly ground pepper to taste
> ¼ cup chopped scallions
> 2 tablespoons chopped fresh dill

Combine beans, oil, lemon juice, cayenne, salt and black pepper in a food processor; process until smooth. Scrape into a bowl; stir in scallions and dill.

Sidebar (Lima Bean Spread)

O

CARBOHYDRATE SERVINGS

MAKES ABOUT 1½ CUPS

PREP TIME: 20 MINUTES
START TO FINISH: 1 HOUR

TO MAKE AHEAD: Cover and refrigerate for up to 4 days or freeze for up to 6 months.

PER TABLESPOON
25 CALORIES
 1 G FAT (0 G SAT, 1 G MONO)
 0 MG CHOLESTEROL
 3 G CARBOHYDRATE
 1 G PROTEIN
 1 G FIBER
56 MG SODIUM

EXCHANGES
FREE FOOD

For White Bean Spread:

O

CARBOHYDRATE SERVINGS

MAKES ABOUT 3 CUPS

PREP TIME: 10 MINUTES
START TO FINISH: 10 MINUTES

TO MAKE AHEAD: Cover and refrigerate for up to 4 days.

PER TABLESPOON
25 CALORIES
 1 G FAT (0 G SAT, 1 G MONO)
 0 MG CHOLESTEROL
 3 G CARBOHYDRATE
 1 G PROTEIN
 1 G FIBER
44 MG SODIUM

EXCHANGES
FREE FOOD

Creamy Herb Dip

Quick ☼ Easy

A perennial favorite with kids, this all-purpose dip can also be used as a sandwich spread.

¼ cup reduced-fat cream cheese (Neufchâtel), softened (2 ounces)
2 tablespoons buttermilk *or* 1% milk
2 tablespoons chopped fresh chives *or* scallions
1 tablespoon chopped fresh dill *or* parsley
1 teaspoon prepared horseradish, or more to taste
Pinch of sugar
⅛ teaspoon salt
Freshly ground pepper to taste

Place cream cheese in a small bowl and stir in buttermilk (or milk) until smooth. Mix in chives (or scallions), dill (or parsley), horseradish, sugar, salt and pepper.

O

CARBOHYDRATE

SERVINGS

MAKES ABOUT ½ CUP

PREP TIME: 15 MINUTES

START TO FINISH: 15 MINUTES

TO MAKE AHEAD: Cover and refrigerate for up to 4 days.

PER TABLESPOON

20 CALORIES
2 G FAT (1 G SAT, 0 G MONO)
5 MG CHOLESTEROL
1 G CARBOHYDRATE
1 G PROTEIN
0 G FIBER
72 MG SODIUM

EXCHANGES

FREE FOOD

Tortilla Chips

Quick ☼ Easy

PREP TIME: 5 MINUTES | **START TO FINISH:** 15 MINUTES | **TO MAKE AHEAD:** Store in an airtight container at room temperature for up to 1 week or in the freezer for up to 2 months.

It's definitely worth making your own—fresh-baked low-fat chips have a more pronounced corn flavor than store-bought.

Preheat oven to 400°F. Lightly brush one side of 4 corn tortillas with about ¼ teaspoon canola oil each and sprinkle with a pinch of salt. Stack the tortillas and cut into 8 wedges; arrange on lightly oiled baking sheets. Bake until crisp, 8 to 10 minutes.

MAKES 32 TORTILLA CHIPS

PER CHIP: 0 CARBOHYDRATE SERVINGS; 8 CALORIES; 0 G FAT (0 G SAT, 0 G MONO); 0 MG CHOLESTEROL; 2 G CARBOHYDRATE; 0 G PROTEIN; 0 G FIBER; 23 MG SODIUM.

Feta-Herb Spread

Quick ☼ Easy

This pungent Greek-inspired dip is sensational on whole-wheat pita crisps or fresh vegetables.

- 1   **32-ounce container low-fat *or* nonfat plain yogurt**
- 1   **clove garlic, crushed and peeled**
- ½ **teaspoon salt, or to taste**
- 1   **cup crumbled feta cheese (about 4 ounces)**
- 1   **tablespoon extra-virgin olive oil**
- 2   **teaspoons chopped fresh parsley**
- 1   **teaspoon dried oregano**

1. Line a sieve with cheesecloth and spoon in yogurt. Set the sieve over a bowl, leaving at least 1 inch clearance at the bottom. Cover and refrigerate for at least 8 hours or overnight.
2. Place garlic on a cutting board, sprinkle with salt and mash into a paste with the side of a chef's knife. Transfer to a medium bowl. Add the drained yogurt (discard whey) and whisk until smooth. Stir in feta cheese, oil, parsley and oregano.

Toasted Pita Crisps

Quick ☼ Easy

PREP TIME: 5 MINUTES | **START TO FINISH:** 15 MINUTES | **TO MAKE AHEAD:** Store in an airtight container at room temperature for up to 1 week or in the freezer for up to 2 months.

Preheat oven to 425°F. Cut 4 whole-wheat pita breads into 4 triangles each. Separate each triangle into 2 halves at the fold. Arrange, rough side up, on a baking sheet. Spritz lightly with olive oil cooking spray or brush lightly with olive oil. Bake until crisp, 8 to 10 minutes.

MAKES 32 PITA CRISPS

PER CRISP: 0 CARBOHYDRATE SERVINGS; 23 CALORIES; 0 G FAT (0 G SAT, 0 G MONO); 0 MG CHOLESTEROL; 4 G CARBOHYDRATE; 1 G PROTEIN; 1 G FIBER; 43 MG SODIUM.

O

CARBOHYDRATE
SERVINGS

MAKES 10 SERVINGS, ¼ CUP EACH

PREP TIME: 15 MINUTES

START TO FINISH: 15 MINUTES (start draining yogurt at least 8 hours before serving)

TO MAKE AHEAD: Cover and refrigerate for up to 4 days.

PER SERVING

65 CALORIES
3 G FAT (1 G SAT, 1 G MONO)
7 MG CHOLESTEROL
4 G CARBOHYDRATE
4 G PROTEIN
0 G FIBER
248 MG SODIUM

EXCHANGES

½ LOW-FAT MILK

Roasted Eggplant Dip

Mellow roasted garlic sets this version of the popular Middle Eastern eggplant dip apart from standard recipes. Roasting the onion and tomato alongside the eggplant also adds an extra dimension of flavor. Serve with sliced raw vegetables, crackers or pita bread.

O

CARBOHYDRATE
SERVINGS

MAKES ABOUT 2½ CUPS

PREP TIME: 20 MINUTES
START TO FINISH: 1 HOUR

TO MAKE AHEAD: Cover and refrigerate for up to 2 days.

PER TABLESPOON

11 CALORIES
0 G FAT (0 G SAT, 0 G MONO)
0 MG CHOLESTEROL
2 G CARBOHYDRATE
0 G PROTEIN
0 G FIBER
30 MG SODIUM

EXCHANGES

FREE FOOD

1 large head garlic
1 eggplant (1-1¼ pounds), cut in half lengthwise
1 small onion, cut into ½-inch-thick slices
1 ripe tomato, cored, sliced in half and seeded
3 tablespoons lemon juice
2 tablespoons chopped fresh mint
1 tablespoon extra-virgin olive oil
½ teaspoon salt, or to taste
Freshly ground pepper, or to taste

1. Set oven racks at the two lowest levels; preheat to 450°F. Peel as much of the papery skin from the garlic as possible and wrap loosely in foil. Bake until the garlic is soft, 30 minutes. Let cool slightly.
2. Meanwhile, coat a baking sheet with cooking spray. Place eggplant halves on the prepared baking sheet, cut-side down. Roast for 10 minutes. Add onion slices and tomato halves to the baking sheet and roast until all the vegetables are soft, 10 to 15 minutes longer. Let cool slightly.
3. Separate the garlic cloves and squeeze the soft pulp into a medium bowl. Mash with the back of a spoon. Slip skins from the eggplant and tomatoes; coarsely chop. Finely chop the onion. Add the chopped vegetables to the garlic pulp and stir in the lemon juice, mint, oil, salt and pepper.

TIPS FOR REAL LIFE

"HOW CAN I EAT HEALTHY DURING THE HOLIDAYS?"

It's one of the most common questions asked by people with diabetes—or anyone who's made a commitment to eating with their health in mind. And no wonder: from Thanksgiving to Passover to Kwanzaa, holidays are all about the food. And not just any food, but the types of rich celebration foods we look forward to all year long. For the most part, forgoing these foods just isn't an option, since they're such a part of who we are. How to do it wisely?

♦ **Lighten up.** Recreate a traditional recipe to fit into your eating plan, while still preserving the goodness that makes it so treasured. That green bean casserole with fried onions, say, might be just as wonderful, or even better, with roasted caramelized onions instead. Of course, this kind of creativity is our stock-in-trade at EATINGWELL. Here you'll find healthful updates of favorites like Sweet Potato Casserole (*page 254*), Rolled Sugar Cookies (*page 301*) and Squash Pie (*page 289*).

♦ **Choose and cull.** While some holiday foods are essential, you might feel less strongly about others. Why not pare those foods from the menu (or, leave them off your plate)? That gives you more leeway to enjoy your "must-haves."

Parmesan Crisps

Quick ☼ Easy

These flavorful wafers, simply baked grated cheese, make a delightful accompaniment to soups or a sophisticated nibble to serve with drinks. As the only ingredient, the cheese matters here. Be sure to use imported Parmigiano-Reggiano (look for the name stenciled on the rind) and grate it yourself.

1¼ cups freshly grated Parmigiano-Reggiano cheese (2¼ ounces)

1. Preheat oven to 350°F. Line a baking sheet with parchment paper or use a nonstick baking sheet. (Do not use cooking spray.)
2. Mound level tablespoonfuls of cheese about 2 inches apart on the baking sheet. Bake until the cheese is melted, soft and a very light golden color, about 6 minutes. Remove from the oven and do not disturb until completely cooled and firm to the touch, about 20 minutes. Using a thin spatula or knife, lift the crackers from the baking sheet.

O

CARBOHYDRATE
SERVINGS

MAKES ABOUT **16** CRISPS

PREP TIME: 10 MINUTES
START TO FINISH: 35 MINUTES

TO MAKE AHEAD: Store in an airtight container for up to 4 days.

PER SERVING
 38 CALORIES
  3 G FAT (1 G SAT, 0 G MONO)
  6 MG CHOLESTEROL
  0 G CARBOHYDRATE
  4 G PROTEIN
  0 G FIBER
156 MG SODIUM

EXCHANGES
 ½ MEDIUM-FAT MEAT

➤ **Plan ahead.** If you're going to a holiday party or restaurant, find out what's on the menu ahead of time, and decide what you're going to eat. That way you can adjust the rest of your day's eating, activity, and medication schedules accordingly.

➤ **Bring your own.** If you're going to an event where you know the foods served will be a challenge for you, offer to bring along your own dish to share. Consider a vegetable-based dish that contains little or no carbohydrate, so you can enjoy it freely. If you'll be staying over for the holidays—say, at Mom's—bring breakfast and lunch items to help you start your days on the right track.

➤ **Navigate the buffet table.** Inspect the offerings first before loading up your plate (choosing a cocktail-size plate, if possible). Make your first trip for vegetables and salad, then go back for small portions of the richer fare.

➤ **Have a drink if you want, but wait until after the meal.** You'll have something in your stomach to blunt the effects of the alcohol. Before and with the meal, sip sparkling water—with lots of lime and lemon wedges to make it festive.

➤ **Focus on the fun, not the feast.** Spend more time in conversation and enjoying the entertainment than worrying about what's on your plate.

Smoked Salmon Canapés

Quick ☀ Easy

Thin cucumber ribbons add a decorative finish to these classic hors d'oeuvres.

O

CARBOHYDRATE
SERVINGS

MAKES **32** PIECES

PREP TIME: 25 MINUTES

START TO FINISH: 25 MINUTES

TO MAKE AHEAD: The cucumber strips and salmon spread will keep, covered, in the refrigerator for up to 1 day.

PER PIECE

39 CALORIES

2 G FAT (1 G SAT, 0 G MONO)

14 MG CHOLESTEROL

4 G CARBOHYDRATE

2 G PROTEIN

1 G FIBER

96 MG SODIUM

EXCHANGES

1/2 FAT

3	medium cucumbers
2/3	cup reduced-fat cream cheese (Neufchâtel) (6 ounces)
1/4	cup chopped smoked salmon (1 ounce)
2	tablespoons prepared horseradish
32	slices cocktail pumpernickel bread, crusts trimmed
1/4	cup salmon roe *or* red caviar (2 ounces)
	Freshly ground pepper to taste
	Dill sprigs for garnish

1. With a vegetable peeler, remove and discard a long strip of dark green skin from one side of one of the cucumbers. On that same side, continue to pare long thin strips edged in dark green until you reach the seedy portion—you should get about 3 strips. Rotate cucumber a quarter turn and continue paring, working your way around the cucumber. Repeat with the remaining cucumbers—you will need about 3 dozen strips in total. Bring a saucepan of water to a boil. Add the cucumber strips and blanch for 5 seconds. Immediately drain and refresh under cold running water. Lay the strips on paper towels to dry.

2. Blend cream cheese, smoked salmon and horseradish in a small bowl. Shortly before serving, spread about 2 teaspoons of the salmon mixture on each slice of bread. Arrange a cucumber strip over each canapé and top with a few eggs of salmon roe (or red caviar). Garnish with pepper and a dill sprig.

Spiced Almonds

Quick ☼ Easy

A high-protein predinner snack—like these simple curry-roasted almonds—is a good way to take the edge off your appetite so that you don't overeat at mealtime.

- **2** cups whole almonds (with skins)
- **2** teaspoons extra-virgin olive oil
- **2** teaspoons curry powder
- **½** teaspoon salt, or to taste
- **¼** teaspoon cayenne pepper

Preheat oven to 300°F. Combine almonds, oil, curry powder, salt and cayenne in a small baking pan; toss to coat well. Bake until the almonds are fragrant and lightly toasted, about 25 minutes. Transfer to a bowl to cool.

Tamari Walnuts

Quick ☼ Easy

Keep these nuts on hand for snacking or to garnish stir-fries or salads.

- **2** cups coarsely chopped walnuts
- **2½** tablespoons tamari *or* reduced-sodium soy sauce

Place walnuts in a large skillet; heat over medium heat until hot. Drizzle with tamari (or soy sauce) and stir until the nuts are coated and the pan is dry, about 1 minute. Transfer to a bowl to cool.

O

CARBOHYDRATE
SERVINGS

MAKES 2 CUPS, FOR 16 SERVINGS

PREP TIME: 5 MINUTES
START TO FINISH: 30 MINUTES

TO MAKE AHEAD: Store in an airtight container for up to 1 week.

PER SERVING
112 CALORIES
10 G FAT (1 G SAT, 6 G MONO)
0 MG CHOLESTEROL
4 G CARBOHYDRATE
4 G PROTEIN
2 G FIBER
73 MG SODIUM

EXCHANGES
2 FAT (MONO)

For Tamari Walnuts:

O

CARBOHYDRATE
SERVINGS

MAKES 2 CUPS, FOR 16 SERVINGS

PREP TIME: 2 MINUTES
START TO FINISH: 5 MINUTES

TO MAKE AHEAD: Cover and refrigerate for up to 1 week.

PER SERVING
100 CALORIES
10 G FAT (1 G SAT, 1 G MONO)
0 MG CHOLESTEROL
2 G CARBOHYDRATE
2 G PROTEIN
1 G FIBER
158 MG SODIUM

EXCHANGES
2 FAT (POLY)

Chili Pecans

A medley of warm spices tempered with a touch of brown sugar is a great match for rich, nutritious pecans. They make a perfect nibble with a drink before dinner or afterward with a cup of espresso.

1½	tablespoons chili powder
1½	teaspoons ground cumin
1	teaspoon ground coriander
1	teaspoon paprika
1	teaspoon brown sugar
¼	teaspoon garlic powder
2	cups pecan halves (about 4 ounces)
1½	tablespoons Worcestershire sauce
½	teaspoon salt

1. Preheat oven to 275°F. Line a large baking sheet with parchment paper.
2. Combine chili powder, cumin, coriander, paprika, brown sugar and garlic powder in a small bowl. Toss pecans and Worcestershire sauce in a large bowl. Sprinkle the spice mixture over the pecans, tossing to coat. Spread the spiced nuts on the prepared baking sheet.
3. Bake the pecans, tossing every 8 to 10 minutes, until lightly browned and very fragrant, about 35 minutes. Transfer to a bowl; sprinkle with salt and toss well. Let cool.

O

CARBOHYDRATE
SERVINGS

MAKES ABOUT **2 CUPS,**
FOR **16** SERVINGS

PREP TIME: 5 MINUTES
START TO FINISH: 1 HOUR

TO MAKE AHEAD: Store in an airtight container for up to 1 week.

PER SERVING

102 CALORIES
10 G FAT (1 G SAT, 6 G MONO)
0 MG CHOLESTEROL
3 G CARBOHYDRATE
1 G PROTEIN
1 G FIBER
96 MG SODIUM

EXCHANGES

2 FAT (MONO)

SUPER SNACK IDEA

GORP

Whenever I travel or go hiking or skiing, I pack a ziplock bag filled with my custom gorp, a mixture of equal amounts of almonds, unsalted peanuts, dried cranberries, chopped pitted dates and a handful of chocolate chips. Gorp is a nutrient-rich energy booster, but go easy, because it's also dense in calories.

—*Patsy Jamieson, Recipe Editor*

PER OUNCE: 1 CARBOHYDRATE SERVING, 102 CALORIES

Greek Split Pea Spread

High ⬆ Fiber

One taste of this simple, rustic spread—a popular *meze* or appetizer throughout Greece—and you are transported to a little seaside taverna. The base of the spread is yellow split peas, a healthful legume that requires no presoaking and cooks in less than 45 minutes. Enjoy this appetizer as the Greeks do, with a generous drizzle of your favorite olive oil.

1	cup yellow split peas, rinsed
6	cloves garlic, crushed and peeled
3	cups water
1	teaspoon salt
2	tablespoons lemon juice
3	tablespoons extra-virgin olive oil, divided
	Freshly ground pepper to taste
¼	cup finely diced red onion
2	tablespoons chopped fresh dill *or* parsley

1. Combine split peas, garlic and water in a large saucepan; bring to a boil, skimming off any froth. Reduce heat to low, cover and simmer for 30 minutes.
2. Uncover and simmer, stirring often, until the mixture has cooked down to a thick puree, 10 to 20 minutes longer. Remove from heat and stir in salt. Press plastic wrap on the surface and let cool.
3. Transfer the pea mixture to a food processor. Add lemon juice and 1 tablespoon oil; process until smooth. Season with pepper. Transfer to a bowl. To serve, drizzle the remaining 2 tablespoons oil over the spread and sprinkle with red onion and dill (or parsley).

¹/₂

CARBOHYDRATE
SERVING

MAKES 10 SERVINGS, ¼ CUP EACH

PREP TIME: 20 MINUTES
START TO FINISH: 1 HOUR 10 MINUTES

TO MAKE AHEAD: Cover and refrigerate for up to 4 days or freeze for up to 6 months.

PER SERVING

87 CALORIES
4 G FAT (1 G SAT, 3 G MONO)
0 MG CHOLESTEROL
13 G CARBOHYDRATE
4 G PROTEIN
5 G FIBER
243 MG SODIUM

EXCHANGES

1 STARCH
1 FAT

Drinks & Nibbles

8 FABULOUS FROSTY ALCOHOL-FREE DRINKS

These simple sippers taste and look festive—but only you have to know they're also alcohol-free. **Each makes 1 serving and starts with a tall, ice-filled glass.**

❧ **Ginger-Lemon Breeze:** Add 2 tablespoons lemon juice. Top with diet ginger ale.

0 CARBOHYDRATE SERVINGS, 8 CALORIES
EXCHANGES: 1½ OTHER CARBOHYDRATE

❧ **Lemon-Mint Spritzer:** Add 2 tablespoons lemon juice, 2 mint sprigs and no-calorie sweetener to taste. Top off with chilled sparkling water.

0 CARBOHYDRATE SERVINGS, 9 CALORIES
EXCHANGES: 2 OTHER CARBOHYDRATE

❧ **Nil & Tonic:** Add lots of gorgeous fruit for garnish (try wedges of orange, lemon, lime, strawberries or starfruit), then fill the glass with diet tonic water.

0 CARBOHYDRATE SERVINGS, 19 CALORIES
EXCHANGES: FREE FOOD

❧ **Mango-Tea Cooler:** Add ½ cup cooled black or green tea and ¼ cup mango nectar; top off with diet ginger ale. Garnish with lemon slices.

½ CARBOHYDRATE SERVING, 36 CALORIES
EXCHANGES: ½ FRUIT

❧ **Pomegranate Splash:** Add ¼ cup pomegranate juice and top off with sparkling water. Garnish with a twist of orange.

½ CARBOHYDRATE SERVING, 38 CALORIES
EXCHANGES: ½ OTHER CARBOHYDRATE

❧ **Sparkling Mary:** Add equal parts reduced-sodium vegetable juice cocktail and lemon-flavored sparkling water; add a spoonful of prepared horseradish and a splash of hot pepper sauce. Stir and garnish with lemon slices and a celery stalk.

½ CARBOHYDRATE SERVING, 29 CALORIES
EXCHANGES: 1 VEGETABLE

❧ **Cranberry Sunrise:** Add ¼ cup diet cranberry juice cocktail, then pour in ½ cup orange-pineapple juice blend. Top off with sparkling water. Garnish with lime wedges.

1 CARBOHYDRATE SERVING, 66 CALORIES
EXCHANGES: 1 FRUIT

❧ **Iced Cinnamocha:** Add ¾ cup cooled strong coffee (regular or decaf), 2 tablespoons 1% milk and 1 tablespoon chocolate syrup; shake until frothy and sprinkle with a pinch of ground cinnamon.

1 CARBOHYDRATE SERVING, 71 CALORIES
EXCHANGES: 1 OTHER CARBOHYDRATE

3 TOASTY WARM BEVERAGES

Lift your spirits and fill your home with the welcoming fragrance of these hot drinks. **Each makes 4 servings, 1 cup each.**

❧ **Chai:** Brew strong tea by steeping 8 chai spice tea bags in 2⅔ cups boiling water in a medium saucepan for 3 to 4 minutes. Heat 1⅓ cups vanilla soymilk (or 1% milk) in the microwave (1 minute on High) or on the stovetop until steaming. Remove tea bags and add hot soymilk (or milk) to the brewed tea. Add no-calorie sweetener to taste, if desired.

½ CARBOHYDRATE SERVING, 50 CALORIES
EXCHANGES: ½ FAT-FREE MILK

❧ **Hot Cocoa:** Place ⅓ cup unsweetened cocoa in a medium saucepan. Gradually whisk in 1 cup 1% milk until smooth. Add 2 cinnamon sticks and bring to a boil, stirring, over medium heat. Whisk in 3 cups milk, 1 teaspoon vanilla extract and ¼ teaspoon almond extracts. Heat, stirring occasionally, until hot. Add no-calorie sweetener to taste. Remove cinnamon sticks and serve.

1 CARBOHYDRATE SERVING, 131 CALORIES
EXCHANGES: 1 FAT-FREE MILK, ½ FAT

❧ **Mulled Apple-Cranberry Cider:** Combine 2 cups apple cider, 2 cups cranberry juice cocktail, 2 strips fresh orange peel and 1 cinnamon stick in a saucepan. Bring to a simmer over low heat. Simmer for 20 minutes. For entertaining, it can be kept steaming in a slow cooker.

2 CARBOHYDRATE SERVINGS, 132 CALORIES
EXCHANGES: 2 FRUIT

7 SUPER SIMPLE SNACK IDEAS

❧ **Edamame Nibbles:** Cook frozen edamame (in pods) according to package directions. Sprinkle with coarse salt.

PER 1/4 CUP: 0 CARBOHYDRATE SERVINGS, 50 CALORIES
EXCHANGES: FREE FOOD

❧ **Eggcetera:** Dip slices of hard-cooked egg in extra-virgin olive oil and sprinkle with kosher salt and paprika.

PER EGG: 0 CARBOHYDRATE SERVINGS, 88 CALORIES
EXCHANGES: FREE FOOD

❧ **Cheesy Popcorn:** Toss hot popcorn with freshly grated Parmesan cheese and cayenne pepper to taste.

PER CUP: 1/2 CARBOHYDRATE SERVING, 74 CALORIES
EXCHANGES: 1/2 STARCH, 1/2 LEAN MEAT

❧ **Sardines on Crackers:** Top a whole-grain Scandinavian-style cracker (Wasa, Ry Krisp, Ryvita, Kavli) with 2 to 3 canned sardines, preferably packed in olive oil. Finish with a squeeze of lemon.

PER CRACKER: 1/2 CARBOHYDRATE SERVING, 64 CALORIES
EXCHANGES: 1/2 STARCH, 1/2 LEAN MEAT

❧ **Sesame Carrots:** Toss 2 cups of baby carrots with 1 tablespoon toasted sesame seeds and a pinch each of dried thyme and kosher salt.

PER 2/3 CUP: 1/2 CARBOHYDRATE SERVING, 50 CALORIES
EXCHANGES: 1 1/2 VEGETABLE

❧ **Turkey Rollups:** Spread slices of deli turkey breast with honey mustard or mango chutney and season with freshly ground pepper. Wrap turkey around breadsticks. For a snappy touch, tie with a blanched chive.

PER 2 ROLLUPS: 1/2 CARBOHYDRATE SERVING, 82 CALORIES
EXCHANGES: 1/2 OTHER CARBOHYDRATE, 1/2 LEAN MEAT

❧ **Pistachios & Cherries:** Combine equal parts dried cherries or cranberries with shelled pistachios.

PER 1 OUNCE: 1 CARBOHYDRATE SERVING, 135 CALORIES
EXCHANGES: 1 FRUIT, 1 FAT

4 ELEGANT EASY APPETIZER IDEAS

❧ **Fennel & Parmesan:** Drizzle fennel slices with extra-virgin olive oil. Top with shaved Parmesan cheese and cracked black pepper.

PER SLICE: 0 CARBOHYDRATE SERVINGS, 25 CALORIES
EXCHANGES: FREE FOOD

❧ **Herbed Olives:** Toss your favorite olives with extra-virgin olive oil, dried oregano, dried basil, crushed garlic and coarsely ground pepper.

PER 4 OLIVES: 0 CARBOHYDRATE SERVINGS, 47 CALORIES
EXCHANGES: FREE FOOD

❧ **Shrimp & Avocado Canapés:** Assemble a whole-wheat cracker with avocado, cooked shrimp and a squeeze of lime juice.

PER CRACKER: 0 CARBOHYDRATE SERVINGS, 43 CALORIES
EXCHANGES: FREE FOOD

❧ **Date Wraps:** Wrap a thin slice of prosciutto around a pitted date. Grind fresh pepper on top.

PER DATE: 1/2 CARBOHYDRATE SERVING, 39 CALORIES
EXCHANGES: 1/2 FRUIT

Soups

> **"** For years, I made potato soup, but after being diagnosed with diabetes I've adapted the recipe to use fewer potatoes. I add 2 or 3 leeks, several stalks of celery and 4 to 5 cloves of garlic (I mash the garlic after cooking, so that it isn't harsh or bitter). Several onions really increase the taste. With the added low-carb vegetables, I have reduced the carb count by almost 50%. **"**
>
> — *Marcia B., Georgia*

1/2

CARBOHYDRATE

SERVING

MAKES 9 SERVINGS, 1 CUP EACH

PREP TIME: 15 MINUTES
START TO FINISH: 25 MINUTES

PER SERVING
164 CALORIES
4 G FAT (1 G SAT, 2 G MONO)
48 MG CHOLESTEROL
10 G CARBOHYDRATE
21 G PROTEIN
2 G FIBER
351 MG SODIUM

EXCHANGES
1 STARCH
2½ LEAN MEAT

For Chicken, Escarole
& Rice Soup:

1

CARBOHYDRATE

SERVING

MAKES 10 SERVINGS, 1 CUP EACH

PREP TIME: 15 MINUTES
START TO FINISH: 30-45 MINUTES

PER SERVING
157 CALORIES
4 G FAT (1 G SAT, 2 G MONO)
30 MG CHOLESTEROL
15 G CARBOHYDRATE
15 G PROTEIN
2 G FIBER
166 MG SODIUM

NUTRITION BONUS: Folate (21%
DAILY VALUE), Vitamin A (20% DV).

EXCHANGES
1 STARCH
1½ LEAN MEAT

Tuscan Chicken & White Bean Soup

Quick ☼ Easy

During the shorter days and long, cold nights of winter, a quick homemade, sage-scented chicken soup is our idea of comfort. This is a good way to use up leftover chicken, but you can also pick up a convenient rotisserie chicken for this recipe.

- 2 teaspoons extra-virgin olive oil
- 2 leeks, white and light green parts, washed and cut into ¼-inch rounds (2 cups)
- 1 tablespoon chopped fresh sage *or* ¼ teaspoon dried
- 2 14-ounce cans reduced-sodium chicken broth
- 2 cups water
- 1 15½-ounce can cannellini (white kidney) beans, rinsed
- 4 cups shredded skinless cooked chicken

Heat oil in a soup pot or large Dutch oven over medium-high heat. Add leeks and cook, stirring often, until soft, about 3 minutes. Stir in sage and continue cooking until aromatic, about 30 seconds. Stir in broth and water, increase heat to high, cover and bring to a boil. Add beans and chicken and cook, stirring occasionally, until heated through, about 3 minutes. Serve hot.

Chicken, Escarole & Rice Soup

Quick ☼ Easy

Based on an Italian classic, this soup blends the goodness of an Old World kitchen with modern convenience.

- 1 tablespoon extra-virgin olive oil
- 1 large onion, chopped
- 2 cloves garlic, minced
- 1 head escarole, trimmed and thinly sliced
- 3 14-ounce cans reduced-sodium chicken broth
- 1 14½-ounce can diced tomatoes
- ½ cup long-grain white rice
- 1 pound boneless, skinless chicken breasts, trimmed and cut into ½-inch pieces
    Freshly ground pepper to taste
- 6 tablespoons freshly grated Romano *or* Parmesan cheese

TO MAKE AHEAD: Both soups will keep, covered, in the refrigerator for up to 2 days or in the freezer for up to 2 months.

1. Heat oil in a large pot over medium-high heat. Add onion and garlic; cook, stirring frequently, until they soften and begin to brown, 5 to 7 minutes. Add escarole and cook, stirring occasionally, until wilted, 2 to 3 minutes. Add broth, tomatoes and rice; bring to a boil. Reduce heat to low, cover and simmer until the rice is almost tender, 12 to 15 minutes.

2. Add chicken and simmer until it is no longer pink in the center and the rice is tender, about 5 minutes. Season with pepper. Serve hot, sprinkled with Romano (or Parmesan).

Roasted Tomato Soup

Quick ☼ Easy

Roasting the vegetables for this simple summer soup enhances their inherent sweetness. The recipe is from EATINGWELL reader Tracey Medeiros of Atlanta, Georgia.

1½	pounds large tomatoes, such as beefsteak, cut in half crosswise
1	medium sweet onion, such as Vidalia, peeled and cut in half crosswise
3	large cloves garlic, unpeeled
1	tablespoon plus 1 teaspoon extra-virgin olive oil, divided
¼	teaspoon salt, or to taste
	Freshly ground pepper to taste
2	cups reduced-sodium chicken broth *or* vegetable broth, divided
¼	cup tomato juice
1	teaspoon tomato paste
¼	teaspoon Worcestershire sauce
1	tablespoon fresh basil, chopped
	Brown sugar to taste (optional)
½	cup corn kernels (fresh, from 1 ear; *see box, page 243*) *or* frozen, thawed

1. Preheat oven to 400°F. Coat a baking sheet with cooking spray.
2. Toss tomatoes, onion, garlic in a mixing bowl with 1 tablespoon oil. Season with salt and pepper. Spread on the prepared baking sheet and roast until the vegetables are soft and caramelized, about 30 minutes. Let cool.
3. Peel and seed the tomatoes. Trim off the onion ends. Peel the garlic. Place the vegetables in a food processor or blender with 1 cup broth and the remaining 1 teaspoon oil. Pulse to desired thickness and texture.
4. Transfer the vegetable puree to a large heavy pot or Dutch oven. Add the remaining 1 cup broth, tomato juice, tomato paste, Worcestershire sauce, basil and brown sugar (if using). Bring to a simmer over medium heat, stirring often. Ladle into 6 soup bowls, garnish with corn and serve.

1

CARBOHYDRATE
SERVING

MAKES 6 SERVINGS, 1 CUP EACH

PREP TIME: 35 MINUTES
START TO FINISH: 45 MINUTES

TO MAKE AHEAD: Cover and refrigerate for up to 2 days or freeze for up to 2 months.

NUTRITION NOTE
Homemade tomato soup is easy to make, a good source of lycopene and so much lower in sodium than any canned tomato soup.

PER SERVING
95 CALORIES
4 G FAT (1 G SAT, 3 G MONO)
1 MG CHOLESTEROL
13 G CARBOHYDRATE
3 G PROTEIN
3 G FIBER
146 MG SODIUM

NUTRITION BONUS: Vitamin C (35% DAILY VALUE), Vitamin A (20% DV).

EXCHANGES
2 VEGETABLE
1 FAT (MONO)

1

CARBOHYDRATE

SERVING

MAKES 6 SERVINGS, 1 CUP EACH

PREP TIME: 30 MINUTES

START TO FINISH: 1 HOUR 10 MINUTES

TO MAKE AHEAD: Cover and refrigerate for up to 1 day.

NUTRITION NOTE
Shrimp generally do not raise blood cholesterol because they are extremely low in saturated fat.

PER SERVING

184 CALORIES

5 G FAT (2 G SAT, 3 G MONO)

94 MG CHOLESTEROL

13 G CARBOHYDRATE

16 G PROTEIN

2 G FIBER

235 MG SODIUM

NUTRITION BONUS: Vitamin C (27% DAILY VALUE).

EXCHANGES

1 STARCH

2 VERY LEAN MEAT

1 FAT

Shrimp Bisque

A broth made from shrimp shells, wine and aromatic vegetables makes a richly flavored base for this bisque. A dollop of reduced-fat sour cream is all you need for a luxurious finish.

12	ounces shrimp (30-40 per pound), shell-on
1	onion, chopped, divided
1	carrot, peeled and sliced
1	stalk celery (with leaves), sliced
½	cup dry white wine
½	teaspoon black peppercorns
1	bay leaf
3	cups water
1	tablespoon extra-virgin olive oil
4	ounces mushrooms, wiped clean and sliced (about 1½ cups)
½	green bell pepper, chopped
¼	cup chopped scallions
2	tablespoons chopped fresh parsley
¼	cup all-purpose flour
1½	cups 1% milk
¼	cup reduced-fat sour cream
¼	cup dry sherry
1	tablespoon lemon juice
¼	teaspoon salt, or to taste
	Freshly ground pepper to taste
	Dash of hot sauce

1. Peel and devein shrimp, reserving the shells. Cut the shrimp into ¾-inch pieces; cover and refrigerate.
2. Combine the shrimp shells with about half the onion, all the carrot, celery, wine, peppercorns and bay leaf in a large heavy saucepan. Add water and simmer over low heat for about 30 minutes. Strain through a sieve, pressing on the solids to extract all the juices; discard the solids. Measure the shrimp stock and add water, if necessary, to make 1½ cups.
3. Heat oil in the same pan over medium heat. Add mushrooms, bell pepper, scallions, parsley and the remaining onion. Cook, stirring, until the mushrooms are soft, about 5 minutes. Sprinkle with flour and cook, stirring constantly, until it starts to turn golden, 2 to 3 minutes. Slowly stir in milk and the shrimp stock. Cook, stirring to loosen any flour sticking to the bottom of the pot, until the soup returns to a simmer and thickens, about 5 minutes. Add the reserved shrimp and cook until they turn opaque in the center, about 2 minutes more. Add sour cream, sherry and lemon juice; stir over low heat until heated through—do not let it come to a boil. Taste and adjust seasonings with salt, pepper and hot sauce.

Pasta & Bean Soup

Quick ☼ Easy

Using basic canned goods and a few other staples, you can make this comforting soup in just minutes. The trick to achieving a full-bodied homemade flavor from canned chicken broth is to freshen it up with a handful of herbs, some garlic cloves and crushed red pepper. For a meatier flavor, add a little crumbled cooked Italian turkey sausage to the soup.

4	14-ounce cans reduced-sodium chicken broth
6	cloves garlic, crushed and peeled
4	4-inch sprigs fresh rosemary *or* 1 tablespoon dried
⅛-¼	teaspoon crushed red pepper
1	15½-ounce *or* 19-ounce can cannellini (white kidney) beans, rinsed, divided
1	14½-ounce can diced tomatoes
1	cup medium pasta shells *or* orecchiette
2	cups individually quick-frozen spinach (6 ounces) (*see Note*)
6	teaspoons extra-virgin olive oil (optional)
6	tablespoons freshly grated Parmesan cheese

1. Combine broth, garlic, rosemary and crushed red pepper in a 4- to 6-quart Dutch oven or soup pot; bring to a simmer. Partially cover and simmer over medium-low heat for 20 minutes to intensify flavor. Meanwhile, mash 1 cup beans in a small bowl.
2. Scoop garlic cloves and rosemary from the broth with a slotted spoon (or pass the soup through a strainer and return to the pot). Add mashed and whole beans to the broth, along with tomatoes; return to a simmer. Stir in pasta, cover and cook over medium heat, stirring occasionally, until the pasta is just tender, 10 to 12 minutes.
3. Stir in spinach, cover and cook just until the spinach has thawed, 2 to 3 minutes. Ladle the soup into bowls and garnish each serving with a drizzle of oil, if desired, and a sprinkling of Parmesan.

MAKES 8 SERVINGS, 1 CUP EACH

PREP TIME: 15 MINUTES
START TO FINISH: 35 MINUTES

VARIATION
Substitute chickpeas (garbanzo beans) for the cannellini beans; use a food processor to puree them.

INGREDIENT NOTE
Individually quick-frozen (IQF) spinach is sold in convenient plastic bags. If you have a 10-ounce box of spinach on hand, use just over half of it and cook according to package directions before adding to the soup in Step 3.

PER SERVING

133	CALORIES
2	G FAT (1 G SAT, 0 G MONO)
6	MG CHOLESTEROL
20	G CARBOHYDRATE
9	G PROTEIN
4	G FIBER
356	MG SODIUM

NUTRITION BONUS: Vitamin A (35% DAILY VALUE), Fiber (16% DV).

EXCHANGES

1½	STARCH
1	VEGETABLE
1	LEAN MEAT

Lentil & Escarole Soup

High ↑ Fiber

A stash of lentil soup in your refrigerator or freezer is like money in the bank. This hearty, fiber-rich soup makes a satisfying lunch at the office or a reviving supper on a busy day.

1	tablespoon extra-virgin olive oil
1	onion, chopped
1	stalk celery, chopped
1	medium carrot, chopped
1	clove garlic, minced
2	large tomatoes, peeled (*see Tip*), seeded and chopped
8	ounces brown lentils, picked over and rinsed (1¼ cups)
6	cups water
½	teaspoon salt, or to taste
	Freshly ground pepper to taste
1	large head escarole (1 pound)
½	cup freshly grated Parmesan cheese

1. Heat oil in a large soup pot or Dutch oven over medium heat. Add onion, celery and carrot. Cook, stirring frequently, until the vegetables are soft, 8 to 10 minutes. Stir in garlic and cook for 1 minute. Add tomatoes, reduce the heat to low and cook, stirring often, for 5 minutes more. Add lentils and water to the pot. Bring to a simmer and cook, partially covered, until the lentils are tender, about 45 minutes. Season with salt and pepper.

2. Meanwhile, wash escarole leaves, stack and cut crosswise into ½-inch-wide strips. When the lentils are tender, stir in the escarole. Return the soup to a simmer; cook until the escarole is tender, about 10 minutes. Ladle into bowls, sprinkle with Parmesan and serve.

1

CARBOHYDRATE
SERVING

MAKES **7** SERVINGS, **1** CUP EACH

PREP TIME: 20 MINUTES

START TO FINISH: 1 HOUR 10 MINUTES

TO MAKE AHEAD: Cover and refrigerate for up to 2 days or freeze for up to 3 months.

TEST KITCHEN TIP
To peel a tomato, make an X in the bottom. Plunge the tomato into boiling water for a few seconds, just until the cut edges of the skin begin to curl. Remove with a slotted spoon. Slip off the skin with a small, sharp knife.

PER SERVING

181 CALORIES
4 G FAT (1 G SAT, 2 G MONO)
4 MG CHOLESTEROL
27 G CARBOHYDRATE
12 G PROTEIN
11 G FIBER
264 MG SODIUM

NUTRITION BONUS: Folate (68% DAILY VALUE), Vitamin A (50% DV), Fiber (42% DV), Iron (25% DV).

EXCHANGES

1 STARCH
2 VEGETABLE
1 VERY LEAN MEAT

Quick Lentil Soups

High ↑ Fiber   Quick ☼ Easy

Canned lentil soup makes a convenient light meal that is low in fat and high in fiber, but it can be a bit mundane. Take it to the next level with any of these sensational seasoning ideas.

CURRY-CILANTRO LENTIL SOUP

Combine one 19-ounce can lentil soup and 1½ teaspoons curry powder in a saucepan; bring to a simmer. Stir in 2 tablespoons chopped fresh cilantro. Ladle into 2 bowls and top each with 1 tablespoon nonfat plain yogurt.

MAKES 2 SERVINGS

PER SERVING: 168 CALORIES; 2 G FAT (0 G SAT, 1 G MONO); 0 MG CHOLESTEROL; 27 G CARBOHYDRATE; 11 G PROTEIN; 8 G FIBER; 848 MG SODIUM

MOROCCAN MINT LENTIL SOUP

Combine one 19-ounce can lentil soup, ¼ teaspoon cayenne pepper and ½ teaspoon each ground coriander, cumin and paprika in a saucepan; bring to a simmer. Stir in 2 tablespoons chopped fresh mint. Ladle into 2 bowls and garnish with lemon slices.

MAKES 2 SERVINGS

PER SERVING: 166 CALORIES; 3 G FAT (0 G SAT, 1 G MONO); 0 MG CHOLESTEROL; 26 G CARBOHYDRATE; 11 G PROTEIN; 9 G FIBER; 842 MG SODIUM

SOUTHERN-STYLE LENTIL SOUP

Combine one 19-ounce can lentil soup, 2 cups individually quick-frozen (IQF) spinach and 1 tablespoon red-wine vinegar in a saucepan; bring to a simmer. Cook, stirring, until the greens are tender. Ladle into 2 bowls and season with pepper.

MAKES 2 SERVINGS

PER SERVING: 186 CALORIES; 3 G FAT (0 G SAT, 1 G MONO); 0 MG CHOLESTEROL; 30 G CARBOHYDRATE; 14 G PROTEIN; 13 G FIBER; 880 MG SODIUM

GREEK DILL & FETA LENTIL SOUP

Combine one 19-ounce can lentil soup and 1 tablespoon fresh lemon juice in a saucepan; bring to a simmer. Stir in 2 tablespoons chopped fresh dill and ½ cup cooked orzo (or rice). Ladle into 2 bowls and garnish each with 1 tablespoon feta cheese.

MAKES 2 SERVINGS

PER SERVING: 244 CALORIES; 4 G FAT (1 G SAT, 2 G MONO); 8 MG CHOLESTEROL; 39 G CARBOHYDRATE; 13 G PROTEIN; 8 G FIBER; 943 MG SODIUM

1

CARBOHYDRATE
SERVING

*For Curry-Cilantro
Lentil Soup:*

EXCHANGES

1½ STARCH
1½ VERY LEAN MEAT

---

*For Moroccan Mint
Lentil Soup:*

EXCHANGES

1½ STARCH
1½ VERY LEAN MEAT

---

*For Southern-Style
Lentil Soup:*

EXCHANGES

1½ STARCH
1 VEGETABLE
1½ VERY LEAN MEAT

---

*For Greek Dill & Feta
Lentil Soup:*

2

CARBOHYDRATE
SERVINGS

EXCHANGES

2 STARCH
1½ LEAN MEAT

$1^1/_2$

CARBOHYDRATE

SERVINGS

Red Lentil Soup with a Spicy Sizzle

High ⬆ Fiber

This Turkish soup features a delicious, healthful combination of lentils and whole-grain bulgur. A drizzle of sizzling spiced olive oil gives the soup a final flourish.

6	teaspoons extra-virgin olive oil, divided
2	onions, chopped (1½ cups)
3	cloves garlic, minced
2	teaspoons ground cumin
8	cups reduced-sodium chicken broth *or* vegetable broth
1½	cups red lentils, rinsed (*see Ingredient Note, page 119*)
⅓	cup bulgur (*see Ingredient Note, page 323*)
2	tablespoons tomato paste
1	bay leaf
3	tablespoons lemon juice
	Freshly ground pepper to taste
1	teaspoon paprika
1	teaspoon cayenne pepper

1. Heat 2 teaspoons oil in a soup pot or Dutch oven over medium heat. Add onions and cook, stirring, until softened, 3 to 5 minutes. Add garlic and cumin; cook for 1 minute. Add broth, lentils, bulgur, tomato paste and bay leaf; bring to a simmer, stirring occasionally. Cover and cook over low heat until the lentils and bulgur are very tender, 25 to 30 minutes. Discard the bay leaf.
2. Ladle about 4 cups of the soup into a food processor and puree. Return the pureed soup to the soup pot and heat through. Stir in lemon juice and season with ground pepper.
3. Just before serving, ladle the soup into bowls. Heat the remaining 4 teaspoons oil in a small skillet and stir in paprika and cayenne. Drizzle about ½ teaspoon of the sizzling spice mixture over each bowlful and serve immediately.

MAKES 8 SERVINGS, ABOUT 1 CUP EACH

PREP TIME: 10 MINUTES

START TO FINISH: 50 MINUTES

TO MAKE AHEAD: Prepare through Step 2. Cover and refrigerate for up to 2 days or freeze for up to 2 months.

SUBSTITUTION TIP
You can replace red lentils with brown lentils; add ½ cup water and simmer 40 to 45 minutes.

PER SERVING

218	CALORIES
5	G FAT (1 G SAT, 3 G MONO)
4	MG CHOLESTEROL
31	G CARBOHYDRATE
13	G PROTEIN
7	G FIBER
126	MG SODIUM

NUTRITION BONUS: Fiber (29% DAILY VALUE), Iron (15% DV).

EXCHANGES

1½	STARCH
1	VEGETABLE
1	LEAN MEAT

Broccoli Chowder

1½

CARBOHYDRATE
SERVINGS

Broccoli-Cheddar soup is a classic winter warmer; this hearty version may not win prizes for its beauty but will get a blue ribbon for taste every time. The broccoli stems are added before the florets so every bite is tender.

- 1 tablespoon extra-virgin olive oil
- 1 large onion, chopped (1½ cups)
- 1 large carrot, diced (½ cup)
- 2 stalks celery, diced (½ cup)
- 1 large potato, peeled and diced (1½ cups)
- 2 cloves garlic, minced
- 1 tablespoon all-purpose flour
- ½ teaspoon dry mustard
- ⅛ teaspoon cayenne pepper
- 3½ cups vegetable broth *or* reduced-sodium chicken broth (two 14-ounce cans)
- 8 ounces broccoli crowns (*see Note*), cut into 1-inch pieces, stems and florets separated (3 cups)
- 1 cup grated reduced-fat Cheddar cheese
- ½ cup reduced-fat sour cream
- ⅛ teaspoon salt, or to taste

1. Heat oil in a Dutch oven or large saucepan over medium-high heat. Add onion, carrot and celery; cook, stirring often, until the onion and celery soften, 5 to 6 minutes. Add potato and garlic; cook, stirring, for 2 minutes. Stir in flour, dry mustard and cayenne; cook, stirring often, for 2 minutes.
2. Add broth and broccoli stems; bring to a boil. Cover and reduce heat to medium. Simmer, stirring occasionally, for 10 minutes. Stir in florets; simmer, covered, until the broccoli is tender, about 10 minutes more. Transfer 2 cups of the chowder to a bowl and mash; return to the pan.
3. Stir in Cheddar and sour cream; cook over medium heat, stirring, until the cheese is melted and the chowder is heated through. Season with salt.

MAKES 6 SERVINGS, 1 CUP EACH

PREP TIME: 25 MINUTES
START TO FINISH: 1 HOUR 5 MINUTES

TO MAKE AHEAD: Prepare through Step 1. Cover and refrigerate for up to 2 days or freeze for up to 2 months.

INGREDIENT NOTE
Most supermarkets sell broccoli crowns, which are the tops of the bunches, with the stalks cut off. Although crowns are more expensive than entire bunches, they are convenient and there is considerably less waste.

PER SERVING

180	CALORIES
8	G FAT (3 G SAT, 3 G MONO)
15	MG CHOLESTEROL
23	G CARBOHYDRATE
6	G PROTEIN
4	G FIBER
354	MG SODIUM

NUTRITION BONUS: Vitamin C (60% DAILY VALUE), Vitamin A (50% DV), Calcium (15% DV).

EXCHANGES

1	STARCH
1	VEGETABLE
1	HIGH-FAT MEAT

1¹/₂

CARBOHYDRATE

SERVINGS

MAKES 8 SERVINGS, 1 CUP EACH

PREP TIME: 10 MINUTES

START TO FINISH: 25 MINUTES

TO MAKE AHEAD: Cover and refrigerate for up to 2 days or freeze for up to 2 months.

VARIATION
Make Curried Sweet Pea Bisque by substituting frozen peas for the corn.

PER SERVING

138 CALORIES

4 G FAT (2 G SAT, 1 G MONO)

1 MG CHOLESTEROL

24 G CARBOHYDRATE

5 G PROTEIN

3 G FIBER

121 MG SODIUM

NUTRITION BONUS:
Fiber (13% DAILY VALUE).

EXCHANGES

1¹/₂ STARCH

1 FAT

Curried Corn Bisque

Quick ☼ Easy

Frozen vegetables are perfect for making soups and we particularly like the fresh flavor of frozen corn. This thick, satisfying soup gets a spicy kick from curry powder and hot sauce, but it's still on the mild side—add more hot sauce to turn the heat up as much as you like. Serve with a squeeze of lime or a dollop of plain yogurt and chopped scallions.

2	teaspoons canola oil
1	cup fresh *or* frozen chopped onions
1	tablespoon curry powder
¹/₂	teaspoon hot sauce, or to taste
¹/₄	teaspoon salt, or to taste
¹/₄	teaspoon freshly ground pepper
2	16-ounce packages frozen corn *or* 3 10-ounce boxes
2	cups reduced-sodium chicken broth
2	cups water
1	cup "lite" coconut milk (*see Ingredient Note, page 323*)

Heat oil in a large saucepan over medium-high heat. Add onions and cook, stirring occasionally, until soft, about 3 minutes. Add curry powder, hot sauce, salt and pepper and stir to coat the onions. Stir in corn, broth and water; increase the heat to high and bring the mixture to a boil. Remove from the heat and puree in a blender or food processor (in batches, if necessary) into a homogeneous mixture that still has some texture. Pour the soup into a clean pot, add coconut milk and heat through. Serve hot or cold.

> **❝**I find excuses to walk. I'll take out the garbage, go for an errand or walk to someone's house instead of calling them. It all adds up.**❞**
>
> — *Marge N.,*
> *Ohio*

Spicy Mushroom & Rice Soup

A hint of sweetness from orange juice and coconut milk balances the heat in this distinctive Southeast Asian soup. (*Photograph: page 162.*)

¾   **cup brown basmati rice (*see Ingredient Note, page 323*)**

1¾   **cups water**

1   **cup "lite" coconut milk (*see page 323*)**

¾   **cup reduced-sodium chicken broth**

1   **tablespoon freshly grated orange zest, preferably organic**

¾   **cup fresh orange juice**

1   **tablespoon fish sauce (*see page 324*)**

1   **teaspoon Thai chile paste *or* Chinese chile-garlic sauce (*see page 323*)**

2   **fresh Thai chile peppers *or* serrano chiles, stemmed, seeded and minced**

2   **cups button mushrooms (about 8 ounces), stems trimmed, caps wiped clean and quartered**

2   **ounces fresh enoki mushrooms (*see Note*), optional**

⅓   **cup plus 1 tablespoon chopped fresh basil**

¼   **teaspoon salt, or to taste**

¼   **teaspoon freshly ground pepper**

1. Place rice and water in a medium saucepan; bring to a simmer. Cover and cook over low heat until the rice is tender and most of the liquid has been absorbed, 40 to 50 minutes.

2. About 15 minutes before the rice is ready, combine coconut milk, broth, orange zest and juice, fish sauce, chile paste (or chile-garlic sauce) and chile peppers in a large saucepan. Bring to a boil, then reduce heat to medium and simmer, uncovered, until foamy and a pale golden orange, about 5 minutes. Add button mushrooms and cook until just tender, about 5 minutes. Add enoki mushrooms, if using, and cook for 1 minute. Stir in ⅓ cup basil, salt and pepper.

3. Divide rice among 4 bowls and spoon the soup over it. Garnish with the remaining 1 tablespoon basil. Serve immediately.

2

CARBOHYDRATE
SERVINGS

MAKES 4 SERVINGS, 1 CUP EACH

PREP TIME: 15 MINUTES
START TO FINISH: 1 HOUR

INGREDIENT NOTE
Enoki mushrooms have long, thin stems and tiny button-sized caps. They have a delicate flavor and pleasant chewy texture. Available in the produce sections of large supermarkets.

PER SERVING

208 CALORIES

5 G FAT (3 G SAT, 0 G MONO)

1 MG CHOLESTEROL

34 G CARBOHYDRATE

7 G PROTEIN

3 G FIBER

370 MG SODIUM

NUTRITION BONUS: Vitamin C (33% DAILY VALUE), Fiber (13% DV).

EXCHANGES

2 STARCH

1 VEGETABLE

1 FAT

CHAPTER FIVE

Salads

Arugula-Mushroom Salad

Quick ☼ Easy

A creamy garlic dressing is a nice foil for peppery greens. Feel free to substitute watercress for the arugula.

> 1 clove garlic, peeled
> ¼ teaspoon salt, or to taste
> 1 tablespoon lemon juice
> 1 tablespoon reduced-fat mayonnaise
> 1 tablespoon extra-virgin olive oil
> 1 tablespoon chopped fresh parsley
> Freshly ground pepper to taste
> 6 cups arugula leaves
> 2 cups sliced mushrooms

Place garlic on a cutting board and crush. Sprinkle with salt and use the flat of a chef's knife blade to mash the garlic to a paste; transfer to a serving bowl. Whisk in lemon juice, mayonnaise, oil and parsley. Season with pepper. Add arugula and mushrooms; toss to coat with the dressing.

Mexican Coleslaw

Quick ☼ Easy

Enjoy this crunchy, refreshing alternative to mayonnaise-based coleslaw on a taco or on the side.

> 6 cups very thinly sliced green cabbage (about ½ head)
>   (*see Tip*)
> 1½ cups grated carrots (2-3 medium)
> ⅓ cup chopped cilantro
> ¼ cup rice vinegar
> 2 tablespoons extra-virgin olive oil
> ¼ teaspoon salt, or to taste

TIP: To make this even faster, use a coleslaw mix containing cabbage and carrots from the produce section of the supermarket.

1. Place cabbage and carrots in a colander; rinse with cold water to crisp. Let drain for 5 minutes.
2. Meanwhile, whisk cilantro, vinegar, oil and salt in a large bowl. Add cabbage; toss well to coat. If not serving right away, cover and refrigerate for up to 1 day. Toss again to refresh just before serving.

O

CARBOHYDRATE
SERVINGS

MAKES 4 SERVINGS

PREP TIME: 10 MINUTES
START TO FINISH: 10 MINUTES

PER SERVING
62 CALORIES
5 G FAT (1 G SAT, 3 G MONO)
1 MG CHOLESTEROL
3 G CARBOHYDRATE
2 G PROTEIN
1 G FIBER
185 MG SODIUM

NUTRITION BONUS: Vitamin C
(15% DAILY VALUE).

EXCHANGES
1 VEGETABLE
1 FAT (MONO)

For Mexican Coleslaw:

O

CARBOHYDRATE
SERVINGS

MAKES 8 SERVINGS

PREP TIME: 20 MINUTES
START TO FINISH: 20 MINUTES

PER SERVING
53 CALORIES
4 G FAT (1 G SAT, 3 G MONO)
0 MG CHOLESTEROL
5 G CARBOHYDRATE
1 G PROTEIN
2 G FIBER
97 MG SODIUM

NUTRITION BONUS: Vitamin A
(50% DAILY VALUE), Vitamin C
(30% DV).

EXCHANGES
1 VEGETABLE
1 FAT (MONO)

Sliced Fennel Salad

Quick ☼ Easy

Serve this crisp salad as an antipasto before an Italian meal.

    1 large fennel bulb
    1 tablespoon extra-virgin olive oil
    1 tablespoon lemon juice
    ⅛ teaspoon salt, or to taste
       Freshly ground pepper to taste

1. Trim base from fennel bulb. Remove and discard the fennel stalks; reserve some of the feathery leaves for garnish. Pull off and discard any discolored parts from the bulb. Stand the bulb upright and cut vertically into very thin slices. Arrange the slices on 4 salad plates.
2. Whisk oil, lemon juice and salt in a small bowl. Drizzle the mixture over the fennel and garnish with a grinding of pepper and a few fennel leaves.

Spinach Salad with Black Olive Vinaigrette

Quick ☼ Easy

Good imported olives in a sophisticated dressing make eating your spinach a special pleasure.

    3   tablespoons extra-virgin olive oil
    1½ tablespoons red-wine vinegar *or* lemon juice
    6   pitted Kalamata olives, finely chopped
    ¼   teaspoon salt, or to taste
        Freshly ground pepper to taste
    6   cups torn spinach leaves
    ½   cucumber, seeded and sliced
    ½   red onion, thinly sliced

Whisk oil, vinegar (or lemon juice) and olives in a salad bowl. Season with salt and pepper. Add spinach, cucumbers and onions; toss well. Serve immediately.

O

CARBOHYDRATE
SERVINGS

MAKES 4 SERVINGS

PREP TIME: 10 MINUTES
START TO FINISH: 10 MINUTES

PER SERVING
  51 CALORIES
   4 G FAT (0 G SAT, 3 G MONO)
   0 MG CHOLESTEROL
   5 G CARBOHYDRATE
   1 G PROTEIN
   2 G FIBER
 103 MG SODIUM

NUTRITION BONUS: Vitamin C (15% DAILY VALUE).

EXCHANGES
   1 VEGETABLE
   1 FAT (MONO)

For Spinach Salad:

O

CARBOHYDRATE
SERVINGS

MAKES 4 SERVINGS

PREP TIME: 20 MINUTES
START TO FINISH: 20 MINUTES

PER SERVING
 128 CALORIES
  12 G FAT (2 G SAT, 9 G MONO)
   0 MG CHOLESTEROL
   4 G CARBOHYDRATE
   2 G PROTEIN
   1 G FIBER
 271 MG SODIUM

NUTRITION BONUS: Vitamin A (80% DAILY VALUE), Folate (22% DV), Vitamin C (20% DV).

EXCHANGES
   1 VEGETABLE
   2 FAT

$1/2$

CARBOHYDRATE

SERVING

Asian Slaw with Tofu & Shiitake Mushrooms

Quick ☼ Easy

A simple slaw is given an Asian twist with bok choy, napa cabbage and a soy-wasabi dressing. The vibrant flavors and rich textures make this a great introduction to tofu for novices and skeptics.

MAKES 4 SERVINGS, ABOUT 2 CUPS EACH

PREP TIME: 15 MINUTES
START TO FINISH: 40 MINUTES

INGREDIENT NOTE
Wasabi, a fiery condiment similar to horseradish, is made from the root of an Asian plant. It is available, as both a paste and a powder, in specialty stores and Asian markets.

PER SERVING
178 CALORIES
12 G FAT (1 G SAT, 6 G MONO)
0 MG CHOLESTEROL
9 G CARBOHYDRATE
9 G PROTEIN
2 G FIBER
603 MG SODIUM

NUTRITION BONUS: Vitamin C (63% DAILY VALUE), Selenium (27% DV).

EXCHANGES
2 VEGETABLE
1 MEDIUM-FAT MEAT
2 FAT (MONO)

¼	cup reduced-sodium soy sauce
2½	tablespoons lemon juice
1	teaspoon wasabi powder (*see Note*)
1	clove garlic, minced
12	ounces firm silken tofu, drained and cut into ½-inch cubes
4	cups lightly packed shredded napa cabbage (*see Ingredient Note, page 324*)
2	cups lightly packed shredded bok choy
2	tablespoons canola oil
2	cups sliced shiitake mushroom caps
2	teaspoons sesame oil

1. Whisk soy sauce, lemon juice, wasabi powder and garlic in a medium bowl. Gently stir in tofu. Cover and marinate in the refrigerator for 15 minutes, stirring occasionally.

2. Place cabbage and bok choy in a large serving bowl.

3. Drain the tofu, reserving the marinade. Heat canola oil in a large skillet or wok over medium-high heat. Add mushrooms and sesame oil; cook, stirring often, for 2 minutes. Add the tofu; cook, stirring often, until the tofu is lightly browned, about 4 minutes.

4. Spoon tofu mixture over cabbage. Add the reserved marinade to the skillet and bring to a boil, stirring. Pour the hot marinade over the salad and toss gently to coat. Serve immediately.

Broccoli Slaw

Quick ☼ Easy

We've lightened this popular potluck classic with a dressing of reduced-fat mayo and yogurt. To speed preparation, use shredded broccoli slaw from the produce aisle.

- 4   slices turkey bacon
- 1   12- to 16-ounce bag shredded broccoli slaw *or* 1 large bunch broccoli (about 1½ pounds)
- ¼   cup low-fat *or* nonfat plain yogurt
- ¼   cup reduced-fat mayonnaise
- 3   tablespoons cider vinegar
- 2   teaspoons sugar
- ½   teaspoon salt, or to taste
      Freshly ground pepper to taste
- 1   8-ounce can low-sodium sliced water chestnuts, rinsed and coarsely chopped
- ½   cup finely diced red onion (½ medium)

1. Cook bacon in a large skillet over medium heat, turning frequently, until crisp, 5 to 8 minutes. (*Alternatively, microwave on High for 2½ to 3 minutes.*) Drain bacon on paper towels. Chop coarsely.
2. If using whole broccoli, trim about 3 inches off the stems. Chop the rest into ¼-inch pieces.
3. Whisk yogurt, mayonnaise, vinegar, sugar, salt and pepper in a large bowl. Add water chestnuts, onion, bacon and broccoli; toss to coat. If not serving right away, cover and refrigerate for up to 2 days.

Lemony Carrot Salad with Dill

Quick ☼ Easy

Carrots are great keepers, so this makes a handy, refreshing salad when you haven't had time to shop for fresh greens. It brightens up a tuna sandwich too.

- 2   tablespoons lemon juice
- 2   tablespoons extra-virgin olive oil
- 1   small clove garlic, minced
- ¼   teaspoon salt, or to taste
      Freshly ground pepper to taste
- 2   cups grated carrots (4 medium-large)
- 3   tablespoons chopped fresh dill
- 2   tablespoons chopped scallions

Whisk lemon juice, oil, garlic, salt and pepper in a medium bowl. Add carrots, dill and scallions; toss to coat. If not serving right away, cover and refrigerate for up to 2 days.

½ CARBOHYDRATE SERVING

MAKES 8 SERVINGS, ¾ CUP EACH

PREP TIME: 15-25 MINUTES
START TO FINISH: 15-25 MINUTES

PER SERVING
- 80   CALORIES
- 4   G FAT (1 G SAT, 1 G MONO)
- 9   MG CHOLESTEROL
- 9   G CARBOHYDRATE
- 3   G PROTEIN
- 3   G FIBER
- 297   MG SODIUM

NUTRITION BONUS: Vitamin C (70% DAILY VALUE).

EXCHANGES
- 2   VEGETABLE
- 1   FAT

For Lemony Carrot Salad:

½ CARBOHYDRATE SERVING

MAKES 4 SERVINGS, ½ CUP EACH

PREP TIME: 15 MINUTES
START TO FINISH: 15 MINUTES

PER SERVING
- 90   CALORIES
- 7   G FAT (1 G SAT, 5 G MONO)
- 0   MG CHOLESTEROL
- 6   G CARBOHYDRATE
- 1   G PROTEIN
- 2   G FIBER
- 184   MG SODIUM

NUTRITION BONUS: Vitamin A (130% DAILY VALUE), Vitamin C (15% DV).

EXCHANGES
- 1   VEGETABLE
- 1½   FAT (MONO)

Mixed Greens with Berries & Honey-Glazed Hazelnuts

High ↑ Fiber   Quick ☼ Easy

For a sophisticated starter, try this colorful salad, which marries fresh berries, caramelized nuts and tangy feta cheese. Pureed berries form the base of the dressing, giving it a velvety texture and rich flavor. (*Photograph: page 166.*)

MAKES 4 SERVINGS, 2½ CUPS EACH (⅓ CUP DRESSING)

PREP TIME: 25 MINUTES

START TO FINISH: 25 MINUTES

TO MAKE AHEAD: The dressing will keep, covered, in the refrigerator for up to 2 days.

PER SERVING

232 CALORIES

17 G FAT (4 G SAT, 10 G MONO)

17 MG CHOLESTEROL

16 G CARBOHYDRATE

7 G PROTEIN

6 G FIBER

349 MG SODIUM

NUTRITION BONUS: Vitamin A (80% DAILY VALUE), Vitamin C (60% DV), Calcium (20% DV).

EXCHANGES

2 VEGETABLE

1 MEDIUM-FAT MEAT

2 FAT

NUTS

1	teaspoon extra-virgin olive oil
1	teaspoon honey
¼	cup chopped hazelnuts *or* walnuts

DRESSING

⅓	cup raspberries, blackberries *and/or* blueberries
2	tablespoons extra-virgin olive oil
1	tablespoon balsamic vinegar
1	tablespoon water
1	teaspoon Dijon mustard
1	small clove garlic, crushed and peeled
½	teaspoon honey
⅛	teaspoon salt, or to taste
	Freshly ground pepper to taste
2	tablespoons finely chopped shallots

SALAD

10	cups mesclun salad greens (about 8 ounces)
1	cup blackberries, raspberries *and/or* blueberries
½	cup crumbled feta *or* goat cheese (4 ounces)

1. **To prepare nuts:** Preheat oven to 350°F. Coat a small baking dish with cooking spray. Combine oil and honey in a small bowl. Add nuts and toss to coat. Transfer to the prepared baking dish and bake, stirring from time to time, until golden, 10 to 14 minutes. Let cool completely.

2. **To prepare dressing:** Combine berries, oil, vinegar, water, mustard, garlic, honey, salt and pepper in a blender or food processor. Blend until smooth. Transfer to a small bowl and stir in shallots.

3. **To prepare salad:** Just before serving, place greens in a large bowl. Drizzle the dressing over the greens and toss to coat. Divide the salad among 4 plates. Scatter berries, cheese and the glazed nuts over each salad; serve immediately.

Mixed Greens with Grapes & Feta

Quick ☼ Easy

Contrasting sweet grapes with savory feta cheese and crisp, colorful greens, this salad makes an elegant first course.

DRESSING

- ¼ cup extra-virgin olive oil
- 2 tablespoons red-wine vinegar
- ¼ teaspoon salt, or to taste
  Freshly ground pepper to taste

SALAD

- 8 cups mesclun salad greens (5 ounces)
- 1 head radicchio, thinly sliced
- 2 cups halved seedless grapes (about 1 pound), preferably red and green
- ¾ cup crumbled feta *or* blue cheese

1. **To prepare dressing:** Whisk (or shake) oil, vinegar, salt and pepper in a small bowl (or jar) until blended.

2. **To prepare salad:** Just before serving, toss greens and radicchio in a large bowl. Drizzle the dressing on top and toss to coat. Divide the salad among 8 plates. Scatter grapes and cheese over each salad; serve immediately.

1/2 CARBOHYDRATE SERVING

MAKES 8 SERVINGS, ABOUT 1½ CUPS EACH

PREP TIME: 15 MINUTES
START TO FINISH: 15 MINUTES

TO MAKE AHEAD: The dressing will keep, covered, in the refrigerator for up to 2 days.

PER SERVING

- 135 CALORIES
- 10 G FAT (3 G SAT, 6 G MONO)
- 13 MG CHOLESTEROL
- 9 G CARBOHYDRATE
- 3 G PROTEIN
- 1 G FIBER
- 239 MG SODIUM

NUTRITION BONUS: Vitamin C (15% DAILY VALUE), Folate (9% DV).

EXCHANGES

- ½ FRUIT
- 1 VEGETABLE
- 2 FAT

**MAKES 6 SERVINGS,
ABOUT 2 CUPS EACH**

PREP TIME: 20 MINUTES
START TO FINISH: 30 MINUTES

TO MAKE AHEAD: The dressing
will keep, covered, in the
refrigerator for up to 2 days.

PER SERVING

194 CALORIES
15 G FAT (5 G SAT, 6 G MONO)
15 MG CHOLESTEROL
10 G CARBOHYDRATE
7 G PROTEIN
2 G FIBER
391 MG SODIUM

NUTRITION BONUS: Vitamin A
(140% DAILY VALUE), Vitamin C
(70% DV), Folate (24% DV).

EXCHANGES

2 VEGETABLE
1 HIGH-FAT MEAT
2 FAT

Spinach Salad with Goat Cheese & Pine Nuts

Quick ☼ Easy

Toasted pine nuts and fresh goat cheese make this salad irresistible; jars of roasted red peppers and marinated mushrooms make it quick and easy.

DRESSING

2 tablespoons extra-virgin olive oil
2 tablespoons balsamic vinegar
2 teaspoons maple syrup
1 teaspoon Dijon mustard
Freshly ground pepper to taste

SALAD

¼ cup pine nuts
8 cups torn spinach leaves (about 10 ounces)
1 12-ounce jar roasted red peppers, drained and thinly sliced
1 8-ounce jar Italian-style marinated mushrooms, drained and cut in half
¾ cup crumbled creamy goat cheese (about 4 ounces)

1. **To prepare dressing:** Combine oil, vinegar, maple syrup, mustard and pepper in a jar with a lid. Shake until well mixed.
2. **To prepare salad:** Toast pine nuts in a small dry skillet over medium-low heat until lightly browned, 2 to 3 minutes. Transfer to a plate to cool.
3. Arrange spinach on a platter or in a shallow bowl. Top with peppers, mushrooms, goat cheese and toasted pine nuts. Drizzle the dressing over the salad; toss to coat.

Sugar Snap Salad

Quick ☼ Easy

Sweet, edible-podded peas make a bright, crisp and colorful salad, which is easily varied by substituting shallots for scallions or adding asparagus to the mix.

- 2 cups sugar snap peas (8 ounces), trimmed
- 2 tablespoons white-wine vinegar
- 2 tablespoons extra-virgin olive oil
- ¼ teaspoon salt, or to taste
- ⅛ teaspoon freshly ground pepper
- 1 bunch scallions, trimmed and thinly sliced on the diagonal
- ½ large red bell pepper, cut into 1½-inch-long slivers

1. Cook peas in lightly salted boiling water in a medium saucepan until tender-crisp, 2 to 3 minutes. Drain and rinse under cold running water.
2. Whisk vinegar, oil, salt and pepper in a large bowl. Add scallions, bell pepper and the peas; toss to coat. Serve within 1 hour.

Bread & Tomato Salad

Quick ☼ Easy

When it's too hot to cook, just step outside and gather tomatoes and basil from your garden, cut up some day-old country bread and make this flavorful, easy salad, our take on the classic Italian bread salad known as *panzanella*.

- 3 tablespoons extra-virgin olive oil
- 3 tablespoons lemon juice
- 1 small clove garlic, minced
- ¼ teaspoon salt, or to taste
  Freshly ground pepper to taste
- 4 cups diced seeded tomatoes (1½ pounds)
- 2 cups cubed whole-wheat country bread (5 ounces), crusts removed
- ¼ cup thinly slivered red onion
- 3 tablespoons chopped fresh basil
- 2 tablespoons capers, rinsed

Whisk oil, lemon juice, garlic, salt and pepper in a large bowl. Add tomatoes, bread, onion, basil and capers. Toss to combine. Let the salad sit for about 5 minutes to allow it to absorb the dressing's flavors, stirring occasionally. Serve at room temperature.

½
CARBOHYDRATE SERVING

MAKES 4 SERVINGS, ¾ CUP EACH

PREP TIME: 15 MINUTES
START TO FINISH: 15 MINUTES

PER SERVING
- 104 CALORIES
- 7 G FAT (1 G SAT, 5 G MONO)
- 0 MG CHOLESTEROL
- 9 G CARBOHYDRATE
- 2 G PROTEIN
- 3 G FIBER
- 153 MG SODIUM

NUTRITION BONUS: Vitamin C (80% DAILY VALUE), Vitamin A (25% DV).

EXCHANGES
- 2 VEGETABLE
- 1½ FAT

For Bread & Tomato Salad:

1
CARBOHYDRATE SERVING

MAKES 6 SERVINGS, 1 CUP EACH

PREP TIME: 15 MINUTES
START TO FINISH: 20 MINUTES

PER SERVING
- 168 CALORIES
- 9 G FAT (1 G SAT, 6 G MONO)
- 0 MG CHOLESTEROL
- 19 G CARBOHYDRATE
- 3 G PROTEIN
- 3 G FIBER
- 275 MG SODIUM

NUTRITION BONUS: Vitamin C (60% DAILY VALUE).

EXCHANGES
- 1 STARCH
- 1 VEGETABLE
- 1½ FAT (MONO)

Chickpea-Spinach Salad with Spiced Yogurt Dressing

High ↑ Fiber   Quick ☼ Easy

A symphony of color and texture, this satisfying, nutrient-rich salad is one we eagerly make for lunch, served with whole-wheat pita and a crisp apple.

**MAKES 6 SERVINGS,
GENEROUS 2 CUPS EACH**

PREP TIME: 25 MINUTES

START TO FINISH: 25 MINUTES

TO MAKE AHEAD: The dressing will keep, covered, in the refrigerator for up to 2 days.

PER SERVING

119 CALORIES

4 G FAT (0 G SAT, 2 G MONO)

0 MG CHOLESTEROL

19 G CARBOHYDRATE

5 G PROTEIN

6 G FIBER

275 MG SODIUM

NUTRITION BONUS: Vitamin A (80% DAILY VALUE), Fiber (23% DV), Vitamin C (20% DV).

EXCHANGES

1 STARCH

1 VEGETABLE

DRESSING

⅓ cup nonfat plain yogurt

1 tablespoon lemon juice

1 tablespoon extra-virgin olive oil

¾ teaspoon ground cumin

½ teaspoon ground ginger

1 clove garlic, minced

¼ teaspoon salt, or to taste

Freshly ground pepper to taste

SALAD

1 15-ounce *or* 19-ounce can chickpeas, rinsed

1 cup diced peeled cucumber

1 cup diced celery *or* fennel

1 cup grated carrots

10 cups small spinach leaves *or* mesclun salad greens (about 8 ounces)

1. **To prepare dressing:** Whisk yogurt, lemon juice, oil, cumin, ginger and garlic in a small bowl until smooth. Season with salt and pepper.

2. **To prepare salad:** Combine chickpeas, cucumber, celery (or fennel) and carrots in a medium bowl. Add half the dressing and toss to coat.

3. Toss spinach (or mesclun) in a large bowl with the remaining dressing. Divide the greens among 6 plates and top with the vegetables. Serve immediately.

Green Mango Salad

Quick ☀ Easy

This refreshing Vietnamese salad is a nice foil for grilled meat, poultry or fish and also makes lovely picnic fare. Green mangoes are simply unripe mangoes. They are readily available in both Asian and Central American groceries. Look for fruit that is evenly colored a deep green. In the absence of green mango, you can use green papaya or, in a pinch, white (Chinese) cabbage or even tart green apple. (*Photograph: page 162.*)

2	tablespoons lime juice (about 1 lime)
1	teaspoon sugar
1	teaspoon chile paste *or* Chinese chile-garlic paste (*see Ingredient Note, page 323*)
1	teaspoon fish sauce (*see Ingredient Note, page 324*)
1	green mango, peeled and grated (about 1½ cups)
1	small cucumber, thinly sliced (about 1 cup)
2	shallots, thinly sliced (about ½ cup)
1	green tomato, thinly sliced (optional)
1	scallion, chopped (about 2 tablespoons)
½	red bell pepper, seeded and cut into 2-inch-long slivers
4	fresh basil leaves *or* cilantro sprigs

Whisk lime juice, sugar, chile paste and fish sauce in a medium bowl. Add mango, cucumber, shallots and tomato (if using). Toss to coat. Garnish with scallion, bell pepper and basil (or cilantro). Serve within 2 hours.

Jícama & Orange Salad

Quick ☀ Easy

Jícama is a large root vegetable with an appealing crunchy texture similar to a water chestnut or radish. You can serve sliced jícama sprinkled with chili powder and lime juice for a simple crudité or in a refreshing salad like this one.

1	small jícama (about 1 pound)
2	navel oranges
6	scallions, thinly sliced
2	tablespoons chopped fresh cilantro
1	tablespoon lime juice
¼	teaspoon salt, or to taste

1. Peel jícama and cut into 8 wedges. Thinly slice each wedge crosswise. With a paring knife, peel oranges, removing all white pith. Halve oranges lengthwise and thinly slice crosswise.
2. Toss jícama, orange slices, scallions, cilantro, lime juice and salt in a large bowl. Cover and chill for at least 15 minutes. Toss again and serve.

1

CARBOHYDRATE
SERVING

MAKES 4 SERVINGS, ¾ CUP EACH

PREP TIME: 15 MINUTES
START TO FINISH: 20 MINUTES

PER SERVING
64 CALORIES
0 G FAT (0 G SAT, 0 G MONO)
0 MG CHOLESTEROL
16 G CARBOHYDRATE
1 G PROTEIN
2 G FIBER
115 MG SODIUM

NUTRITION BONUS: Vitamin C (80% DAILY VALUE), Vitamin A (20% DV).

EXCHANGES
1 FRUIT

For Jícama & Orange Salad:

1

CARBOHYDRATE
SERVING

MAKES 6 SERVINGS

PREP TIME: 20 MINUTES
START TO FINISH: 20 MINUTES

PER SERVING
52 CALORIES
0 G FAT (0 G SAT, 0 G MONO)
0 MG CHOLESTEROL
13 G CARBOHYDRATE
1 G PROTEIN
4 G FIBER
102 MG SODIUM

NUTRITION BONUS: Vitamin A (73% DAILY VALUE).

EXCHANGES
1 FRUIT

1

CARBOHYDRATE
SERVING

MAKES **4** SERVINGS,
ABOUT 1½ CUPS EACH

PREP TIME: 10 MINUTES
START TO FINISH: 10 MINUTES

PER SERVING

64 CALORIES

1 G FAT (0 G SAT, 0 G MONO)

0 MG CHOLESTEROL

12 G CARBOHYDRATE

2 G PROTEIN

2 G FIBER

182 MG SODIUM

NUTRITION BONUS: Vitamin A
(120% DAILY VALUE), Vitamin C
(30% DV), Folate (16% DV).

EXCHANGES

2 VEGETABLE

Salad of Boston Lettuce with Creamy Orange-Shallot Dressing

Quick ☼ Easy

Light mayonnaise makes a velvety base for this zesty dressing, which can easily be doubled if you want enough for another meal later in the week.

DRESSING

¼ cup reduced-fat mayonnaise

½ teaspoon Dijon mustard

¼ cup orange juice

2 teaspoons finely chopped shallot

Freshly ground pepper to taste

SALAD

1 large head Boston lettuce, torn into bite-size pieces (5 cups)

1 cup julienned *or* grated carrot (1 carrot)

1 cup cherry *or* grape tomatoes, rinsed and cut in half

2 tablespoons snipped fresh tarragon *or* chives (optional)

1. **To prepare dressing:** Whisk mayonnaise and mustard in a small bowl. Slowly whisk in orange juice until smooth. Stir in shallot. Season with pepper.

2. **To prepare salad:** Divide lettuce among 4 plates and scatter carrot and tomatoes on top. Drizzle the dressing over the salads and sprinkle with tarragon (or chives), if desired. Serve immediately.

Spinach, Avocado & Mango Salad

High ⬆ Fiber   **Quick ☼ Easy**

Reader Jennifer Sanders contributed this salad, which offers a wealth of color and texture, as well as antioxidants.

DRESSING

- ⅓ cup orange juice
- 1 tablespoon red-wine vinegar
- 2 tablespoons hazelnut oil, almond oil *or* canola oil
- 1 teaspoon Dijon mustard
- ¼ teaspoon salt, or to taste
   Freshly ground pepper to taste

SALAD

- 10 cups baby spinach leaves (about 8 ounces)
- 1½ cups radicchio, torn into bite-size pieces
- 8-12 small red radishes (1 bunch), sliced
- 1 small ripe mango, sliced
- 1 medium avocado, sliced

1. **To prepare dressing:** Whisk juice, vinegar, oil, mustard, salt and pepper in a bowl.
2. **To prepare salad:** Just before serving, combine spinach, radicchio, radishes and mango in a large bowl. Add the dressing; toss to coat. Garnish each serving with avocado slices.

Barbecue Bean Salad

High ⬆ Fiber   **Quick ☼ Easy**

Perfect for picnics or a side for grilled chicken, this fast salad has all the flavor of baked barbecued beans, without the hassle or the heat.

- ⅓ cup prepared spicy barbecue sauce
- 3 tablespoons cider vinegar
- 2 teaspoons molasses
- 1 15½-ounce can pinto beans, rinsed
- 2 medium tomatoes, seeded and coarsely chopped
- 1 bunch scallions, trimmed and chopped (1 cup)
   Freshly ground pepper to taste
   Hot sauce to taste

Whisk barbecue sauce, vinegar and molasses in a large bowl. Add beans, tomatoes and scallions; toss to coat. Season with pepper and hot sauce. If not serving immediately, cover and refrigerate for up to 2 days. Serve at room temperature.

1

CARBOHYDRATE
SERVING

MAKES 4 SERVINGS, 2 CUPS EACH

PREP TIME: 20 MINUTES
START TO FINISH: 20 MINUTES

PER SERVING

- 210 CALORIES
- 14 G FAT (2 G SAT, 10 G MONO)
- 0 MG CHOLESTEROL
- 22 G CARBOHYDRATE
- 3 G PROTEIN
- 6 G FIBER
- 258 MG SODIUM

NUTRITION BONUS: Vitamin C (70% DAILY VALUE), Vitamin A (40% DV), Fiber (26% DV).

EXCHANGES

- 3 VEGETABLE
- 3 FAT (MONO)

For Barbecue Bean Salad:

1½

CARBOHYDRATE
SERVINGS

MAKES 4 SERVINGS, ¾ CUP EACH

PREP TIME: 15 MINUTES
START TO FINISH: 15 MINUTES

PER SERVING

- 142 CALORIES
- 0 G FAT (0 G SAT, 0 G MONO)
- 0 MG CHOLESTEROL
- 30 G CARBOHYDRATE
- 6 G PROTEIN
- 8 G FIBER
- 409 MG SODIUM

EXCHANGES

- 1 STARCH
- 1 VEGETABLE
- 1 VERY LEAN MEAT

117

Roasted Corn, Black Bean & Mango Salad

Quick ☼ Easy

This simple, fresh-tasting salad adds delicious variety to grilled foods, such as salmon, halibut, chicken or pork. Browning the corn in a skillet gives it a nutty, caramelized flavor that contrasts with the sweetness of the mango. (*Photograph: page 164.*)

MAKES 8 SERVINGS,
GENEROUS ½ CUP EACH

PREP TIME: 35 MINUTES

START TO FINISH: 45 MINUTES

TO MAKE AHEAD: Cover and refrigerate for up to 8 hours. Serve at room temperature.

PER SERVING

125 CALORIES
2 G FAT (0 G SAT, 1 G MONO)
0 MG CHOLESTEROL
26 G CARBOHYDRATE
4 G PROTEIN
4 G FIBER
245 MG SODIUM

NUTRITION BONUS: Vitamin C (70% DAILY VALUE), Fiber (18% DV).

EXCHANGES

1 STARCH
1 FRUIT

2	teaspoons canola oil
1	clove garlic, minced
1½	cups corn kernels (from 3 ears; *see box, page 243*)
1	large ripe mango (about 1 pound), peeled and diced
1	15½-ounce *or* 19-ounce can black beans, rinsed
½	cup chopped red onion
½	cup diced red bell pepper
3	tablespoons lime juice
1	small canned chipotle pepper in adobo sauce (*see Ingredient Note, page 323*), drained and chopped
1½	tablespoons chopped fresh cilantro
¼	teaspoon ground cumin
¼	teaspoon salt, or to taste

Heat oil in a large nonstick skillet over medium-high heat. Add garlic and cook, stirring, until fragrant, about 30 seconds. Stir in corn and cook, stirring occasionally, until browned, about 8 minutes. Transfer the corn mixture to a large bowl. Stir in mango, beans, onion, bell pepper, lime juice, chipotle, cilantro, cumin and salt.

Red Lentil Salad with Dried Fruit & Toasted Pine Nuts

High ⬆ Fiber

Quick-cooking red lentils and bulgur team up to make this hearty fiber-rich salad. Tart lemon juice plays against the sweet flavors of dried fruits, mint and cinnamon for a distinctive Middle Eastern flair; serve alongside grilled lamb or chicken.

2½
CARBOHYDRATE
SERVINGS

1½ cups water
½ teaspoon ground cinnamon
½ teaspoon salt, divided
1 cup bulgur (*see Ingredient Note, page 323*)
½ cup red lentils (*see Note*), rinsed and picked over
3 tablespoons pine nuts
½ cup chopped pitted dates
½ cup chopped dried apricots
½ cup chopped fresh parsley
⅓ cup chopped fresh mint
2 tablespoons extra-virgin olive oil
¼ cup lemon juice
2 teaspoons freshly grated lemon zest, preferably organic

1. Bring water, cinnamon and ¼ teaspoon salt to a boil in a small saucepan; stir in bulgur, remove from the heat, cover the pan and set aside until the water has been absorbed, about 30 minutes. Transfer to a large bowl and let cool to room temperature, about 15 minutes.

2. Meanwhile, combine lentils and the remaining ¼ teaspoon salt in a saucepan; add enough water to cover by 1 inch. Bring to a simmer and cook until the lentils are just tender, 10 to 15 minutes. Drain and rinse under cold water, pressing firmly to remove excess water.

3. Toast pine nuts in a small dry skillet over medium-low heat until lightly browned, 2 to 3 minutes. Transfer to a plate to cool.

4. Add lentils, dates, apricots, parsley, mint, oil, lemon juice and zest, and half the pine nuts to the bulgur. Toss well. Sprinkle the remaining pine nuts on top.

MAKES 6 SERVINGS, 1 CUP EACH

PREP TIME: 25 MINUTES
START TO FINISH: 50 MINUTES

TO MAKE AHEAD: Cover and refrigerate for up to 2 days.

INGREDIENT NOTE
Red lentils are a useful addition to your pantry because they cook in just 10 to 15 minutes. They are excellent in soups, salads and vegetarian stews. You can find them in the natural-foods section of your supermarket or through online sources (*see page 323*).

PER SERVING
285 CALORIES
8 G FAT (1 G SAT, 4 G MONO)
0 MG CHOLESTEROL
49 G CARBOHYDRATE
8 G PROTEIN
9 G FIBER
209 MG SODIUM

NUTRITION BONUS: Fiber (37% DAILY VALUE), Vitamin C (25% DV), Iron (20% DV).

EXCHANGES
2 STARCH
1 FRUIT
1 VERY LEAN MEAT
1 FAT (MONO)

Salad Dressings

Light Ranch Dressing

Quick ☼ Easy

If you love ranch dressing, this horseradish-spiked version could be your new house favorite.

- ¾ cup buttermilk
- ¼ cup reduced-fat mayonnaise
- ¼ cup chopped scallions
- 3 tablespoons chopped fresh dill
- 1 tablespoon chopped fresh parsley
- 1 tablespoon lemon juice
- 1 tablespoon prepared horseradish
- ⅛ teaspoon salt, or to taste
  Freshly ground pepper to taste

Combine buttermilk, mayonnaise, scallions, dill, parsley, lemon juice, horseradish, salt and pepper in a blender. Puree until smooth.

Honey-Mustard Vinaigrette

Quick ☼ Easy

Here is a great, all-purpose salad dressing. The pleasing pungency of Dijon mustard makes it a good match for slightly bitter greens, such as escarole, chicory, radicchio or Belgian endive. It also makes an irresistible dipping sauce for crunchy vegetables (especially fennel) and crusty whole-wheat bread.

- 1 clove garlic, minced
- 1 tablespoon white-wine vinegar
- 1½ teaspoons Dijon mustard (coarse or smooth)
- ½ teaspoon honey
- ⅛ teaspoon salt, or to taste
  Freshly ground pepper to taste
- ⅓ cup extra-virgin olive oil *or* canola oil

Whisk garlic, vinegar, mustard, honey, salt and pepper in a small bowl. Slowly whisk in oil.

O

CARBOHYDRATE
SERVINGS

MAKES ABOUT 1 CUP

PREP TIME: 10 MINUTES
START TO FINISH: 10 MINUTES

TO MAKE AHEAD: Cover and refrigerate for up to 4 days.

PER TABLESPOON
12 CALORIES
1 G FAT (0 G SAT, 0 G MONO)
0 MG CHOLESTEROL
1 G CARBOHYDRATE
0 G PROTEIN
0 G FIBER
66 MG SODIUM

EXCHANGES
FREE FOOD

For Honey-Mustard Vinaigrette:

O

CARBOHYDRATE
SERVINGS

MAKES ABOUT ½ CUP

PREP TIME: 5 MINUTES
START TO FINISH: 5 MINUTES

TO MAKE AHEAD: Cover and refrigerate for up to 1 week.

PER TABLESPOON
85 CALORIES
9 G FAT (1 G SAT, 7 G MONO)
0 MG CHOLESTEROL
1 G CARBOHYDRATE
0 G PROTEIN
0 G FIBER
49 MG SODIUM

EXCHANGES
2 FAT (MONO)

Orange-Ginger Vinaigrette

Quick ☼ Easy

This easy Asian dressing is great over greens, but also try it as a sauce for cooked asparagus or fish, such as salmon or halibut.

1   tablespoon miso (*see Ingredient Note, page 324*)
1   tablespoon hot water
2   tablespoons orange juice
1   tablespoon canola oil
1   tablespoon rice vinegar
2   teaspoons sugar
1   teaspoon reduced-sodium soy sauce
½   teaspoon minced fresh ginger

Stir miso and water in a small bowl until smooth. Add orange juice, oil, vinegar, sugar, soy sauce and ginger; whisk to blend.

MINI INDEX

COUNT YOUR DRESSINGS

Other recipes in this chapter (and beyond) that can be mixed and matched to dress other salads:

O

CARBOHYDRATE
SERVINGS

MAKES ABOUT ⅓ **CUP**

PREP TIME: 10 MINUTES
START TO FINISH: 10 MINUTES

TO MAKE AHEAD: Cover and refrigerate for up to 2 days.

PER TABLESPOON
39 CALORIES
 3 G FAT (0 G SAT, 2 G MONO)
 0 MG CHOLESTEROL
 3 G CARBOHYDRATE
 0 G PROTEIN
 0 G FIBER
122 MG SODIUM

EXCHANGES
 1 FAT (MONO)

Vegetarian Main Dishes

1/2

CARBOHYDRATE

SERVING

MAKES 4 SERVINGS

PREP TIME: 30 MINUTES
START TO FINISH: 45 MINUTES

PER SERVING
209 CALORIES
16 G FAT (2 G SAT, 11 G MONO)
0 MG CHOLESTEROL
10 G CARBOHYDRATE
9 G PROTEIN
2 G FIBER
682 MG SODIUM

NUTRITION BONUS: Vitamin C
(50% DAILY VALUE), Iron (15% DV).

EXCHANGES
1 VEGETABLE
1 MEDIUM-FAT MEAT
2 FAT (MONO)

For Chopped Salad:

MAKES 4 SERVINGS, 3/4 CUP EACH

PREP TIME: 20 MINUTES
START TO FINISH: 20 MINUTES

PER SERVING
113 CALORIES
10 G FAT (1 G SAT, 8 G MONO)
0 MG CHOLESTEROL
5 G CARBOHYDRATE
1 G PROTEIN
1 G FIBER
328 MG SODIUM

NUTRITION BONUS: Vitamin C
(40% DAILY VALUE), Vitamin A
(15% DV).

EXCHANGES
1 VEGETABLE
2 FAT (MONO)

Grilled Tofu with a Mediterranean Chopped Salad

Quick ☼ Easy

Mild-flavored tofu benefits from this intensely flavored lemon juice-and-garlic-based marinade. If you have the time, marinate the tofu early in the day (up to 8 hours before serving) so it can absorb all the flavors.

¼ cup lemon juice
1 tablespoon extra-virgin olive oil
3 cloves garlic, minced
2 teaspoons dried oregano
½ teaspoon salt, or to taste
  Freshly ground pepper to taste
14 ounces extra-firm tofu, preferably water-packed
  Mediterranean Chopped Salad (*recipe follows*)

> **TIP:** To make attractive grill marks on the tofu, rotate it 90° halfway through grilling for a cross-hatch pattern.

1. Preheat grill.
2. Whisk lemon juice, oil, garlic, oregano, salt and pepper in a small bowl. Reserve 2 tablespoons of this mixture for basting.
3. Drain and rinse tofu; pat dry. Cut the block crosswise into eight ½-inch-thick slices and place in a shallow glass dish. Add remaining marinade and turn to coat. Cover and refrigerate for at least 30 minutes or for up to 8 hours.
4. Meanwhile, make Mediterranean Chopped Salad.
5. Lightly oil the grill rack (hold a piece of oil-soaked paper towel with tongs and rub it over the grate). Drain the tofu, discarding marinade. Grill the tofu over medium-high heat, basting occasionally with reserved lemon juice mixture, until lightly browned, 3 to 4 minutes per side. Serve immediately, topped with the salad.

Mediterranean Chopped Salad

Quick ☼ Easy

A summer staple, this flavorful salad is also good with grilled fish or chicken. Like all fresh tomato salads, it provides some fiber and a healthy dose of vitamin C.

2 medium tomatoes, seeded and diced
1 cup diced seedless cucumber (¼ medium)
¼ cup chopped scallions
¼ cup coarsely chopped fresh parsley
¼ cup Kalamata olives, pitted and coarsely chopped
2 tablespoons extra-virgin olive oil
1 tablespoon white-wine vinegar
¼ teaspoon salt, or to taste
  Freshly ground pepper to taste

Combine all ingredients in a medium bowl; toss gently to mix. Serve within 1 hour.

Tofu with Tomato-Mushroom Sauce

Quick ☼ Easy

Sautéed tofu makes a simple fresh tomato-and-mushroom sauce hearty and substantial. Serve over polenta or toss with pasta.

14	ounces extra-firm tofu, preferably water-packed
2	teaspoons extra-virgin olive oil
2	medium tomatoes, coarsely chopped (about 1½ cups)
1½	cups sliced mushrooms (4 ounces)
2	tablespoons prepared pesto
2	tablespoons crumbled feta cheese

1. Drain and rinse tofu; pat dry. Slice the block crosswise into eight ½-inch-thick slabs. Coarsely crumble each slice into smaller, uneven pieces.
2. Heat oil in a large nonstick skillet over high heat. Add tofu and cook in a single layer, without stirring, until the pieces begin to turn golden brown on the bottom, about 5 minutes. Then gently stir and continue cooking, stirring occasionally, until all sides are golden brown, 5 to 7 minutes more.
3. Add tomatoes and mushrooms and cook, stirring, until the vegetables are just cooked, 1 to 2 minutes more. Remove from the heat and stir in pesto and feta.

$\frac{1}{2}$

CARBOHYDRATE
SERVING

MAKES 4 SERVINGS, ¾ CUP EACH

PREP TIME: 5 MINUTES
START TO FINISH: 20 MINUTES

PER SERVING

136 CALORIES
9 G FAT (2 G SAT, 3 G MONO)
6 MG CHOLESTEROL
6 G CARBOHYDRATE
9 G PROTEIN
2 G FIBER
111 MG SODIUM

NUTRITION BONUS: Calcium (16% DAILY VALUE), Folate (15% DV).

EXCHANGES

1 VEGETABLE
1 MEDIUM-FAT MEAT
1 FAT (MONO)

1

CARBOHYDRATE

SERVING

Tofu with Peanut-Ginger Sauce

High ⬆ Fiber   Quick ☼ Easy

Tofu and vegetables get a dramatic lift from a spicy peanut sauce. Serve with a cucumber salad for a low-calorie, nutrient-packed vegetarian supper.

MAKES 4 SERVINGS,
GENEROUS ¾ CUP EACH

PREP TIME: 15 MINUTES
START TO FINISH: 25 MINUTES

PER SERVING
225 CALORIES
14 G FAT (2 G SAT, 3 G MONO)
0 MG CHOLESTEROL
16 G CARBOHYDRATE
12 G PROTEIN
5 G FIBER
229 MG SODIUM

NUTRITION BONUS: Calcium
(16% DAILY VALUE), Iron (16% DV).

EXCHANGES
2 VEGETABLE
2 MEDIUM-FAT MEAT

SAUCE
5 tablespoons water
4 tablespoons smooth natural peanut butter
1 tablespoon rice vinegar (*see Ingredient Note, page 324*) *or* white vinegar
2 teaspoons reduced-sodium soy sauce
2 teaspoons honey
2 teaspoons minced ginger
2 cloves garlic, minced

TOFU & VEGETABLES
14 ounces extra-firm tofu, preferably water-packed
2 teaspoons extra-virgin olive oil
4 cups baby spinach (6 ounces)
1½ cups sliced mushrooms (4 ounces)
4 scallions, sliced (1 cup)

1. **To prepare sauce:** Whisk the sauce ingredients in a small bowl.
2. **To prepare tofu:** Drain and rinse tofu; pat dry. Slice the block crosswise into eight ½-inch-thick slabs. Coarsely crumble each slice into smaller, uneven pieces.
3. Heat oil in a large nonstick skillet over high heat. Add tofu and cook in a single layer, without stirring, until the pieces begin to turn golden brown on the bottom, about 5 minutes. Then gently stir and continue cooking, stirring occasionally, until all sides are golden brown, 5 to 7 minutes more.
4. Add spinach, mushrooms, scallions and the peanut sauce and cook, stirring, until the vegetables are just cooked, 1 to 2 minutes more.

Tofu with Thai Curry Sauce

Quick ☀ Easy

Creamy Thai curry sauce gives tofu a spicy, satisfying kick. You can adjust the amount of curry paste depending on your spice preference. Serve with brown basmati rice and lime wedges.

SAUCE

- 1 cup "lite" coconut milk (*see Ingredient Note, page 323*)
- 2 tablespoons chopped fresh cilantro
- 1 teaspoon red curry paste, or to taste (*see Ingredient Note, page 324*)
- ½ teaspoon brown sugar
- ½ teaspoon salt, or to taste

TOFU & VEGETABLES

- 14 ounces extra-firm tofu, preferably water-packed
- 2 teaspoons extra-virgin olive oil
- 4 cups baby spinach (6 ounces)
- 1 medium red bell pepper, sliced (1½ cups)

1. **To prepare sauce:** Whisk the sauce ingredients in a small bowl.
2. **To prepare tofu:** Drain and rinse tofu; pat dry. Slice the block crosswise into eight ½-inch-thick slabs. Coarsely crumble each slice into smaller, uneven pieces.
3. Heat oil in a large nonstick skillet over high heat. Add tofu and cook in a single layer, without stirring, until the pieces begin to turn golden brown on the bottom, about 5 minutes. Then gently stir and continue cooking, stirring occasionally, until all sides are golden brown, 5 to 7 minutes more.
4. Add spinach, bell pepper and the curry sauce and cook, stirring, until the vegetables are just cooked, 1 to 2 minutes more.

1

CARBOHYDRATE
SERVING

MAKES 4 SERVINGS,
GENEROUS ¾ CUP EACH

PREP TIME: 5 MINUTES
START TO FINISH: 20 MINUTES

PER SERVING

179	CALORIES
11	G FAT (4 G SAT, 3 G MONO)
0	MG CHOLESTEROL
13	G CARBOHYDRATE
10	G PROTEIN
4	G FIBER
405	MG SODIUM

NUTRITION BONUS: Vitamin A (90% DAILY VALUE), Calcium (20% DV).

EXCHANGES

- 2 VEGETABLE
- 1 MEDIUM-FAT MEAT
- 1 FAT (SATURATED)

1

CARBOHYDRATE
SERVING

Roasted Red Pepper Subs

Quick ☼ Easy

When the occasion calls for a sophisticated sandwich, simply layer roasted red peppers, goat cheese and peppery arugula on a crusty baguette.

MAKES 4 SANDWICHES

PREP TIME: 15 MINUTES

START TO FINISH: 15 MINUTES

TO MAKE AHEAD: Wrap in plastic wrap and store in the refrigerator or in a cooler with a cold pack for up to 8 hours.

PER SERVING

221 CALORIES

15 G FAT (5 G SAT, 3 G MONO)

13 MG CHOLESTEROL

16 G CARBOHYDRATE

7 G PROTEIN

1 G FIBER

429 MG SODIUM

NUTRITION BONUS: Vitamin A (50% DAILY VALUE).

EXCHANGES

1 STARCH

1 VEGETABLE

1 HIGH-FAT MEAT

1/2 FAT

1	12-ounce jar roasted red peppers, rinsed
1	clove garlic, minced
1	tablespoon red-wine vinegar
1	teaspoon extra-virgin olive oil
	Pinch of salt
	Freshly ground pepper to taste
1	16- to 20-inch baguette, preferably whole-wheat
3	tablespoon olive paste (*olivada*)
4	ounces creamy goat cheese
1½	cups arugula leaves

1. Combine peppers, garlic, vinegar and oil in a small bowl; toss to combine. Season with salt and pepper.

2. Slice baguette in half lengthwise. Spread one half with olive paste and the other half with goat cheese. Layer pepper mixture and arugula over olive paste. Top with remaining baguette. Cut across into 4 pieces.

Open-Face Spinach, Mushroom & Pine Nut Sandwiches

High ⬆ Fiber   Quick ☼ Easy

Warm sandwiches are ideal for weekend lunches and light suppers. Open-faced versions like this one can help keep carbohydrate counts under control—you'll be rewarded with a topping of gooey melted cheese.

> 8 ounces portobello mushrooms, wiped clean
> 2 tablespoons pine nuts
> 1 tablespoon extra-virgin olive oil, divided
> 5 scallions, trimmed and sliced
> ¼ cup chopped fresh parsley
> ⅛ teaspoon salt, or to taste
>   Freshly ground pepper to taste
> 1 clove garlic, minced
> 1½ pounds fresh spinach, stems trimmed, coarsely chopped
> 4 ½-inch slices whole-wheat country bread
> ¾ cup grated part-skim mozzarella, preferably smoked

1. Preheat oven to 400°F.
2. Cut mushroom stems off at the base and reserve for another use. Cut mushroom caps in quarters. With a paring knife, remove gills from caps and discard. Thinly slice caps.
3. Toast pine nuts in a small dry skillet over medium-low heat until lightly browned, 2 to 3 minutes. Transfer to a plate to cool.
4. Heat ½ tablespoon oil in a large skillet over high heat. Add mushrooms, scallions and parsley. Cook, stirring constantly, until mushrooms are browned in spots, 4 to 5 minutes. Season with salt and pepper. Transfer to a large bowl.
5. Add the remaining ½ tablespoon oil and garlic to the pan. Cook, stirring, until fragrant, about 30 seconds. Add spinach and toss until wilted, about 2 minutes. Remove from heat and add to the mushroom mixture. Toss to combine. Stir in the pine nuts. Adjust seasoning with salt and pepper.
6. Meanwhile, place bread on a baking sheet and lightly toast in the oven. Divide the spinach-mushroom mixture over the toasted bread and sprinkle with mozzarella. Bake until cheese is melted, about 5 minutes. Serve immediately.

1
CARBOHYDRATE
SERVING

MAKES 4 SERVINGS

PREP TIME: 25 MINUTES
START TO FINISH: 35 MINUTES

PER SERVING
245 CALORIES
12 G FAT (3 G SAT, 5 G MONO)
14 MG CHOLESTEROL
24 G CARBOHYDRATE
15 G PROTEIN
6 G FIBER
480 MG SODIUM

NUTRITION BONUS: Folate (96% DAILY VALUE), Calcium (38% DV), Iron (33% DV).

EXCHANGES
1 STARCH
2 VEGETABLE
1 MEDIUM-FAT MEAT
1 FAT

Tofu & Veggies with Maple Barbecue Sauce

Nestled in the foothills of the Green Mountains, Mary's Restaurant is an idyllic retreat in Bristol, Vermont. Chef-owner Doug Mack works with farmers to highlight seasonal ingredients on his menu. He keeps vegetarian diners happy with this untraditional stir-fry, which jazzes up tofu with a zesty sauce.

- ½ cup Maple Barbecue Sauce (*recipe follows*)
- 14 ounces extra-firm tofu, preferably water-packed
- 4 teaspoons canola oil, divided
- 1 cup broccoli florets
- 1 cup cauliflower florets
- 1 cup sliced mushrooms (3 ounces)
- 1 cup grated carrots (2 medium)

1. Make Maple Barbecue Sauce.
2. Drain and rinse tofu; pat dry. Cut into 1-inch cubes. Heat 2 teaspoons oil in a large non-stick skillet over medium-high heat. Add tofu and cook, turning from time to time, until browned on all sides, 5 to 7 minutes. Transfer to a plate.
3. Add the remaining 2 teaspoons oil to the pan. Add broccoli, cauliflower, mushrooms and carrots; cook, stirring often, until just tender, about 4 minutes. Add the barbecue sauce and bring to a simmer. Stir in tofu and serve.

Maple Barbecue Sauce

Quick ☼ Easy

A splash of Southern Comfort gives a kick to Chef Doug Mack's easy sauce. For nonvegetarians, the recipe is also great with chicken or pork.

- 2 teaspoons canola oil
- 1 small onion, finely chopped
- ¾ cup reduced-sodium ketchup (*see Note*)
- ½ cup Southern Comfort liqueur *or* apple juice
- ¼ cup maple syrup
- ¾ cup cider vinegar
- 1 tablespoon Dijon mustard
- 1 tablespoon Worcestershire sauce *or* reduced-sodium soy sauce
- 1½ teaspoons hot sauce, such as Tabasco
- 5 cloves garlic, minced

> **INGREDIENT NOTE:**
>
> We recommend using reduced-sodium ketchup whenever possible. Look for it in your supermarket.

Heat oil in a medium saucepan over medium-low heat. Add onion and cook, stirring often, until softened but not browned, 3 to 5 minutes. Add remaining ingredients and bring to a simmer. Reduce heat to low and simmer, uncovered, stirring occasionally, until thickened, about 30 minutes. Let cool for about 10 minutes. Transfer to a food processor or blender and puree until smooth. (Use caution when blending hot liquids.)

1½

CARBOHYDRATE
SERVINGS

MAKES 4 SERVINGS, 1 CUP EACH

PREP TIME: 15 MINUTES
START TO FINISH: 1 HOUR 10 MINUTES

PER SERVING
215 CALORIES
10 G FAT (1 G SAT, 4 G MONO)
0 MG CHOLESTEROL
21 G CARBOHYDRATE
9 G PROTEIN
3 G FIBER
102 MG SODIUM

NUTRITION BONUS: Vitamin A (80% DAILY VALUE), Vitamin C (62% DV), Calcium (15% DV).

EXCHANGES
½ OTHER CARBOHYDRATE
1 VEGETABLE
1 MEDIUM-FAT MEAT
1 FAT (MONO)

For Maple Barbecue Sauce:

MAKES 1¼ CUPS

PREP TIME: 10 MINUTES
START TO FINISH: 30 MINUTES

TO MAKE AHEAD: Cover and refrigerate for up to 2 weeks.

PER TABLESPOON
42 CALORIES
1 G FAT (0 G SAT, 0 G MONO)
0 MG CHOLESTEROL
7 G CARBOHYDRATE
0 G PROTEIN
0 G FIBER
30 MG SODIUM

EXCHANGES
½ OTHER CARBOHYDRATE

Miso-Glazed Tofu with Cabbage & Peppers

High ⬆ Fiber

Roasting fresh vegetables and tofu with a gingery Asian marinade makes a comforting one-dish winter meal. Be sure to schedule enough time for the tofu to marinate before roasting.

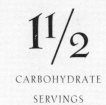

1¹/₂

CARBOHYDRATE
SERVINGS

3 tablespoons mirin *or* dry sherry (*see Ingredient Note, page 324*)

3 tablespoons miso, preferably dark (*see page 324*)

2 tablespoons minced fresh ginger

1 tablespoon lemon juice

1 tablespoon reduced-sodium soy sauce

1 tablespoon sugar

1 teaspoon chile-garlic sauce (*see page 323*)

½ teaspoon sesame oil

14 ounces extra-firm tofu, preferably water-packed

1 small green cabbage, cored and cut into 8 wedges

2 large red bell peppers, seeded and sliced

1 bunch scallions, trimmed and thinly sliced

1½ tablespoons sesame seeds

1. Whisk mirin (or sherry), miso, ginger, lemon juice, soy sauce, sugar, chile paste and sesame oil in a small bowl until blended. Drain and rinse tofu; pat dry. Cut the block into eight ½-inch-thick slabs. Arrange tofu slices in a single layer in a shallow nonreactive pan; pour ⅓ cup of the marinade over it, turning to coat. Cover and marinate in the refrigerator for 30 minutes to 1 hour.

2. Preheat oven to 425°F. Coat a 9-by-13-inch roasting pan with cooking spray. Arrange cabbage wedges, cut-side down, in 2 rows. Scatter bell peppers around the cabbage. Sprinkle with scallions. Pour the remaining marinade over the vegetables. Cover tightly with foil.

3. Bake the vegetables until tender, 25 to 35 minutes.

4. Meanwhile, toast sesame seeds in a small dry skillet over low heat, stirring constantly, until fragrant, 3 to 5 minutes. Transfer to a small bowl.

5. When the vegetables are tender, overlap tofu slices in the center of the pan and baste with any pan juices. Roast, uncovered, until the tofu is heated through, 12 to 15 minutes more. Sprinkle with sesame seeds and serve.

MAKES 4 SERVINGS

PREP TIME: 20 MINUTES
START TO FINISH: 1½ HOURS

PER SERVING

262 CALORIES

8 G FAT (1 G SAT, 1 G MONO)

0 MG CHOLESTEROL

32 G CARBOHYDRATE

17 G PROTEIN

10 G FIBER

681 MG SODIUM

NUTRITION BONUS: Vitamin C (360% DAILY VALUE), Fiber (40% DV), Folate (25% DV).

EXCHANGES

1½ OTHER CARBOHYDRATE

2 LEAN MEAT

Vegetarian Chili

High ⬆ Fiber

Corn and zucchini boost the vegetable quota in this hearty bean chili. Try serving it over quinoa or brown rice, and sprinkle with grated Monterey Jack cheese and chopped scallions, if desired.

1	tablespoon canola oil
1	large onion, chopped
1	clove garlic, minced
2	tablespoons chili powder
2	teaspoons ground cumin
1	pound zucchini (2 medium), cut into ½-inch chunks
¼	cup thinly sliced sun-dried tomatoes (*not* packed in oil)
1½	tablespoons all-purpose flour
2	15½-ounce cans pinto beans, rinsed
2	cups vegetable broth
2	cups fresh corn kernels (from 4 ears; *see box, page 243*) *or* frozen
1	14½-ounce can diced tomatoes
⅓	cup chopped fresh cilantro
	Freshly ground pepper to taste

1. Heat oil in a Dutch oven over medium-high heat. Add onion and cook, stirring, until golden, 2 to 3 minutes. Reduce heat to medium-low. Add garlic, chili powder and cumin; cook, stirring constantly, until fragrant, about 1 minute. Add zucchini and sun-dried tomatoes; cook, stirring, for 2 minutes more.

2. Add flour and beans; cook, stirring, for 1 minute. Add broth, corn and tomatoes. Bring to a boil, reduce heat to low and simmer, partially covered, until the zucchini is tender, 15 to 20 minutes. Stir in cilantro and season with pepper.

1½

CARBOHYDRATE

SERVINGS

MAKES 9 SERVINGS, 1 CUP EACH

PREP TIME: 20 MINUTES

START TO FINISH: 50 MINUTES

TO MAKE AHEAD: Cover and refrigerate for up to 2 days.

PER SERVING

173 CALORIES

3 G FAT (0 G SAT, 1 G MONO)

0 MG CHOLESTEROL

33 G CARBOHYDRATE

8 G PROTEIN

9 G FIBER

293 MG SODIUM

NUTRITION BONUS: Vitamin C (30% DAILY VALUE), Fiber (36% DV), Vitamin A (25% DV).

EXCHANGES

1½ STARCH

1 VEGETABLE

1 VERY LEAN MEAT

Mushroom & Spinach Lasagna

High ↑ Fiber

Soy "sausage," layered with tomato, creamy ricotta and whole-wheat noodles, gives this crowd-pleasing lasagna a satisfying, meaty texture and flavor. Keep one in the freezer for a great last-minute homemade Italian special.

8	ounces lasagna noodles, preferably whole-wheat (*see Note*)
1	pound soy sausage, such as Gimme Lean
4	cups sliced mushrooms (10 ounces)
¼	cup water
1	pound frozen spinach, thawed
1	28-ounce can crushed tomatoes, preferably chunky
¼	cup chopped fresh basil
½	teaspoon salt, or to taste
	Freshly ground pepper to taste
1	pound part-skim ricotta cheese (2 cups)
8	ounces part-skim mozzarella cheese, shredded (about 2 cups), divided

1. Preheat oven to 350°F. Coat a 9-by-13-inch glass baking dish with cooking spray. Put a large pot of water on to boil.
2. Cook noodles in the boiling water until not quite al dente, about 2 minutes less than the package directions. Drain; return the noodles to the pot, cover with cool water and set aside.
3. Coat a large nonstick skillet with cooking spray and heat over medium-high heat. Add sausage and cook, crumbling with a wooden spoon, until browned, about 4 minutes. Add mushrooms and water; cook, stirring occasionally until the water has evaporated and the mushrooms are tender, 8 to 10 minutes. Squeeze spinach to remove excess water, then stir into the pan; remove from heat.
4. Mix tomatoes with basil, salt and pepper in a medium bowl.
5. **To assemble lasagna:** Spread ½ cup of the tomatoes in the prepared baking dish. Arrange a layer of noodles on top, trimming to fit if necessary. Evenly dollop half the ricotta over the noodles. Top with half the spinach mixture, one-third of the remaining tomatoes and one-third of the mozzarella. Continue with another layer of noodles, the remaining ricotta, the remaining spinach mixture, half the remaining tomatoes and half the remaining mozzarella. Top with a third layer of noodles and the remaining tomatoes.
6. Cover the lasagna with foil and bake until bubbling and heated through, 1 hour to 1 hour 10 minutes. Remove the foil and sprinkle the remaining mozzarella on the lasagna. Return to the oven and bake until the cheese is just melted but not browned, 8 to 10 minutes. Let rest for 10 minutes before serving.

2

CARBOHYDRATE

SERVINGS

MAKES 10 SERVINGS

PREP TIME: 30 MINUTES

START TO FINISH: 2 HOURS

TO MAKE AHEAD: Prepare through Step 5 up to 1 day ahead.

VARIATION
For a nonvegetarian version, use 1 pound lean spicy Italian turkey sausage, casings removed.

INGREDIENT NOTE
Whole-wheat lasagna noodles are higher in fiber than white noodles. They can be found in health-food stores and some large supermarkets.

PER SERVING

303	CALORIES
8	G FAT (5 G SAT, 2 G MONO)
28	MG CHOLESTEROL
33	G CARBOHYDRATE
25	G PROTEIN
7	G FIBER
535	MG SODIUM

NUTRITION BONUS: Vitamin A (90% DAILY VALUE), Calcium (40% DV), Folate (15% DV).

EXCHANGES

2	STARCH
1	VEGETABLE
2½	MEDIUM-FAT MEAT

2

CARBOHYDRATE
SERVINGS

MAKES **8** SERVINGS, ½ CUP EACH

PREP TIME: 15 MINUTES

START TO FINISH: 45 MINUTES

TO MAKE AHEAD: The filling will keep, covered, in the refrigerator for up to 2 days.

TEST KITCHEN TIP
If you have a smaller group, make the full amount of filling, serve half with tortillas for dinner and puree the leftovers with broth or water the next day for a thick, rich soup.

PER SERVING
(WITHOUT GARNISHES)

235 CALORIES

5 G FAT (2 G SAT, 2 G MONO)

6 MG CHOLESTEROL

40 G CARBOHYDRATE

12 G PROTEIN

10 G FIBER

581 MG SODIUM

NUTRITION BONUS: Vitamin C (50% DAILY VALUE), Iron (20% DV).

EXCHANGES

2 STARCH

1 VEGETABLE

1½ MEAT

Black Bean Burritos

High ⬆ Fiber   Quick ☼ Easy

Supper's a wrap in no time flat with simple spiced black beans and tortillas. Set out diced tomatoes, reduced-fat sour cream and chopped fresh cilantro for garnishing the wraps.

1   tablespoon extra-virgin olive oil
2   green bell peppers, cut into ½ inch dice (about 2 cups)
3   cloves garlic, minced
2   teaspoons dried oregano
2   teaspoons ground cumin
1   14½-ounce can no-salt-added diced tomatoes
1   4-ounce can chopped green chiles
2   15½-ounce cans black beans, rinsed
3   tablespoons red-wine vinegar
8   7-inch whole-wheat tortillas
½   cup grated Monterey Jack cheese

1. Heat oil in a Dutch oven over medium heat. Add bell peppers, garlic, oregano and cumin; cook, stirring, until softened, 4 to 5 minutes. Add tomatoes, green chiles, beans and vinegar. Return to a simmer; reduce heat to medium-low and cook, stirring occasionally, until thickened, about 25 minutes. Add a little water if liquid evaporates too quickly.

2. Meanwhile, preheat oven to 300°F. About 15 minutes before the beans are ready, wrap tortillas in foil and bake until heated through, 10 to 15 minutes.

3. With the back of a large spoon, coarsely mash some of the beans. Spoon about ½ cup of the filling into each tortilla, sprinkle with 2 tablespoons cheese, wrap and serve.

Veggie-Burger Pitas

High ⬆ Fiber

Mushrooms and pine nuts give these "burgers" a terrific flavor. A food processor comes in handy for making the breadcrumbs and chopping the onions and mushrooms.

- ⅓ **cup bulgur (*see Note*)**
- **Yogurt-Garlic Sauce (*page 264*)**
- 3 **slices whole-wheat bread**
- 3 **large cloves garlic, peeled**
- ⅓ **cup pine nuts, toasted**
- 1 **large onion, cut into 8 pieces**
- 10 **ounces button mushrooms, trimmed**
- 1 **tablespoon canola oil *or* extra-virgin olive oil**
- ¼ **teaspoon salt, or to taste**
- **Freshly ground pepper to taste**
- 1 **large egg, lightly beaten**
- 6 **whole-wheat pita breads (4-inch), toasted**
- 6 **lettuce leaves**
- 1 **cup diced tomato**

1. Place bulgur in a bowl and pour in boiling water to cover by 1 inch. Let stand until softened, 20 to 30 minutes.
2. Meanwhile, prepare Yogurt-Garlic Sauce.
3. Place bread in a food processor and process into fine crumbs. Transfer to a mixing bowl. With the motor running, drop garlic through the feed tube and process until minced. Add pine nuts and pulse until chopped. Add onion and pulse until chopped. Transfer to another bowl. Put mushrooms in the food processor and pulse until coarsely chopped.
4. Heat oil in a large nonstick skillet over medium-high heat. Add the onion mixture and sauté until softened, about 3 minutes. Increase heat to high. Add the mushrooms and cook, stirring, until softened and most of their liquid has evaporated, about 5 minutes more. Add the vegetables to the breadcrumbs.
5. Drain the bulgur and stir into the vegetable-breadcrumb mixture. Season with salt and pepper. Add egg and mix well.
6. Preheat broiler. Coat a baking sheet with cooking spray.
7. Shape the burger mixture into 6 patties and place on the prepared baking sheet. Broil until lightly browned, 5 to 7 minutes per side. Tuck the burgers into pitas along with lettuce, tomato and the yogurt sauce.

2

CARBOHYDRATE

SERVINGS

MAKES 6 SERVINGS

PREP TIME: 30 MINUTES
START TO FINISH: 50 MINUTES

INGREDIENT NOTE
Bulgur, a staple in the Middle East, is made from wheat kernels that have been steamed, dried and crushed. It can be simmered in broth or water for a fiber-rich pilaf, or it can simply be plumped in boiling water for use in salads or vegetarian patties.

PER SERVING

267	CALORIES
11	G FAT (1 G SAT, 4 G MONO)
36	MG CHOLESTEROL
37	G CARBOHYDRATE
10	G PROTEIN
6	G FIBER
377	MG SODIUM

NUTRITION BONUS: Fiber (23% DAILY VALUE), Vitamin C (20% DV), Iron (15% DV).

EXCHANGES

2½ STARCH
1½ FAT

2

CARBOHYDRATE
SERVINGS

Spicy Tofu Hotpot

High ⬆ Fiber   Quick ☼ Easy

Warm up a winter evening with this light but satisfying one-pot meal. The tofu absorbs the flavors of this fragrant, spicy broth, making it anything but bland. Look for fresh Chinese-style noodles in the refrigerated case of your supermarket alongside wonton wrappers.

MAKES **6** SERVINGS, 1½ CUPS EACH

PREP TIME: 20 MINUTES
START TO FINISH: 30 MINUTES

PER SERVING
251 CALORIES
7 G FAT (1 G SAT, 1 G MONO)
0 MG CHOLESTEROL
39 G CARBOHYDRATE
13 G PROTEIN
7 G FIBER
639 MG SODIUM

NUTRITION BONUS: Vitamin A (45% DAILY VALUE), Vitamin C (40% DV), Fiber (27% DV), Iron (20% DV).

EXCHANGES
2 STARCH
1 VEGETABLE
½ MEDIUM-FAT MEAT
1 FAT

14	ounces firm tofu, preferably water-packed
2	teaspoons canola oil
2	tablespoons grated fresh ginger
6	cloves garlic, minced
4	ounces fresh shiitake mushrooms, stemmed and sliced (about 2 cups)
1	tablespoon brown sugar
4	cups vegetable broth *or* reduced-sodium chicken broth
¼	cup reduced-sodium soy sauce
2	teaspoons chile-garlic sauce, or to taste (*see Ingredient Note, page 323*)
4	cups thinly sliced tender bok choy greens
8	ounces fresh Chinese-style (lo mein) noodles
½	cup chopped fresh cilantro

1. Drain and rinse tofu; pat dry. Cut the block into 1-inch cubes.
2. Heat oil in a Dutch oven over medium heat. Add ginger and garlic; cook, stirring, until fragrant, about 1 minute. Add mushrooms and cook until slightly soft, 2 to 3 minutes. Stir in sugar, broth, soy sauce and chile-garlic sauce; cover and bring to a boil. Add bok choy and tofu, cover and simmer until greens are wilted, about 2 minutes. Raise heat to high and add the noodles, pushing them down into the broth. Cook, covered, until the noodles are tender, 2 to 3 minutes. Remove from the heat and stir in cilantro.

Ravioli with Bell Pepper Sauce

Quick ☼ Easy

Freezer staples—frozen bell peppers with onions and individually quick-frozen spinach—give a simple tomato-based pasta sauce complexity and a big boost of nutrients.

2 teaspoons extra-virgin olive oil

2 cloves garlic, minced

2 teaspoons finely chopped fresh rosemary, divided

1 16-ounce package frozen stir-fry vegetables
   (bell peppers and onions)

1 14½-ounce can diced tomatoes, undrained

1 cup individually quick-frozen spinach
   Freshly ground pepper to taste

24 ounces fresh *or* frozen cheese ravioli

½ cup freshly grated Parmesan cheese

> **SUBSTITUTION:**
> In place of the frozen stir-fry mixture, use 1 onion and 2 bell peppers, sliced.

1. Put a large pot of lightly salted water on to boil for cooking ravioli.
2. Heat oil in a large nonstick skillet over medium heat. Add garlic and 1 teaspoon rosemary; cook, stirring, until fragrant, about 1 minute. Add stir-fry vegetables and tomatoes. Bring to a simmer. Cook until vegetables are tender, 5 to 10 minutes. Stir in spinach; cook until tender, about 2 minutes more. Add the remaining 1 teaspoon rosemary and season with pepper.
3. Meanwhile, cook ravioli in the boiling water until they float, 5 to 7 minutes. Drain and transfer to a large bowl. Toss with the sauce. Serve with Parmesan.

2

CARBOHYDRATE
SERVINGS

MAKES 8 SERVINGS, 1 CUP EACH

PREP TIME: 10 MINUTES
START TO FINISH: 25 MINUTES

PER SERVING

267 CALORIES

9 G FAT (4 G SAT, 3 G MONO)

38 MG CHOLESTEROL

34 G CARBOHYDRATE

13 G PROTEIN

4 G FIBER

309 MG SODIUM

NUTRITION BONUS: Vitamin A (20% DAILY VALUE), Vitamin C (20% DV), Calcium (20% DV).

EXCHANGES

1½ STARCH

1 VEGETABLE

1 HIGH-FAT MEAT

½ VERY LEAN MEAT

2½

CARBOHYDRATE
SERVINGS

Fettuccine with Shiitake Mushrooms & Basil

High ↑ Fiber   Quick ☼ Easy

EatingWell reader Sidra Goldman of Washington, D.C., contributed this fresh-tasting whole-wheat pasta recipe. Lemon zest accents the basil beautifully.

MAKES 4 SERVINGS, 1½ CUPS EACH

PREP TIME: 10 MINUTES
START TO FINISH: 20 MINUTES

INGREDIENT NOTE
Whole-wheat pastas are higher in fiber than white pastas. They can be found in health-food stores and some large supermarkets.

PER SERVING

311 CALORIES
 11 G FAT (3 G SAT, 6 G MONO)
  9 MG CHOLESTEROL
 44 G CARBOHYDRATE
 13 G PROTEIN
  8 G FIBER
307 MG SODIUM

NUTRITION BONUS: Fiber (28% DAILY VALUE), Calcium (14% DV).

EXCHANGES
2½ STARCH
 1 LEAN MEAT
 1 FAT

2	tablespoons extra-virgin olive oil
3	cloves garlic, minced
2	ounces shiitake mushrooms, stemmed and sliced (1½ cups)
2	teaspoons freshly grated lemon zest
2	tablespoons lemon juice
¼	teaspoon salt, or to taste
	Freshly ground pepper to taste
8	ounces whole-wheat fettuccine *or* spaghetti (*see Note*)
½	cup freshly grated Parmesan cheese (1 ounce)
½	cup chopped fresh basil, divided

1. Bring a large pot of lightly salted water to a boil for cooking pasta.
2. Heat oil in large nonstick skillet over low heat. Add garlic and cook, stirring, until fragrant but not browned, about 1 minute. Add mushrooms and increase heat to medium-high; cook, stirring occasionally, until tender and lightly browned, 4 to 5 minutes. Stir in lemon zest, lemon juice, salt and pepper. Remove from the heat.
3. Meanwhile, cook pasta, stirring occasionally, until just tender, 9 to 11 minutes or according to package directions. Drain, reserving ½ cup cooking liquid.
4. Add the pasta, the reserved cooking liquid, Parmesan and ¼ cup basil to the mushrooms in the skillet; toss to coat well. Serve immediately, garnished with remaining basil.

TIP

TASTE TEST: WHOLE-WHEAT PASTAS

In a comparison of several brands of whole-wheat pasta, our tasters gave top marks to DeBoles, Bionaturae and Ronzoni Healthy Harvest (not a true whole-wheat pasta, but a blend that includes wheat germ and bran). Other brands to look for are Hodgson Mill and DeCecco. You can find a selection in the natural-foods section of large markets and in natural-foods stores.

Macaroni & Cheese

With its irresistibly creamy interior and crusty topping, old-fashioned macaroni and cheese is always a winner. This version has been updated using whole-grain macaroni and breadcrumbs. Low-fat cottage cheese replaces some of the Cheddar, reducing saturated fat and contributing a rich dairy flavor.

2½

CARBOHYDRATE
SERVINGS

8   ounces whole-wheat elbow macaroni (2 cups; *see Tip, page 138*)
4   slices whole-wheat sandwich bread
2   teaspoons butter, melted
3   teaspoons extra-virgin olive oil, divided
3   cups 1% milk, divided
¼   cup all-purpose flour
½   teaspoon dry mustard
1   medium white onion, grated, liquid drained
2   cups grated extra-sharp Cheddar cheese
1   cup 1% cottage cheese
1   teaspoon salt, or to taste
½   teaspoon freshly ground pepper

1. Preheat oven to 350°F. Coat a 9-by-13-inch baking dish with cooking spray. Put a large pot of lightly salted water on to boil.
2. Cook macaroni until just tender, 8 to 10 minutes or according to package directions. Drain and rinse under cold water. Set aside.
3. Pulse bread into fine crumbs in a food processor. Add butter and 2 teaspoons oil; pulse to moisten. Place in a small bowl and set aside.
4. Combine ½ cup milk, flour and dry mustard in a small bowl; whisk until smooth. Heat the remaining 1 teaspoon oil in a large heavy-bottomed saucepan over medium-low heat. Add onion; cook, stirring occasionally, until softened but not browned, 6 to 8 minutes. Add the remaining 2½ cups milk, increase heat to medium and bring to a bare simmer. Whisk in the milk-flour mixture and cook, whisking constantly, until the sauce is thickened, 5 to 7 minutes.
5. Remove from heat and whisk in Cheddar, cottage cheese, salt and pepper. Stir in reserved pasta and transfer to the prepared baking dish. Sprinkle with the reserved breadcrumbs.
6. Bake the casserole, uncovered, until bubbly and lightly browned, 30 to 35 minutes.

MAKES 8 SERVINGS

PREP TIME: 25 MINUTES
START TO FINISH: 1 HOUR

TO MAKE AHEAD: Prepare through Step 5. Cover and refrigerate for up to 2 days or freeze for up to 3 months. Thaw in the refrigerator, if necessary, before baking.

PER SERVING
353   CALORIES
14   G FAT (8 G SAT, 2 G MONO)
36   MG CHOLESTEROL
39   G CARBOHYDRATE
19   G PROTEIN
3   G FIBER
699   MG SODIUM

NUTRITION BONUS: Calcium (35% DAILY VALUE).

EXCHANGES
2½   STARCH
2   HIGH-FAT MEAT

3

CARBOHYDRATE
SERVINGS

MAKES **8** SERVINGS,
ABOUT **1½** CUPS EACH

PREP TIME: 20 MINUTES
START TO FINISH: 20 MINUTES

TO MAKE AHEAD: Prepare
through Step 2, up to 2 hours in
advance.

PER SERVING

345 CALORIES
 12 G FAT (2 G SAT, 5 G MONO)
  0 MG CHOLESTEROL
 51 G CARBOHYDRATE
 12 G PROTEIN
 10 G FIBER
542 MG SODIUM

NUTRITION BONUS: Vitamin C
(100% DAILY VALUE), Fiber (40% DV),
Vitamin A (40% DV).

EXCHANGES

3 STARCH
1 VEGETABLE
2 FAT

Elise's Sesame Noodles

High ↑ Fiber   Quick ☼ Easy

Whole-wheat pasta bolsters fiber and nutrients in this popular Asian noodle salad. The recipe is from Annelise Stuart of Germantown, New York. (*Photograph: front cover.*)

1	pound whole-wheat spaghetti (*see Tip, page 138*)
½	cup reduced-sodium soy sauce
2	tablespoons sesame oil
2	tablespoons canola oil
2	tablespoons rice-wine vinegar *or* lime juice
1½	teaspoons crushed red pepper
1	bunch scallions, sliced, divided
¼	cup chopped fresh cilantro, divided (optional)
4	cups snow peas, trimmed and sliced on the bias
1	medium red bell pepper, thinly sliced
½	cup toasted sesame seeds

1. Bring a large pot of water to a boil. Cook spaghetti until just tender, 9 to 11 minutes or according to package directions. Drain; rinse under cold water.

2. Meanwhile, whisk soy sauce, sesame oil, canola oil, vinegar (or lime juice), crushed red pepper, ¼ cup scallions and 2 tablespoons cilantro (if using). Add noodles, snow peas and bell pepper; toss to coat.

3. To serve, mix in sesame seeds and garnish with the remaining scallions and cilantro.

Indian Vegetable Stew

High ⬆ Fiber

Sweet sautéed onions and a rich mixture of spices create a complex, flavorful base for this extraordinary vegetarian stew.

- 1 tablespoon extra-virgin olive oil
- 3 large onions, coarsely chopped (4 cups)
- 4 cloves garlic, minced
- 1 teaspoon cumin seed
- 1 teaspoon ground cumin
- 1 teaspoon ground coriander
- ½ teaspoon ground cinnamon
- ¼ teaspoon cardamom
- ⅛ teaspoon cayenne pepper
- 1 pound new potatoes, scrubbed and quartered
- 1½ cups water
- ½ teaspoon salt, or to taste
- 1 19-ounce can chickpeas, rinsed
- 1 14½-ounce can crushed tomatoes, preferably fire-roasted
- 1 pound mini carrots
- ¾ cup chopped fresh cilantro
- ¾ cup low-fat plain yogurt (optional)

1. Heat oil in a Dutch oven over medium heat. Add onions and cook, stirring often, until fragrant and beginning to brown, 5 to 6 minutes. Add garlic and cook, stirring, until fragrant, about 1 minute. Add cumin seed, ground cumin, coriander, cinnamon, cardamom and cayenne; cook, stirring, until fragrant, 30 to 60 seconds. Add potatoes, water and salt; bring to a simmer. Cover and cook for 10 minutes.

2. Add chickpeas, tomatoes and carrots; stir to combine. Bring to a simmer. Reduce heat to low and simmer, partially covered, stirring occasionally and adding ½ cup water, if needed, until the potatoes and the carrots are tender, 30 to 35 minutes. Stir in cilantro. Serve with yogurt, if desired.

3

CARBOHYDRATE
SERVINGS

MAKES 6 SERVINGS, 1¼ CUPS EACH

PREP TIME: 20 MINUTES
START TO FINISH: 1 HOUR

PER SERVING

- 264 CALORIES
- 4 G FAT (1 G SAT, 2 G MONO)
- 0 MG CHOLESTEROL
- 51 G CARBOHYDRATE
- 9 G PROTEIN
- 10 G FIBER
- 603 MG SODIUM

NUTRITION BONUS: Vitamin C (53% DAILY VALUE), Fiber (40% DV), Folate (25% DV).

EXCHANGES

- 2 STARCH
- 2 VEGETABLE
- 1 VERY LEAN MEAT

3

CARBOHYDRATE

SERVINGS

MAKES 6 SERVINGS

PREP TIME: 20 MINUTES

START TO FINISH: 40 MINUTES

PER SERVING

329 CALORIES

8 G FAT (3 G SAT, 2 G MONO)

11 MG CHOLESTEROL

57 G CARBOHYDRATE

10 G PROTEIN

10 G FIBER

523 MG SODIUM

NUTRITION BONUS: Fiber (40% DAILY VALUE), Vitamin C (40% DV).

EXCHANGES

3 STARCH

1 VEGETABLE

1 FAT

Pasta with Eggplant Ragu

High ⬆ Fiber   Quick ☼ Easy

Spiking prepared marinara sauce with meaty eggplant, garlic and basil transforms it into a deliciously hearty sauce for whole-wheat pasta.

2 teaspoons extra-virgin olive oil

1 onion, chopped

2 cloves garlic, minced

1 eggplant (1-1¼ pounds), cut into ¾-inch dice

Freshly ground pepper to taste

2 cups prepared marinara sauce

1 yellow *or* red bell pepper, diced

3 tablespoons chopped fresh basil

12 ounces whole-wheat penne *or* rigatoni

½ cup crumbled feta cheese *or* ¼ cup freshly grated Parmesan cheese

1. Put a large pot of lightly salted water on to boil.
2. Heat oil in a large nonstick skillet over medium heat. Add onion and garlic; cook, stirring, until softened, about 4 minutes. Add eggplant and cook, stirring, for 2 minutes more. Season with pepper. Stir in marinara sauce and bring to a simmer. Cover and cook, stirring occasionally, until the eggplant is almost tender, about 20 minutes. Add bell pepper and basil; cover and cook for 5 minutes more.
3. Meanwhile, cook pasta in the boiling water until just tender, 8 to 10 minutes or according to package directions. Drain and toss with sauce. Sprinkle with feta (or Parmesan) and serve.

Whole-Wheat Spaghetti with Roasted Onions & Chard

High ↑ Fiber   Quick ☼ Easy

This rustic pasta dish offers health and happiness in every bite. Dark leafy greens like Swiss chard contain the phytochemicals lutein and zeaxanthine, which help protect against cataracts and macular degeneration.

¼	cup chopped walnuts
2	large red onions, peeled and cut into 12 wedges each
2	large cloves garlic, minced
2	tablespoons extra-virgin olive oil
1	teaspoon minced fresh thyme
¼	teaspoon salt, or to taste
	Freshly ground pepper to taste
2	pounds Swiss chard, ribs removed, leaves coarsely chopped (24 cups)
¾	cup vegetable broth *or reduced-sodium chicken broth*
1	pound whole-wheat spaghetti (*see Tip, page 138*)

1. Preheat oven to 400°F. Put a large pot of lightly salted water on to boil.
2. Place walnuts in a small baking dish and bake until fragrant, about 5 minutes. Set aside.
3. Combine onions, garlic, oil and thyme in a roasting pan. Season with salt and pepper. Roast until the onions are caramelized, stirring once or twice, 25 to 30 minutes. Stir in the chard and broth; roast until the chard is wilted, 8 to 10 minutes more. Adjust seasoning with salt and pepper.
4. Meanwhile, cook spaghetti until just tender, 9 to 11 minutes or according to package directions. Drain and transfer to a warmed serving bowl. Toss with the onion mixture. Serve garnished with the toasted walnuts.

3
CARBOHYDRATE
SERVINGS

MAKES 8 SERVINGS

PREP TIME: 10 MINUTES
START TO FINISH: 35-45 MINUTES

TEST KITCHEN TIP
Save the chard ribs and serve as a vegetable side dish. Cut them in ½-inch pieces and braise in a little broth until tender.

PER SERVING
291 CALORIES
7 G FAT (1 G SAT, 3 G MONO)
0 MG CHOLESTEROL
51 G CARBOHYDRATE
11 G PROTEIN
10 G FIBER
297 MG SODIUM

NUTRITION BONUS: Vitamin A (120% DAILY VALUE), Fiber (40% DV), Vitamin C (35% DV), Iron (25% DV).

EXCHANGES
3 STARCH
1 VEGETABLE
1 FAT (MONO)

Chicken & Turkey

CARBOHYDRATE
SERVINGS

Grilled Chicken Breasts with Salsa Verde

Quick ☼ Easy

Salsa verde, a piquant Italian herb sauce, dresses up basic grilled chicken breasts. The versatile sauce is also excellent with fish or pasta.

MAKES 4 SERVINGS

PREP TIME: 15 MINUTES
START TO FINISH: 20 MINUTES

TO MAKE AHEAD: The salsa verde will keep, covered, in the refrigerator for up to 2 days. Bring to room temperature before serving.

SALSA VERDE

½	cup chopped fresh parsley
1½	tablespoons capers, rinsed
1	clove garlic, peeled and smashed
1	tablespoon extra-virgin olive oil
1	tablespoon lemon juice
1	tablespoon water
1	teaspoon anchovy paste
	Freshly ground pepper to taste

CHICKEN

4	boneless, skinless chicken breast halves (about 1 pound total), trimmed of fat
1	teaspoon extra-virgin olive oil
⅛	teaspoon salt, or to taste
	Freshly ground pepper to taste

PER SERVING

183	CALORIES
7	G FAT (1 G SAT, 4 G MONO)
70	MG CHOLESTEROL
1	G CARBOHYDRATE
27	G PROTEIN
0	G FIBER
471	MG SODIUM

NUTRITION BONUS: Selenium (28% DAILY VALUE), Vitamin C (20% DV).

EXCHANGES

4 VERY LEAN MEAT
1 FAT (MONO)

1. **To prepare salsa verde:** Combine parsley, capers and garlic in a blender or food processor; process until finely chopped. Add oil, lemon juice, water and anchovy paste and process until blended. Season with pepper.

2. **To prepare chicken:** Prepare a grill or preheat broiler. Rub chicken with oil and season with salt and pepper. Grill or broil until no longer pink inside, 3 to 4 minutes per side. Serve with salsa verde.

Turkey Cutlets with Sage & Lemon

Quick ☼ Easy

Lean turkey cutlets are ideal for a quick sauté. Here, a simple pan sauce with wine, sage and a whisper of butter delivers a luxurious finish. Serve with mashed winter squash and sautéed spinach.

3	tablespoons all-purpose flour
1	pound turkey breast cutlets
¼	teaspoon salt, or to taste
	Freshly ground pepper to taste
3	teaspoons extra-virgin olive oil, divided
2	cloves garlic, minced
2	teaspoons chopped fresh sage
¼	cup dry white wine
¾	cup reduced-sodium chicken broth
1	teaspoon lemon juice
1	teaspoon butter

1. Spread flour on a large plate. Cut several small slits in outer edges of the turkey to prevent curling. Pat dry with paper towels and season with salt and pepper. Dredge lightly in flour. Discard any remaining flour.
2. Heat 1 teaspoon oil in a large nonstick skillet over medium-high heat. Add half the turkey and cook until golden outside and no longer pink inside, 1 to 2 minutes per side. Transfer to a platter and tent with foil to keep warm. Sauté the remaining turkey in another 1 teaspoon oil until golden; transfer to platter.
3. Add the remaining 1 teaspoon oil to the pan. Add garlic and sage; cook, stirring, until fragrant, about 1 minute. Add wine and cook, scraping up any browned bits, until reduced by half, about 1 minute. Add broth and cook until the liquid is reduced by half, 4 to 5 minutes. Stir in lemon juice and any juices accumulated from the turkey and simmer for 1 minute more. Remove from heat and swirl in butter. Serve, spooning the sauce over the turkey.

O
CARBOHYDRATE
SERVINGS

MAKES 4 SERVINGS

PREP TIME: 10 MINUTES
START TO FINISH: 25 MINUTES

PER SERVING

205 CALORIES
5 G FAT (1 G SAT, 3 G MONO)
74 MG CHOLESTEROL
5 G CARBOHYDRATE
29 G PROTEIN
0 G FIBER
228 MG SODIUM

NUTRITION BONUS: Selenium
(47% DAILY VALUE).

EXCHANGES

4 VERY LEAN MEAT
1 FAT

$\frac{1}{2}$

CARBOHYDRATE

SERVING

MAKES 4 SERVINGS

PREP TIME: 10 MINUTES

START TO FINISH: 40 MINUTES

TO MAKE AHEAD: The roasted lemons will keep, covered, in the refrigerator for up to 2 days.

PER SERVING

219 CALORIES

7 G FAT (2 G SAT, 3 G MONO)

72 MG CHOLESTEROL

10 G CARBOHYDRATE

28 G PROTEIN

1 G FIBER

396 MG SODIUM

NUTRITION BONUS: Vitamin C (40% DAILY VALUE).

EXCHANGES

1/2 FRUIT

4 VERY LEAN MEAT

1 FAT

Chicken Breasts with Roasted Lemons

Quick ☼ Easy

Tangy roasted lemons harmonize beautifully with chicken. They are also delicious chopped and sprinkled over fish.

ROASTED LEMONS

3 medium lemons, preferably organic, scrubbed, thinly sliced and seeded

1 teaspoon extra-virgin olive oil

1/8 teaspoon salt, or to taste

CHICKEN

4 boneless, skinless chicken breast halves (about 1 pound total), trimmed of fat

1/8 teaspoon salt, or to taste

Freshly ground pepper to taste

1/4 cup all-purpose flour

2 teaspoons extra-virgin olive oil

1¼ cups reduced-sodium chicken broth

2 tablespoons drained capers, rinsed

2 teaspoons butter

3 tablespoons chopped fresh parsley, divided

1. **To prepare roasted lemons:** Preheat oven to 325°F. Line a baking sheet with parchment paper. Arrange lemon slices in a single layer on it. Brush the lemon slices with oil and sprinkle with salt. Roast the lemons until slightly dry and beginning to brown around the edges, 25 to 30 minutes.

2. **Meanwhile, prepare chicken:** Cover chicken with plastic wrap and pound with a rolling pin or heavy skillet until flattened to about 1/2 inch thick. Sprinkle the chicken with salt and pepper. Place flour in a shallow dish and dredge the chicken to coat both sides; shake off excess (discard remaining flour).

3. Heat oil in a large nonstick skillet over medium-high heat. Add the chicken and cook until golden brown, 2 to 3 minutes per side. Add broth and bring to a boil, scraping up any browned bits. Stir in capers. Boil until the liquid is reduced to syrup consistency, 5 to 8 minutes, turning the chicken halfway. Add the roasted lemons, butter, 2 tablespoons parsley and more pepper, if desired; simmer until the butter melts and the chicken is cooked through, about 2 minutes. Transfer to a platter. Sprinkle with the remaining 1 tablespoon parsley and serve.

Chicken with Green Olives & Prunes

Quick ☼ Easy

The delicious combination of sweet, tart and savory flavors makes a simple dish the star of a weeknight meal. Serve with whole-wheat couscous (*page 237*), to soak up the tasty sauce, and North African Spiced Carrots (*page 233*).

  1¼ **pounds boneless, skinless chicken thighs, trimmed of fat**
   1 **teaspoon extra-virgin olive oil**
   1 **cup reduced-sodium chicken broth**
  ¼ **cup red-wine vinegar**
  ¼ **cup chopped pitted green olives, such as Spanish, Cerignola *or* cracked green**
  ¼ **cup chopped pitted prunes (dried plums)**
     Freshly ground pepper to taste

Pat chicken dry with a paper towel. Heat oil in a large nonstick skillet over medium-high heat. Add the chicken and cook until browned, about 2 minutes per side. Add broth and vinegar to the pan; bring to a simmer, stirring. Add olives, prunes and pepper; reduce heat to low. Cover and cook until the chicken is tender and no longer pink in the center, 12 to 15 minutes. Transfer the chicken to a plate. Spoon sauce over the chicken and serve.

Chutney-Glazed Chicken

Taking a minute to remove the skin from chicken breasts is definitely worth the effort—it trims off about 80% of the fat. In this recipe, a lively curry, lime and chutney glaze replaces the skin and ensures a succulent result.

   4 **bone-in chicken breasts (2½-3 pounds total), skinned and trimmed of fat**
  ¼ **teaspoon salt, or to taste**
   5 **teaspoons curry powder, divided**
   3 **tablespoons prepared chutney, preferably Major Grey**
   2 **tablespoons fresh lime juice**

1. Preheat oven to 400°F. Coat a shallow baking dish with cooking spray.
2. Season chicken on both sides with salt, then rub all over with 4 teaspoons curry powder. Place bone-side up in prepared dish.
3. Bake the chicken for 20 minutes. Meanwhile, combine chutney, lime juice and the remaining 1 teaspoon curry powder in a small bowl.
4. Turn the chicken pieces over and spoon the chutney mixture on top. Bake until no longer pink in the center, 15 to 20 minutes more. Serve, spooning pan juices over the chicken.

CARBOHYDRATE

SERVING

MAKES 4 SERVINGS

PREP TIME: 10 MINUTES
START TO FINISH: 30 MINUTES

PER SERVING
  224 CALORIES
    8 G FAT (2 G SAT, 4 G MONO)
 118 MG CHOLESTEROL
    7 G CARBOHYDRATE
  29 G PROTEIN
    1 G FIBER
 339 MG SODIUM

NUTRITION BONUS: Selenium
(20% DAILY VALUE).

EXCHANGES
 ½ FRUIT
 4 LEAN MEAT

For Chutney-Glazed Chicken:

CARBOHYDRATE

SERVING

MAKES 4 SERVINGS

PREP TIME: 10 MINUTES
START TO FINISH: 50 MINUTES

PER SERVING
  232 CALORIES
    3 G FAT (1 G SAT, 1 G MONO)
 107 MG CHOLESTEROL
    7 G CARBOHYDRATE
  43 G PROTEIN
    1 G FIBER
 269 MG SODIUM

NUTRITION BONUS: Selenium
(47% DAILY VALUE).

EXCHANGES
 ½ FRUIT
 7½ VERY LEAN MEAT

Orange-Rosemary Glazed Chicken

Shine up plain baked chicken with a tart rosemary and citrus glaze. Serve with roasted potatoes and sautéed spinach.

4	bone-in chicken breast halves (2½-3 pounds total), skin removed, trimmed of fat
¼	teaspoon salt, or to taste
	Freshly ground pepper to taste
1½	teaspoons chopped fresh rosemary, divided
3	tablespoons orange marmalade
2	tablespoons sherry vinegar, malt vinegar *or* cider vinegar
1	teaspoon extra-virgin olive oil

1. Preheat oven to 400°F. Coat a roasting pan with cooking spray.
2. Season chicken on both sides with salt and pepper and place, bone-side up, in the prepared pan. Sprinkle with 1 teaspoon rosemary.
3. Bake the chicken for 20 minutes. Meanwhile, combine the remaining ½ teaspoon rosemary, marmalade, vinegar and oil in a small bowl.
4. Turn the chicken pieces over and top with the marmalade mixture. Bake until the chicken is no longer pink in the center, 15 to 20 minutes more. Serve immediately, spooning the sauce over the chicken.

½
CARBOHYDRATE
SERVING

MAKES 4 SERVINGS

PREP TIME: 10 MINUTES
START TO FINISH: 50 MINUTES

PER SERVING

252	CALORIES
3	G FAT (1 G SAT, 1 G MONO)
107	MG CHOLESTEROL
10	G CARBOHYDRATE
43	G PROTEIN
0	G FIBER
274	MG SODIUM

NUTRITION BONUS: Selenium (47% DAILY VALUE).

EXCHANGES

1 OTHER CARBOHYDRATE
7 VERY LEAN MEAT

> **❝**'Melted' peppers make a wonderful topping for fish or sautéed chicken breasts, and are a really nice side dish. To make them, slice 4 bell peppers of any combination of colors into strips and cook slowly in ¼ cup balsamic vinegar for an hour, stirring often.**❞**
>
> —*Marilyn C., Minnesota*

Pampered Chicken

An ovenproof skillet is the key to this easy recipe. Breaded stuffed chicken breasts are browned on one side on the top of the stove, carefully flipped and transferred—still in the pan—to the oven to finish cooking. This guarantees a nice brown crust and moist, tender chicken.

CARBOHYDRATE
SERVING

4 boneless, skinless chicken breast halves (about 1 pound), trimmed of fat
4 slices Monterey Jack cheese (2 ounces)
2 egg whites
⅓ cup seasoned (Italian-style) breadcrumbs
2 tablespoons freshly grated Parmesan cheese
2 tablespoons chopped fresh parsley
¼ teaspoon salt, or to taste
½ teaspoon freshly ground pepper
2 teaspoons extra-virgin olive oil
   Lemon wedges for garnish

1. Preheat oven to 400°F. Place a chicken breast, skinned-side down, on a cutting board. Keeping the blade of a sharp knife parallel to the board, make a horizontal slit along the thinner, long edge of the breast, cutting nearly through to the opposite side. Open the breast so it forms two flaps, hinged at the center. Place a slice of cheese on one flap, leaving a ½-inch border at the edge. Press remaining flap down firmly over the cheese and set aside. Repeat with the remaining breasts.
2. Lightly beat egg whites with a fork in a medium bowl. Mix breadcrumbs, Parmesan, parsley, salt and pepper in a shallow dish. Holding a stuffed breast together firmly, dip it in the egg whites and then roll in the breadcrumbs. Repeat with the remaining breasts.
3. Heat oil in a large ovenproof skillet over medium-high heat. Add the stuffed breasts and cook until browned on one side, about 2 minutes. Turn the breasts over and place the skillet in the oven.
4. Bake the chicken until no longer pink in the center, about 20 minutes. Serve with lemon wedges.

MAKES 4 SERVINGS

PREP TIME: 25 MINUTES
START TO FINISH: 50 MINUTES

PER SERVING
258 CALORIES
9 G FAT (4 G SAT, 4 G MONO)
81 MG CHOLESTEROL
7 G CARBOHYDRATE
34 G PROTEIN
1 G FIBER
536 MG SODIUM

NUTRITION BONUS: Selenium (40% DAILY VALUE), Calcium (15% DV).

EXCHANGES
½ STARCH
4 VERY LEAN MEAT
1 MEDIUM-FAT MEAT

Tandoori Chicken

A highly seasoned yogurt marinade tenderizes these chicken thighs. Baking them at an extremely high temperature simulates a tandoori clay oven, creating a deliciously caramelized surface.

MAKES 4 SERVINGS

PREP TIME: 20 MINUTES

START TO FINISH: 2 HOURS 50 MINUTES (including 2 hours marinating time)

PER SERVING

227 CALORIES
10 G FAT (3 G SAT, 4 G MONO)
87 MG CHOLESTEROL
8 G CARBOHYDRATE
27 G PROTEIN
1 G FIBER
398 MG SODIUM

NUTRITION BONUS: Selenium (24% DAILY VALUE), Zinc (18% DV).

EXCHANGES

1/2 OTHER CARBOHYDRATE
4 LEAN MEAT

1	cup nonfat plain yogurt
1	small onion, minced
2	cloves garlic, minced
1½	tablespoons lemon juice
1	teaspoon chopped fresh cilantro
½	teaspoon paprika
½	teaspoon ground cumin
½	teaspoon ground turmeric
½	teaspoon ground ginger
½	teaspoon salt, or to taste
¼	teaspoon freshly ground pepper
¼	teaspoon ground cinnamon
	Pinch of ground cloves
4	bone-in chicken thighs (about 1½ pounds), skinned and trimmed of fat

1. Stir together yogurt, onion and garlic in a shallow glass dish. Add lemon juice, cilantro, paprika, cumin, turmeric, ginger, salt, pepper, cinnamon and cloves. Add chicken and coat well. Cover and marinate in the refrigerator for at least 2 hours or overnight.
2. Preheat oven to 500°F. Coat a wire rack with cooking spray and set it over a foil-covered baking sheet. Place the chicken on the prepared rack.
3. Bake the chicken until browned and no trace of pink remains in the center, 25 to 30 minutes. Serve hot.

Asian Chicken Salad

Quick ☼ Easy

Crunchy vegetables and tender chicken breasts tossed in a tangy vinaigrette make a refreshing main-dish salad. If you poach the chicken yourself, reserve ¾ cup of the cooking liquid to make the dressing. (*Photograph: page 167.*)

DRESSING

- ¼ cup reduced-sodium soy sauce
- 3 tablespoons rice-wine vinegar
- 1½ tablespoons brown sugar
- 1½ teaspoons sesame oil
- 1½ teaspoons chile-garlic sauce (*see Ingredient Note, page 323*)
- 3 tablespoons canola oil
- 1 tablespoon minced fresh ginger
- 2 cloves garlic, minced
- 1 tablespoon tahini paste
- ¾ cup reduced-sodium chicken broth *or reserved chicken-poaching liquid*

SALAD

- 2 tablespoons sesame seeds
- 8 cups shredded napa cabbage (1 small head; *see Note*)
- 1½ cups grated carrots (2-3 medium)
- 5 radishes, sliced (about 1 cup)
- ½ cup chopped scallions
- 3½ cups shredded skinless cooked chicken (about 1½ pounds boneless, skinless chicken breast; *see box, page 177*)

1. **To prepare dressing:** Combine soy sauce, vinegar, brown sugar, sesame oil and chile-garlic sauce in a glass measuring cup; stir to blend. Heat canola oil in a small saucepan over medium-high heat. Add ginger and garlic; cook, stirring, until fragrant, 1 to 2 minutes. Add the soy sauce mixture to the pan; bring to a simmer. Whisk in tahini and broth (or poaching liquid); cook until reduced slightly, 3 to 4 minutes. Let cool.
2. **To prepare salad:** Heat a small dry skillet over medium-low heat. Add sesame seeds and cook, stirring, until lightly browned and fragrant, 1 to 2 minutes. Transfer to a small plate to cool.
3. Combine cabbage, carrots, radishes, scallions and chicken in a large shallow bowl. Stir dressing to recombine and drizzle over the salad; toss to coat. Sprinkle the sesame seeds on top.

1
CARBOHYDRATE
SERVING

MAKES **6** SERVINGS, **2** CUPS EACH

PREP TIME: 30 MINUTES
START TO FINISH: 40 MINUTES

TO MAKE AHEAD: The dressing will keep, covered, in the refrigerator for up to 2 days.

INGREDIENT NOTE
Napa cabbage has an elongated head and is pale green in color with tender, tapered white ribs. Its tightly packed, crinkled leaves have a crisp texture. Discard the cone-shaped core.

PER SERVING
289 CALORIES
14 G FAT (2 G SAT, 7 G MONO)
64 MG CHOLESTEROL
14 G CARBOHYDRATE
28 G PROTEIN
3 G FIBER
518 MG SODIUM

NUTRITION BONUS: Vitamin A (100% DAILY VALUE), Vitamin C (60% DV).

EXCHANGES
2 VEGETABLE
4 VERY LEAN MEAT
2 FAT

1

MAKES 4 SERVINGS

PREP TIME: 20 MINUTES
START TO FINISH: 50 MINUTES

SUBSTITUTION NOTE
You can use 1½ teaspoons dried tarragon instead of fresh. Add it all at once in Step 3.

PER SERVING

404 CALORIES

10 G FAT (3 G SAT, 5 G MONO)

138 MG CHOLESTEROL

18 G CARBOHYDRATE

48 G PROTEIN

1 G FIBER

406 MG SODIUM

NUTRITION BONUS: Selenium (60% DAILY VALUE), Vitamin A (50% DV).

EXCHANGES

1 STARCH

6½ LEAN MEAT

Chicken Fricassee with Tarragon

Fricassee is a classic French stew of chicken and vegetables, cooked in white wine and finished with a touch of cream. The light tarragon-infused sauce begs to be sopped up with crusty bread.

2½ pounds bone-in chicken pieces, skin removed
¼ teaspoon salt, or to taste
    Freshly ground pepper to taste
2 tablespoons all-purpose flour
1 tablespoon extra-virgin olive oil
5 large shallots, finely chopped (about 1 cup)
1 cup dry white wine
1½ cups reduced-sodium chicken broth
1 medium carrot, peeled and thinly sliced
1 pound button mushrooms, wiped clean and halved or quartered
4 sprigs fresh tarragon plus 4 teaspoons chopped (*see Substitution Note*)
1 tablespoon cornstarch mixed with 1 tablespoon water
¼ cup reduced-fat sour cream
2 teaspoons Dijon mustard

1. Season chicken with salt and pepper. Dredge in flour, shaking off the excess. Heat oil in a large deep skillet or Dutch oven. Add chicken; cook until browned, about 4 minutes per side. Transfer to a plate.

2. Add shallots to the pan; cook, stirring, until fragrant, about 30 seconds. Add wine and scrape up any browned bits. Simmer until reduced slightly, about 3 minutes.

3. Add broth; bring to a simmer. Return the chicken to the pan; add carrot, mushrooms and tarragon sprigs. Reduce heat to low, cover and simmer gently until the chicken is tender and no longer pink in the center, about 20 minutes.

4. Transfer the chicken to a plate; cover with foil to keep warm. Discard tarragon sprigs. Increase heat to medium-high. Simmer the cooking liquid for 2 to 3 minutes to intensify flavor. Add cornstarch mixture and cook, stirring, until slightly thickened, about 2 minutes. Whisk in sour cream, mustard and chopped tarragon. Serve immediately.

Chicken Paprikash

Quick ☼ Easy

When you are craving a creamy chicken dish, try this streamlined version of a Hungarian classic. Instead of egg noodles, serve it over Steamed Vegetable Ribbons (*page 234*).

1 pound boneless, skinless chicken breasts, trimmed of fat and cut into
  ½-inch strips
¼ teaspoon salt, or to taste
  Freshly ground pepper to taste
1 tablespoon extra-virgin olive oil, divided
2 medium onions, sliced
2 cloves garlic, minced
2 teaspoons paprika, preferably Hungarian
2 tablespoons all-purpose flour
1 cup reduced-sodium chicken broth
1 large red bell pepper, cut into thin strips
3 tablespoons reduced-fat sour cream
2 tablespoons chopped fresh dill

1. Pat chicken strips dry. Season with salt and pepper.
2. Heat ½ tablespoon oil in a large nonstick skillet over medium-high heat. Add the chicken and cook, stirring, until no trace of pink remains, 3 to 5 minutes. Transfer to a bowl and cover to keep warm.
3. Reduce heat to medium and add the remaining ½ tablespoon oil to the pan. Add onions and cook, stirring, until softened, about 5 minutes. Season with salt and pepper. Add garlic and paprika; cook, stirring, until fragrant, about 1 minute more. Add flour and cook, stirring, for 1 minute. Add broth and bring to a simmer, stirring constantly. Stir in bell pepper. Cover and cook, stirring occasionally, until the peppers are softened and the sauce is slightly thickened, 4 to 5 minutes. Add the reserved chicken and cook, uncovered, until heated through, 1 to 2 minutes.
4. Remove from heat and stir in sour cream. Sprinkle with dill and serve immediately.

1

CARBOHYDRATE
SERVING

**MAKES 4 SERVINGS,
ABOUT 1¼ CUPS EACH**

PREP TIME: 15 MINUTES
START TO FINISH: 35 MINUTES

PER SERVING
234 CALORIES
  7 G FAT (2 G SAT, 3 G MONO)
 71 MG CHOLESTEROL
 13 G CARBOHYDRATE
 29 G PROTEIN
  2 G FIBER
262 MG SODIUM

NUTRITION BONUS: Vitamin C
(140% DAILY VALUE), Vitamin A
(40% DV).

EXCHANGES
  1 VEGETABLE
  4 VERY LEAN MEAT

Grilled Chicken Caesar Salad

Quick ☼ Easy

Our Grilled Chicken Caesar is far lighter, and just as good, as the popular full-fat version.

1 pound boneless, skinless chicken breasts, trimmed of fat
1 teaspoon canola oil
¼ teaspoon salt, or to taste
  Freshly ground pepper to taste
8 cups washed, dried and torn romaine lettuce
1 cup fat-free croutons
½ cup Caesar Salad Dressing (*recipe follows*)
½ cup Parmesan curls (*see Tip*)
  Lemon wedges

> **TO MAKE PARMESAN CURLS:**
> Start with a piece of cheese that is at least 4 ounces. Use a swivel-bladed vegetable peeler to shave off curls.

1. Prepare a grill or preheat broiler.
2. Rub chicken with oil and season with salt and pepper. Grill or broil chicken until browned and no trace of pink remains in the center, 3 to 4 minutes per side.
3. Combine lettuce and croutons in a large bowl. Toss with Caesar Salad Dressing and divide among 4 plates. Cut chicken into ½-inch slices and fan over salad. Top with Parmesan curls. Serve immediately, with lemon wedges.

Caesar Salad Dressing

Quick ☼ Easy

This dressing has just 13 calories and less than half a gram of fat per tablespoon, compared to 115 calories and 12 grams of fat for its traditional counterpart.

1 clove garlic, crushed
⅓ cup low-fat cottage cheese
½ cup nonfat plain yogurt
¼ cup freshly grated Parmesan cheese
5 teaspoons white-wine vinegar
½ teaspoon Worcestershire sauce
⅛ teaspoon salt, or to taste
  Freshly ground pepper to taste

Puree garlic and cottage cheese in a blender or food processor until smooth. Add yogurt, Parmesan, vinegar and Worcestershire and pulse to blend. Season with salt and pepper.

1

CARBOHYDRATE
SERVING

MAKES 4 SERVINGS

PREP TIME: 15 MINUTES
START TO FINISH: 25 MINUTES

PER SERVING
278 CALORIES
6 G FAT (3 G SAT, 2 G MONO)
76 MG CHOLESTEROL
16 G CARBOHYDRATE
36 G PROTEIN
1 G FIBER
724 MG SODIUM

NUTRITION BONUS: Vitamin A (50% DAILY VALUE), Vitamin C (35% DV), Calcium (25% DV).

EXCHANGES
½ STARCH
2 VEGETABLE
4 VERY LEAN MEAT

For Caesar Salad Dressing:

MAKES ABOUT 1 CUP

PREP TIME: 10 MINUTES
START TO FINISH: 10 MINUTES

TO MAKE AHEAD: Cover and refrigerate for up to 2 days.

PER TABLESPOON
13 CALORIES
0 G FAT (0 G SAT, 0 G MONO)
1 MG CHOLESTEROL
1 G CARBOHYDRATE
1 G PROTEIN
0 G FIBER
62 MG SODIUM

EXCHANGES
FREE FOOD

Grilled Rosemary-Scented Chicken

Grilling chicken breasts on a bed of rosemary sprigs is an effective and easy way to infuse them with flavor. Savory black olive paste, contrasted with a sweet confit of caramelized onion, provides a sophisticated finish.

Sweet & Sour Onion Jam (*recipe follows*)
- 4   boneless, skinless chicken breast halves, trimmed of fat (1-1¼ pounds total)
- 1½   teaspoons extra-virgin olive oil
- ¼   teaspoon salt, or to taste
-   Freshly ground pepper to taste
- 4   large sprigs fresh rosemary
- 4   teaspoons black olive paste (*see Note*)

> **SUBSTITUTION NOTE:** An equal amount of minced black olives can be substituted for the black olive paste.

1. Prepare Sweet & Sour Onion Jam.
2. Prepare a charcoal fire or preheat a gas grill.
3. Rub chicken breasts with oil and season with salt and pepper. Place rosemary sprigs on the grill and lay a chicken breast over each one. Grill until chicken is browned on the bottom, about 5 minutes. Turn, keeping rosemary under chicken, and grill until no trace of pink remains in the center, about 5 minutes more. Discard rosemary. Serve chicken with black olive paste and the onion jam.

Sweet & Sour Onion Jam

Quick ☼ Easy

This is a convenient condiment to keep on hand. It makes a delicious topping for grilled meats and also enlivens sandwich fillings.

- 2   teaspoons extra-virgin olive oil
- 2   large sweet onions, such as Vidalia, halved lengthwise and sliced
- 2½   tablespoons sugar
- 1   large clove garlic, minced
- 1   teaspoon chopped fresh rosemary
- ¼   cup distilled white vinegar, plus more to taste
-   Pinch of salt
-   Freshly ground pepper to taste

1. Heat oil in a 12-inch skillet (not nonstick) over medium heat. Add onions and sugar. Cover and cook, stirring occasionally, until onions are soft and most of their liquid has evaporated, 10 to 20 minutes. Uncover and cook, stirring, until onions turn deep golden, 10 to 20 minutes more. (Add 1 or 2 tablespoons water if onions start to scorch.)
2. Add garlic and rosemary; cook, stirring, until fragrant, about 1 minute. Add ¼ cup vinegar and cook until most of the liquid has evaporated, about 3 minutes. Season with salt, pepper and more vinegar, if desired.

1

CARBOHYDRATE

SERVING

MAKES 4 SERVINGS

PREP TIME: 25 MINUTES
START TO FINISH: 55 MINUTES

PER SERVING
250   CALORIES
9   G FAT (1 G SAT, 4 G MONO)
66   MG CHOLESTEROL
15   G CARBOHYDRATE
27   G PROTEIN
1   G FIBER
287   MG SODIUM

NUTRITION BONUS: Selenium (30% DAILY VALUE).

EXCHANGES
1   OTHER CARBOHYDRATE
4   VERY LEAN MEAT

For Sweet & Sour Onion Jam:

MAKES ABOUT ¾ CUP, FOR 4 SERVINGS

PREP TIME: 10 MINUTES
START TO FINISH: 40 MINUTES

TO MAKE AHEAD: Cover and refrigerate for up to 4 days.

PER SERVING
81   CALORIES
2   G FAT (0 G SAT, 2 G MONO)
0   MG CHOLESTEROL
15   G CARBOHYDRATE
1   G PROTEIN
1   G FIBER
38   MG SODIUM

EXCHANGES
1   OTHER CARBOHYDRATE

CARBOHYDRATE

SERVING

Lemony Sugar Snap & Chicken Stir-Fry

Quick ☼ Easy

This recipe uses the speedy cooking technique of a stir-fry, but instead of the typical Asian seasonings, it is brightened with lemon zest and parsley.

MAKES **4** SERVINGS,
ABOUT **1**½ CUPS EACH

PREP TIME: 20 MINUTES
START TO FINISH: 35 MINUTES

PER SERVING

263 CALORIES

6 G FAT (1 G SAT, 3 G MONO)

68 MG CHOLESTEROL

15 G CARBOHYDRATE

31 G PROTEIN

3 G FIBER

290 MG SODIUM

NUTRITION BONUS: Vitamin C
(26% DAILY VALUE).

EXCHANGES

½ OTHER CARBOHYDRATE

1 VEGETABLE

4 VERY LEAN MEAT

1	pound boneless, skinless chicken breasts, trimmed of fat
¼	teaspoon salt, or to taste
	Freshly ground pepper to taste
⅓	cup all-purpose flour
3	teaspoons extra-virgin olive oil, divided
12	ounces sugar snap peas *or* snow peas (4 cups), trimmed of stem ends and strings
1	14-ounce can reduced-sodium chicken broth
3	cloves garlic, minced
¼	cup finely chopped fresh parsley
1	tablespoon freshly grated lemon zest
1	tablespoon lemon juice

1. Cut chicken into 1-by-2-inch strips; season with salt and pepper. Place flour in a shallow pan and dredge the chicken strips in it, shaking off excess. (Discard any leftover flour.)

2. Heat 1 teaspoon oil in a large nonstick skillet over medium-high heat. Add peas and stir-fry until bright green, 2 to 3 minutes. Transfer to a large bowl.

3. Add the remaining 2 teaspoons oil to the pan and heat on medium-high until shimmering. Add chicken and cook, stirring, until lightly browned and opaque in the center, 4 to 5 minutes. Transfer the chicken to the bowl with the peas.

4. Add broth and garlic to the pan; cook until reduced to 1 cup, 6 to 8 minutes. Reduce heat to medium and return the chicken and peas to the pan. Cook until heated through. Add parsley, lemon zest and lemon juice. Serve immediately.

Sauté of Chicken with Apples & Leeks

Quick ☼ Easy

Fragrant with flavors of fall, this easy chicken sauté turns a weeknight supper into a special occasion.

4	boneless, skinless chicken breast halves (1-1¼ pounds), trimmed of fat
3	teaspoons extra-virgin olive oil, divided
¼	teaspoon salt, or to taste
	Freshly ground pepper to taste
2	large leeks, white parts only, washed and cut into julienne strips (2 cups)
2	large cloves garlic, minced
1	tablespoon sugar
2	teaspoons minced fresh rosemary *or* ½ teaspoon dried
¼	cup cider vinegar
2	firm tart apples, such as York *or* Granny Smith, peeled, cored and thinly sliced
1	cup reduced-sodium chicken broth

1. Place chicken breasts between 2 sheets of plastic wrap. Use a rolling pin or a small heavy pot to pound them to a thickness of ½ inch.
2. Heat 1½ teaspoons oil in a large nonstick skillet over medium-high heat. Season the chicken breasts with salt and pepper and add to the pan. Cook until browned on both sides, 4 to 5 minutes per side. Transfer to a plate and keep warm.
3. Reduce the heat to low. Add the remaining 1½ teaspoons oil and leeks. Cook, stirring, until the leeks are soft, about 5 minutes. Add garlic, sugar and rosemary and cook until fragrant, about 2 minutes more. Increase the heat to medium-high, stir in vinegar and cook until most of the liquid has evaporated.
4. Add apples and broth and cook, stirring once or twice, until the apples are tender, about 3 minutes. Reduce the heat to low and return the chicken and any juices to the pan. Simmer gently until the chicken is heated through. Serve immediately.

1

CARBOHYDRATE
SERVING

MAKES 4 SERVINGS

PREP TIME: 20 MINUTES
START TO FINISH: 40 MINUTES

PER SERVING

239 CALORIES
5 G FAT (1 G SAT, 3 G MONO)
67 MG CHOLESTEROL
20 G CARBOHYDRATE
28 G PROTEIN
2 G FIBER
256 MG SODIUM

NUTRITION BONUS: Vitamin C (18% DAILY VALUE).

EXCHANGES

1 FRUIT
4 VERY LEAN MEAT
1 FAT

1

CARBOHYDRATE

SERVING

MAKES 4 SERVINGS

PREP TIME: 20 MINUTES

START TO FINISH: 30 MINUTES

PER SERVING

268 CALORIES

11 G FAT (1 G SAT, 8 G MONO)

45 MG CHOLESTEROL

13 G CARBOHYDRATE

29 G PROTEIN

0 G FIBER

350 MG SODIUM

NUTRITION BONUS: Iron (10% DAILY VALUE).

EXCHANGES

1 OTHER CARBOHYDRATE

4 LEAN MEAT

Turkey Cutlets with Cider-Dijon Sauce

Quick ☼ Easy

This terrific recipe illustrates the basic principles of a sauté: First dredge the cutlets in flour so they brown beautifully, then cook them quickly in a hot skillet. Finally, splash one or more flavorful liquids (such as wine, broth or, here, cider) into the pan to create an instant sauce.

3	tablespoons instant *or* all-purpose flour
½	teaspoon dried thyme
½	teaspoon dried marjoram
¼	teaspoon salt, or to taste
½	teaspoon freshly ground pepper, plus more to taste
	Pinch of cayenne pepper
1	pound turkey cutlets
3	teaspoons extra-virgin olive oil, divided
1	large shallot, minced
1	cup apple cider *or* unsweetened apple juice
2	tablespoons Dijon mustard

1. Combine flour, thyme, marjoram, salt, pepper and cayenne in a shallow pan. Dredge turkey lightly in the flour mixture, shaking off excess. (Discard any leftover flour.)

2. Heat 1 teaspoon oil in a large skillet over medium-high heat. Add half the turkey and cook until golden outside and no longer pink inside, 1 to 2 minutes per side. Transfer to a plate and tent with foil to keep warm. Sauté the remaining turkey in another 1 teaspoon oil; add to the previous batch.

3. Add the remaining 1 teaspoon oil to the pan. Add shallot and cook, stirring, until softened, about 1 minute. Add cider (or juice) and mustard. Bring to a boil, scraping up any browned bits. Cook until liquid is reduced by half, about 4 minutes. Stir in any accumulated juices from the turkey. Divide turkey among 4 plates and spoon sauce over. Serve immediately.

Overnight Oatmeal (PAGE 57)

THE EATINGWELL DIABETES COOKBOOK

ABOVE: *Fragrant Bulgur Pilaf* (PAGE 236)

OPPOSITE, TOP: *Spicy Mushroom & Rice Soup* (PAGE 103)

OPPOSITE, BOTTOM: *Green Mango Salad* (PAGE 115)

ABOVE: *Roasted Corn, Black Bean & Mango Salad* (PAGE 118)

OPPOSITE, TOP: *Spiced Apple Butter Bran Muffins* (PAGE 69)

OPPOSITE, BOTTOM: *Scrambled Egg Burritos* (PAGE 59)

Mixed Greens with Berries & Honey-Glazed Hazelnuts (PAGE 110)

Asian Chicken Salad (PAGE 153)

Shrimp Spedini with Basil & Peppers (PAGE 189)

THE EATINGWELL DIABETES COOKBOOK

Zucchini Frittata (PAGE 48)

ABOVE: *Lamb Chops with a Mustard Crust* (PAGE 210)

OPPOSITE: *Rosemary & Garlic Crusted Pork Loin with
Butternut Squash & Potatoes* (PAGE 225)

ABOVE: *Southwestern Steak & Peppers* (PAGE 222)

OPPOSITE: *Turkey Potpie* (PAGE 182)

ABOVE: *Roasted Pineapple Shortcakes* (PAGE 274)
OPPOSITE: *Mixed Berry-Almond Gratin* (PAGE 285)

THE EATINGWELL DIABETES COOKBOOK

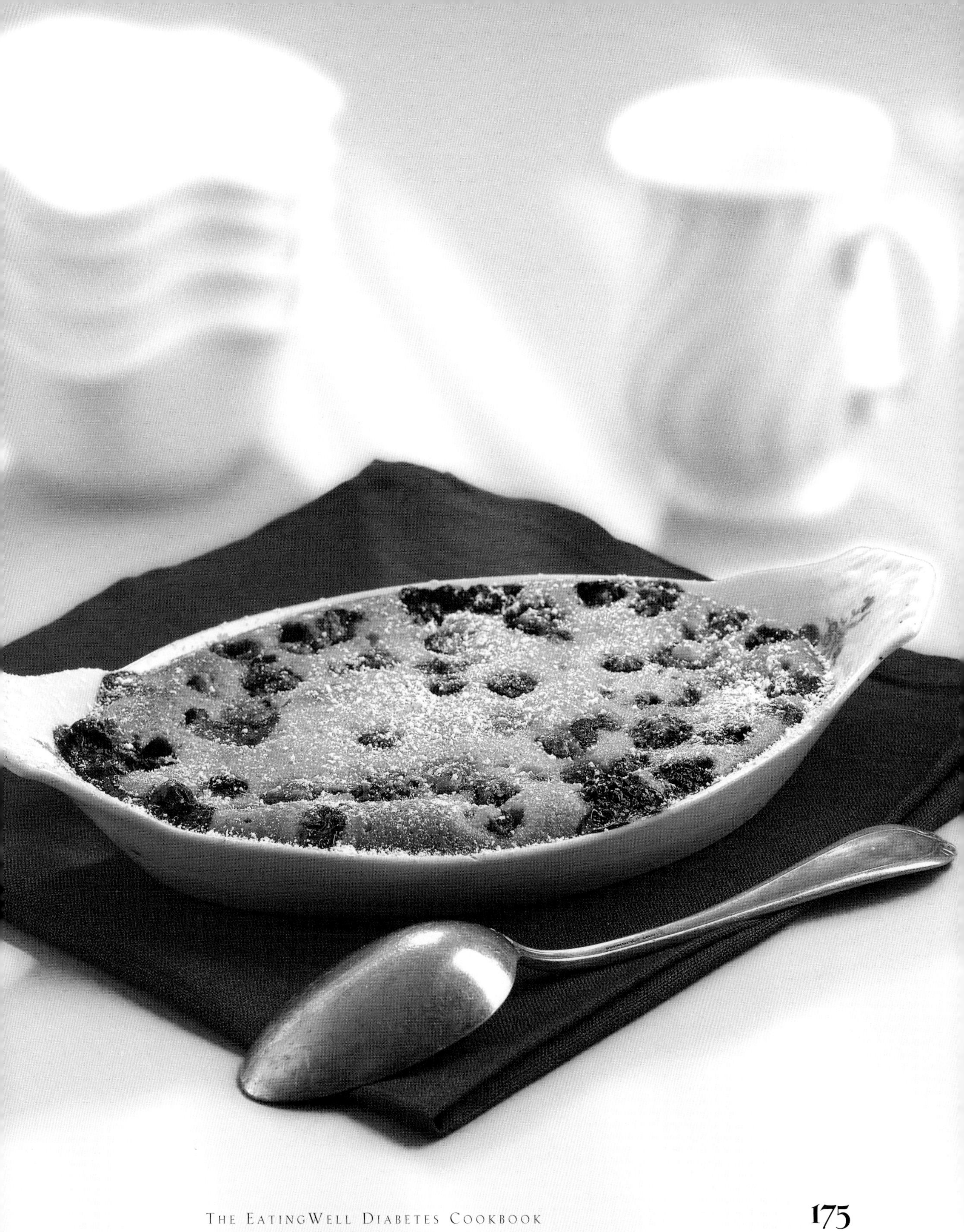

Strawberries-and-Cream Parfaits (PAGE 277)

Chicken Tabbouleh

High ⬆ Fiber   Quick ☼ Easy

On a hot summer day, make this hearty salad using roasted chicken from the deli counter and whole-grain bulgur (it doesn't require cooking, just plumping in hot water). Round out the meal with tomato wedges and Toasted Pita Crisps (*page 83*).

1¹⁄₂
CARBOHYDRATE
SERVINGS

3	**cups water**
1	**cup bulgur (*see Ingredient Note, page 323*)**
3	**cups cubed skinless cooked chicken (1-inch cubes) (*see box, below*)**
1	**cup chopped fresh parsley**
1	**cup chopped scallions**
¹⁄₃	**cup currants**
¹⁄₄	**cup frozen orange juice concentrate**
2	**tablespoons lemon juice**
1	**tablespoon extra-virgin olive oil**
1	**teaspoon ground cumin**
¹⁄₄	**teaspoon cayenne pepper, or to taste**
¹⁄₄	**teaspoon salt, or to taste**
	Freshly ground pepper to taste

1. Bring water to a boil in a large saucepan. Add bulgur and remove from the heat. Let stand until most of the water is absorbed, 20 to 30 minutes.
2. Drain bulgur well, squeezing out excess moisture. Transfer to a large bowl. Add chicken, parsley, scallions and currants.
3. Whisk orange juice concentrate, lemon juice, oil, cumin and cayenne in a small bowl until blended. Toss with the bulgur mixture. Season with salt and pepper and serve.

> **TO POACH CHICKEN:**
> Combine two 14-ounce cans reduced-sodium chicken broth, 2 chopped scallions, 2 slivers fresh ginger (optional) and 2 cloves garlic in a large skillet; bring to a simmer. Add 1½ pounds boneless, skinless chicken breast and cook over medium heat until no longer pink inside, 10 to 15 minutes. The flavorful poaching liquid will keep, tightly covered, in the refrigerator for up to 2 days or in the freezer for up to 6 months.

MAKES 6 SERVINGS,
ABOUT 1¹⁄₃ CUPS EACH

PREP TIME: 20 MINUTES
START TO FINISH: 40 MINUTES

TEST KITCHEN TIP
One 2-pound roasted chicken yields approximately 1 pound (4 cups) of meat.

PER SERVING
260 CALORIES
5 G FAT (1 G SAT, 3 G MONO)
54 MG CHOLESTEROL
31 G CARBOHYDRATE
24 G PROTEIN
6 G FIBER
157 MG SODIUM

NUTRITION BONUS: Vitamin C (60% DAILY VALUE), Fiber (24% DV).

EXCHANGES
2 STARCH
3 VERY LEAN MEAT

Curried Chicken Wraps

Quick ☀ Easy

This East-West fusion "burrito" combines a quick curried stir-fry with sweet grapes and healthy, convenient whole-wheat tortillas. Any leftover filling makes a delicious cold wrap sandwich the following day.

1½	cups Cucumber Raita (*page 261*)
8	10-inch whole-wheat tortillas
1	pound boneless, skinless chicken breasts, trimmed of fat
1	tablespoon canola oil
½	cup chopped scallions (1 bunch)
1	tablespoon minced fresh ginger
1	tablespoon freshly grated orange zest, preferably organic
1	tablespoon minced jalapeño *or* serrano pepper (2 small peppers)
1	teaspoon curry powder
1	tablespoon rice wine, sake *or* orange juice
½	teaspoon salt, or to taste
	Freshly ground pepper to taste
1½	cups red seedless grapes (8 ounces), washed, dried and halved

1. Prepare Cucumber Raita.
2. Preheat oven to 300°F. Wrap tortillas in foil and bake until heated through, 10 to 15 minutes.
3. Meanwhile, cut chicken into ¼-inch-thick slices. Turn slices on their sides and cut into ¼-inch strips.
4. Heat a wok or large nonstick skillet over medium-high heat. Add oil and tilt pan to coat it evenly. Add scallions, ginger, orange zest and jalapeño (or serrano). Cook, stirring, until fragrant, about 1 minute.
5. Add chicken; stir-fry for 1 minute. Add curry powder, rice wine (or sake or orange juice), salt and pepper. Cook, stirring, until chicken is browned and no longer pink in the center, about 2 minutes. Transfer to a medium bowl. Add grapes; toss to mix.
6. To assemble wraps: Spoon about ½ cup of the chicken mixture into each warm tortilla. Top with 2 tablespoons Cucumber Raita. Roll up the tortilla and serve with the remaining raita for dipping.

2
CARBOHYDRATE
SERVINGS

MAKES 8 SERVINGS, 1 WRAP EACH

PREP TIME: 15 MINUTES
START TO FINISH: 20 MINUTES

PER SERVING

180 CALORIES
3 G FAT (0 G SAT, 1 G MONO)
33 MG CHOLESTEROL
27 G CARBOHYDRATE
17 G PROTEIN
3 G FIBER
359 MG SODIUM

NUTRITION BONUS: Niacin (50% DAILY VALUE), Selenium (15% DV).

EXCHANGES

1½ STARCH
1 VEGETABLE
2 VERY LEAN MEAT

Honey-Mustard Turkey Burgers

High ⬆ Fiber   Quick ☼ Easy

Burgers made with ground turkey are a lean alternative to beef burgers, providing you choose turkey ground from the breast. Regular ground turkey, which is a mixture of light and dark meat and some skin, contains almost as much fat as lean ground beef. A honey-mustard mixture keeps these low-fat patties moist and succulent.

- ¼ cup coarse-grained mustard
- 2 tablespoons honey
- 1 pound ground turkey breast
- ¼ teaspoon salt, or to taste
- ¼ teaspoon freshly ground pepper
- 2 teaspoons canola oil
- 4 whole-wheat hamburger rolls, split and toasted
  Lettuce, tomato slices and red onion slices for garnish

1. Prepare a grill.
2. Whisk mustard and honey in a small bowl until smooth.
3. Combine turkey, 3 tablespoons of the mustard mixture, salt and pepper in a bowl; mix well. Form into four 1-inch-thick burgers.
4. Lightly brush the burgers on both sides with oil. Grill until no pink remains in center, 5 to 7 minutes per side. Brush the burgers with the remaining mustard mixture. Serve on rolls with lettuce, tomato and onion slices.

2

CARBOHYDRATE
SERVINGS

MAKES 4 SERVINGS

PREP TIME: 10 MINUTES
START TO FINISH: 25 MINUTES

NUTRITION NOTE: Ground turkey breast has 6 grams of fat per pound, compared to 32 grams of fat in regular ground turkey, which contains leg meat.

PER SERVING
(WITHOUT GARNISHES)

313	CALORIES
6	G FAT (0 G SAT, 1 G MONO)
45	MG CHOLESTEROL
39	G CARBOHYDRATE
32	G PROTEIN
5	G FIBER
526	MG SODIUM

NUTRITION BONUS: Folate (20% DAILY VALUE), Iron (20% DV), Calcium (15% DV).

EXCHANGES
2 STARCH
4 LEAN MEAT

2

CARBOHYDRATE
SERVINGS

**MAKES 4 SERVINGS,
2½ CUPS EACH**

PREP TIME: 30 MINUTES
START TO FINISH: 40 MINUTES

TO MAKE AHEAD: The dressing
will keep, covered, in the
refrigerator for up to 2 days.

TO TOAST ALMONDS
Spread on a baking sheet and bake
at 350°F until golden brown and
fragrant, 5 to 7 minutes. Toasted
almonds will keep, tightly covered,
at room temperature for up to 1
week.

PER SERVING
456 CALORIES
20 G FAT (3 G SAT, 13 G MONO)
66 MG CHOLESTEROL
38 G CARBOHYDRATE
35 G PROTEIN
10 G FIBER
434 MG SODIUM

NUTRITION BONUS: Vitamin A
(230% DAILY VALUE), Vitamin C
(110% DV), Fiber (41% DV).

EXCHANGES
1 FRUIT
3 VEGETABLE
4 LEAN MEAT
1 FAT (MONO)

Romaine Salad with Chicken, Apricots & Mint

High ⬆ Fiber   Quick ☼ Easy

This bright and summery entree salad, which uses a savory apricot puree as both marinade and dressing, makes a refreshing change from the standby Chicken Caesar. The salad also works well with sliced peaches or nectarines.

MARINADE & DRESSING
½ cup dried apricots
1 cup hot water
2 cups loosely packed mint leaves (about 1 bunch)
1 teaspoon freshly grated orange zest
½ cup orange juice
2 tablespoons honey
4 teaspoons Dijon mustard
4 teaspoons red-wine vinegar
½ teaspoon salt, or to taste
Freshly ground pepper to taste
¼ cup extra-virgin olive oil

SALAD
1 pound boneless, skinless chicken breast, trimmed of fat
1 large head romaine lettuce, torn into bite-size pieces (10 cups)
6 fresh apricots *or* plums, pitted and cut into wedges
1 cup loosely packed mint leaves (about ½ bunch), roughly chopped
½ cup sliced almonds, toasted (*see Tip*)

1. Preheat grill.
2. **To prepare marinade & dressing:** Soak dried apricots in hot water for 10 minutes. Drain and transfer apricots to a food processor. Add 2 cups mint, orange zest, orange juice, honey, mustard, vinegar, salt and pepper. Process until smooth. With the motor running, gradually drizzle in oil. Reserve 1 cup for the dressing.
3. **To prepare salad:** Transfer the remaining marinade to a large sealable plastic bag. Add chicken, seal and turn to coat. Marinate in the refrigerator for 20 minutes.
4. Lightly oil the grill rack (hold a piece of oil-soaked paper towel with tongs and rub it over the grate). Grill the chicken over medium-high heat until no longer pink in the center, 6 to 8 minutes per side. (Discard the marinade.)
5. Meanwhile, combine lettuce, apricot (or plum) wedges and chopped mint in a large bowl. Add the reserved dressing and toss to coat. Divide the salad among 4 plates. Slice the chicken and arrange over the salads. Sprinkle with almonds and serve.

Spicy Chicken Tacos

High ⬆ Fiber   Quick ☀ Easy

While many North Americans think of tacos as having crisp, fried shells, authentic Mexican tacos are made with soft, fresh corn tortillas. It's also a smart choice, as unfried corn tortillas are low in fat and made with whole grains.

8	corn tortillas
1	pound boneless, skinless chicken breasts, trimmed of fat and cut into thin strips
¼	teaspoon salt, or to taste
2	teaspoons canola oil, divided
1	large onion, sliced
1	large green bell pepper, seeded and sliced
3	large cloves garlic, minced
1	jalapeño pepper, seeded and minced
1	tablespoon ground cumin
½	cup prepared hot salsa, plus more for garnish
¼	cup chopped fresh cilantro
	Sliced scallions, chopped fresh tomatoes and reduced-fat sour cream for garnish

1. Preheat oven to 300°F. Wrap tortillas in foil and bake until heated through, 10 to 15 minutes.
2. Meanwhile, season chicken with salt. Heat 1 teaspoon oil in a large heavy skillet over high heat until very hot. Add chicken and cook, stirring until browned on all sides, about 6 minutes. Transfer to a bowl.
3. Reduce heat to medium and add the remaining 1 teaspoon oil to skillet. Add onion and cook, stirring, until they start to brown around the edges, 3 to 5 minutes. Add bell peppers, garlic, jalapeños and cumin. Cook, stirring, until peppers are bright green but still crisp, 2 to 3 minutes more.
4. Stir in salsa and reserved chicken. Cook, stirring, until chicken is heated through, about 2 minutes. Remove from heat and stir in cilantro. Spoon into warmed tortillas and garnish with scallions, tomatoes and sour cream.

2 CARBOHYDRATE SERVINGS

MAKES 4 SERVINGS, 2 TACOS EACH

PREP TIME: 20 MINUTES
START TO FINISH: 35 MINUTES

PER SERVING (WITHOUT GARNISHES)
308 CALORIES
6 G FAT (1 G SAT, 2 G MONO)
66 MG CHOLESTEROL
34 G CARBOHYDRATE
31 G PROTEIN
5 G FIBER
504 MG SODIUM

NUTRITION BONUS: Vitamin C (68% DAILY VALUE), Folate (25% DV), Fiber (20% DV).

EXCHANGES
2 STARCH
1 VEGETABLE
3½ VERY LEAN MEAT

Turkey Potpie

The familiar blend of poultry, vegetables and pastry is a comforting part of American food culture, but traditional versions are not as nourishing as the cozy name implies. Our enlightened potpie uses reduced-fat sour cream to make a rich sauce and tops the filling with scrumptious whole-wheat buttermilk biscuits. (*Photograph: page 172.*)

MAKES 6 SERVINGS

PREP TIME: 15 MINUTES

START TO FINISH: 1 HOUR 5 MINUTES

PER SERVING

375 CALORIES

11 G FAT (4 G SAT, 4 G MONO)

55 MG CHOLESTEROL

39 G CARBOHYDRATE

26 G PROTEIN

4 G FIBER

666 MG SODIUM

NUTRITION BONUS: Vitamin A (70% DAILY VALUE), Fiber (16% DV).

EXCHANGES

2 STARCH

1 VEGETABLE

3 LEAN MEAT

FILLING

3 teaspoons canola oil, divided

1 cup frozen small onions, thawed

1 cup peeled baby carrots

10 ounces cremini mushrooms, wiped clean and halved

2½ cups reduced-sodium chicken broth, divided

¼ cup cornstarch

2½ cups diced cooked turkey *or* chicken

1 cup frozen peas, thawed

¼ cup reduced-fat sour cream

¼ teaspoon salt, or to taste

Freshly ground pepper to taste

BISCUIT TOPPING

¾ cup whole-wheat pastry flour

¾ cup all-purpose flour

2 teaspoons sugar

1¼ teaspoons baking powder

½ teaspoon baking soda

½ teaspoon salt

1 teaspoon dried thyme

1½ tablespoons cold butter, cut into small pieces

1 cup buttermilk *or* equivalent buttermilk powder (*see page 323*)

1 tablespoon canola oil

1. **To prepare filling:** Heat 1 teaspoon oil in a large skillet or Dutch oven over medium-high heat. Add onions and carrots; cook, stirring, until golden brown and tender, about 7 minutes. Transfer to a bowl. Heat the remaining 2 teaspoons oil in the pan over medium-high heat. Add mushrooms and cook, stirring often, until browned and their liquid has evaporated, 5 to 7 minutes. Return the onions and carrots to the pan. Add 2 cups broth and bring to a boil; reduce heat to a simmer. Mix cornstarch with the remaining ½ cup broth; add to the pan and cook, stirring, until the sauce thickens. Stir in turkey (or chicken), peas, sour cream, salt and pepper. Transfer the filling to a 2-quart baking dish.

2. **To prepare biscuit topping & bake potpie:** Preheat oven to 400°F. Whisk whole-wheat flour, all-purpose flour, sugar, baking powder, baking soda, salt and thyme in a large bowl. Using your fingertips or 2 knives, cut butter into the dry ingredients until crumbly. Add buttermilk and oil; stir until just combined. Drop the dough onto the filling in 5 or 6 even portions. Set the baking dish on a baking sheet.

3. Bake the potpie until the topping is golden and the filling is bubbling, 30 to 35 minutes. Let cool for 10 minutes; serve.

Easy Chicken Burritos

High ⬆ Fiber   Quick ☀ Easy

This is a great way to turn leftover cooked chicken (or supermarket rotisserie chicken) into a healthful lunch or supper that's sure to be a hit with kids.

4	cups shredded skinless cooked chicken
½	cup prepared barbecue sauce
1	cup canned black beans, rinsed
½	cup corn kernels (frozen, thawed, *or* canned, drained)
¼	cup reduced-fat sour cream
4	leaves romaine lettuce
4	10-inch whole-wheat tortillas
2	limes, cut in wedges

1. Combine chicken, barbecue sauce, beans, corn and sour cream in a large nonstick skillet. Cook over medium-high heat, stirring often, until heated through, 4 to 5 minutes.
2. **To assemble wraps:** Place a lettuce leaf in the center of each tortilla and top with one-fourth of the chicken mixture; roll as you would a burrito. Slice in half diagonally and serve warm, with a wedge of lime.

White Chili

High ⬆ Fiber   Quick ☀ Easy

This fragrant "white" chili is an unusual, delicious alternative to traditional tomato-based chilis. Serve with lime wedges and a dollop of sour cream or a sprinkling of cheese.

1	tablespoon canola oil
1½	cups chopped onion
2	4-ounce cans chopped green chiles
1	teaspoon dried oregano
1	teaspoon ground cumin
⅛-¼	teaspoon cayenne pepper
3	15-ounce cans great northern beans, rinsed
4	cups reduced-sodium chicken broth
4	cups diced cooked skinless turkey *or* chicken
2	tablespoons cider vinegar

Heat oil in a large pot or Dutch oven over medium-high heat. Add onion; cook, stirring occasionally, until softened, about 5 minutes. Stir in chiles, oregano, cumin and cayenne. Cook, stirring occasionally, for 5 minutes. Stir in beans and broth; bring to a simmer. Cook, stirring occasionally, for 20 minutes. Add turkey (or chicken) and vinegar; cook for 5 minutes more. Serve.

2½
CARBOHYDRATE
SERVINGS

MAKES 4 SERVINGS, 1 WRAP EACH

PREP TIME: 5 MINUTES
START TO FINISH: 10 MINUTES

PER SERVING
371 CALORIES
9 G FAT (3 G SAT, 3 G MONO)
82 MG CHOLESTEROL
44 G CARBOHYDRATE
34 G PROTEIN
6 G FIBER
604 MG SODIUM

NUTRITION BONUS: Fiber (24% DAILY VALUE), Iron (20% DV).

EXCHANGES
2½ STARCH
1 VEGETABLE
4 VERY LEAN MEAT

For White Chili:

3
CARBOHYDRATE
SERVINGS

MAKES 6 SERVINGS, 1⅓ CUPS EACH

PREP TIME: 10 MINUTES
START TO FINISH: 45 MINUTES

PER SERVING
453 CALORIES
7 G FAT (2 G SAT, 2 G MONO)
68 MG CHOLESTEROL
52 G CARBOHYDRATE
47 G PROTEIN
11 G FIBER
215 MG SODIUM

NUTRITION BONUS: Niacin (80% DAILY VALUE), Fiber (45% DV), Vitamin C (30% DV), Iron (25% DV).

EXCHANGES
3 STARCH
1 VEGETABLE
5 VERY LEAN MEAT

CHAPTER EIGHT

Fish & Seafood

Halibut Picante

Quick ☼ Easy

Fish cookery doesn't get any easier than this. Look for the freshest fish you can find—just about any firm, mild white fish will be a fine foil for this spicy tomato sauce.

O

CARBOHYDRATE
SERVINGS

MAKES 4 SERVINGS

PREP TIME: 10 MINUTES

START TO FINISH: 25 MINUTES

PER SERVING

188 CALORIES

5 G FAT (1 G SAT, 3 G MONO)

45 MG CHOLESTEROL

3 G CARBOHYDRATE

30 G PROTEIN

1 G FIBER

673 MG SODIUM

EXCHANGES

4 VERY LEAN MEAT

1 FAT (MONO)

1¼ pounds halibut, striped bass *or* tilapia fillet, cut into 4 portions
1 teaspoon ground cumin, divided
¼ teaspoon salt, or to taste
Freshly ground pepper to taste
1 10-ounce can diced tomatoes with green chiles
¼ cup sliced green olives with pimientos
2 tablespoons chopped fresh cilantro
1 teaspoon extra-virgin olive oil

1. Preheat oven to 450°F. Coat a baking sheet with cooking spray. Arrange fish on baking sheet. Season with ½ teaspoon cumin, salt and pepper.
2. Combine tomatoes, olives, cilantro, oil and the remaining ½ teaspoon cumin in a small bowl. Spoon over the fish.
3. Bake the fish until flaky and opaque in the center, 12 to 15 minutes. Serve immediately.

Halibut with Herbs & Capers

Quick ☼ Easy

A vibrant herb paste brings robust flavor to a delicate fish.

- ¼ cup chopped onion
- ¼ cup fresh parsley leaves
- 1 tablespoon fresh cilantro leaves
- 2 teaspoons freshly grated lemon zest
- 1 tablespoon lemon juice
- 1 tablespoon chopped pitted green olives
- 2 teaspoons drained capers, rinsed
- 1 clove garlic, minced
- ⅛ teaspoon freshly ground pepper
- 2 tablespoons extra-virgin olive oil
- 1 1-pound halibut fillet, cut into 4 portions

1. Place onion, parsley, cilantro, lemon zest, lemon juice, olives, capers, garlic and pepper in a food processor; pulse several times to chop. Add oil and process, scraping down the sides several times, until a pesto-like paste forms. Pat halibut with the herb paste. Cover and refrigerate for 30 minutes.
2. Preheat oven to 450°F. Coat a 7-by-11-inch baking dish with cooking spray. Arrange the halibut in the dish and spoon any extra herb mixture on top. Bake, uncovered, until the fish is opaque in the center, 15 to 20 minutes. Serve immediately.

O

CARBOHYDRATE
SERVINGS

MAKES 4 SERVINGS

PREP TIME: 15 MINUTES
START TO FINISH: 40 MINUTES

PER SERVING

- 199 CALORIES
- 10 G FAT (1 G SAT, 6 G MONO)
- 36 MG CHOLESTEROL
- 2 G CARBOHYDRATE
- 24 G PROTEIN
- 1 G FIBER
- 125 MG SODIUM

NUTRITION BONUS: Selenium (60% DAILY VALUE), Vitamin C (15% DV).

EXCHANGES

- 3 VERY LEAN MEAT
- 2 FAT (MONO)

Herbed Scallop Kebabs

Quick ☼ Easy

Grilled under a watchful eye to avoid overcooking, these skewers are a snap to prepare. A light lemon-and-herb marinade allows the sweet, succulent flavor of the scallops to shine. Be sure to purchase sea scallops, which are a good size for kebabs.

MAKES 4 SERVINGS

PREP TIME: 20 MINUTES

START TO FINISH: 30-35 MINUTES

PER SERVING

152 CALORIES

3 G FAT (0 G SAT, 2 G MONO)

47 MG CHOLESTEROL

5 G CARBOHYDRATE

24 G PROTEIN

0 G FIBER

374 MG SODIUM

NUTRITION BONUS: Selenium (44% DAILY VALUE), Vitamin C (20% DV).

EXCHANGES

3½ VERY LEAN MEAT

3	tablespoons lemon juice
1½	tablespoons chopped fresh thyme
2	teaspoons extra-virgin olive oil
2	teaspoons freshly grated lemon zest
1	teaspoon freshly ground pepper
¼	teaspoon salt, or to taste
1¼	pounds sea scallops, trimmed
1	lemon, cut into 8 wedges

1. Preheat grill to medium-high. Place a fine-mesh nonstick grill topper on grill to heat.
2. Whisk lemon juice, thyme, oil, lemon zest, pepper and salt in a small bowl.
3. Toss scallops with 2 tablespoons of the lemon mixture; reserve the remaining mixture for basting the kebabs. Thread the scallops and the lemon wedges onto four 10-inch-long skewers, placing 6 to 7 scallops and 2 lemon wedges on each skewer.
4. Lightly oil the grill rack (hold a piece of oil-soaked paper towel with tongs and rub it over the grate). Cook the kebabs, turning from time to time and basting with the reserved lemon mixture, until the scallops are opaque in the center, 8 to 12 minutes. Serve immediately.

Shrimp Spedini with Basil & Peppers

Spedini are Italian kebabs. These shrimp ones are packed with flavor, thanks to their skewers: sprigs of fresh rosemary. You'll need fairly stiff branches, the sort you find on a small rosemary bush at a plant shop and often in plastic bags in the supermarket produce section. For a simplified version, use bamboo skewers. (*Photograph: page 168.*)

24	large shrimp, peeled and deveined (about 12 ounces)
1	tablespoon lemon juice
1	tablespoon extra-virgin olive oil
1	clove garlic, minced
12	stiff sprigs fresh rosemary, each 4 to 5 inches long
½	small red bell pepper, cut into 1-inch triangles
½	small yellow bell pepper, cut into 1-inch triangles
12	leaves fresh basil, rinsed
¼	teaspoon salt, or to taste
	Freshly ground pepper to taste

1. Combine shrimp, lemon juice, oil and garlic in a glass bowl and toss to mix. Cover and refrigerate for 15 minutes. Drain, discarding marinade.

2. Preheat grill to medium-high.

3. **To prepare spedini:** Strip the leaves off the bottom 2 inches of each rosemary sprig. Use a wooden or metal skewer to pierce holes in peppers and the shrimp, then thread a piece of red pepper, followed by 2 shrimp (through head and tail), yellow pepper and a basil leaf on each rosemary sprig. Season the shrimp with salt and pepper.

4. Lightly oil the grill rack (hold a piece of oil-soaked paper towel with tongs and rub it over the grate). Grill the spedini until the shrimp are pink and opaque in the center, 2 to 3 minutes per side.

O

CARBOHYDRATE
SERVINGS

MAKES 12 SPEDINI,
FOR 3 MAIN-DISH *OR*
6 APPETIZER SERVINGS

PREP TIME: 30 MINUTES
START TO FINISH: 1 HOUR

PER MAIN-DISH SERVING
156 CALORIES
4 G FAT (1 G SAT, 2 G MONO)
172 MG CHOLESTEROL
4 G CARBOHYDRATE
24 G PROTEIN
1 G FIBER
363 MG SODIUM

NUTRITION BONUS: Vitamin C
(140% DAILY VALUE), Selenium
(61% DV), Iron (15% DV).

EXCHANGES
3½ VERY LEAN MEAT
1 FAT

Coconut-Curry Salmon Kebabs

Coconut milk and curry seasonings give these salmon kebabs an enticing tropical fragrance. Sugarcane makes interesting skewers and imparts a subtle sweetness to the salmon. If unavailable, use small bamboo skewers.

MARINADE & SAUCE

1	cup canned "lite" coconut milk (*see Ingredient Note, page 323*)
½	red bell pepper, coarsely chopped
2	scallions, whites coarsely chopped, greens finely chopped for garnish
2	tablespoons chopped fresh cilantro *or* parsley
1	jalapeño pepper, seeded and coarsely chopped
1	clove garlic, coarsely chopped
2	tablespoons lime juice
2	teaspoons curry powder
½	teaspoon salt, or to taste
	Freshly ground pepper to taste

KEBABS

6	sugarcane swizzle sticks, about 8 inches long (*see Note*)
1½	pounds salmon fillet
1	lime, cut into wedges, for garnish

1. **To prepare marinade:** Place coconut milk, bell pepper, scallion whites, cilantro (or parsley), jalapeño, garlic, lime juice, curry powder, salt and pepper in a food processor or blender and puree. Measure out ½ cup and refrigerate to use as a sauce in Step 4.

2. **To prepare kebabs:** Cut each swizzle stick in half crosswise, angling your knife so the cuts form sharp points.

3. Remove salmon skin and cut the salmon into 12 strips about 3½ inches long and 1 inch wide. Using a metal skewer, make a lengthwise tunnel through each salmon strip. Insert a piece of sugarcane through this tunnel. Arrange the resulting kebabs in a baking dish. Pour the marinade over the kebabs, turning several times. Cover and marinate in the refrigerator for at least 2 hours or for up to 4 hours.

4. Preheat grill to high. Lightly oil the grill rack (hold a piece of oil-soaked paper towel with tongs and rub it over the grate). Arrange the kebabs diagonally on the grill. Grill, turning as necessary, until cooked through, 2 to 3 minutes per side. Transfer to a platter, sprinkle with the reserved scallion greens and serve immediately, with lime wedges and the reserved sauce.

O

CARBOHYDRATE
SERVINGS

MAKES 6 SERVINGS

PREP TIME: 40 MINUTES

START TO FINISH: 2 HOURS
50 MINUTES

INGREDIENT NOTE
Melissa's (www.melissas.com) and Frieda's (www.friedas.com) sell vacuum-packed, precut sugarcane swizzle sticks, which are terrific for grilling pork, chicken, shrimp and even fruit (*see Sources, page 323*).

PER SERVING

234 CALORIES
14 G FAT (4 G SAT, 4 G MONO)
67 MG CHOLESTEROL
2 G CARBOHYDRATE
23 G PROTEIN
0 G FIBER
199 MG SODIUM

NUTRITION BONUS: Selenium (60% DAILY VALUE), Vitamin C (30% DV).

EXCHANGES
3 LEAN MEAT
1 FAT (SATURATED)

Crab Salad with Pimiento Mayonnaise

Quick ☼ Easy

Pimientos and a touch of cayenne enrich a light creamy dressing for a luxurious but healthful seafood salad that makes a sensational lunch or light supper.

¼	cup nonfat plain yogurt
2	tablespoons reduced-fat mayonnaise
2	tablespoons pimientos, rinsed and patted dry
1	small clove garlic, minced
⅛	teaspoon salt, or to taste
⅛	teaspoon cayenne pepper, or to taste
2⅔	cups cooked crab *or* lobster meat, picked over
6	cups mixed salad greens
	Lemon wedges for garnish

1. Combine yogurt, mayonnaise, pimientos, garlic, salt and cayenne in a blender. Blend until smooth. Scrape into a bowl and mix in crab (or lobster). Adjust seasoning with salt and cayenne.
2. Divide greens among 4 large plates and spoon salad on top. Serve with lemon wedges.

O

CARBOHYDRATE
SERVINGS

MAKES 4 SERVINGS

PREP TIME: 20 MINUTES
START TO FINISH: 20 MINUTES

PER SERVING

107 CALORIES
2 G FAT (0 G SAT, 0 G MONO)
71 MG CHOLESTEROL
5 G CARBOHYDRATE
18 G PROTEIN
2 G FIBER
378 MG SODIUM

NUTRITION BONUS: Vitamin A (50% DAILY VALUE), Vitamin C (35% DV), Folate (34% DV), Zinc (27% DV).

EXCHANGES

1 VEGETABLE
3 VERY LEAN MEAT

$1/2$
CARBOHYDRATE
SERVING

MAKES 4 SERVINGS

PREP TIME: 20 MINUTES
START TO FINISH: 30 MINUTES

INGREDIENT NOTES
Miso (fermented bean paste) and mirin (a low-alcohol sweet rice wine) are sold at health-food stores and Asian markets. The dry rice wine called sake is generally available where wines are sold.

Pickled ginger is found at natural-foods stores, Asian markets and in the produce department of some supermarkets.

PER SERVING
258 CALORIES
5 G FAT (1 G SAT, 2 G MONO)
54 MG CHOLESTEROL
9 G CARBOHYDRATE
37 G PROTEIN
0 G FIBER
562 MG SODIUM

NUTRITION BONUS: Selenium (89% DAILY VALUE), Magnesium (37% DV).

EXCHANGES
1/2 OTHER CARBOHYDRATE
5 VERY LEAN MEAT

Broiled Halibut with Miso Glaze
Quick ☼ Easy

Miso, mirin and sake—three standard ingredients used in Japanese cooking—enhance the mild sweetness of halibut. Deboning halibut steaks is actually a simple procedure, which creates delightful tender morsels of fish. You can substitute halibut fillet, if desired.

¼	cup shiro miso (sweet white miso paste) (*see Note*)
2	tablespoons Japanese sake *or* Chinese rice wine
2	tablespoons mirin
1½	pounds halibut steak
1	tablespoon sesame seeds
	Lime wedges for garnish
	Pickled ginger for garnish (*see Note*)

1. Whisk miso, sake (or rice wine) and mirin in a small bowl into a smooth paste.
2. With a large sharp boning knife, remove skin from halibut steaks. Following the natural divisions created by the bone and cartilage, cut fish from the bone to create 4 small boneless steaks (also called medallions). Trim any dark areas.
3. Preheat broiler. Line a heavy baking sheet with foil and coat the foil with cooking spray.
4. Place the halibut medallions on the prepared baking sheet and brush the tops with half the miso glaze. Broil, 3 to 4 inches from the flame, until golden brown, 4 to 5 minutes. Turn the medallions over and brush with the remaining miso mixture. Sprinkle sesame seeds on top and broil until the fish is opaque in the center, 3 to 4 minutes. Serve with lime wedges and pickled ginger.

Baja-Style Shrimp

Quick ☀ Easy

Inspired by the famous fish tacos served up on the Baja Peninsula, this tequila- and lime-spiked sauté should be served with warm corn tortillas (though it's nice with rice too). You might not think of pairing shrimp with cabbage, but the marriage is magical, especially when accented by garlic, chiles and cilantro.

MARINADE & SHRIMP

- 2 tablespoons tequila
- 1 tablespoon lime juice
- ½ teaspoon salt, or to taste
- 1 pound shrimp (30-40 per pound), peeled and deveined

SAUCE

- 3 teaspoons extra-virgin olive oil, divided
- 2 cloves garlic, minced
- ¼ teaspoon ground cumin
- 3 cups shredded Savoy *or* green cabbage (*see Tip*)
- 1 medium tomato, chopped
- 1 jalapeño pepper, seeded and minced
- 4 scallions, thinly sliced (⅔ cup)
- ¼ cup chopped fresh cilantro
- 2 tablespoons lime juice

1. Combine tequila, lime juice and salt in a medium bowl. Add the shrimp and toss to coat. Cover and marinate in the refrigerator for 10 to 15 minutes, tossing occasionally. Drain well, reserving marinade.

2. Heat 1 teaspoon oil in a 12-inch nonstick skillet over medium-high heat. Add the shrimp and cook, turning once, until barely pink, about 30 seconds per side; transfer to a plate. Add the remaining 2 teaspoons oil to the pan. Add garlic and cumin; cook, stirring, until fragrant, about 30 seconds. Stir in cabbage, tomato and jalapeño; cook until the cabbage starts to soften, 3 to 4 minutes. Add the reserved marinade; simmer for 2 minutes. Add scallions and return the shrimp and any accumulated juices to the pan; heat through. Serve immediately, sprinkled with cilantro and lime juice.

½

CARBOHYDRATE
SERVING

MAKES **4 SERVINGS,**
1 GENEROUS CUP EACH

PREP TIME: 30 MINUTES (including peeling shrimp)

START TO FINISH: 40 MINUTES

TEST KITCHEN TIP
To cut down on prep time, use packaged coleslaw mix.

PER SERVING

194 CALORIES
6 G FAT (1 G SAT, 3 G MONO)
172 MG CHOLESTEROL
7 G CARBOHYDRATE
25 G PROTEIN
2 G FIBER
477 MG SODIUM

NUTRITION BONUS: Vitamin C (45% DAILY VALUE), Iron (20% DV), Vitamin A (20% DV), Folate (15% DV).

EXCHANGES

1 VEGETABLE
3 VERY LEAN MEAT
1 FAT (MONO)

Italian Seafood Stew

The fishermen's catch of the day is transformed into a succulent seafood stew.

1	cup bottled clam juice
4	cloves garlic (2 smashed, 2 minced)
1	pound mussels, scrubbed and debearded, *or* small cherrystone clams
2	tablespoons extra-virgin olive oil, divided
1	onion, thinly sliced
8	ounces squid, cleaned and cut into ½-inch-thick rings
½	cup dry white wine
⅓	cup red-wine vinegar, plus more to taste
1	14½-ounce can diced tomatoes
2	pounds firm white-fleshed fish fillet, such as halibut, skinned and cut into 1-inch chunks
8	ounces medium shrimp, peeled and deveined
4	tablespoons chopped fresh parsley, divided
2	tablespoons fine dry breadcrumbs
	Freshly ground pepper to taste

1. Bring clam juice and smashed garlic to a simmer in a large pot. Add mussels (or clams) and cook, covered, until open, 3 to 5 minutes. Discard garlic; remove mussels from the pot, discarding any that did not open. Using a fine-mesh sieve lined with cheesecloth, strain broth into a bowl; set aside. Wipe out the pot.

2. Add 1 tablespoon oil to the pot and heat over medium-low heat. Add onion and minced garlic and cook, stirring, until softened, 5 to 7 minutes. Increase heat to high; add squid and cook, stirring, until the squid turns opaque, about 1 minute. Add wine and ⅓ cup vinegar; cook, stirring occasionally, until the liquid has reduced by half, 5 to 7 minutes.

3. Add tomatoes and the reserved mussel broth. Reduce heat to low, cover and simmer until the squid is tender, 18 to 20 minutes.

4. Just before serving, add fish and shrimp to the simmering stew and cook, covered, just until the fish is opaque in the center, 3 to 5 minutes. Stir in the reserved mussels and heat through, about 1 minute. With a slotted spoon, remove solids to a bowl and cover to keep warm. Stir 3 tablespoons parsley, breadcrumbs and the remaining 1 tablespoon oil into the sauce. Simmer until the sauce thickens to the consistency of heavy cream, 1 to 2 minutes. Adjust seasoning with pepper and vinegar. Return the solids to the sauce. Serve immediately, garnished with the remaining 1 tablespoon parsley.

½
CARBOHYDRATE
SERVING

MAKES 8 SERVINGS

PREP TIME: 30 MINUTES

START TO FINISH: 1¼ HOURS

TO MAKE AHEAD: Prepare through Step 3. Cover and refrigerate mussels and stew separately for up to 1 day.

PER SERVING

280 CALORIES

8 G FAT (1 G SAT, 4 G MONO)

156 MG CHOLESTEROL

8 G CARBOHYDRATE

39 G PROTEIN

1 G FIBER

405 MG SODIUM

NUTRITION BONUS: Selenium (118% DAILY VALUE), Magnesium (31% DV), Vitamin C (20% DV).

EXCHANGES

1 VEGETABLE

5 VERY LEAN MEAT

1 FAT (MONO)

Salmon with Cucumbers & Dill

Quick  Easy

Seared first to add color and flavor, the salmon is then combined with braised cucumbers—an unexpected yet delicious way to enjoy that vegetable's subtle taste.

2 tablespoons all-purpose flour

¼ teaspoon salt, or to taste

   Freshly ground pepper to taste

1¾ pounds salmon fillet, preferably center-cut, skin removed (*see box, page 203*), cut into 1½-inch cubes

4 teaspoons extra-virgin olive oil, divided

2 seedless cucumbers (1½ pounds), cut into 2-by-½-inch sticks

⅓ cup reduced-sodium chicken broth

   Pinch of sugar

¼ cup chopped fresh dill, plus sprigs for garnish

   Lemon wedges for garnish

1. Combine flour, salt and pepper in a shallow dish. Dredge salmon pieces in the flour mixture, shaking off the excess.

2. Heat 2 teaspoons oil in a large nonstick skillet over high heat. Add half the salmon and sauté until lightly browned on the outside but still pink inside, 4 to 5 minutes. Transfer to a plate. Wipe out the pan, add the remaining 2 teaspoons oil and return to the heat. Sauté the remaining salmon and transfer to the plate.

3. Wipe out the pan again and add cucumbers, broth and sugar. Bring to a simmer over medium heat. Cover and simmer until the cucumbers are tender-crisp, 3 to 4 minutes.

4. Uncover, increase the heat to high and boil until the pan juices are reduced to 2 tablespoons, about 3 minutes. Add the reserved salmon and dill to the pan, cover and simmer just until the salmon is opaque in the center, 2 to 3 minutes. Garnish with dill sprigs and lemon wedges.

1/2

CARBOHYDRATE

SERVING

MAKES 6 SERVINGS

PREP TIME: 20 MINUTES

START TO FINISH: 40 MINUTES

PER SERVING

240 CALORIES

12 G FAT (2 G SAT, 5 G MONO)

72 MG CHOLESTEROL

6 G CARBOHYDRATE

27 G PROTEIN

1 G FIBER

164 MG SODIUM

NUTRITION BONUS: Selenium (86% DAILY VALUE).

EXCHANGES

1 VEGETABLE

4 LEAN MEAT

Spicy Cornmeal-Crusted Catfish

Farmed domestic catfish these days is a pleasure to cook—mild, clean-tasting and economical. These fillets—moist within, lightly crusted on the outside—also make excellent sandwiches.

1	pound catfish fillets, cut into 4 portions
1	cup 1% milk
¼	cup Tangy Tartar Sauce (*recipe follows*)
½	cup cornmeal
½	cup chopped fresh parsley
1	clove garlic, minced
½-1	teaspoon cayenne pepper
¼	teaspoon salt, or to taste
	Cooking spray
1	lemon, cut into wedges

1. Place fillets in a single layer in a shallow glass dish. Pour milk over the fish; cover and refrigerate for at least 30 minutes or for up to 2 hours.
2. Meanwhile, make Tangy Tartar Sauce.
3. Preheat oven to 500°F. Combine cornmeal, parsley, garlic and cayenne to taste in a shallow dish. Remove the fish from the milk, sprinkle both sides with salt and dredge it in the cornmeal mixture. Coat a baking sheet with cooking spray. Place the fish on it and lightly coat the fish with cooking spray.
4. Bake until the fish is firm to the touch and opaque in the center, 10 to 15 minutes. Serve immediately, with the tartar sauce and lemon wedges.

Tangy Tartar Sauce

Quick ☼ Easy

¼	cup reduced-fat mayonnaise
¼	cup low-fat *or* nonfat plain yogurt
1	tablespoon lemon juice
1	teaspoon capers, finely chopped
1	teaspoon sweet pickle relish
½	teaspoon freshly grated lemon zest
½	teaspoon Dijon mustard
1	clove garlic, minced

Whisk mayonnaise, yogurt and lemon juice in a small bowl until smooth. Stir in remaining ingredients.

Sidebar

½ CARBOHYDRATE SERVING

MAKES 4 SERVINGS

PREP TIME: 15 MINUTES

START TO FINISH: 1 HOUR 20 MINUTES

PER SERVING

220 CALORIES
11 G FAT (2 G SAT, 5 G MONO)
56 MG CHOLESTEROL
10 G CARBOHYDRATE
19 G PROTEIN
1 G FIBER
137 MG SODIUM

EXCHANGES

½ STARCH
2½ LEAN MEAT
1 FAT (MONO)

For Tangy Tartar Sauce:

MAKES ½ CUP

PREP TIME: 10 MINUTES

START TO FINISH: 10 MINUTES

TO MAKE AHEAD: Cover and refrigerate for up to 1 week.

PER TABLESPOON

29 CALORIES
2 G FAT (0 G SAT, 0 G MONO)
2 MG CHOLESTEROL
2 G CARBOHYDRATE
0 G PROTEIN
0 G FIBER
70 MG SODIUM

EXCHANGES

1 FAT

Mexican Tuna Salad

Quick ☼ Easy

South-of-the-border seasonings spice up a basic tuna salad. Serve over lettuce or try as an appetizer dip with baked corn chips.

- 1 6-ounce can chunk light tuna in water, drained and flaked
- 1 green bell pepper, minced
- 2 scallions, minced
- ¼ cup prepared green salsa
- 6 pimiento-stuffed olives, chopped
- 2 tablespoons reduced-fat mayonnaise
- 1 tablespoon lime juice
- ½ teaspoon ground cumin
- Freshly ground pepper to taste

Combine tuna, bell pepper, scallions, salsa, olives, mayonnaise, lime juice and cumin in a medium bowl. Mix with a fork; season with pepper.

1/2 CARBOHYDRATE SERVING

MAKES **2** SERVINGS, ABOUT **1** CUP EACH

PREP TIME: 10 MINUTES
START TO FINISH: 10 MINUTES

TO MAKE AHEAD: Cover and refrigerate for up to 2 days.

PER SERVING

192	CALORIES
8	G FAT (1 G SAT, 1 G MONO)
31	MG CHOLESTEROL
8	G CARBOHYDRATE
23	G PROTEIN
2	G FIBER
841	MG SODIUM

NUTRITION BONUS: Vitamin C (100% DAILY VALUE), Selenium (97% DV).

EXCHANGES

- 1 VEGETABLE
- 3 VERY LEAN MEAT
- 1 FAT (MONO)

❝We don't go out to eat very often, because I feel I can control my portions better at home. Besides that, I like my own cooking!❞

—Beverly D., California

Tuna & White Bean Salad

High ↟ Fiber   Quick ☼ Easy

The time-honored Italian pairing of canned tuna and cannellini beans makes a super-simple, satisfying lunch. Serve over salad greens, on grilled whole-wheat country bread or tucked in a whole-wheat pita pocket.

- 3   tablespoons lemon juice
- 2   tablespoons extra-virgin olive oil
- 1   clove garlic, minced
- ⅛   teaspoon salt, or to taste
      Freshly ground pepper to taste
- 1   19-ounce can cannellini (white kidney) beans, rinsed
- 1   6-ounce can chunk light tuna in water, drained and flaked
- ¼   cup chopped red onion
- 3   tablespoons chopped fresh parsley
- 3   tablespoons chopped fresh basil

Whisk lemon juice, oil, garlic, salt and pepper in a medium bowl. Add beans, tuna, onion, parsley and basil; toss to coat well.

1

CARBOHYDRATE
SERVING

MAKES 4 SERVINGS, 1 CUP EACH

PREP TIME: 10 MINUTES

START TO FINISH: 10 MINUTES

TO MAKE AHEAD: Cover and refrigerate for up to 2 days.

PER SERVING

226 CALORIES
  8 G FAT (1 G SAT, 5 G MONO)
 13 MG CHOLESTEROL
 21 G CARBOHYDRATE
 16 G PROTEIN
  6 G FIBER
498 MG SODIUM

NUTRITION BONUS: Fiber (24% DAILY VALUE), Iron (16% DV), Vitamin C (15% DV).

EXCHANGES

1 STARCH
2 VERY LEAN MEAT
1 FAT (MONO)

Oven-Fried Fish Fillets

Quick ☼ Easy

Toasting the breadcrumbs in a skillet ensures a crisp and golden crust on the fish.

- ⅓ cup fine, dry, unseasoned breadcrumbs
- ¼ teaspoon salt, or to taste
  Freshly ground pepper to taste
- 1 pound sole fillets
- 1 tablespoon extra-virgin olive oil
- ½ cup Tangy Tartar Sauce (*page 196*)
  Lemon wedges

1. Preheat oven to 450°F. Coat a baking sheet with cooking spray.
2. Place breadcrumbs, salt and pepper in a small dry skillet over medium heat. Cook, stirring, until toasted, about 5 minutes. Remove from heat. Brush both sides of each fish fillet with oil and dredge in the breadcrumb mixture. Place on the prepared baking sheet.
3. Bake the fish until opaque in the center, 5 to 6 minutes.
4. Meanwhile, make Tangy Tartar Sauce.
5. To serve, carefully transfer the fish to plates using a spatula. Garnish with a dollop of the sauce and serve with lemon wedges.

1

CARBOHYDRATE
SERVING

MAKES **4** SERVINGS

PREP TIME: 10 MINUTES
START TO FINISH: 25 MINUTES

PER SERVING

229 CALORIES
10 G FAT (2 G SAT, 4 G MONO)
59 MG CHOLESTEROL
11 G CARBOHYDRATE
23 G PROTEIN
1 G FIBER
444 MG SODIUM

NUTRITION BONUS: Selenium
(57% DAILY VALUE).

EXCHANGES

½ STARCH
3 LEAN MEAT

1

CARBOHYDRATE
SERVING

MAKES 4 SERVINGS

PREP TIME: 20 MINUTES (including peeling shrimp)

START TO FINISH: 30 MINUTES

PER SERVING

208 CALORIES
5 G FAT (1 G SAT, 2 G MONO)
173 MG CHOLESTEROL
13 G CARBOHYDRATE
27 G PROTEIN
4 G FIBER
407 MG SODIUM

NUTRITION BONUS: Vitamin C (30% DAILY VALUE), Iron (22% DV), Fiber (16% DV).

EXCHANGES

1 STARCH
3 VERY LEAN MEAT

Pan-Seared Shrimp with Peas

Quick ☼ Easy

Spoon the shrimp over fresh lo mein noodles or rice.

8	scallions, divided
2	cloves garlic
1	1-inch piece fresh ginger, peeled
1	pound shrimp (30-40 per pound), peeled and deveined
1	tablespoon curry powder, divided
2	teaspoon canola oil, divided
1½	cups frozen peas
1	cup reduced-sodium chicken broth
¼	teaspoon salt, or to taste
	Freshly ground pepper to taste

1. Combine 7 scallions, garlic and ginger in a food processor; pulse until finely chopped. Slice remaining scallion; set aside.
2. Toss shrimp in a bowl with ½ tablespoon curry powder.
3. Heat 1 teaspoon oil in a large nonstick skillet over high heat. Add the shrimp and cook, stirring, until firm and pink, 2 to 4 minutes. Transfer the shrimp to a plate.
4. Reduce heat to low and add the remaining 1 teaspoon oil. Add the chopped scallion mixture and the remaining ½ tablespoon curry powder; cook, stirring, until fragrant, about 2 minutes. Add peas and broth, increase heat to medium-high and bring to a simmer. Cook until the peas are heated through, about 3 minutes. Add the shrimp and cook about 1 minute more. Season with salt and pepper. Garnish with the reserved sliced scallion and serve.

Shrimp with Artichokes & Lemon

Quick ☼ Easy

Convenient canned artichokes provide a delicate counterpoint to sherry- and lemon-infused shrimp.

MARINADE & SHRIMP

- 2 tablespoons dry sherry
- 1 tablespoon lemon juice
- ½ teaspoon salt, or to taste
- 1 pound shrimp (30-40 per pound), peeled and deveined

SAUCE

- 3 teaspoons extra-virgin olive oil, divided
- ½ cup finely chopped shallots *or* onion
- 2 cloves garlic, minced
- 1 14-ounce can artichoke hearts, rinsed and halved
- 2 tablespoons water
- 2 teaspoons freshly grated lemon zest

1. Combine sherry, lemon juice and salt in a medium bowl. Add shrimp and toss to coat. Cover and marinate in the refrigerator for 10 to 15 minutes, tossing occasionally. Drain well, reserving marinade.

2. Heat 1 teaspoon oil in a 12-inch nonstick skillet over medium-high heat. Add the shrimp and cook, turning once, until barely pink, about 30 seconds per side; transfer to a plate. Add the remaining 2 teaspoons oil to the pan. Add shallots (or onion); cook, stirring often, until translucent, 2 to 3 minutes. Add garlic; cook, stirring, for 30 seconds. Add artichoke hearts and cook, stirring, until heated through. Add water and the reserved marinade; simmer for 1 minute. Add lemon zest and return the shrimp and any accumulated juices to the pan; heat through. Serve immediately.

1

CARBOHYDRATE
SERVING

MAKES 4 SERVINGS, ABOUT 1 CUP EACH

PREP TIME: 25 MINUTES (including peeling shrimp)

START TO FINISH: 40 MINUTES

PER SERVING

228 CALORIES
5 G FAT (1 G SAT, 3 G MONO)
172 MG CHOLESTEROL
16 G CARBOHYDRATE
27 G PROTEIN
4 G FIBER
1,064 MG SODIUM

NUTRITION BONUS: Vitamin C (33% DAILY VALUE), Fiber (16% DV).

EXCHANGES

1 VEGETABLE
4 VERY LEAN MEAT
1 FAT

1

CARBOHYDRATE

SERVING

MAKES 4 SERVINGS,
1½ CUPS EACH

PREP TIME: 20 MINUTES (including peeling shrimp)

START TO FINISH: 25 MINUTES

TO MAKE AHEAD: Refrigerate for up to 4 days. Reheat before serving.

INGREDIENT NOTE
Madras curry powder is made with a hotter blend of spices than standard curry powder.

PER SERVING
253 CALORIES
7 G FAT (1 G SAT, 3 G MONO)
259 MG CHOLESTEROL
13 G CARBOHYDRATE
35 G PROTEIN
4 G FIBER
488 MG SODIUM

NUTRITION BONUS: Selenium (93% DAILY VALUE), Vitamin C (70% DV).

EXCHANGES
1 FRUIT
5 VERY LEAN MEAT
1 FAT (MONO)

Curry-Roasted Shrimp with Oranges

Quick ☼ Easy

Shrimp, oranges and curry make a great flavor trio. Serve over rice as a main course or as is for an appetizer.

>   2   large seedless oranges, preferably organic, scrubbed
>   ½   teaspoon coarse salt, divided
>   1½ pounds shrimp (30-40 per pound), peeled and deveined
>   1   tablespoon extra-virgin olive oil
>   1   tablespoon curry powder, preferably Madras (*see Note*)
>   ½   teaspoon freshly ground pepper

1. Preheat oven to 400°F. Line a baking sheet (with sides) with parchment paper. Finely grate the zest of 1 orange; set aside. Using a sharp knife, peel both oranges, removing all the bitter white pith. Thinly slice the oranges crosswise, then cut the slices into quarters. Spread the orange slices on the prepared baking sheet and sprinkle with ¼ teaspoon salt. Roast until the oranges are slightly dry, about 12 minutes.
2. Meanwhile, toss shrimp with oil, curry powder, pepper, the orange zest and the remaining ¼ teaspoon salt in a large bowl. Transfer the shrimp to the baking sheet with the oranges and roast until pink and curled, about 6 minutes. Divide the oranges and the shrimp among 4 plates and serve.

Salmon Roasted with Tomatoes & Olives

Although you can use any firm-fleshed fish, such as halibut or cod, salmon is especially pretty with the roasted tomatoes and black olives. Serve with steamed green beans or broccoli florets and boiled new potatoes.

2	pounds ripe plum tomatoes, stem ends trimmed, cut into thin wedges
½	medium onion, peeled and cut into thin wedges
2	strips orange zest, cut into thin slivers
2	cloves garlic, minced
1	tablespoon extra-virgin olive oil
⅓	cup pitted Kalamata olives, coarsely chopped
1	tablespoon chopped fresh rosemary
¼	teaspoon salt, or to taste
	Freshly ground pepper to taste
1¼	pounds salmon fillet (about 1½ inches thick), skin removed (*see box, below*), cut into 4 portions

1. Preheat oven to 400°F. Combine tomatoes, onion, orange zest and garlic in a large roasting pan or on a large baking sheet with sides. Drizzle with oil and toss to coat.
2. Roast, uncovered, stirring occasionally, until the tomatoes and onion are tender and beginning to brown on the edges, about 45 minutes. Remove pan from the oven. Increase oven temperature to 450°.
3. Add olives and rosemary to the pan; season with salt and pepper. Clear four spaces in the pan and place a salmon piece in each. Spoon some of the tomato mixture on top.
4. Roast until the salmon is opaque in the center, 10 to 15 minutes, depending on the thickness.

TIP

HOW TO SKIN A FISH FILLET

You can ask to have the skin removed from a piece of salmon or halibut fillet at the fish counter, but it is also easy to do it yourself. Place the fillet, skin-side down, on a cutting board. Use a thin, sharp knife to cut between the skin and flesh at the tip. Grasp the skin with your free hand and ease the knife carefully between the skin and flesh, keeping the knife pointed slightly toward the skin, until the skin is removed.

1

CARBOHYDRATE

SERVING

MAKES 4 SERVINGS

PREP TIME: 20 MINUTES

START TO FINISH: 1 HOUR 20 MINUTES

PER SERVING

372 CALORIES

20 G FAT (3 G SAT, 6 G MONO)

90 MG CHOLESTEROL

14 G CARBOHYDRATE

34 G PROTEIN

3 G FIBER

585 MG SODIUM

NUTRITION BONUS: Vitamin C (40% DAILY VALUE), Potassium (37% DV), Vitamin A (25% DV), Folate (18% DV).

EXCHANGES

2 VEGETABLE

5 LEAN MEAT

1 FAT (MONO)

1

CARBOHYDRATE

SERVING

MAKES 4 SERVINGS

PREP TIME: 20 MINUTES

START TO FINISH: 30 MINUTES

TEST KITCHEN TIP
To clean mussels, scrub them with a stiff brush under cold running water. Scrape off any barnacles using the shell of another mussel. Just before cooking, pull off the bit of weed, or "beard" from each one. Discard any mussels with broken shells or any that do not close when tapped.

PER SERVING

267 CALORIES

6 G FAT (1 G SAT, 2 G MONO)

64 MG CHOLESTEROL

14 G CARBOHYDRATE

28 G PROTEIN

1 G FIBER

427 MG SODIUM

NUTRITION BONUS: Selenium (146% DAILY VALUE), Vitamin C (50% DV), Iron (45% DV), Potassium (17% DV).

EXCHANGES

1 VEGETABLE

4 VERY LEAN MEAT

Steamed Mussels in Tomato Broth

Quick ☼ Easy

With fresh mussels increasingly available at supermarket fish counters, you can easily make this bistro favorite at home.

1	teaspoon extra-virgin olive oil
4	cloves garlic, finely chopped
6	ripe plum tomatoes, cored and coarsely chopped
1	cup dry white wine
3	pounds mussels, scrubbed and debearded (*see Tip*)
2	teaspoons chopped fresh parsley

1. Warm oil in a large pot with a tight-fitting lid over low heat. Add garlic and cook, stirring, until golden, about 3 minutes. Add tomatoes, increase the heat to high and stir for 1 minute more. Pour in wine and bring to a boil.
2. Add mussels, cover and steam, occasionally giving the pan a vigorous shake, until all the mussels have opened, 3 to 4 minutes. Discard any that do not open. Transfer the mussels to a serving bowl. Spoon the broth over the mussels and sprinkle with parsley.

Beer-Battered Tilapia with Mango Salsa

Quick ☼ Easy

Lovers of fried fish get the taste without the calories in this recipe.

　　　Mango Salsa (*recipe follows*)
　3　tablespoons whole-wheat flour
　2　tablespoons all-purpose flour
　¼　teaspoon ground cumin
　¼　teaspoon salt, or to taste
⅛-¼　teaspoon cayenne pepper
　½　cup beer
　1　pound tilapia fillets (about 3), cut in half lengthwise
　4　teaspoons canola oil, divided

1. Make Mango Salsa.
2. Combine whole-wheat flour, all-purpose flour, cumin, salt and cayenne in a medium bowl. Whisk in beer to create a batter.
3. Coat half the tilapia pieces in the batter. Heat 2 teaspoons oil in a large nonstick skillet over medium-high heat. Letting excess batter drip back into the bowl, add the fish to the pan; cook until crispy and golden, 2 to 4 minutes per side. Transfer to a plate and loosely cover with foil. Coat the remaining fish with batter and cook in the remaining 2 teaspoons oil; adjust heat as necessary for even browning. Serve immediately with Mango Salsa.

Mango Salsa

Quick ☼ Easy

While this quick, tropical salsa pairs perfectly with Beer-Battered Tilapia, it also complements chicken, pork or other mild white fish.

　1　ripe mango, diced (1½ cups) (*see Cooking Tip, page 325*)
　¼　cup finely chopped red onion
　2　tablespoons lime juice
　2　tablespoons rice vinegar
　1　tablespoon chopped fresh cilantro

Combine all ingredients in a medium bowl. Let stand for 15 minutes; stir before serving.

1½ CARBOHYDRATE SERVINGS

MAKES 4 SERVINGS

PREP TIME: 20 MINUTES
START TO FINISH: 35 MINUTES

PER SERVING
242　CALORIES
　7　G FAT (1 G SAT, 4 G MONO)
　48　MG CHOLESTEROL
　21　G CARBOHYDRATE
　23　G PROTEIN
　2　G FIBER
234　MG SODIUM

NUTRITION BONUS: Selenium (77% DAILY VALUE), Vitamin C (35% DV), Calcium (13% DV).

EXCHANGES
½　STARCH
1　FRUIT
3　VERY LEAN MEAT
1　FAT (MONO)

For Mango Salsa:

MAKES 4 SERVINGS, ABOUT ⅓ CUP EACH

PREP TIME: 10 MINUTES
START TO FINISH: 10 MINUTES

PER SERVING
50　CALORIES
　0　G FAT (0 G SAT, 0 G MONO)
　0　MG CHOLESTEROL
　13　G CARBOHYDRATE
　0　G PROTEIN
　1　G FIBER
　2　MG SODIUM

EXCHANGES
1　FRUIT

Curried Corn & Crab Cakes

Quick ☼ Easy

Many cooks think crab cakes require a lot of effort, but they're actually not difficult. And with this corn-studded version, accented with fresh lime, mint and cilantro, the time you do spend will be rewarded with raves. Browning the cakes in a skillet and then finishing them in the oven produces a crisp crust and ensures even cooking.

**MAKES 4 SERVINGS,
2 CRAB CAKES EACH**

PREP TIME: 15 MINUTES
START TO FINISH: 45 MINUTES

INGREDIENT NOTE
Crabmeat can be purchased in three forms: canned, frozen or pasteurized. The pasteurized usually has the best flavor (it is heated to a lower temperature than canned); look for it in the fresh seafood section of the market. Once opened, the crabmeat should be used within 4 days.

- 5   teaspoons canola oil, divided
- 1   cup fresh corn kernels (from 2 ears; *see box, page 243*) *or* frozen
- ¼   cup finely chopped onion
- ½   teaspoon curry powder
- 1   clove garlic, minced
- 1   pound lump crabmeat, shells removed (*see Note*)
- ⅓   cup reduced-fat mayonnaise
- 2   large egg whites
- 2   tablespoons lime juice
- 3   tablespoons chopped fresh cilantro
- 2   tablespoons chopped fresh mint
- ¼   teaspoon salt, or to taste
- 1   cup fine, dry, unseasoned breadcrumbs, divided
     Lime wedges

PER SERVING

343 CALORIES
14   G FAT (2 G SAT, 5 G MONO)
72   MG CHOLESTEROL
29   G CARBOHYDRATE
26   G PROTEIN
2   G FIBER
784 MG SODIUM

NUTRITION BONUS: Zinc (33% DAILY VALUE), Vitamin C (22% DV), Magnesium (20% DV), Potassium (18% DV).

EXCHANGES

2 STARCH
3 LEAN MEAT

1. Preheat oven to 450°F. Coat a baking sheet with cooking spray.
2. Heat 1 teaspoon oil in a large nonstick skillet over medium-high heat. Add corn, onion, curry powder and garlic; cook, stirring often, until vegetables are soft, about 5 minutes. Transfer mixture to a large bowl and let cool completely. Stir in crabmeat.
3. Whisk mayonnaise, egg whites, lime juice, cilantro, mint and salt in a small bowl. Fold into the crab mixture. Stir in ½ cup breadcrumbs. Using about ⅓ cup per patty, form the mixture into eight ¾-inch-thick patties. Dredge the patties in the remaining breadcrumbs.
4. Heat 2 teaspoons oil in a large nonstick skillet over medium heat. Add 4 crab cakes and cook until the undersides are golden, 2 to 3 minutes. Using a wide spatula, turn cakes over onto the prepared baking sheet. Add the remaining 2 teaspoons oil to the skillet and repeat with the remaining 4 crab cakes.
5. Bake the crab cakes until golden on the second side and heated through, 15 to 20 minutes. Serve with lime wedges.

Pasta, Tuna & Roasted Pepper Salad

High ⬆ Fiber   Quick ☼ Easy

The secret to this delicious pasta salad is a creamy low-fat dressing made with bottled roasted red peppers. If you have cooked chicken on hand, you can substitute it for the tuna.

1	6-ounce can chunk light tuna in water, drained
1	7-ounce jar roasted red peppers, rinsed and sliced (⅔ cup), divided
½	cup finely chopped red onion *or* scallions
2	tablespoons capers, rinsed, coarsely chopped if large
2	tablespoons nonfat plain yogurt
2	tablespoons chopped fresh basil
1	tablespoon extra-virgin olive oil
1½	teaspoons lemon juice
1	small clove garlic, crushed and peeled
⅛	teaspoon salt, or to taste
	Freshly ground pepper to taste
6	ounces whole-wheat penne *or* rigatoni (1¾ cups; *see Tip, page 138*)

1. Put a large pot of lightly salted water on to boil.
2. Combine tuna, ⅓ cup red peppers, onion (or scallions) and capers in a large bowl.
3. Combine yogurt, basil, oil, lemon juice, garlic, salt, pepper and the remaining ⅓ cup red peppers in a blender or food processor. Puree until smooth.
4. Cook pasta until just tender, 10 to 14 minutes or according to package directions. Drain and rinse under cold water. Add to the tuna mixture along with the red pepper sauce; toss to coat.

2

CARBOHYDRATE
SERVINGS

**MAKES 4 SERVINGS,
ABOUT 1 CUP EACH**

PREP TIME: 20 MINUTES
START TO FINISH: 30 MINUTES

PER SERVING

270	CALORIES
5	G FAT (1 G SAT, 3 G MONO)
13	MG CHOLESTEROL
39	G CARBOHYDRATE
18	G PROTEIN
6	G FIBER
539	MG SODIUM

NUTRITION BONUS: Vitamin C (30% DAILY VALUE), Fiber (23% DV), Magnesium (19% DV).

EXCHANGES

2 STARCH
2 VERY LEAN MEAT

CHAPTER NINE

Beef, Pork & Lamb

Lamb Chops with a Mustard Crust

Quick ☼ Easy

Giving lamb chops the classic garlicky breadcrumb crust that's usually reserved for a rack of lamb, creates an elegant but less pricey dish, ideal for either midweek meals or entertaining. If the chops weigh less than 4 ounces, you can double the recipe and allow 2 chops per serving. (Recommended portion size is 3 ounces cooked, boneless meat.) Fresh breadcrumbs give the crust an appealing texture—commercial dry crumbs are not recommended for this recipe. (*Photograph: page 170.*)

1	small clove garlic, crushed and peeled
¼	teaspoon salt, divided
2	teaspoons coarse-grained Dijon mustard
2	teaspoons chopped fresh rosemary
½	teaspoon Worcestershire sauce
	Freshly ground pepper to taste
¼	cup fresh whole-wheat breadcrumbs (*see Tip*)
2	tablespoons chopped fresh flat-leaf parsley
1	tablespoon plus 1 teaspoon extra-virgin olive oil
4	4- to 5-ounce loin *or* rib lamb chops, trimmed of fat

1. Preheat oven to 450°F.
2. In a mortar and pestle or with the side of a chef's knife, mash garlic and ⅛ teaspoon salt into a paste. Transfer to a small bowl; stir in mustard, rosemary, Worcestershire sauce and pepper. Mix breadcrumbs, parsley, 1 tablespoon oil and remaining ⅛ teaspoon salt in another small bowl. Set aside.
3. Heat remaining 1 teaspoon oil in a large nonstick skillet over medium-high heat. Add lamb chops and cook until one side is nicely browned, 1 to 2 minutes. Place the chops, browned-side up, on a broiler pan or baking sheet.
4. Spread the reserved mustard mixture over the browned side of each chop. Pat the breadcrumb mixture on top of the mustard mixture. Roast until the chops are cooked to your liking, 6 to 8 minutes for medium-rare.

O

CARBOHYDRATE
SERVINGS

MAKES 4 SERVINGS

PREP TIME: 20 MINUTES

START TO FINISH: 35 MINUTES

TO MAKE FRESH BREADCRUMBS
Trim crust from 1 slice firm bread. Tear bread into pieces and process in a food processor until coarse crumbs form. Makes ⅓ cup.

PER SERVING

151 CALORIES

9 G FAT (2 G SAT, 5 G MONO)

40 MG CHOLESTEROL

5 G CARBOHYDRATE

14 G PROTEIN

1 G FIBER

266 MG SODIUM

NUTRITION BONUS: Selenium (21% DAILY VALUE).

EXCHANGES

2 MEDIUM-FAT MEAT

Grilled Lamb with Fresh Mint Chutney

Quick ☼ Easy

For a refreshing change from mint sauce or mint jelly, try serving lamb chops with an Indian-inspired fresh mint chutney.

Fresh Mint Chutney (*recipe follows*)
8 rib lamb chops (about 3 ounces each), trimmed of fat
1 clove garlic, cut in half
1 teaspoon extra-virgin olive oil *or* canola oil
¼ teaspoon kosher salt, or to taste
Freshly ground pepper to taste

1. Prepare Fresh Mint Chutney.
2. Heat gas grill. Rub lamb chops with garlic, then brush with oil and season with salt and pepper. Grill the chops until cooked to desired doneness, 4 to 5 minutes per side for medium-rare. Serve with Fresh Mint Chutney.

Fresh Mint Chutney

Quick ☼ Easy

This tangy herb chutney is delicious with grilled salmon as well as the lamb. For the best results, make it shortly before serving.

2 teaspoons sugar
½ teaspoon kosher salt, or to taste
1 tablespoon coarsely chopped fresh ginger
1 small serrano *or* jalapeño pepper, seeded and coarsely chopped
1 clove garlic, crushed and peeled
2 cups lightly packed fresh mint leaves
2 tablespoons rice-wine vinegar
1 teaspoon canola oil

Place sugar and salt in a food processor. With the motor running, drop ginger, peppers and garlic through the feed tube; process until very finely chopped. Add mint and pulse until finely chopped. Add vinegar and oil and pulse to mix. Transfer to a small serving bowl.

1/2
CARBOHYDRATE
SERVING

MAKES 4 SERVINGS

PREP TIME: 20 MINUTES
START TO FINISH: 30 MINUTES

PER SERVING
296 CALORIES
13 G FAT (4 G SAT, 6 G MONO)
112 MG CHOLESTEROL
7 G CARBOHYDRATE
37 G PROTEIN
0 G FIBER
560 MG SODIUM

NUTRITION BONUS: Selenium (57% DAILY VALUE), Vitamin C (50% DV), Zinc (36% DV).

EXCHANGES
1 VEGETABLE
5 LEAN MEAT

For Fresh Mint Chutney:

MAKES 4 SERVINGS,
ABOUT 2 TABLESPOONS EACH

PREP TIME: 10 MINUTES
START TO FINISH: 10 MINUTES

PER SERVING
41 CALORIES
2 G FAT (0 G SAT, 1 G MONO)
0 MG CHOLESTEROL
7 G CARBOHYDRATE
1 G PROTEIN
0 G FIBER
327 MG SODIUM

NUTRITION BONUS: Vitamin C (50% DAILY VALUE).

EXCHANGES
1 VEGETABLE

Grilled Pork Tenderloin with Mustard, Rosemary & Apple Marinade

This recipe gets added depth and a pretty finish from a balsamic vinaigrette that's enriched with either port or black tea. Try the boldly flavored marinade with chicken too.

¼ cup frozen apple juice concentrate

2 tablespoons plus 1½ teaspoons Dijon mustard

2 tablespoons extra-virgin olive oil, divided

2 tablespoons chopped fresh rosemary *or* thyme

4 cloves garlic, minced

1 teaspoon crushed black peppercorns

2 12-ounce pork tenderloins, trimmed of fat

1 tablespoon minced shallot

3 tablespoons port *or* brewed black tea

2 tablespoons balsamic vinegar

¼ teaspoon salt, or to taste

Freshly ground pepper to taste

1. Whisk apple juice concentrate, 2 tablespoons mustard, 1 tablespoon oil, rosemary (or thyme), garlic and peppercorns in a small bowl. Reserve 3 tablespoons marinade for basting. Place tenderloins in a shallow glass dish and pour the remaining marinade over them, turning to coat. Cover and marinate in the refrigerator for at least 20 minutes or for up to 2 hours, turning several times.

2. Heat a grill or broiler.

3. Combine shallot, port (or tea), vinegar, salt, pepper and the remaining 1½ teaspoons mustard and 1 tablespoon oil in a small bowl or a jar with a tight-fitting lid; whisk or shake until blended. Set aside.

4. Grill or broil the tenderloins, turning several times and basting the browned sides with the reserved marinade, until just cooked through, 15 to 20 minutes. (An instant-read thermometer inserted in the center should register 155°F. The temperature will increase to 160° during resting.)

5. Transfer the tenderloins to a clean cutting board, tent with foil and let them rest for about 5 minutes before carving them into ½-inch-thick slices. Arrange the pork slices on plates and drizzle with the shallot dressing. Serve immediately.

1/2

CARBOHYDRATE
SERVING

MAKES 6 SERVINGS

PREP TIME: 20 MINUTES

START TO FINISH: 1 HOUR

PER SERVING

214 CALORIES

9 G FAT (2 G SAT, 5 G MONO)

63 MG CHOLESTEROL

8 G CARBOHYDRATE

23 G PROTEIN

0 G FIBER

229 MG SODIUM

NUTRITION BONUS: Vitamin C
(20% DAILY VALUE).

EXCHANGES

½ OTHER CARBOHYDRATE

3 LEAN MEAT

Pork Chops with Apples & Thyme

Quick ☼ Easy

Round out this lovely autumn meal with barley (*see page 237*) and pureed winter squash (*see page 325*; for added convenience, look for frozen squash).

1/2

CARBOHYDRATE
SERVING

¾	cup reduced-sodium chicken broth, divided
2	teaspoons cornstarch
2	teaspoons canola oil
4	4-ounce boneless pork chops, ½ inch thick, trimmed of fat
1	small onion, sliced
1	tart apple, such as Granny Smith, peeled and sliced
¼	cup apple cider *or* apple juice
2	teaspoons Dijon mustard
¼	teaspoon dried thyme

1. Mix 2 tablespoons broth and cornstarch in a small bowl.
2. Heat oil in a large nonstick skillet over high heat. Add chops and cook until browned, 2 to 3 minutes per side. Transfer to a plate.
3. Reduce heat to medium-high and add onion to the pan. Cook, stirring often, until it starts to soften and brown, 2 to 3 minutes. Add apple and cook, stirring often, until tender, 3 to 5 minutes. Stir in the remaining broth, cider (or juice), mustard, thyme and the cornstarch mixture. Bring to a boil, stirring, until thickened and glossy, about 1 minute. Return the chops to the pan and heat through. Serve immediately.

MAKES 4 SERVINGS

PREP TIME: 15 MINUTES
START TO FINISH: 30 MINUTES

PER SERVING

219	CALORIES
9	G FAT (3 G SAT, 4 G MONO)
67	MG CHOLESTEROL
9	G CARBOHYDRATE
24	G PROTEIN
1	G FIBER
102	MG SODIUM

NUTRITION BONUS: Selenium (50% DAILY VALUE).

EXCHANGES

1/2	FRUIT
3	LEAN MEAT

Branding Iron Beef & Beans

High ⬆ Fiber

This distinctive chili recipe, perfect for serving a large gathering, comes from ranchers Mike and Linda Bentz of the V-Dash Cattle Company in Drewsey, Oregon. They mash a portion of the beans, a great technique for adding extra body. Serve with corn or whole-wheat tortillas.

1	pound dried pinto beans (2½ cups)
3	pounds beef rump roast, trimmed of fat
½	cup chopped onion
1	4-ounce can chopped green chiles
2	tablespoons chili powder
1	tablespoon ground cumin
1	teaspoon dried oregano
½	teaspoon garlic powder
5	cups water
1	cup shredded Monterey Jack cheese (4 ounces)
1	cup shredded jalapeño pepper Jack cheese (4 ounces)
1½	teaspoons salt, or to taste

1. Soak beans overnight in 2 quarts water. (*Alternatively, place beans and 2 quarts water in a large pot. Bring to a boil. Boil for 2 minutes. Remove from heat and let stand for 1 hour.*) Drain beans, discarding soaking liquid. Rinse beans thoroughly under cool water.

2. Preheat oven to 325°F. Place beef, onion, chiles, chili powder, cumin, oregano, garlic powder, water and the beans in a Dutch oven. Bring to a simmer over medium-high heat. Cover the pot and transfer it to the oven. Bake, turning the beef halfway through cooking, until the beef falls apart and the beans are tender, 4 to 5 hours.

3. Remove the beef to a cutting board and shred it with two forks. Mash about 1 cup of the beans in a small bowl with a fork. Return the shredded beef and the mashed beans to the pot. Add cheeses and salt; stir over medium heat until melted.

1

CARBOHYDRATE

SERVING

MAKES 14 SERVINGS, 1 CUP EACH

PREP TIME: 25 MINUTES

START TO FINISH: 5 HOURS
(including 1 hour bean-soaking time)

PER SERVING

341 CALORIES

14 G FAT (7 G SAT, 4 G MONO)

70 MG CHOLESTEROL

21 G CARBOHYDRATE

32 G PROTEIN

7 G FIBER

445 MG SODIUM

NUTRITION BONUS: Iron (20% DAILY VALUE), Calcium (15% DV).

EXCHANGES

1 STARCH

4 LEAN MEAT

Lettuce Wraps with Spiced Pork

High ⬆ Fiber   **Quick ☼ Easy**

Serve this quick stir-fry family-style: set out a bowl of stir-fried pork and the lettuce leaves and let people make their own wraps.

SAUCE

- 2 tablespoons oyster sauce
- 2 tablespoons water
- 1 tablespoon hoisin sauce
- 1 tablespoon rice vinegar
- 1 tablespoon dry sherry *or* rice wine
- 2 teaspoons cornstarch
- 1 teaspoon brown sugar
- 1 teaspoon reduced-sodium soy sauce
- 1 teaspoon sesame oil

STIR-FRY

- 3 teaspoons canola oil, divided
- 1 pound thin center-cut boneless pork chops, trimmed of fat and cut into thin julienne strips
- 2 cloves garlic, minced
- 1 tablespoon minced fresh ginger
- 1 8-ounce can sliced water chestnuts, rinsed and coarsely chopped
- 1 8-ounce can sliced bamboo shoots, rinsed and coarsely chopped
- 8 ounces shiitake mushrooms, stemmed, cut into julienne strips
- 4 scallions, greens only, sliced
- 1 head iceberg lettuce, leaves separated

1. **To prepare sauce:** Combine oyster sauce, water, hoisin sauce, vinegar, sherry (or rice wine), cornstarch, brown sugar, soy sauce and sesame oil in a small bowl.
2. **To prepare stir-fry:** Heat 2 teaspoons canola oil over medium-high heat in a large non-stick skillet or wok. Add pork; cook, stirring constantly, until no longer pink, about 4 minutes. Transfer to a plate. Wipe out the pan.
3. Add remaining 1 teaspoon oil, garlic and ginger; cook, stirring constantly, until fragrant, 30 seconds. Add water chestnuts, bamboo shoots and mushrooms; cook, stirring often, until the mushrooms have softened, about 4 minutes. Return the pork to the pan and add the sauce. Cook, stirring constantly, until a thick glossy sauce has formed, about 1 minute. Serve sprinkled with scallions and wrapped in lettuce leaves.

1

CARBOHYDRATE
SERVING

**MAKES 4 SERVINGS,
1 CUP FILLING EACH**

PREP TIME: 25 MINUTES
START TO FINISH: 45 MINUTES

TO MAKE AHEAD: The sauce will keep, covered, in the refrigerator for up to 2 days.

PER SERVING

331	CALORIES
16	G FAT (5 G SAT, 8 G MONO)
59	MG CHOLESTEROL
22	G CARBOHYDRATE
25	G PROTEIN
6	G FIBER
628	MG SODIUM

NUTRITION BONUS: Vitamin C (20% DAILY VALUE), Iron (15% DV).

EXCHANGES

- ½ OTHER CARBOHYDRATE
- 2 VEGETABLE
- 3 MEDIUM-FAT MEAT

Pizza-Style Meatloaf

The idea for this playful meatloaf came from reader Jane Sveska of South Lyon, Michigan.

1	teaspoon extra-virgin olive oil
1	medium onion, sliced
1	red *or* yellow bell pepper, sliced
4	ounces mushrooms, sliced
¼	cup chopped fresh basil
1	pound lean ground beef
1	clove garlic, minced
⅓	cup seasoned (Italian-style) breadcrumbs
⅓	cup 1% milk
½	teaspoon salt, or to taste
½	cup prepared marinara sauce
¼	cup shredded sharp Cheddar cheese

1. Preheat oven to 400°F. Coat a 12-inch pizza pan with cooking spray and place it on a large baking sheet with sides.
2. Heat oil in a large skillet over medium heat. Add onion, bell pepper, mushrooms and basil; cook, stirring, until softened, about 10 minutes.
3. Meanwhile, combine beef, garlic, breadcrumbs, milk and salt in a large bowl. Mix well.
4. Transfer the meat mixture to the prepared pan. With dampened hands, pat into a 10-inch circle. Top with marinara sauce. Spoon the vegetable mixture over the sauce and sprinkle with cheese.
5. Bake until the meat is browned and the cheese has melted, about 30 minutes. Drain off any fat. Cut into wedges and serve.

1

CARBOHYDRATE
SERVING

MAKES 6 SERVINGS

PREP TIME: 20 MINUTES

START TO FINISH: 50 MINUTES

EQUIPMENT TIP
Use a perforated pizza pan so excess fat drips away.

PER SERVING
195 CALORIES
8 G FAT (3 G SAT, 2 G MONO)
53 MG CHOLESTEROL
11 G CARBOHYDRATE
20 G PROTEIN
2 G FIBER
471 MG SODIUM

NUTRITION BONUS: Vitamin C (48% DAILY VALUE), Zinc (27% DV), Selenium (21% DV), Vitamin A (18% DV).

EXCHANGES
1 OTHER CARBOHYDRATE
2½ LEAN MEAT

Mushroom-Beef Stroganoff

Braising is an excellent way to tenderize an inexpensive cut of meat like top round—and create a rich-tasting sauce. Embellished with mushrooms, colorful bell peppers and a dollop of low-fat sour cream, it becomes downright luxurious. Try serving this over barley (*see page 237*) instead of the usual egg noodles.

8	ounces beef top round, trimmed of fat
3	teaspoons extra-virgin olive oil, divided
1	large onion, finely chopped
3	cloves garlic, minced
1	tablespoon all-purpose flour
2	teaspoons paprika
1	14-ounce can reduced-sodium beef broth
2	teaspoons Dijon mustard
2	red bell peppers, sliced
1	pound button mushrooms, sliced (about 6 cups)
¼	teaspoon salt, or to taste
	Freshly ground pepper to taste
¼	cup reduced-fat sour cream
2	tablespoons chopped fresh parsley

1. Preheat oven to 325°F.
2. Slice beef across the grain into thin strips. Heat 1 teaspoon oil in a Dutch oven over high heat. Add beef and cook, turning from time to time, until browned on all sides, 1 to 2 minutes. Transfer to a plate. Reduce heat to medium.
3. Add 1 teaspoon oil to the pot. Add onion and cook, stirring, until golden, about 5 minutes. Add garlic, flour and paprika; cook, stirring, for 1 minute more. Add broth, mustard and the reserved beef. Bring to a simmer, cover the pot and transfer to the oven.
4. Bake the stroganoff until the beef is very tender, 1 to 1½ hours.
5. Meanwhile, heat the remaining 1 teaspoon oil in a large skillet over high heat. Add bell peppers and cook, stirring, about 1 minute. Add mushrooms and cook, stirring, until the mushroom liquid has evaporated, about 5 minutes. Season with salt and pepper.
6. Add the vegetables and sour cream to the stroganoff; stir to combine. Season with salt and pepper and garnish with parsley.

1

CARBOHYDRATE
SERVING

MAKES 4 SERVINGS, ¾ CUP EACH

PREP TIME: 20 MINUTES
START TO FINISH: 2 HOURS

PER SERVING

196	CALORIES
8	G FAT (2 G SAT, 4 G MONO)
38	MG CHOLESTEROL
15	G CARBOHYDRATE
19	G PROTEIN
4	G FIBER
260	MG SODIUM

NUTRITION BONUS: Vitamin C (200% DAILY VALUE), Vitamin A (20% DV).

EXCHANGES

2 VEGETABLE
2½ LEAN MEAT

Orange-Scented Beef Stir-Fry

High ⬆ Fiber   Quick ☼ Easy

Orange marmalade is the secret ingredient in this quick stir-fry. For variations, substitute chicken, shrimp, pork or tofu for the beef; adjusting the cooking time accordingly.

½ cup reduced-sodium chicken broth, divided

1 tablespoon cornstarch

2 tablespoons reduced-sodium soy sauce

2 tablespoons orange marmalade

1 tablespoon oyster-flavored sauce

1 tablespoon rice vinegar

1½-2 teaspoons chile-garlic sauce

4 teaspoons canola oil, divided

12 ounces beef top sirloin, trimmed of fat and cut into ¼-inch strips

1 tablespoon minced fresh ginger

1 large onion, slivered (1½-2 cups)

1 small red bell pepper, diced (1 cup)

1 pound broccoli florets (about 4 cups)

1. Combine ¼ cup broth, cornstarch, soy sauce, marmalade, oyster sauce, vinegar and chile-garlic sauce in a small bowl; mix well.

2. Heat 1 teaspoon oil in a wok or large nonstick skillet over high heat. Add half the beef; stir-fry until browned, about 2 minutes. Transfer to a plate. Stir-fry the remaining beef in 1 teaspoon oil; transfer to the plate.

3. Add the remaining 2 teaspoons oil to the wok. Add ginger and stir-fry until fragrant, 10 to 20 seconds. Add onion; stir-fry for 30 seconds. Add bell pepper and broccoli; stir-fry for 30 seconds. Pour in the remaining ¼ cup broth, cover and cook until the vegetables are crisp-tender, 2 to 4 minutes. Push the vegetables to the sides. Stir the sauce mixture and add it to the wok. Cook, stirring, until the sauce becomes thick and translucent. Stir the vegetables into the sauce and return the beef to the wok; toss to coat. Serve immediately.

1

CARBOHYDRATE
SERVING

MAKES 4 SERVINGS,
1¼ CUPS EACH

PREP TIME: 20 MINUTES
START TO FINISH: 30 MINUTES

PER SERVING

266 CALORIES

11 G FAT (3 G SAT, 5 G MONO)

42 MG CHOLESTEROL

23 G CARBOHYDRATE

20 G PROTEIN

5 G FIBER

408 MG SODIUM

NUTRITION BONUS: Vitamin C
(273% DAILY VALUE), Vitamin A
(100% DV), Fiber (20% DV),
Iron (20% DV).

EXCHANGES

½ OTHER CARBOHYDRATE

2 VEGETABLE

3 LEAN MEAT

Quick Pork Sauté with Blackberries

Quick ☼ Easy

A snappy pan sauce made with shallots, port and fruity blackberry nectar transforms basic pork chops into a special-occasion dinner. A touch of butter swirled in at the end of cooking gives the sauce a rich finish. You can substitute flattened boneless chicken breast, turkey cutlets or veal scallops for pork; adjust cooking time accordingly.

4	4-ounce boneless pork loin chops, ½ inch thick, trimmed of fat
¼	teaspoon salt, or to taste
¼	teaspoon freshly ground pepper
3	teaspoons extra-virgin olive oil, divided
⅓	cup finely chopped shallot (1 large)
1	tablespoon chopped fresh thyme *or* 1 teaspoon dried
½	cup port *or* brewed black tea
½	cup black currant nectar, blackberry *or* blueberry juice (*see Note*)
½	cup reduced-sodium chicken broth
2	tablespoons balsamic vinegar
1½	teaspoons cornstarch
1½	teaspoons water
1	cup fresh *or* frozen and thawed blackberries
2	teaspoons butter

1. Season pork chops with salt and pepper. Heat 2 teaspoons oil in a large nonstick skillet over medium-high heat. Add the pork and cook until browned and just cooked through, 2 to 3 minutes per side. Transfer to a plate. (Do not wash skillet.)

2. Add remaining 1 teaspoon oil to the pan. Add shallot and thyme; cook, stirring, for 30 seconds. Add port (or tea), black currant nectar (or blackberry or blueberry juice), broth and vinegar; bring to a boil, scraping up any browned bits. Cook, stirring occasionally, for 5 minutes to reduce sauce and intensify flavor.

3. Mix cornstarch and water in a small bowl. Add to the sauce and stir until lightly thickened. Reduce heat to low. Add blackberries and butter. Simmer, stirring, just until the butter has melted. Return the pork chops and any accumulated juices to the pan; turn to coat with sauce. Serve immediately.

1

CARBOHYDRATE
SERVING

MAKES 4 SERVINGS

PREP TIME: 25 MINUTES

START TO FINISH: 30 MINUTES

INGREDIENT NOTE
You can find a variety of berry juices and nectars in natural-foods stores or the natural-foods section of your supermarket. Enjoy some in a refreshing spritzer.

PER SERVING

264	CALORIES
8	G FAT (3 G SAT, 4 G MONO)
57	MG CHOLESTEROL
18	G CARBOHYDRATE
22	G PROTEIN
2	G FIBER
338	MG SODIUM

NUTRITION BONUS: Selenium (34% DAILY VALUE), Vitamin C (30% DV).

EXCHANGES

1	OTHER CARBOHYDRATE
3	LEAN MEAT

Ranch Barbecue Beef

A flavorful, easy barbecue from the kitchen of Max and Jean Mallory of the Walking Cane Ranch in Wallowa, Oregon, this recipe makes great sandwiches. It also works well in a slow cooker.

1	2½-pound beef chuck roast, trimmed of fat
4	cups chopped celery
1	cup chopped onion
¾	cup ketchup
¾	cup prepared barbecue sauce
1	cup water
2	medium-large tomatoes, seeded and diced
2	tablespoons cider vinegar
2	tablespoons Worcestershire sauce
2	tablespoons brown sugar
1	teaspoon chili powder
1	teaspoon garlic powder

1. Preheat oven to 350°F.
2. Place beef, celery and onion in a Dutch oven. Combine remaining ingredients in a medium bowl; pour over the beef. Bring to a simmer over medium-high heat. Cover, transfer to the oven and bake, turning the beef occasionally, until it is fork-tender, 4 to 4½ hours.
3. Transfer the beef to a cutting board and shred it with two forks. Serve hot.

1

CARBOHYDRATE

SERVING

MAKES **12** SERVINGS, ABOUT ½ CUP EACH

PREP TIME: 10 MINUTES

START TO FINISH: 4 HOURS 40 MINUTES

TO MAKE AHEAD: Cover and refrigerate for up to 2 days or freeze for up to 3 months.

PER SERVING

368 CALORIES

23 G FAT (9 G SAT, 10 G MONO)

94 MG CHOLESTEROL

12 G CARBOHYDRATE

27 G PROTEIN

2 G FIBER

417 MG SODIUM

NUTRITION BONUS: Iron (20% DAILY VALUE), Vitamin C (20% DV).

EXCHANGES

1 OTHER CARBOHYDRATE

4 MEDIUM-FAT MEAT

Salt & Pepper Sirloin

Quick ☼ Easy

A simple grilled steak topped with tangy tomatillo salsa is a favorite of EATINGWELL's Food Editor, Jim Romanoff. Instead of serving a slab of steak, he likes to slice it and fan it on the plates. Not only is it more attractive this way, it is easier to control portion sizes. Barbecue Bean Salad (*page 117*) or Roasted Corn Salsa (*page 267*) also make great accompaniments.

>   2   cups Grilled Tomatillo Salsa (*recipe follows*)
>   1   pound boneless top sirloin steak, trimmed of fat
>   1   teaspoon extra-virgin olive oil
>   ½   teaspoon coarse kosher salt, or to taste
>   Freshly ground pepper to taste

1. Make Grilled Tomatillo Salsa.
2. Preheat grill to high.
3. Rub steak with oil; season both sides with salt and pepper. Lightly oil the grill rack (hold a piece of oil-soaked paper towel with tongs and rub it over the grate). Grill the steak until cooked to desired doneness, 4 to 6 minutes per side for medium-rare. Transfer it to a cutting board and let it rest for 5 minutes. Slice the steak thinly across the grain and serve with tomatillo salsa.

Grilled Tomatillo Salsa

Quick ☼ Easy

Tomatillos are delicious raw, but they take on a sweet, smoky flavor when cooked on the grill. This quick salsa makes a great topping for grilled meats and fish and it's excellent with eggs and corn tortillas. If you like, add some diced avocado just before serving.

>   1   pound tomatillos, husked and rinsed (*see Ingredient Note, page 324*)
>   1   small red onion, cut into ½-inch-thick slices
>   2   jalapeño peppers
>   1   tablespoon lime juice
>   1   tablespoon rice vinegar *or* cider vinegar
>   2   teaspoons dark brown sugar
>   ⅛   teaspoon salt, or to taste

1. Preheat grill.
2. Grill tomatillos, onion slices and jalapeños, turning occasionally, until soft and a bit charred, 10 to 15 minutes. Remove vegetables as they are ready. Let cool for about 10 minutes.
3. Peel, seed and stem the jalapeños. Place the tomatillos, onions, jalapeños, lime juice, vinegar, brown sugar and salt in a food processor. Pulse until the mixture is well blended but still has a chunky texture. Serve warm or chilled.

1

CARBOHYDRATE

SERVING

MAKES 4 SERVINGS

PREP TIME: 15 MINUTES
START TO FINISH: 45 MINUTES

PER SERVING
294 CALORIES
17 G FAT (6 G SAT, 7 G MONO)
53 MG CHOLESTEROL
11 G CARBOHYDRATE
24 G PROTEIN
3 G FIBER
370 MG SODIUM

NUTRITION BONUS: Selenium (37% DAILY VALUE), Zinc (26% DV).

EXCHANGES
3 MEDIUM-FAT MEAT
2 VEGETABLE

For Grilled Tomatillo Salsa:

MAKES 4 SERVINGS, ½ CUP EACH

PREP TIME: 10 MINUTES
START TO FINISH: 35 MINUTES

TO MAKE AHEAD: Cover and refrigerate for up to 4 days.

PER SERVING
55 CALORIES
1 G FAT (0 G SAT, 0 G MONO)
0 MG CHOLESTEROL
11 G CARBOHYDRATE
1 G PROTEIN
2 G FIBER
76 MG SODIUM.

NUTRITION BONUS: Vitamin C (30% DAILY VALUE).

EXCHANGES
2 VEGETABLE

Southwestern Steak & Peppers

Quick ☼ Easy

This juicy spice-crusted steak gets finished with a dynamite sauce made with an unusual ingredient—coffee, which adds depth and richness to the dish. Slice the steak very thinly across the grain to ensure the most tender results. (*Photograph: page 173.*)

½   teaspoon ground cumin

½   teaspoon ground coriander

½   teaspoon chili powder

¼   teaspoon salt, or to taste

¾   teaspoon coarsely ground pepper, plus more to taste

1   pound boneless top sirloin steak, trimmed of fat

3   cloves garlic, peeled, 1 halved and 2 minced

3   teaspoons canola oil *or* extra-virgin olive oil, divided

2   red bell peppers, thinly sliced

1   medium white onion, halved lengthwise and thinly sliced

1   teaspoon brown sugar

½   cup brewed coffee *or* prepared instant coffee

¼   cup balsamic vinegar

4   cups watercress sprigs

1. Mix cumin, coriander, chili powder, salt and ¾ teaspoon pepper in a small bowl. Rub steak with the cut garlic. Rub the spice mix all over the steak.

2. Heat 2 teaspoons oil in a large heavy skillet, preferably cast iron, over medium-high heat. Add the steak and cook to desired doneness, 4 to 6 minutes per side for medium-rare. Transfer to a cutting board and let rest.

3. Add remaining 1 teaspoon oil to the skillet. Add bell peppers and onion; cook, stirring often, until softened, about 4 minutes. Add minced garlic and brown sugar; cook, stirring often, for 1 minute. Add coffee, vinegar and any accumulated meat juices; cook for 3 minutes to intensify flavor. Season with pepper.

4. To serve, mound 1 cup watercress on each plate. Top with the sautéed peppers and onion. Slice the steak thinly across the grain and arrange on the vegetables. Pour the sauce from the pan over the steak. Serve immediately.

1

CARBOHYDRATE
SERVING

MAKES 4 SERVINGS

PREP TIME: 15 MINUTES

START TO FINISH: 35 MINUTES

PER SERVING

226 CALORIES

9 G FAT (2 G SAT, 4 G MONO)

64 MG CHOLESTEROL

12 G CARBOHYDRATE

24 G PROTEIN

3 G FIBER

213 MG SODIUM

NUTRITION BONUS: Vitamin C (210% DAILY VALUE), Vitamin A (60% DV), Iron (25% DV).

EXCHANGES

2 VEGETABLE

3 LEAN MEAT

Picadillo

Quick ☀ Easy

Picadillo, which means "small bits and pieces," is a sweet-and-savory spiced ground-meat mixture from Latin America. Serve with warm corn or whole-wheat flour tortillas.

1½
CARBOHYDRATE
SERVINGS

- 2 eggs (optional)
- 1 pound lean ground beef *or* ground turkey breast
- 2 teaspoons extra-virgin olive oil
- 1 medium onion, chopped
- ½ cup chopped scallions, divided
- 3 cloves garlic, minced
- 4 teaspoons chili powder
- 1½ teaspoons dried oregano
- 1½ teaspoons ground cumin
- ¾ teaspoon ground cinnamon
- ⅛ teaspoon cayenne pepper
- ½ cup golden raisins
- ½ cup chopped pitted green olives
- 2 tablespoons tomato paste
- 1 cup water
- ½ teaspoon freshly ground pepper

MAKES 4 SERVINGS, 1 CUP EACH

PREP TIME: 20 MINUTES
START TO FINISH: 40 MINUTES

PER SERVING (WITH BEEF)
- 313 CALORIES
- 13 G FAT (3 G SAT, 7 G MONO)
- 70 MG CHOLESTEROL
- 25 G CARBOHYDRATE
- 26 G PROTEIN
- 4 G FIBER
- 558 MG SODIUM

NUTRITION BONUS: Iron (25% DAILY VALUE), Vitamin A (20% DV), Vitamin C (15% DV).

1. If using eggs, place in a small saucepan and cover with cold water. Bring to a boil; simmer on medium-low for 15 minutes. Drain; let cool; peel and slice.
2. Meanwhile, cook meat in a large nonstick skillet over medium-high heat, crumbling it with a wooden spoon, until no longer pink, about 5 minutes. Transfer to a colander; drain off fat.
3. Add oil to the skillet. Add onion, ¼ cup scallions and garlic; cook over medium heat, stirring often, until softened, 2 to 3 minutes. Stir in chili powder, oregano, cumin, cinnamon and cayenne; cook, stirring, until fragrant, about 1 minute. Add raisins, olives, tomato paste, water and the browned meat; stir to blend. Reduce heat to low, cover and simmer, stirring occasionally, for 10 minutes. Season with pepper. Garnish with the remaining scallions and the hard-cooked eggs, if desired.

PER SERVING (WITH TURKEY)
- 277 CALORIES
- 9 G FAT (0 G SAT, 5 G MONO)
- 45 MG CHOLESTEROL
- 25 G CARBOHYDRATE
- 30 G PROTEIN
- 4 G FIBER
- 548 MG SODIUM

NUTRITION BONUS: Vitamin A (20% DAILY VALUE), Iron (15% DV), Vitamin C (15% DV).

EXCHANGES
- 1 OTHER CARBOHYDRATE
- 1 VEGETABLE
- 4 LEAN MEAT

Pork, Sweet Potato & Pineapple Stew

To make this Southwestern stew into a complete meal, serve with brown rice (*see page 237*) and Mexican Coleslaw (*page 106*).

12	ounces pork tenderloin, trimmed of fat
4	cups water
2	small onions, 1 halved, 1 sliced
4	cloves garlic, 2 whole, 2 minced
3	black peppercorns
½	teaspoon salt, or to taste
1	teaspoon extra-virgin olive oil
2	28-ounce cans whole tomatoes, drained and chopped
1	medium sweet potato, peeled and cut into ½-inch chunks
1½	tablespoons raisins
1	tablespoon sugar
½	teaspoon adobo sauce from canned chipotle peppers (*see Ingredient Note, page 323*) or chile-garlic paste
½	teaspoon ground cinnamon
¼	teaspoon dried oregano
	Pinch of ground cloves
1	cup diced fresh pineapple
8	green olives, pitted and coarsely chopped
¼	cup chopped fresh cilantro

1. Combine pork, water, halved onion, whole garlic, peppercorns and ¼ teaspoon salt in a large saucepan. Bring to a simmer; cook, partially covered, over low heat until the pork is no longer pink inside, 30 to 40 minutes.

2. Meanwhile, heat oil in a Dutch oven over medium heat. Add sliced onion and cook, stirring frequently, until softened, 4 to 5 minutes. Add remaining ¼ teaspoon salt, minced garlic, tomatoes, sweet potato, raisins, sugar, adobo sauce (or chile paste), cinnamon, oregano and cloves. Bring to a simmer; cover and cook, stirring occasionally, until the sweet potato is just tender, about 15 minutes.

3. Transfer the pork to a cutting board and cut into ½-inch pieces. Strain the cooking liquid through a fine sieve, reserving ¾ cup. (Refrigerate or freeze extra broth for another use.)

4. Add the pork, ¾ cup cooking liquid, pineapple and olives to the vegetable mixture. Cook, stirring occasionally, for 15 minutes. Stir in cilantro.

Sidebar

1½

CARBOHYDRATE
SERVINGS

**MAKES 6 SERVINGS,
1¼ CUPS EACH**

PREP TIME: 30 MINUTES
START TO FINISH: 50 MINUTES

TO MAKE AHEAD: Cover and refrigerate for up to 2 days.

PER SERVING
201 CALORIES
4 G FAT (1 G SAT, 2 G MONO)
45 MG CHOLESTEROL
23 G CARBOHYDRATE
19 G PROTEIN
4 G FIBER
321 MG SODIUM

NUTRITION BONUS: Vitamin A (46% DAILY VALUE), Vitamin C (27% DV).

EXCHANGES
1 STARCH
1 VEGETABLE
2 LEAN MEAT

Rosemary & Garlic Crusted Pork Loin with Butternut Squash & Potatoes

Pork today is so lean, the meat will be dry and crumbly if overcooked, but there are a couple of tricks to help avoid that fate. The first is to turn the pork over halfway through the cooking time so the juices will concentrate in the center of the roast instead of settling on the bottom. Second, take the roast out of the oven when it is about 5° below the recommended internal temperature, which is 160°F. The meat will continue to cook as it stands. (*Photograph: page 171.*)

1½

CARBOHYDRATE
SERVINGS

3	tablespoons chopped fresh rosemary *or* 1 tablespoon dried
4	cloves garlic, minced
1	teaspoon coarse salt, divided
½	teaspoon freshly ground pepper, plus more to taste
1	2-pound boneless center-cut pork loin roast, trimmed of fat
1½	pounds small Yukon Gold potatoes, scrubbed and cut into 1-inch cubes
4	teaspoons extra-virgin olive oil, divided
1	pound butternut squash, peeled, seeded and cut into 1-inch cubes
½	cup port *or* prune juice
½	cup reduced-sodium chicken broth

1. Preheat oven to 400°F.
2. Combine rosemary, garlic, ½ teaspoon salt and ½ teaspoon pepper in a mortar and crush with the pestle to form a paste. (*Alternatively, finely chop the ingredients together on a cutting board.*)
3. Coat a large roasting pan with cooking spray. Place pork in the pan and rub the rosemary mixture all over it. Toss potatoes with 2 teaspoons oil and ¼ teaspoon salt in a medium bowl; scatter along one side of the pork.
4. Roast the pork and potatoes for 30 minutes. Meanwhile, toss squash with the remaining 2 teaspoons oil, ¼ teaspoon salt and pepper in a medium bowl.
5. Remove the roasting pan from the oven. Carefully turn the pork over. Scatter the squash along the other side of the pork.
6. Roast the pork until an instant-read thermometer inserted in the center registers 155°F, 30 to 40 minutes more. Transfer the pork to a carving board; tent with foil and let stand for 10 to 15 minutes. If the vegetables are tender, transfer them to a bowl, cover and keep them warm. If not, continue roasting until they are browned and tender, 10 to 15 minutes more.
7. After removing the vegetables, place the roasting pan over medium heat and add port (or prune juice); bring to a boil, stirring to scrape up any browned bits. Simmer for 2 minutes. Add broth and bring to a simmer. Simmer for a few minutes to intensify the flavor. Add any juices that have accumulated on the carving board.
8. To serve, cut the strings from the pork and carve. Serve with the roasted vegetables and pan sauce.

MAKES 8 SERVINGS

PREP TIME: 20 MINUTES
START TO FINISH: 1¾ HOURS

TEST KITCHEN TIP
By placing the potatoes along one side of the roast and the squash along the other, you have the flexibility of removing one of the vegetables if it is done before the other.

PER SERVING

299	CALORIES
10	G FAT (3 G SAT, 5 G MONO)
63	MG CHOLESTEROL
23	G CARBOHYDRATE
25	G PROTEIN
3	G FIBER
358	MG SODIUM

NUTRITION BONUS: Vitamin A (110% DAILY VALUE), Vitamin C (45% DV).

EXCHANGES

1½	STARCH
3	LEAN MEAT

Middle Eastern Burgers

High ↑ Fiber   Quick ☼ Easy

Exotic-tasting spices and chopped prunes give Middle Eastern flair to these truly succulent burgers. Serve with Yogurt-Garlic Sauce (*page 264*), slices of ripe tomato, lettuce and sharp red onion.

MAKES 4 SERVINGS

PREP TIME: 30 MINUTES
START TO FINISH: 40 MINUTES

INGREDIENT NOTE
Fiber-rich bulgur is made from whole-wheat kernels that are precooked, dried and cracked. You can find it in natural-foods stores and large markets.

PER SERVING (WITH 90%-LEAN BEEF)

339	CALORIES
12	G FAT (4 G SAT, 5 G MONO)
108	MG CHOLESTEROL
36	G CARBOHYDRATE
24	G PROTEIN
6	G FIBER
373	MG SODIUM

NUTRITION BONUS: Zinc (30% DAILY VALUE), Fiber (24% DV), Iron (20% DV).

EXCHANGES
2½ STARCH
3 LEAN MEAT

- ⅓ cup bulgur (*see Note*)
- ½ cup plus 2 tablespoons warm water, divided
- 1 teaspoon canola oil
- ½ cup chopped onion (1 small)
- 2 cloves garlic, minced
- ⅓ cup pitted prunes, finely chopped (2 ounces)
- ½ teaspoon ground cumin
- ½ teaspoon ground coriander
- ¼ teaspoon ground allspice
- 12 ounces lean ground beef
- 1 large egg, lightly beaten
- ¼ teaspoon salt, or to taste
- ¼ teaspoon freshly ground pepper
- 4 small whole-wheat pita breads

1. Preheat grill.
2. Combine bulgur with ½ cup warm water in a small bowl; let soak until the bulgur is tender and most of the water has been absorbed, 20 to 30 minutes. Drain any excess liquid.
3. Meanwhile, heat oil in a large nonstick skillet over medium heat. Add onion; cook, stirring often, until the onion softens, about 4 minutes. Add garlic and prunes; cook, stirring often, until fragrant, about 2 minutes. Don't let the garlic burn. Stir in cumin, coriander and allspice; cook, stirring constantly, for 1 minute. Add remaining 2 tablespoons water; cook until it is absorbed, about 1 minute. Remove from the heat.
4. Combine beef, egg, salt, pepper, the onion-prune mixture and the bulgur in a mixing bowl; mix thoroughly. Shape into four ¾-inch-thick patties.
5. Lightly oil the grill rack (hold a piece of oil-soaked paper towel with tongs and rub it over the grate). Grill the burgers over medium heat, turning once, until browned and cooked through, about 4 minutes per side. Warm pitas on the grill, if desired. Serve the burgers with the pitas.

Pork Tenderloin with Roasted Plums & Rosemary

Lush vanilla- and rosemary-scented plums marry beautifully with succulent pork tenderloin. Serve with Green Beans with Toasted Nuts (*page 230*).

ROASTED PLUMS

1	pound black *or* red plums, pitted and cut into eighths (6-7 plums)
2	sprigs fresh rosemary, plus more for garnish
½	cup water
½	cup balsamic vinegar
6	tablespoons sugar, divided
10	black peppercorns, crushed
1	vanilla bean, split (*see Substitution Tip*)

PORK

2	teaspoons extra-virgin olive oil
1	pound pork tenderloin, trimmed of fat
¼	teaspoon freshly ground pepper
⅛	teaspoon salt, or to taste

1. **To roast plums:** Preheat oven to 400°F. Place plums and 2 rosemary sprigs in an 8-inch-square baking dish. Whisk water, vinegar, 4 tablespoons sugar and peppercorns in a small bowl until the sugar dissolves. Scrape seeds from vanilla bean; add the seeds and bean to the vinegar mixture. Pour the mixture over the plums. Sprinkle with the remaining 2 tablespoons sugar.

2. Roast the plums, uncovered, until tender and beginning to break down, 20 to 25 minutes. Discard the rosemary and the vanilla bean. Transfer the plums to a serving platter and cover with foil. Strain the roasting liquid into a small saucepan and bring to a boil. Reduce heat to medium-high; cook until reduced to ½ cup, 6 to 8 minutes. Pour the sauce over the plums; keep warm.

3. **To prepare pork:** Meanwhile, heat oil in a large ovenproof skillet over medium-high heat. Sprinkle pork with pepper and salt. Add to the skillet and brown on all sides, 5 to 8 minutes.

4. Transfer the skillet to the oven; bake at 400° until an instant-read thermometer registers 155° and the pork has just a hint of pink in the center, 10 to 15 minutes. Transfer the pork to a cutting board and let rest for 10 minutes. (The internal temperature will increase to 160° during resting.) Cut the pork into thin slices and serve with the roasted plums.

2½

CARBOHYDRATE
SERVINGS

MAKES 4 SERVINGS

PREP TIME: 20 MINUTES
START TO FINISH: 1 HOUR

TO MAKE AHEAD: The roasted plums will keep, covered, in the refrigerator for up to 2 days.

SUBSTITUTION TIP
You can use ¼ teaspoon vanilla extract instead of the vanilla bean.

PER SERVING

298	CALORIES
7	G FAT (2 G SAT, 4 G MONO)
63	MG CHOLESTEROL
37	G CARBOHYDRATE
24	G PROTEIN
2	G FIBER
127	MG SODIUM

NUTRITION BONUS: Selenium (56% DAILY VALUE), Vitamin C (20% DV).

EXCHANGES

2	FRUIT
5	LEAN MEAT

CHAPTER TEN

Side Dishes

Vegetables

CARBOHYDRATE SERVINGS

CARBOHYDRATE SERVING

1

CARBOHYDRATE SERVING

1¹/₂

CARBOHYDRATE SERVINGS

CARBOHYDRATE SERVINGS

Beans & Grains

1

CARBOHYDRATE SERVING

1¹/₂

CARBOHYDRATE SERVINGS

2

CARBOHYDRATE SERVINGS

2¹/₂

CARBOHYDRATE SERVINGS

Creamy Cauliflower Puree

High ⬆ Fiber   Quick ☼ Easy

This savory side dish is a healthy stand-in for mashed potatoes. Vary it by adding shredded low-fat cheese or chopped fresh herbs.

8	cups bite-size cauliflower florets (about 1 head)
4	cloves garlic, crushed and peeled
⅓	cup buttermilk *or* equivalent buttermilk powder *(see page 323)*
4	teaspoons extra-virgin olive oil, divided
1	teaspoon butter
½	teaspoon salt, or to taste
	Freshly ground pepper to taste
	Snipped fresh chives for garnish

NUTRITION BONUS: Cauliflower is a good source of vitamin C, a powerful antioxidant, and has a modest amount of calcium.

1. Place cauliflower florets and garlic in a steamer basket over boiling water, cover and steam until very tender, 12 to 15 minutes. (*Alternatively, place florets and garlic in a microwave-safe bowl with ¼ cup water, cover and microwave on High for 3 to 5 minutes.*)
2. Place the cooked cauliflower and garlic in a food processor. Add buttermilk, 2 teaspoons oil, butter, salt and pepper; pulse several times, then process until smooth and creamy. Transfer to a serving bowl. Drizzle with the remaining 2 teaspoons oil and garnish with chives, if desired. Serve hot.

Green Beans with Toasted Nuts

High ⬆ Fiber   Quick ☼ Easy

Toasted nuts are a simple way to embellish green beans. If you have hazelnut or walnut oil on hand, use it in place of the olive oil to enhance the nutty flavor.

1	pound green beans, stem ends trimmed
2	teaspoons extra-virgin olive oil
2	tablespoons chopped peeled hazelnuts *or* walnuts
¼	teaspoon salt, or to taste
	Freshly ground pepper to taste

1. Cook beans in a large pot of boiling salted water until just tender, 5 to 7 minutes. Drain.
2. Heat oil in a large nonstick skillet over low heat. Add nuts and cook, stirring, until golden, about 1 minute. Return the reserved beans to the pot and toss to coat. Season with salt and pepper.

Sidebar (left column)

O

CARBOHYDRATE
SERVINGS

MAKES **4** SERVINGS, **¾** CUP EACH

PREP TIME: 15 MINUTES
START TO FINISH: 30 MINUTES

PER SERVING
108 CALORIES
7 G FAT (2 G SAT, 4 G MONO)
3 MG CHOLESTEROL
10 G CARBOHYDRATE
4 G PROTEIN
5 G FIBER
342 MG SODIUM

EXCHANGES
2 VEGETABLE
1½ FAT

For Green Beans:

O

CARBOHYDRATE
SERVINGS

MAKES **4** SERVINGS

PREP TIME: 10 MINUTES
START TO FINISH: 20 MINUTES

PER SERVING
104 CALORIES
6 G FAT (0 G SAT, 4 G MONO)
0 MG CHOLESTEROL
11 G CARBOHYDRATE
3 G PROTEIN
7 G FIBER
145 MG SODIUM

NUTRITION BONUS: Fiber (28% DAILY VALUE), Vitamin C (22% DV).

EXCHANGES
1 VEGETABLE
1 FAT (MONO)

230

Broccoli with Black Bean-Garlic Sauce

Quick ☼ Easy

The bold taste of black bean-garlic sauce mellows into a rich and warming glaze in this fast Asian-style dish.

- 1 teaspoon sesame seeds
- ½ cup water, divided
- 1 teaspoon rice-wine vinegar *or* white-wine vinegar
- 1 teaspoon cornstarch
- 2 teaspoons black bean-garlic sauce (*see Note*)
- 2 teaspoons canola oil
- 1 clove garlic, minced
- 4 cups broccoli florets

1. Toast sesame seeds in a small dry skillet over medium-low heat, stirring constantly, until lightly browned and fragrant, 2 to 3 minutes. Transfer to a bowl to cool.
2. Mix ¼ cup water, vinegar and cornstarch in a small bowl. Add black bean sauce and stir until smooth.
3. Heat oil in a large nonstick skillet or stir-fry pan over medium-high heat. Add garlic and stir-fry until fragrant, about 30 seconds. Add broccoli and stir to coat. Add the remaining ¼ cup water; cover and steam just until the broccoli is tender-crisp, 1 to 3 minutes. Push broccoli to the sides and pour the sauce mixture in the center. Stir until the sauce begins to thicken, about 1 minute. Stir in the broccoli to coat. Serve immediately, sprinkled with sesame seeds.

1/2

CARBOHYDRATE
SERVING

MAKES 4 SERVINGS, ¾ CUP EACH

PREP TIME: 10 MINUTES
START TO FINISH: 15 MINUTES

INGREDIENT NOTE
Black bean-garlic sauce, made from pureed salted and fermented black soybeans, is a widely used condiment in Chinese cooking and can be found with the Asian food in most supermarkets.

PER SERVING
- 53 CALORIES
- 3 G FAT (0 G SAT, 2 G MONO)
- 0 MG CHOLESTEROL
- 6 G CARBOHYDRATE
- 2 G PROTEIN
- 2 G FIBER
- 133 MG SODIUM

NUTRITION BONUS: Vitamin C (110% DAILY VALUE), Vitamin A (45% DV), Folate (13% DV).

EXCHANGES
- 1 VEGETABLE
- ½ FAT (MONO)

Sidebar

$\frac{1}{2}$

CARBOHYDRATE
SERVING

MAKES 4 SERVINGS, 1½ CUPS EACH

PREP TIME: 15 MINUTES
START TO FINISH: 20 MINUTES

PER SERVING
136 CALORIES
6 G FAT (3 G SAT, 2 G MONO)
18 MG CHOLESTEROL
13 G CARBOHYDRATE
10 G PROTEIN
5 G FIBER
247 MG SODIUM

NUTRITION BONUS: Vitamin C
(145% DAILY VALUE), Calcium
(24% DV), Folate (23% DV).

EXCHANGES
2 VEGETABLE
1 HIGH-FAT MEAT

For Roasted Florets:

$\frac{1}{2}$

CARBOHYDRATE
SERVING

MAKES 4 SERVINGS, 1½ CUPS EACH

PREP TIME: 5 MINUTES
START TO FINISH: 30 MINUTES

PER SERVING (CAULIFLOWER)
113 CALORIES
7 G FAT (1 G SAT, 5 G MONO)
0 MG CHOLESTEROL
11 G CARBOHYDRATE
4 G PROTEIN
5 G FIBER
351 MG SODIUM

EXCHANGES
2 VEGETABLE
1½ FAT (MONO)

Cauliflower with Gruyère Sauce

High ↑ Fiber   Quick ☼ Easy

Plain steamed or microwaved cauliflower turns into something extraordinary when you cover it with this rich-tasting twist on a classic cheese sauce.

8 cups bite-size cauliflower florets (about 1 head)
4 teaspoons all-purpose flour
1 cup 1% milk, divided
½ cup shredded Gruyère cheese (2 ounces)
1 tablespoon snipped fresh chives *or* chopped fresh parsley
½ teaspoon minced garlic (1 small clove)
¼ teaspoon salt, or to taste
Freshly ground pepper to taste

1. Place cauliflower florets in a steamer basket over boiling water, cover and steam until tender, 8 to 10 minutes. (*Alternatively, place florets in a microwave-safe bowl with ¼ cup water, cover and microwave on High for 2 to 4 minutes.*)

2. Meanwhile, whisk flour with 2 tablespoons milk until smooth. Heat the remaining milk in a saucepan over medium heat until steaming. Add the flour mixture; cook, whisking, until the sauce bubbles and thickens, 2 to 3 minutes. Remove from heat; stir in Gruyère, chives (or parsley), garlic, salt and pepper. Spoon over the cauliflower and serve.

Roasted Florets

High ↑ Fiber   Quick ☼ Easy

Roasting members of the brassica family brings out a hidden nutty sweetness that could change a few minds about these oft-maligned root vegetables. Use either broccoli or cauliflower or a colorful mix.

8 cups bite-size cauliflower *or* broccoli florets (about 1 head), sliced
2 tablespoons extra-virgin olive oil
½ teaspoon salt, or to taste
Freshly ground pepper to taste
Lemon wedges (optional)

NUTRITION BONUS: Vitamin C
(150% DAILY VALUE), Folate
(28% DV), Fiber (20% DV).

Preheat oven to 450°F. Place florets in a large bowl with oil, salt and pepper and toss to coat. Spread out on a baking sheet. Roast the vegetables, stirring once, until tender-crisp and browned in spots, 15 to 25 minutes. Serve hot or warm with lemon wedges, if desired.

Roasted Green Beans with Sesame Seeds

Quick ☀ Easy

Here's a quick way to glamorize a family favorite.

> 1 **pound green beans, trimmed**
> 1 **teaspoon canola oil**
> 2 **teaspoons sesame seeds**
> ¼ **teaspoon salt, or to taste**
> **Freshly ground pepper to taste**

1. Preheat oven to 450°F. On a baking sheet with sides, toss beans with oil, then spread the beans out in a single layer. Roast the beans until wrinkled, brown and tender, about 12 minutes, stirring once.
2. Meanwhile, toast sesame seeds in a small dry skillet, stirring constantly over medium-low heat, until lightly browned and fragrant, about 2 to 3 minutes. Crush the seeds lightly and toss with the beans. Season with salt and pepper.

North African Spiced Carrots

Quick ☀ Easy

The trinity of North African seasonings, cumin, coriander and paprika, lends exotic appeal to this simple carrot preparation.

> 1 **tablespoon extra-virgin olive oil**
> 4 **cloves garlic, minced**
> 2 **teaspoons paprika**
> 1 **teaspoon ground cumin**
> 1 **teaspoon ground coriander**
> 3 **cups sliced carrots (4 medium-large)**
> 1 **cup water**
> 3 **tablespoons lemon juice**
> ⅛ **teaspoon salt, or to taste**
> ¼ **cup chopped fresh parsley**

Heat oil in a large nonstick skillet over medium heat. Add garlic, paprika, cumin and coriander; cook, stirring, until fragrant but not browned, about 20 seconds. Add carrots, water, lemon juice and salt; bring to a simmer. Reduce heat to low, cover and cook until almost tender, 5 to 7 minutes. Uncover and simmer, stirring often, until the carrots are just tender and the liquid is syrupy, 2 to 4 minutes. Stir in parsley. Serve hot or at room temperature.

½

CARBOHYDRATE
SERVING

MAKES 4 SERVINGS

PREP TIME: 10 MINUTES
START TO FINISH: 25 MINUTES

PER SERVING
54 CALORIES
2 G FAT (0 G SAT, 1 G MONO)
0 MG CHOLESTEROL
7 G CARBOHYDRATE
2 G PROTEIN
4 G FIBER
146 MG SODIUM

NUTRITION BONUS: Fiber (16% DAILY VALUE), Vitamin C (13% DV).

EXCHANGES
1 VEGETABLE

For North African Carrots:

½

CARBOHYDRATE
SERVING

MAKES 6 SERVINGS, ½ CUP EACH

PREP TIME: 10 MINUTES
START TO FINISH: 20 MINUTES

PER SERVING
51 CALORIES
3 G FAT (0 G SAT, 2 G MONO)
0 MG CHOLESTEROL
7 G CARBOHYDRATE
1 G PROTEIN
2 G FIBER
86 MG SODIUM

NUTRITION BONUS: Vitamin A (210% DAILY VALUE), Vitamin C (15% DV).

EXCHANGES
1 VEGETABLE
½ FAT (MONO)

1/2

CARBOHYDRATE
SERVING

MAKES **4** SERVINGS,
ABOUT **1** CUP EACH

PREP TIME: 15 MINUTES
START TO FINISH: 20 MINUTES

PER SERVING

51 CALORIES

3 G FAT (0 G SAT, 2 G MONO)

0 MG CHOLESTEROL

7 G CARBOHYDRATE

1 G PROTEIN

2 G FIBER

179 MG SODIUM

NUTRITION BONUS: Vitamin A
(90% DAILY VALUE), Vitamin C
(30% DV).

EXCHANGES

1 VEGETABLE

1/2 FAT (MONO)

Steamed Vegetable Ribbons

Quick ☼ Easy

Graceful ribbons of carrot and zucchini make a dramatic side dish that's surprisingly easy to prepare; just use a vegetable peeler to carve long paper-thin strips and steam until tender-crisp.

2	large carrots, peeled
3	small zucchini
2	teaspoons extra-virgin olive oil
2	teaspoons lemon juice, or to taste
1/4	teaspoon salt, or to taste
	Freshly ground pepper to taste

1. With a swivel vegetable peeler, shave carrots lengthwise into wide ribbons. Repeat with zucchini, shaving long, wide strips from all sides until you reach the seedy core. Discard the core.

2. Bring 2 inches of water to a boil in a large saucepan fitted with a steamer basket. Add the carrots; cover and steam for 2 minutes. Place the zucchini over the carrots; cover and steam until the vegetables are just tender, 2 to 3 minutes more. Transfer the vegetables to a large bowl. Toss with oil, lemon juice, salt and pepper. Serve immediately.

Tex-Mex Summer Squash Casserole

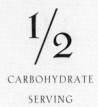

Chiles and cheese turn mild summer squash into a zesty, satisfying casserole. The jalapeños make this dish quite hot; if you prefer a milder version, use a second can of diced green chiles instead.

2¼	pounds summer squash, quartered lengthwise and thinly sliced crosswise (about 10 cups)
⅔	cup finely chopped yellow onion
1	4-ounce can chopped green chiles
1	4½-ounce can chopped jalapeños (about ½ cup), drained
½	teaspoon salt, or to taste
2¼	cups grated extra-sharp Cheddar cheese (about 7 ounces), divided
¼	cup all-purpose flour
¾	cup mild salsa
4	scallions, thinly sliced, for garnish
¼	cup finely chopped red onion for garnish

1. Preheat oven to 400°F. Coat a 9-by-13-inch baking dish with cooking spray.
2. Combine squash, onion, chiles, jalapeños, salt and ¾ cup cheese in a large bowl. Sprinkle with flour; toss to coat. Spread the mixture in the prepared pan and cover with foil.
3. Bake the casserole until it is bubbling and the squash is tender, 35 to 45 minutes. Spoon salsa over the casserole and sprinkle with the remaining 1½ cups cheese. Bake, uncovered, until golden and heated through, 20 to 30 minutes. Sprinkle with scallions and red onion.

MAKES 12 SERVINGS

PREP TIME: 20 MINUTES
START TO FINISH: 1½ HOURS

TO MAKE AHEAD: Cover and refrigerate for up to 2 days. Reheat, covered, at 350°F for about 40 minutes. Garnish just before serving.

PER SERVING

101 CALORIES
5 G FAT (4 G SAT, 0 G MONO)
15 MG CHOLESTEROL
8 G CARBOHYDRATE
5 G PROTEIN
3 G FIBER
258 MG SODIUM

NUTRITION BONUS: Vitamin C (30% DAILY VALUE).

EXCHANGES

1 VEGETABLE
1 FAT (SATURATED)

1

CARBOHYDRATE

SERVING

Fragrant Bulgur Pilaf

High ⬆ Fiber   Quick ☼ Easy

Vibrant with color and perfumed with the scents of Morocco and Tunisia, this tantalizing bulgur-and-almond pilaf is a perfect accompaniment for simple grilled chicken or fish. Although the ingredient list might seem long, it's largely spices you probably have on hand. (*Photograph: page 163.*)

**MAKES 8 SERVINGS,
ABOUT ¾ CUP EACH**

PREP TIME: 20 MINUTES
START TO FINISH: 40 MINUTES

PER SERVING

176 CALORIES
  6 G FAT (1 G SAT, 4 G MONO)
  0 MG CHOLESTEROL
 28 G CARBOHYDRATE
  6 G PROTEIN
  8 G FIBER
181 MG SODIUM

NUTRITION BONUS: Fiber
(36% DAILY VALUE).

EXCHANGES

2 STARCH
1 FAT (MONO)

1	tablespoon extra-virgin olive oil
1	medium onion, chopped
1	clove garlic, minced
1½	teaspoons ground cumin
¾	teaspoon ground cinnamon
½	teaspoon ground ginger
	Pinch of cayenne pepper
1½	cups bulgur (*see Ingredient Note, page 323*)
2½	cups water
½	teaspoon salt, or to taste
½	cup slivered almonds
2	cups frozen peas and carrots
1	teaspoon freshly grated lemon zest
2-3	tablespoons lemon juice
	Freshly ground pepper to taste
3	tablespoons coarsely chopped fresh mint *or* parsley

1. Heat oil in a large heavy saucepan over medium heat. Add onion and cook, stirring often, until softened, 3 to 4 minutes. Add garlic, cumin, cinnamon, ginger and cayenne; cook, stirring, until fragrant, about 30 seconds. Add bulgur and stir to coat. Add water and salt; bring just to a simmer. Reduce heat to low, cover and simmer until the bulgur is tender and most of the liquid has been absorbed, 15 to 20 minutes.

2. Meanwhile, toast almonds in a small dry skillet over medium-low heat, stirring constantly, until golden and fragrant, 2 to 3 minutes. Transfer to a plate to cool. Cook peas and carrots according to package directions.

3. When the bulgur is ready, add lemon zest, lemon juice, pepper, the peas and carrots; fluff and mix with a fork. Sprinkle with mint (or parsley) and the almonds; serve hot.

Grain-Cooking Guide

Directions are for 1 cup of uncooked grain.

GRAIN	LIQUID (water/broth)	DIRECTIONS	YIELD	PER ½-CUP SERVING	CARBOHYDRATE SERVINGS (per ½ cup)
Barley Quick-cooking	1¾ cups	Bring liquid to a boil; add barley. Reduce heat to low and simmer, covered, 10-12 minutes.	2 cups	86 CALORIES; 1 G FAT (0 G SAT, 0 G MONO); 0 MG CHOLESTEROL; 19 G CARBOHYDRATE; 3 G PROTEIN; 3 G FIBER; 2 MG SODIUM.	1
Pearl	2½ cups	Bring barley and liquid to a boil. Reduce heat to low and simmer, covered, 35-50 minutes.	3-3½ cups	117 CALORIES; 0 G FAT; 0 MG CHOLESTEROL; 26 G CARBOHYDRATE; 3 G PROTEIN; 5 G FIBER; 6 MG SODIUM.	1½
Bulgur	1½ cups	Bring bulgur and liquid to a boil. Reduce heat to low and simmer, covered, until tender and most of the liquid has been absorbed, 10-15 minutes.	2½-3 cups	96 CALORIES; 0 G FAT; 0 MG CHOLESTEROL; 21 G CARBOHYDRATE; 3 G PROTEIN; 5 G FIBER; 7 MG SODIUM.	1
Couscous Whole-wheat	1¾ cups	Bring liquid to a boil; stir in couscous. Remove from heat and let stand, covered, 5 minutes. Fluff with a fork.	3-3½ cups	140 CALORIES; 1 G FAT (0 G SAT, 0 G MONO); 0 MG CHOLESTEROL; 30 G CARBOHYDRATE; 5 G PROTEIN; 5 G FIBER; 1 MG SODIUM.	1½
Millet	2½ cups	Bring liquid to a boil; add millet. Reduce heat to low and simmer, covered, until tender, 20-25 minutes.	3 cups	126 CALORIES; 1 G FAT (0 G SAT, 0 G MONO); 0 MG CHOLESTEROL; 24 G CARBOHYDRATE; 4 G PROTEIN; 3 G FIBER; 3 MG SODIUM.	1½
Quinoa	2 cups	Rinse in several changes of cold water. Bring quinoa and liquid to a boil. Reduce heat to low and simmer, covered, until tender and most of the liquid has been absorbed, 15-20 minutes. Fluff with a fork.	3 cups	106 CALORIES; 2 G FAT (0 G SAT, 0 G MONO); 0 MG CHOLESTEROL; 20 G CARBOHYDRATE; 4 G PROTEIN; 2 G FIBER; 8 MG SODIUM.	1
Rice Brown	2½ cups	Bring rice and liquid to a boil. Reduce heat to low and simmer, covered, until tender and most of the liquid has been absorbed, 40-50 minutes. Let stand 5 minutes, then fluff with a fork.	3 cups	98 CALORIES; 1 G FAT (0 G SAT, 0 G MONO); 0 MG CHOLESTEROL; 20 G CARBOHYDRATE; 2 G PROTEIN; 1 G FIBER; 3 MG SODIUM.	1
Wild	At least 4 cups	Cook rice in a large saucepan of lightly salted boiling water until tender, 45-55 minutes. Drain.	2-2½ cups	82 CALORIES; 0 G FAT; 0 MG CHOLESTEROL; 17 G CARBOHYDRATE; 3 G PROTEIN; 1 G FIBER; 4 MG SODIUM.	1

1

CARBOHYDRATE
SERVING

MAKES 4 SERVINGS, 1 CUP EACH

PREP TIME: 10 MINUTES
START TO FINISH: 25 MINUTES

PER SERVING

183 CALORIES
6 G FAT (1 G SAT, 3 G MONO)
0 MG CHOLESTEROL
25 G CARBOHYDRATE
10 G PROTEIN
5 G FIBER
208 MG SODIUM

NUTRITION BONUS: Vitamin C
(180% DAILY VALUE), Vitamin A
(150% DV), Fiber (21% DV),
Iron (15% DV).

EXCHANGES

1 STARCH
1 VEGETABLE
1 VERY LEAN MEAT
1 FAT (MONO)

Broccoli Rabe with Chickpeas

High ↑ Fiber   Quick ☼ Easy

Broccoli rabe, also know as rapini, has an assertive, slightly bitter flavor, which is complemented by olive oil, garlic and comforting chickpeas.

1 pound broccoli rabe, trimmed, washed and cut into 1-inch pieces
1 tablespoon extra-virgin olive oil
3 cloves garlic, peeled and thinly sliced
1 19 ounce *or* 15½ ounce can chickpeas, rinsed
¼ teaspoon crushed red pepper
½ cup water
¼ teaspoon salt, or to taste
Freshly ground pepper to taste

1. Bring a large pot of lightly salted water to a boil. Add the broccoli rabe and cook until almost tender, about 5 minutes. Drain well.
2. Heat oil in a large skillet over medium-low heat. Add garlic and stir until pale golden, about 1 minute. Stir in chickpeas, crushed red pepper and water. Simmer for 5 minutes, stirring occasionally.
3. Stir in the broccoli rabe and cook until tender, about 3 minutes. Season with salt and pepper. Serve hot or at room temperature.

Carrot Sauté with Ginger & Orange

Quick ☼ Easy

Spiked with fresh ginger and orange juice, sautéed grated carrots make an appealing, textural side dish. To speed up preparation time, use a food processor to grate the carrots or purchase them already grated.

2 teaspoons canola oil
3 cups grated carrots (6 medium-large)
2 teaspoons minced fresh ginger
½ cup orange juice
¼ teaspoon salt, or to taste
Freshly ground pepper to taste

Heat oil in a large nonstick skillet over medium-high heat. Add carrots and ginger; cook, stirring often, until wilted, about 2 minutes. Stir in orange juice and salt; simmer, uncovered, until the carrots are tender and most of the liquid has evaporated, 1 to 2 minutes. Season with pepper and serve.

Glazed Mini Carrots

Quick ☼ Easy

Take advantage of convenient mini ("baby") carrots to make this simple but sophisticated classic French side dish.

3 cups mini carrots (1 pound)
⅓ cup water
1 tablespoon honey
2 teaspoons butter
¼ teaspoon salt, or to taste
1 tablespoon lemon juice
Freshly ground pepper to taste
2 tablespoons chopped fresh parsley

Combine carrots, water, honey, butter and salt in a large skillet. Bring to a simmer over medium-high heat. Cover and cook until tender, 5 to 7 minutes. Uncover and cook, stirring often, until the liquid is a syrupy glaze, 1 to 2 minutes. Stir in lemon juice and pepper. Sprinkle with parsley and serve.

1

CARBOHYDRATE
SERVING

MAKES 4 SERVINGS, ½ CUP EACH

PREP TIME: 10 MINUTES
START TO FINISH: 15 MINUTES

PER SERVING
69 CALORIES
3 G FAT (0 G SAT, 1 G MONO)
0 MG CHOLESTEROL
11 G CARBOHYDRATE
1 G PROTEIN
3 G FIBER
203 MG SODIUM

NUTRITION BONUS: Vitamin A (200% DAILY VALUE), Vitamin C (35% DV).

EXCHANGES
2 VEGETABLE
½ FAT (MONO)

For Glazed Mini Carrots:

1

CARBOHYDRATE
SERVING

MAKES 4 SERVINGS, ½ CUP EACH

PREP TIME: 5 MINUTES
START TO FINISH: 10 MINUTES

PER SERVING
74 CALORIES
2 G FAT (1 G SAT, 1 G MONO)
5 MG CHOLESTEROL
14 G CARBOHYDRATE
1 G PROTEIN
2 G FIBER
236 MG SODIUM

NUTRITION BONUS: Vitamin A (320% DAILY VALUE), Vitamin C (23% DV).

EXCHANGES
2 VEGETABLE

1

CARBOHYDRATE
SERVING

MAKES 6 SERVINGS, 3/4 CUP EACH

PREP TIME: 30 MINUTES

START TO FINISH: 1 HOUR

TO MAKE AHEAD: Prepare recipe
through Step 3. Cover and
refrigerate walnuts and shallots
separately for up to 2 days.

TIP
To ensure even cooking, make sure
that the Brussels sprouts are more
or less the same size, halve; quarter
or leave them whole.

PER SERVING

162 CALORIES

10 G FAT (2 G SAT, 2 G MONO)

5 MG CHOLESTEROL

17 G CARBOHYDRATE

5 G PROTEIN

3 G FIBER

288 MG SODIUM

NUTRITION BONUS: Vitamin C
(93% DAILY VALUE), Fiber (16% DV),
Folate (15% DV).

EXCHANGES

2 VEGETABLE

2 FAT

Brussels Sprouts with Shallots & Walnuts

Brussels sprouts, like many hearty vegetables, taste best after a cold snap—the chilly temperature actually sweetens their flavor. Tossing the sprouts with glazed shallots and toasted walnuts gives them a festive air—perfect for a holiday menu.

½ cup walnut halves

8 large shallots, unpeeled, separated at their natural divisions

1 tablespoon butter

½ teaspoon salt, divided

  Freshly ground pepper to taste

1 cup vegetable broth, reduced-sodium chicken broth *or* water

1 pound Brussels sprouts, trimmed (*see Tip*)

1 tablespoon walnut oil *or* extra-virgin olive oil

2 tablespoons chopped fresh marjoram

1. Preheat oven to 350°F. Bring several cups of water to a boil in a large saucepan. Blanch walnuts for 1 minute, then scoop them out. Using a towel, rub off what you can of the skins. Spread the walnuts in a small baking pan and dry in the oven for 7 to 8 minutes.

2. Meanwhile, blanch the shallots in the same water for 1 minute. Drain, slip off the outer skins and trim the roots as short as possible without cutting off the root end.

3. Heat butter in a 10-inch skillet over medium heat. Add the shallots and season with ¼ teaspoon salt and pepper. Reduce heat to low, cover and cook, giving the pan a shake every few minutes, until lightly browned and nearly tender, about 12 minutes.

4. Add the broth (or water) and bring to a simmer. Reduce heat to low, cover and simmer until it has reduced to a few tablespoons of syrupy juices, about 35 minutes. Stir in the walnuts.

5. Bring a large pot of lightly salted water to a boil. Drop in the Brussels sprouts and boil, uncovered, until just tender, 7 to 8 minutes. Drain, then add to the pan with the shallots and walnuts. Add oil and marjoram, the remaining ¼ teaspoon salt and pepper. Gently stir everything together with a rubber spatula. Serve immediately.

Green Beans with Poppy Seed Dressing

Quick ☼ Easy

These warm, fresh-tasting beans offer an exciting alternative to old standby mushroom-soup-based green-bean casseroles. Toasting the poppy seeds brings out their nutty flavor.

- 1 teaspoon poppy seeds
- 2 tablespoons extra-virgin olive oil
- 1 tablespoon white-wine *or* rice-wine vinegar
- 1 teaspoon Dijon mustard
- ½ teaspoon honey
- 1 tablespoon minced shallot
- ⅛ teaspoon salt, or to taste
  Freshly ground pepper to taste
- 1 pound green beans, stem ends trimmed

1. **To prepare dressing:** Heat a small dry skillet over medium-low heat. Add poppy seeds and toast, stirring, until fragrant, about 1 minute. Transfer to a small bowl (or jar) and let cool. Add oil, vinegar, mustard, honey, shallot, salt and pepper; whisk (or shake) until blended.

2. **To prepare beans:** Cook beans in a large pot of boiling water until just tender, 5 to 7 minutes. Drain. Warm the dressing in a large skillet over medium heat. Add beans and toss to coat.

1

CARBOHYDRATE
SERVING

MAKES 4 SERVINGS, ¾ CUP EACH

PREP TIME: 20 MINUTES
START TO FINISH: 25 MINUTES

TO MAKE AHEAD: The dressing will keep, covered, in the refrigerator for up to 2 days.

PER SERVING

113 CALORIES
8 G FAT (1 G SAT, 5 G MONO)
0 MG CHOLESTEROL
11 G CARBOHYDRATE
3 G PROTEIN
4 G FIBER
104 MG SODIUM

NUTRITION BONUS: Vitamin C (20% DAILY VALUE), Fiber (15% DV), Vitamin A (15% DV).

EXCHANGES

1½ VEGETABLE
1½ FAT (MONO)

Herbed Corn & Edamame Succotash

Quick ☼ Easy

Fresh green soybeans, called edamame or sweet beans, are a great addition to this classic American dish, where they stand in for the traditional lima beans. The succotash is wonderful as it is or topped with grilled shrimp, salmon or chicken.

1½ cups frozen *or* fresh shelled edamame (*see Ingredient Note, page 324*)

1 tablespoon canola oil

½ cup chopped red bell pepper

¼ cup chopped onion

2 cloves garlic, minced

2 cups fresh corn kernels (from 4 ears; *see box, page 243*)

3 tablespoons dry white wine *or* water

2 tablespoons rice vinegar

2 tablespoons chopped fresh parsley

2 tablespoons chopped fresh basil *or* 1 teaspoon dried

½ teaspoon salt, or to taste

Freshly ground pepper to taste

1. Cook edamame in a large saucepan of lightly salted water until tender, about 4 minutes or according to package directions. Drain well.
2. Heat oil in a large nonstick skillet over medium heat. Add bell pepper, onion and garlic; cook, stirring frequently, until vegetables start to soften, about 2 minutes. Stir in corn, wine (or water) and the edamame; cook, stirring frequently, for 4 minutes. Remove from the heat. Stir in vinegar, parsley, basil, salt and pepper. Serve immediately.

1
CARBOHYDRATE
SERVING

MAKES 6 SERVINGS, ¾ CUP EACH

PREP TIME: 15 MINUTES

START TO FINISH: 25 MINUTES

TO MAKE AHEAD: Cover and refrigerate for up to 2 days.

PER SERVING

128 CALORIES

4 G FAT (0 G SAT, 2 G MONO)

0 MG CHOLESTEROL

16 G CARBOHYDRATE

6 G PROTEIN

4 G FIBER

218 MG SODIUM

NUTRITION BONUS: Vitamin C (45% DAILY VALUE), Vitamin A (20% DV).

EXCHANGES

1 STARCH

1 LEAN MEAT

Southwestern Corn & Zucchini Sauté

Quick ☼ Easy

A traditional dish of the Pueblo Indians, this dish is known as *calabacitas* in Spanish, which means "little squash."

1   tablespoon canola oil
1   large onion, thinly sliced
2   cloves garlic, minced
2   large zucchini, cut into ¼-inch dice
1   cup fresh corn kernels (from 2 ears; *see box, below*) *or* frozen
1   4-ounce can chopped green chiles
¼   teaspoon salt, or to taste
    Freshly ground pepper to taste

Heat oil in a large nonstick skillet over medium heat. Add onion and garlic; cook, stirring, until golden and tender, 5 to 10 minutes. Stir in zucchini, corn and chiles. Cover and cook, stirring once, until the zucchini is tender, about 10 minutes. Season with salt and pepper. Serve hot.

1

CARBOHYDRATE
SERVING

**MAKES 6 SERVINGS,
ABOUT ¾ CUP EACH**

PREP TIME: 10 MINUTES
START TO FINISH: 20 MINUTES

TO MAKE AHEAD: Cover and refrigerate for up to 2 days.

PER SERVING

    76   CALORIES
     3   G FAT (0 G SAT, 1 G MONO)
     0   MG CHOLESTEROL
    12   G CARBOHYDRATE
     2   G PROTEIN
     2   G FIBER
   138   MG SODIUM

NUTRITION BONUS: Vitamin C (48% DAILY VALUE), Folate (12% DV).

EXCHANGES

     2   VEGETABLE
    ½   FAT (MONO)

TIP

REMOVING CORN FROM THE COB

Stand an uncooked ear of corn on its stem end in a shallow bowl and slice the kernels off with a sharp, thin-bladed knife. This technique produces whole kernels that are good for adding to salads and salsas. If you want to use the corn kernels for soups, fritters or puddings, you can add another step to the process. After cutting the kernels off, reverse the knife and, using the dull side, press it down the length of the ear to push out the rest of the corn and its milk.

Roasted Asparagus with Pine Nuts

Quick ☀ Easy

Roasting is one of the easiest and tastiest ways to cook asparagus. Here we give it an extra flourish with a quick sauce of reduced balsamic vinegar and a sprinkling of toasted pine nuts.

MAKES **4** SERVINGS

PREP TIME: 15 MINUTES

START TO FINISH: 20 MINUTES

PER SERVING

112 CALORIES

5 G FAT (1 G SAT, 3 G MONO)

0 MG CHOLESTEROL

12 G CARBOHYDRATE

5 G PROTEIN

4 G FIBER

153 MG SODIUM

NUTRITION BONUS: Vitamin C (30% DAILY VALUE), Vitamin A (20% DV).

EXCHANGES

2 VEGETABLE

1 FAT (MONO)

2	tablespoons pine nuts
1½	pounds asparagus
1	large shallot, thinly sliced
2	teaspoons extra-virgin olive oil
¼	teaspoon salt, divided
	Freshly ground pepper to taste
¼	cup balsamic vinegar

1. Preheat oven to 350°F. Spread pine nuts in a small baking pan and toast in the oven until golden and fragrant, 7 to 10 minutes. Transfer to a small bowl to cool.

2. Increase oven temperature to 450°. Snap off the tough ends of asparagus. Toss the asparagus with shallot, oil, ⅛ teaspoon salt and pepper. Spread in a single layer on a large baking sheet with sides. Roast, turning twice, until the asparagus is tender and browned, 10 to 15 minutes.

3. Meanwhile, bring vinegar and the remaining ⅛ teaspoon salt to a simmer in a small skillet over medium-high heat. Reduce heat to medium-low and simmer, swirling the pan occasionally, until slightly syrupy and reduced to 1 tablespoon, about 5 minutes. To serve, toss the asparagus with the reduced vinegar and sprinkle with the pine nuts.

❝The gas grill is a great way to cook, because I can make just one portion of something, especially vegetables. Grilled asparagus is a treat in the summer months. In the winter, I make some kind of soup every week. Hot soup makes a good breakfast that fits into my meal plan.❞

— *Marcia B.,*
Georgia

Mediterranean Lima Beans

High ⬆ Fiber   Quick ☀ Easy

Canned tomatoes and frozen chopped onions and lima beans make this hearty side dish a cinch. If you like, make it more substantial with the addition of crumbled feta cheese or chopped Greek olives.

2	tablespoons extra-virgin olive oil
2	cups chopped fresh *or* frozen onions
4	cloves garlic, minced
1	teaspoon dried oregano
1	teaspoon ground cinnamon
½	teaspoon crushed red pepper, or to taste
2	14½-ounce cans diced tomatoes
2	10-ounce packages frozen baby lima beans (4 cups)

Heat oil in a large nonstick skillet over medium-high heat. Add onions and cook, stirring occasionally, until soft, 3 to 5 minutes. Add garlic and cook 1 minute more. Stir in oregano, cinnamon, crushed red pepper, tomatoes and lima beans. Cook, stirring occasionally, until the beans are fully cooked and the mixture is heated through, 10 to 15 minutes. Serve hot.

1½
CARBOHYDRATE
SERVINGS

MAKES 6 SERVINGS, 1 CUP EACH

PREP TIME: 5 MINUTES
START TO FINISH: 25 MINUTES

PER SERVING

190	CALORIES
5	G FAT (1 G SAT, 4 G MONO)
0	MG CHOLESTEROL
30	G CARBOHYDRATE
8	G PROTEIN
9	G FIBER
208	MG SODIUM

NUTRITION BONUS: Fiber (37% DAILY VALUE), Vitamin C (30% DV), Magnesium (15% DV).

EXCHANGES

1	STARCH
2	VEGETABLE
1	LEAN MEAT

$1\frac{1}{2}$

CARBOHYDRATE

SERVINGS

Peppers Stuffed with Zucchini & Corn

High ↑ Fiber

Late summer, when corn, zucchini and bell peppers are abundant, is the perfect time for creating these savory stuffed vegetables. Serve them as a special side for grilled or roasted chicken, or with cooked quinoa (*see page 237*) for a spectacular vegetarian entree.

MAKES 4 SERVINGS

PREP TIME: 20 MINUTES

START TO FINISH: 1 HOUR 10 MINUTES

TO MAKE AHEAD: Prepare through Step 5. Cover and refrigerate for up to 2 days.

INGREDIENT TIP
For a hot and spicy dish, don't seed the jalapeño.

PER SERVING

198 CALORIES

8 G FAT (3 G SAT, 3 G MONO)

14 MG CHOLESTEROL

28 G CARBOHYDRATE

9 G PROTEIN

7 G FIBER

402 MG SODIUM

NUTRITION BONUS: Vitamin C (558% DAILY VALUE), Fiber (28% DV), Folate (21% DV).

EXCHANGES

2 VEGETABLE

1 STARCH

1 MEDIUM-FAT MEAT

4	large, plump red bell peppers
2	teaspoons extra-virgin olive oil
1	onion, finely chopped
2	cloves garlic, minced
1-2	jalapeño peppers, seeded and minced
3	cups diced zucchini
1½	cups fresh corn kernels (from 3 ears; *see box, page 243*) *or frozen*
½	teaspoon salt, or to taste
½	cup grated Muenster *or* Monterey Jack cheese
¼	cup chopped fresh cilantro
	Freshly ground pepper to taste
	Paprika for garnish

1. Preheat oven to 450°F. Coat a baking sheet with cooking spray.

2. Halve peppers lengthwise, leaving stems intact. With a paring knife, remove seeds and ribs. Place peppers, cut-side down, on the prepared baking sheet. Bake until the peppers are just tender, 10 to 15 minutes. Set aside.

3. Reduce oven temperature to 375°. Coat a 9-by-13-inch baking dish with cooking spray.

4. Heat oil in a large skillet over medium heat. Add onion and cook, stirring occasionally, until softened, 3 to 5 minutes. Add garlic and jalapeño; cook, stirring, for 1 minute. Add zucchini, corn and salt; cook, stirring occasionally, until the vegetables are tender, about 10 minutes. Let cool. Stir in cheese and cilantro. Season with pepper.

5. Divide the mixture among the pepper halves. Place in the prepared baking dish.

6. Add 2 to 3 tablespoons water to the baking dish. Cover with foil and bake the peppers until heated through, about 20 minutes. Uncover and bake for 5 minutes more. Sprinkle with paprika and serve.

Spiced Corn & Rice Pilaf

Quick  Easy

This corn-flecked rice pilaf has a distinctive Indian flavor, thanks to the addition of cumin seeds, cinnamon and cardamom. It makes a delicious accompaniment to grilled meats and poultry.

2	teaspoons extra-virgin olive oil
¼	cup finely chopped onion
1	3-inch cinnamon stick
¾	teaspoon cumin seeds
¼	teaspoon ground cardamom
¼	teaspoon salt, or to taste
1	cup brown basmati (*see Ingredient Note, page 323*) *or* long-grain brown rice
2¾	cups reduced-sodium chicken broth *or* vegetable broth
2	tablespoons hulled pumpkin seeds
1	cup fresh corn kernels (from 2 ears; *see box, page 243*) *or* frozen

1. Heat oil in a large saucepan over medium-high heat. Add onion and cook, stirring often, until lightly browned, about 3 minutes. Add cinnamon stick, cumin seeds, cardamom, salt and rice; cook, stirring often, until spices are fragrant, about 1 minute.

2. Stir in broth and bring to a boil. Reduce heat to low; cover and simmer until the liquid is absorbed and the rice is tender, 35 to 40 minutes.

3. Meanwhile, toast pumpkin seeds in a small dry skillet over medium-low heat, stirring constantly, until fragrant, 1 to 2 minutes. Transfer to a bowl to cool.

4. When the rice is ready, stir in corn, cover and cook until heated through, about 5 minutes. Remove the cinnamon stick. Fluff the pilaf with a fork and fold in the toasted pumpkin seeds.

1½

CARBOHYDRATE SERVINGS

MAKES 8 SERVINGS, ½ CUP EACH

PREP TIME: 10 MINUTES
START TO FINISH: 45 MINUTES

PER SERVING

129 CALORIES
3 G FAT (1 G SAT, 2 G MONO)
2 MG CHOLESTEROL
22 G CARBOHYDRATE
4 G PROTEIN
2 G FIBER
126 MG SODIUM

EXCHANGES

1½ STARCH
1 FAT (MONO)

1¹/₂

CARBOHYDRATE

SERVINGS

MAKES **6** SERVINGS, ¾ CUP EACH

PREP TIME: 10 MINUTES

START TO FINISH: 1 HOUR 5 MINUTES

PER SERVING

159 CALORIES

4 G FAT (1 G SAT, 2 G MONO)

4 MG CHOLESTEROL

25 G CARBOHYDRATE

8 G PROTEIN

3 G FIBER

60 MG SODIUM

NUTRITION BONUS: Magnesium (18% DAILY VALUE), Zinc (13% DV), Folate (12% DV).

EXCHANGES

1 STARCH

1 VEGETABLE

1 FAT (MONO)

Wild Rice with Shiitakes
& Toasted Almonds

Toasted almonds enhance the nutty flavor of wild rice in this simple yet luxurious side dish. You could give it an Asian twist by substituting sesame oil for the butter and adding a drizzle of soy sauce.

2¼ cups reduced-sodium chicken broth *or* vegetable broth
2 cups sliced shiitake mushroom caps *or* button mushrooms (3 ounces)
1 cup wild rice
6 tablespoons sliced almonds
1 teaspoon butter
1 bunch scallions, trimmed and thinly sliced (about 2 cups)
Freshly ground pepper to taste

1. Bring broth to a boil in a medium saucepan over high heat. Stir in mushrooms and wild rice. Return to a boil. Reduce heat to very low, cover, and simmer until the rice has "blossomed" and is just tender, 45 to 55 minutes. Drain any remaining liquid and transfer the rice to a serving bowl.
2. Meanwhile, toast almonds in a small dry skillet over medium-low heat, stirring constantly until golden brown and fragrant, 2 to 3 minutes. Transfer to a plate to cool.
3. About 5 minutes before the rice is done, melt butter in a medium nonstick skillet over medium heat. Add scallions and cook, stirring often, until softened and still bright green, 2 to 3 minutes. Stir the scallions, almonds and pepper into the rice. Serve warm.

Baked Curried Brown Rice & Lentil Pilaf

High ⬆ Fiber

Pop this quickly assembled, fiber-rich side dish (or vegetarian main dish) into the oven and forget it till the timer rings. Serve with spinach to add color and maximize iron absorption.

1	tablespoon butter
1	cup brown basmati (*see Ingredient Note, page 323*) *or* brown jasmine rice
4¼	cups water
1	cup brown lentils
4	cloves garlic, peeled
1	cinnamon stick
4	⅛-inch-thick slices peeled fresh ginger
1-2	teaspoons red curry paste (*see Note*) *or* 1 tablespoon curry powder
½	teaspoon salt, or to taste
4	scallions, sliced

1. Place rack in lower third of oven; preheat to 350°F.
2. Melt butter over medium-high heat in a large ovenproof Dutch oven; add rice and cook, stirring, until lightly toasted, about 1½ minutes. (If using curry powder, add it now and cook, stirring, until fragrant, about 15 seconds.) Add water. Stir in lentils, garlic cloves, cinnamon stick, ginger, curry paste, if using, and salt; bring to a boil, stirring to dissolve the curry paste.
3. Cover the pot tightly with a lid or foil. Transfer to the oven and bake until the rice and lentils are tender and all the water is absorbed, 50 to 55 minutes. Fluff with a fork, removing the cinnamon stick and ginger slices. Serve garnished with scallions.

2

CARBOHYDRATE
SERVINGS

MAKES 6 SERVINGS, ¾ CUP EACH

PREP TIME: 5 MINUTES
START TO FINISH: 1 HOUR

INGREDIENT NOTE
A blend of chile peppers, garlic, lemongrass and galanga (a root with a flavor similar to ginger), red curry paste is a convenient way to add heat and complexity to a recipe with just one ingredient. Look for it in jars or cans in the Asian section of the supermarket or specialty stores.

PER SERVING

232	CALORIES
3	G FAT (1 G SAT, 1 G MONO)
5	MG CHOLESTEROL
42	G CARBOHYDRATE
11	G PROTEIN
9	G FIBER
216	MG SODIUM

NUTRITION BONUS: Folate (43% DAILY VALUE), Fiber (36% DV), Iron (22% DV).

EXCHANGES

2½	STARCH
1	LEAN MEAT

2

CARBOHYDRATE

SERVINGS

MAKES **4** SERVINGS, ABOUT
1¼ CUPS EACH

PREP TIME: 20 MINUTES
START TO FINISH: 35 MINUTES

PER SERVING

280 CALORIES

12 G FAT (2 G SAT, 6 G MONO)

2 MG CHOLESTEROL

37 G CARBOHYDRATE

11 G PROTEIN

9 G FIBER

244 MG SODIUM

NUTRITION BONUS: Vitamin A
(160% DAILY VALUE), Fiber (38% DV),
Vitamin C (35% DV), Folate
(18% DV).

EXCHANGES

1½ STARCH

1 VEGETABLE

2½ FAT (MONO)

Braised Bulgur & Cabbage

High ⬆ Fiber   Quick ☼ Easy

Cooking hearty cabbage with nutty-tasting bulgur makes for a practical and nutrient-rich braise that marries nicely with pork or chicken.

2	teaspoons canola oil
¾	cup bulgur (*see Ingredient Note, page 323*)
1	large onion, chopped
2	cups chopped green cabbage
2	cups sliced carrots
1½	cups reduced-sodium chicken broth *or* vegetable broth
1	tablespoon reduced-sodium soy sauce *or* tamari
½	cup chopped unsalted dry-roasted peanuts
2	tablespoons chopped fresh parsley

Heat oil in a Dutch oven or large saucepan over medium heat. Add bulgur, onion, cabbage and carrots; cook, stirring, until the vegetables begin to soften, about 1 minute. Add broth and soy sauce (or tamari); bring to a boil. Reduce heat to low, cover and simmer until the bulgur is tender and the broth is absorbed, 10 to 15 minutes. Serve hot, sprinkled with peanuts and parsley.

Bulgur-Chickpea Pilaf

High ⬆ Fiber   Quick ☼ Easy

Chickpeas and bulgur are a popular pairing in Middle Eastern cooking—a smart choice too because both ingredients provide a healthy amount of fiber.

1	cup bulgur (*see Ingredient Note, page 323*)
1	cup boiling water
1	teaspoon sesame oil
½	teaspoon canola oil
1	onion, chopped
1	clove garlic, finely chopped
1	teaspoon ground cumin
¾	cup canned chickpeas, rinsed
1	cup reduced-sodium chicken broth *or* vegetable broth
	Freshly ground pepper to taste

1. Place bulgur in a medium bowl and cover with boiling water. Let stand for 10 minutes to soften.
2. Meanwhile, heat sesame oil and canola oil in a Dutch oven over medium heat. Add onion, garlic and cumin; cook, stirring often, until the onion is softened but not browned, about 5 minutes. Stir in chickpeas. Add broth and the bulgur; mix well. Bring to a boil, reduce heat to low, cover and simmer over low heat until the liquid is absorbed, about 10 minutes.
3. If the bulgur seems too wet, uncover the pan and cook over medium heat until the liquid is absorbed. Fluff with a fork and season with pepper.

2

CARBOHYDRATE
SERVINGS

MAKES 4 SERVINGS

PREP TIME: 10 MINUTES
START TO FINISH: 35 MINUTES

PER SERVING

201	CALORIES
3	G FAT (0 G SAT, 1 G MONO)
1	MG CHOLESTEROL
38	G CARBOHYDRATE
8	G PROTEIN
9	G FIBER
87	MG SODIUM

NUTRITION BONUS: Fiber
(36% DAILY VALUE).

EXCHANGES
2½ STARCH
1 LEAN MEAT

2

CARBOHYDRATE

SERVINGS

MAKES 6 SERVINGS,
ABOUT 1 CUP EACH

PREP TIME: 20 MINUTES

START TO FINISH: 30 MINUTES

TO MAKE AHEAD: Cover and refrigerate for up to 2 hours.

PER SERVING

206 CALORIES

7 G FAT (1 G SAT, 5 G MONO)

0 MG CHOLESTEROL

32 G CARBOHYDRATE

5 G PROTEIN

5 G FIBER

358 MG SODIUM

NUTRITION BONUS: Vitamin C (78% DAILY VALUE), Fiber (20% DV).

EXCHANGES

2 STARCH

1 FAT (MONO)

Citrusy Couscous Salad with Olives

High ⬆ Fiber   Quick ☼ Easy

Try this refreshing grain salad as an accompaniment to grilled chicken or fish. Chilled, it's also great for picnics. Look for whole-wheat couscous in the natural-foods section of supermarkets or in specialty stores.

1½	cups whole-wheat couscous
¼	cup orange juice concentrate, thawed
2	tablespoons extra-virgin olive oil
1	tablespoon Dijon mustard
1	tablespoon chopped fresh thyme *or* 1 teaspoon dried thyme leaves
1	teaspoon freshly grated orange zest, preferably organic
½	teaspoon salt, or to taste
2	cups boiling water
1	cup chopped fresh parsley
½	cup chopped scallions (4 scallions)
¼	cup chopped pitted Kalamata olives (12 olives)
1	navel orange, peeled, sectioned and diced
1	tablespoon lemon juice
	Freshly ground pepper to taste

1. Stir together couscous, orange juice concentrate, oil, mustard, thyme, orange zest and salt in a large bowl. Stir in boiling water, cover and set aside until the liquid has been absorbed, about 5 minutes.

2. Fluff the couscous with a fork. Add parsley, scallions, olives, diced orange and lemon juice; toss to blend. Season with pepper.

Quinoa with Sun-Dried Tomatoes

Quick ☼ Easy

This ancient Peruvian grain has a nutty, almost sweet flavor that really needs no accent but is excellent with sun-dried tomatoes and shallots. It can be found in the natural-foods section of supermarkets and specialty stores.

- 1 cup quinoa
- 1 teaspoon butter *or* extra-virgin olive oil
- 8 sun-dried tomatoes (*not* oil-packed), chopped
- 2 shallots, finely chopped
- 1 clove garlic, minced
- 2 cups reduced-sodium chicken broth *or* vegetable broth
  Pinch of cayenne pepper
- 2 tablespoons chopped fresh parsley
  Freshly ground pepper to taste

1. Place quinoa in a fine-meshed sieve and rinse under cold running water until the water runs clear.
2. Heat butter (or oil) in a heavy medium saucepan over medium heat. Add tomatoes, shallots and garlic; cook, stirring often, until the shallots are softened, 3 to 5 minutes. Add broth and bring to a boil. Stir in the quinoa and cayenne and return to a boil.
3. Reduce heat to low and simmer, covered, until the quinoa is tender and the liquid has been absorbed, 15 to 20 minutes. Let sit for 5 minutes. Fluff with a fork. Stir in parsley and season with pepper.

2

CARBOHYDRATE

SERVINGS

MAKES 4 SERVINGS

PREP TIME: 10 MINUTES

START TO FINISH: 40 MINUTES

PER SERVING

200 CALORIES

4 G FAT (1 G SAT, 1 G MONO)

4 MG CHOLESTEROL

34 G CARBOHYDRATE

8 G PROTEIN

3 G FIBER

148 MG SODIUM

EXCHANGES

2 STARCH

1 VEGETABLE

Sweet Potato Casserole

With a scrumptious, crunchy nut topping, this casserole can be a side dish or even a sweet ending to a holiday meal. We reworked this traditional Southern recipe for the *Rx for Recipes* column, reducing calories by 42 percent and saturated fat by 60 percent.

2½ pounds sweet potatoes (3 medium), peeled and cut into 2-inch chunks
2 large eggs
1 tablespoon canola oil
1 tablespoon honey
½ cup 1% milk
2 teaspoons freshly grated orange zest, preferably organic
1 teaspoon vanilla extract
½ teaspoon salt, or to taste

TOPPING
½ cup whole-wheat flour
⅓ cup packed brown sugar
4 teaspoons frozen orange juice concentrate
1 tablespoon canola oil
1 tablespoon butter, melted
½ cup chopped pecans (1¾ ounces)

1. Place sweet potatoes in a large saucepan; cover with lightly salted water and bring to a boil. Cover and cook over medium heat until tender, 10 to 15 minutes. Drain well and return to the pan. Mash with a potato masher. Measure out 3 cups. (Reserve any extra for another use.)

2. Preheat oven to 350°F. Coat an 8-inch-square (or similar 2-quart) baking dish with cooking spray.

3. Whisk eggs, oil and honey in a medium bowl. Add mashed sweet potato and mix well. Stir in milk, orange zest, vanilla and salt. Spread the mixture in the prepared baking dish.

4. **To prepare topping:** Mix flour, brown sugar, orange juice concentrate, oil and butter in a small bowl. Blend with a fork or your fingertips until crumbly. Stir in pecans. Sprinkle over the sweet potato mixture.

5. Bake the casserole until heated through and the top is lightly browned, 35 to 45 minutes.

2
CARBOHYDRATE SERVINGS

MAKES **10** SERVINGS, ABOUT ½ CUP EACH

PREP TIME: 30 MINUTES
START TO FINISH: 1¼ HOURS

TO MAKE AHEAD: Prepare through Step 4; cover and refrigerate for up to 2 days.

PER SERVING
223 CALORIES
10 G FAT (2 G SAT, 5 G MONO)
46 MG CHOLESTEROL
31 G CARBOHYDRATE
4 G PROTEIN
4 G FIBER
163 MG SODIUM

NUTRITION BONUS: Vitamin A (280% DAILY VALUE), Vitamin C (25% DV).

EXCHANGES
2 STARCH
1½ FAT (MONO)

Black Beans & Barley

High ↑ Fiber   Quick ☼ Easy

Quick-cooking barley replaces rice in the classic Caribbean combo. Barley makes a good whole-grain choice because it's rich in soluble fiber and is digested slowly, leaving you feeling satisfied longer.

2½

CARBOHYDRATE
SERVINGS

2	teaspoons canola oil
1	medium onion, chopped
½	red bell pepper, chopped
2	cloves garlic, minced
¼	teaspoon ground cumin
1½	cups reduced-sodium chicken broth *or* vegetable broth
¾	cup quick-cooking barley
½	teaspoon dried oregano
1	15½-ounce *or* 19-ounce can black beans, rinsed
2	tablespoons chopped fresh cilantro (optional)

1. Heat oil in a large nonstick skillet over medium heat. Add onion, bell pepper and garlic; cook, stirring frequently, until onion is barely tender, about 5 minutes. Add cumin and cook for 30 seconds more.

2. Add broth, barley and oregano; increase heat and bring to a boil. Reduce heat to low; cover and simmer until the barley is tender and most of the liquid has been absorbed, about 10 minutes.

3. Gently stir in beans and heat through. Sprinkle with cilantro (if using) just before serving.

MAKES 4 SERVINGS, 1 CUP EACH

PREP TIME: 15 MINUTES
START TO FINISH: 35 MINUTES

PER SERVING
279 CALORIES
4 G FAT (1 G SAT, 1 G MONO)
1 MG CHOLESTEROL
49 G CARBOHYDRATE
12 G PROTEIN
13 G FIBER
113 MG SODIUM

NUTRITION BONUS: Vitamin C (53% DAILY VALUE), Fiber (52% DV), Selenium (20% DV).

EXCHANGES
2½ STARCH
1 LEAN MEAT

Bean-Cooking Guide

BESIDES BEING DELICIOUS and accepting of just about any flavoring, virtually all types of beans are nutrient powerhouses—rich in protein, folic acid, magnesium and protective phytochemicals. (Choose darker-colored beans, and you'll benefit even more; recent research confirms that black, red and brown beans are richest in heart-healthy, cancer-protective anti-oxidants.) Most beans are high in both soluble and insoluble fiber, and the carbohydrates they contain are slowly digested, with a gentler effect on blood-sugar levels. That makes beans especially filling and satisfying, even though they're fairly low in calories—about 100 to 125 calories per half-cup serving. Hearty, protein-packed and toothsome, beans closely match meat's nutrition and flavor profile, without the accompanying dose of saturated fat.

Cooking dried beans from scratch gives you the firmest texture and best flavor, and it's easy to do with a little advance planning. But there's no denying that canned beans are wonderfully convenient, and you're more likely to eat beans regularly if there are canned beans in your cupboard. So we're advocates of having both types on hand.

When you use canned beans in a recipe, be sure to rinse them first in a colander under cold running water, as their canning liquid often contains a fair amount of sodium.

Equivalents

A pound of dried beans (about 2 cups) will yield 5 to 6 cups cooked beans.

One 19-ounce can yields about 2 cups cooked beans; a 15-ounce can, about 1½ cups.

Soaking

Our preferred method for cooking most types of dried beans is to soak them first, to shorten their cooking time. (Lentils and split peas do not need to be soaked, as they cook quickly.) For the best results, use the overnight soaking method; if you're in a hurry and don't mind risking a few burst bean skins, use the quick-soak method.

OVERNIGHT SOAK: Rinse and pick over the beans, then place them in a large bowl with enough cold water to cover them by 2 inches. Let the beans soak for at least 8 hours or overnight. (For longer soaking, or in warm weather, place the bowl of beans in the refrigerator.) Drain.

QUICK SOAK: Rinse and pick over the beans, then place them in a large pot with enough cold water to cover them by 2 inches. Bring to a boil. Boil for 2 minutes. Remove from the heat and let stand, covered, for 1 hour; drain.

Cooking

CONVENTIONAL METHOD: Place the drained, soaked beans in a large pot and add enough cold water to cover them by 2 inches (about 2 quarts of water for 1 pound of beans). Bring to a boil, skimming off any debris that rises to the surface. Reduce the heat to low and simmer gently, stirring occasionally, until the beans are tender, 1 to 2 hours (cooking time will vary with the type and age of the bean). Wait until the end of the cooking time to add salt or acidic ingredients, such as tomatoes, vinegar or molasses; these ingredients prevent the beans from softening.

SLOW-COOKER METHOD: Place the drained, soaked beans in a slow cooker and pour in 5 cups boiling water. Cover and cook on high until tender, 2 to 3½ hours. Add salt, if using, and cook 15 minutes more.

Herbed White Bean Puree

High ⬆ Fiber   Quick ☼ Easy

A velvety puree of white beans makes a fiber-rich alternative to mashed potatoes. Serve with lamb chops or steak.

- 3   large cloves garlic, peeled and cut in half
- 2   15½-ounce *or* 19-ounce cans cannellini beans (white kidney beans), rinsed
- 2   tablespoons finely chopped fresh parsley
- 1   tablespoon extra-virgin olive oil
- 1   teaspoon finely chopped fresh sage *or* ½ teaspoon dried rubbed sage
- ¼   teaspoon salt, or to taste
     Freshly ground pepper to taste

1. Fill a large saucepan with cold water, add garlic and bring to a boil over high heat. Add beans and return to a boil. Reserve ½ cup of the cooking liquid, then drain the beans and garlic in a strainer or colander.

2. Transfer the beans and garlic to a food processor. Add parsley, oil and sage. Process, adding some of the reserved cooking liquid if necessary, to make a thick puree. Season with salt and pepper.

MAKES 4 SERVINGS

PREP TIME: 5 MINUTES
START TO FINISH: 15 MINUTES

PER SERVING

285   CALORIES
  4   G FAT (1 G SAT, 3 G MONO)
  0   MG CHOLESTEROL
 48   G CARBOHYDRATE
 16   G PROTEIN
 10   G FIBER
157   MG SODIUM

NUTRITION BONUS: Fiber (40% DAILY VALUE), Folate (35% DV), Calcium (16% DV).

EXCHANGES

2½   STARCH
  2   LEAN MEAT

Sauces & Condiments

0

CARBOHYDRATE
SERVINGS

1/2

CARBOHYDRATE
SERVING

1

CARBOHYDRATE
SERVING

2

CARBOHYDRATE
SERVINGS

Citrus-Rosemary Sauce

Quick ☼ Easy

Reducing orange juice with shallots and rosemary intensifies its sweetness; finishing it with just a smidgen of butter makes it magically rich. This is an elegant sauce for salmon, halibut or chicken.

1 cup orange juice (from 2-3 oranges)
2 tablespoons finely chopped shallot (1 medium)
1 tablespoon chopped fresh rosemary
2 teaspoons butter
1 teaspoon balsamic vinegar
¼ teaspoon salt, or to taste
   Freshly ground pepper to taste

Combine orange juice, shallot and rosemary in small saucepan; bring to a boil over medium-high heat. Cook, uncovered, until reduced to ½ cup, 6 to 8 minutes. Remove from heat. Add butter, vinegar, salt and pepper; stir until the butter has melted. Serve warm.

Creamy Dill Sauce

Quick ☼ Easy

Cutting mayonnaise with yogurt is an excellent technique for reducing calories and fat. Here, it makes a simple sauce that goes perfectly with delicate preparations, such as Oven-Fried Fish Fillets (*page 199*).

¼ cup reduced-fat mayonnaise
¼ cup nonfat plain yogurt
2 scallions, finely chopped
1 tablespoon lemon juice
1 tablespoon finely chopped fresh dill *or* parsley
   Freshly ground pepper to taste

Combine ingredients in a small bowl and mix well.

O

CARBOHYDRATE
SERVINGS

MAKES ABOUT ½ CUP

PREP TIME: 10 MINUTES
START TO FINISH: 20 MINUTES

PER TABLESPOON
25 CALORIES
1 G FAT (1 G SAT, 0 G MONO)
3 MG CHOLESTEROL
4 G CARBOHYDRATE
0 G PROTEIN
0 G FIBER
80 MG SODIUM

NUTRITION BONUS: Vitamin C
(26% DAILY VALUE).

EXCHANGES
FREE FOOD

For Creamy Dill Sauce:

CARBOHYDRATE
SERVINGS

MAKES ABOUT ½ CUP

PREP TIME: 5 MINUTES
START TO FINISH: 5 MINUTES

TO MAKE AHEAD: Cover and
refrigerate for up to 2 days.

PER TABLESPOON
28 CALORIES
2 G FAT (0 G SAT, 0 G MONO)
2 MG CHOLESTEROL
2 G CARBOHYDRATE
0 G PROTEIN
0 G FIBER
50 MG SODIUM

EXCHANGES
FREE FOOD

Cucumber Raita

Quick ☀ Easy

An easy, cooling accompaniment to spicy dishes. Try it with Tandoori Chicken (*page 152*).

- ½ teaspoon canola oil
- 1 clove garlic, minced
- 1 medium cucumber, peeled, seeded and finely diced
- ⅔ cup nonfat plain yogurt
- 1 tablespoon chopped fresh cilantro
- ½ teaspoon honey
- ½ teaspoon rice-wine vinegar
-   Pinch of ground cumin
-   Dash of Tabasco *or* other hot sauce
-   Freshly ground pepper to taste

Heat oil in a small skillet over medium heat. Add garlic and cook, stirring, until fragrant, about 30 seconds. Transfer to a bowl. Add cucumber, yogurt, cilantro, honey, vinegar, cumin and hot sauce. Stir to combine. Season with pepper.

Light Cheese Sauce

Quick ☀ Easy

A spoonful of cheese sauce helps the broccoli (and other vegetables) go down. This lightened version is thickened with a flour and milk "slurry," instead of the traditional roux, which is made with melted butter and flour.

- 4 teaspoons all-purpose flour
- 1 cup 1% milk, divided
- ½ cup grated sharp Cheddar cheese
- 1 teaspoon dry mustard
- ½ teaspoon sweet paprika
-   Cayenne pepper to taste (optional)
- ¼ teaspoon salt, or to taste

Whisk flour with 2 tablespoons milk in a small bowl until smooth. Heat the remaining milk in a small saucepan over medium heat until steaming. Add the flour mixture and cook, whisking constantly, until the sauce bubbles and thickens, 2 to 3 minutes. Remove from the heat; stir in Cheddar, dry mustard, paprika, cayenne (if using) and salt.

O

CARBOHYDRATE
SERVINGS

MAKES 1 CUP

PREP TIME: 10 MINUTES
START TO FINISH: 10 MINUTES

TO MAKE AHEAD: Cover and refrigerate for up to 1 day.

PER SERVING
- 41 CALORIES
- 1 G FAT (0 G SAT, 1 G MONO)
- 2 MG CHOLESTEROL
- 5 G CARBOHYDRATE
- 3 G PROTEIN
- 0 G FIBER
- 30 MG SODIUM

EXCHANGES
- 1 VEGETABLE

For Light Cheese Sauce:

O

CARBOHYDRATE
SERVINGS

MAKES ½ CUP

PREP TIME: 5 MINUTES
START TO FINISH: 10 MINUTES

TO MAKE AHEAD: Cover and refrigerate for up to 2 days. Reheat before serving.

PER TABLESPOON
- 47 CALORIES
- 3 G FAT (1 G SAT, 0 G MONO)
- 9 MG CHOLESTEROL
- 3 G CARBOHYDRATE
- 3 G PROTEIN
- 0 G FIBER
- 131 MG SODIUM

EXCHANGES
- 1 FAT

CARBOHYDRATE
SERVINGS

MAKES ABOUT 1 CUP

PREP TIME: 10 MINUTES
START TO FINISH: 10 MINUTES

TO MAKE AHEAD: Cover and refrigerate for up to 4 days.

PER TABLESPOON
26 CALORIES
2 G FAT (0 G SAT, 1 G MONO)
0 MG CHOLESTEROL
2 G CARBOHYDRATE
0 G PROTEIN
0 G FIBER
61 MG SODIUM

EXCHANGES
FREE FOOD

For Orange & Sesame Sauce:

CARBOHYDRATE
SERVINGS

MAKES ABOUT ½ CUP

PREP TIME: 10 MINUTES
START TO FINISH: 20 MINUTES

PER TABLESPOON
28 CALORIES
1 G FAT (0 G SAT, 1 G MONO)
0 MG CHOLESTEROL
4 G CARBOHYDRATE
1 G PROTEIN
0 G FIBER
34 MG SODIUM

NUTRITION BONUS: Vitamin C (20% DAILY VALUE).

EXCHANGES
FREE FOOD

262

Mediterranean Red Pepper Sauce

Quick ☼ Easy

Jarred roasted red peppers are an invaluable addition to any cook's pantry. Paired with almonds, garlic and spices, they make a simple, rich-tasting sauce to serve with grilled fish or vegetables.

- ¼ cup slivered almonds
- 1 small clove garlic, crushed
- 1 teaspoon ground cumin
- ½ teaspoon paprika
- ¼ teaspoon salt, or to taste
- Pinch of crushed red pepper
- 1 7-ounce jar roasted red peppers, drained and rinsed
- 1 tablespoon extra-virgin olive oil
- 1 tablespoon red-wine vinegar

Combine almonds, garlic, cumin, paprika, salt and crushed red pepper in a food processor; pulse until the almonds are ground. Add peppers, oil and vinegar; process until smooth, stopping several times to scrape down the sides of the workbowl.

Orange & Sesame Seed Sauce

Quick ☼ Easy

We love to dress up steamed asparagus or broccoli with this sauce. When tangerines are in season, squeeze them fresh for an especially interesting variation.

- 1 teaspoon canola oil
- 1 tablespoon sesame seeds
- 2 tablespoons finely chopped shallots (1 medium)
- 1½ teaspoons freshly grated orange zest
- 1 cup orange juice (from 2-3 oranges)
- 1 tablespoon sherry vinegar *or* rice-wine vinegar
- 1½ teaspoons reduced-sodium soy sauce
- 2 tablespoons chopped fresh chives *or* scallion greens

Heat oil in a small saucepan over low heat. Add sesame seeds and stir until lightly toasted, about 20 seconds. Add shallots and stir until softened, about 1 minute. Add zest and juice, vinegar and soy sauce. Simmer until reduced to ½ cup, about 6 minutes. Stir in chives (or scallion greens).

Orange-Miso Sauce

Quick ☼ Easy

Mild, nutty flaxseed oil, the richest plant source of omega-3 fatty acids, provides the perfect base for salty miso and sweet orange juice. This sauce is delightful over grilled eggplant, fish and chicken or used as a salad dressing.

¼ cup sweet white miso (*see Ingredient Note, page 324*)
1 tablespoon orange zest
¼ cup orange juice
¼ cup flaxseed oil (*see Note*) *or* canola oil
1 tablespoon minced fresh ginger
1 tablespoon rice vinegar
1 teaspoon mirin (optional)

INGREDIENT NOTE: Flaxseed oil contains alpha-linoleic acid, an omega-3 similar to the fatty acids in fish. This is a perishable oil—be sure to keep it in the refrigerator and note the expiration date. Flaxseed oil should not be heated. You can find it in natural-foods stores.

Combine all ingredients in a small bowl and whisk until thoroughly blended.

O

CARBOHYDRATE SERVINGS

MAKES ¾ **CUP**

PREP TIME: 10 MINUTES
START TO FINISH: 10 MINUTES

TO MAKE AHEAD: Cover and refrigerate for up to 4 days.

PER TABLESPOON
53 CALORIES
5 G FAT (0 G SAT, 1 G MONO)
0 MG CHOLESTEROL
2 G CARBOHYDRATE
0 G PROTEIN
0 G FIBER
135 MG SODIUM

EXCHANGES
1 FAT (MONO)

Rémoulade Sauce

Quick ☼ Easy

This is a classic mayonnaise-based sauce that we've lightened using a combination of reduced-fat mayonnaise and yogurt. In addition to seafood, the sauce complements cold roast beef, chicken or hard-boiled eggs.

⅓ cup reduced-fat mayonnaise
⅓ cup low-fat plain yogurt
1 tablespoon coarse-grained mustard
1 tablespoon lemon juice
½ teaspoon anchovy paste
Pinch of cayenne pepper
4 teaspoons drained capers, rinsed
4 teaspoons chopped fresh parsley

Whisk mayonnaise, yogurt, mustard, lemon juice, anchovy paste and cayenne in a small bowl until smooth. Stir in capers and parsley.

For Rémoulade Sauce:

O

CARBOHYDRATE SERVINGS

MAKES ABOUT ¾ **CUP**

PREP TIME: 10 MINUTES
START TO FINISH: 10 MINUTES

TO MAKE AHEAD: Cover and refrigerate for up to 4 days.

PER TABLESPOON
18 CALORIES
1 G FAT (0 G SAT, 0 G MONO)
1 MG CHOLESTEROL
3 G CARBOHYDRATE
1 G PROTEIN
0 G FIBER
153 MG SODIUM

EXCHANGES
FREE FOOD

CARBOHYDRATE
SERVINGS

O

MAKES ½ CUP

PREP TIME: 10 MINUTES
START TO FINISH: 10 MINUTES

TO MAKE AHEAD: Cover and refrigerate for up to 2 days.

PER TABLESPOON
  60 CALORIES
  6 G FAT (1 G SAT, 3 G MONO)
  0 MG CHOLESTEROL
  3 G CARBOHYDRATE
  0 G PROTEIN
  0 G FIBER
  132 MG SODIUM

EXCHANGES
  1 FAT (MONO)

For Yogurt-Garlic Sauce:

O

CARBOHYDRATE
SERVINGS

MAKES ½ CUP

PREP TIME: 5 MINUTES
START TO FINISH: 35 MINUTES

TO MAKE AHEAD: Cover and refrigerate for up to 1 day. Stir before using.

PER TABLESPOON
  30 CALORIES
  1 G FAT (0 G SAT, 1 G MONO)
  1 MG CHOLESTEROL
  4 G CARBOHYDRATE
  2 G PROTEIN
  0 G FIBER
  98 MG SODIUM

EXCHANGES
FREE FOOD

Watercress Mayonnaise

Quick ☼ Easy

Watercress adds a subtle peppery bite to a creamy sauce to serve with seafood and poultry.

  ⅓ cup finely chopped watercress leaves
  ¼ cup reduced-fat mayonnaise
  2 tablespoons finely chopped scallions
  1 tablespoon extra-virgin olive oil
  1 tablespoon lemon juice
  1 clove garlic, minced
  ½ teaspoon freshly grated lemon zest
    Freshly ground pepper to taste

Stir all ingredients together in a small bowl until creamy.

Yogurt-Garlic Sauce

Quick ☼ Easy

We created this cool, savory sauce for Middle Eastern Burgers (*page 226*) and Veggie-Burger Pitas (*page 135*), but it's excellent with grilled chicken and lamb too.

  1 6-ounce container (¾ cup) nonfat plain yogurt
    (see *Note*)
  1 clove garlic, minced
  1 teaspoon extra-virgin olive oil
  ⅛ teaspoon salt, or to taste

INGREDIENT NOTE: It's now possible to buy Greek strained yogurt (we like the brand Total, available in many natural-foods stores or www.fageusa.com). If you use that, skip Step 1.

1. Line a sieve or colander with cheesecloth and set over a bowl, leaving at least ½-inch clearance from the bottom. (*Alternatively, use a coffee filter lined with filter paper.*) Spoon in yogurt, cover and let drain in the refrigerator for at least 30 minutes and up to 1 hour. Discard whey.
2. Whisk drained yogurt, garlic, oil and salt in a small bowl.

Fast Fruit Chutney

Quick ☼ Easy

You can use this formula to turn just about any soft fruit you may have on hand into a complex, spicy chutney. Serve with meat and poultry and use to perk up sandwiches.

- 1 teaspoon coriander seeds
- ½ cup sugar
- ¼ cup water
- ⅓ cup cider vinegar
- 2 cups diced soft fruit, such as peaches, nectarines, papayas *or* bananas
- 2 tablespoons minced serrano chiles *or* jalapeño peppers
- 2 teaspoons minced fresh ginger
- Pinch of salt

1. Toast coriander seeds in a small dry skillet over medium-low heat, stirring or shaking the pan constantly, until fragrant, about 1 minute. Transfer to a spice grinder or mortar and pestle and grind to a coarse powder. Set aside.

2. Combine sugar and water in a heavy medium saucepan. Bring to a boil over medium-high heat, stirring occasionally to dissolve sugar. Once it starts boiling, cook without stirring until syrup turns amber, 3 to 6 minutes.

3. Remove from heat and carefully pour in vinegar. (Stand back, as caramel may sputter slightly.) Add fruit, serranos (or jalapeños), ginger, salt and the reserved ground coriander. Return saucepan to medium-high heat and bring to a simmer, stirring occasionally. Reduce heat to low and simmer, stirring occasionally, until the fruit is tender and the chutney has thickened, 3 to 5 minutes. Let cool.

1/2

CARBOHYDRATE
SERVING

MAKES ABOUT 1½ CUPS

PREP TIME: 10 MINUTES
START TO FINISH: 25 MINUTES

TO MAKE AHEAD: Cover and refrigerate for up to 4 days.

PER TABLESPOON

- 23 CALORIES
- 0 G FAT (0 G SAT, 0 G MONO)
- 0 MG CHOLESTEROL
- 6 G CARBOHYDRATE
- 0 G PROTEIN
- 0 G FIBER
- 6 MG SODIUM

EXCHANGES

- ½ FRUIT

Rainbow Pepper Sauté

Use these colorful, versatile peppers to top crostini, on a sandwich or as a condiment on fish or chicken. Reader Maggie Poppa from Yorkshire, England, contributed the recipe.

> 2 tablespoons extra-virgin olive oil
> 2 medium onions, chopped
> 6 red, yellow *and/or* orange bell peppers, seeded and cut into 2-inch slivers
> 1 teaspoon dried oregano
> ¼ teaspoon salt, or to taste
> Freshly ground pepper to taste

Heat oil in a large nonstick skillet over medium heat. Add onions and cook, stirring often, until softened, 3 to 5 minutes. Add peppers; cook, stirring occasionally, until softened, 7 to 10 minutes. Stir in oregano, salt and pepper; cover. Cook, stirring occasionally and adjusting the heat as necessary so the mixture doesn't burn, until the peppers are very tender, 15 to 20 minutes. Serve warm or at room temperature.

Sidebar

1/2 CARBOHYDRATE SERVING

MAKES 12 SERVINGS, ¼ CUP EACH

PREP TIME: 15 MINUTES
START TO FINISH: 50 MINUTES

TO MAKE AHEAD: Cover and refrigerate for up to 4 days.

PER SERVING

47 CALORIES
2 G FAT (0 G SAT, 2 G MONO)
0 MG CHOLESTEROL
6 G CARBOHYDRATE
1 G PROTEIN
1 G FIBER
51 MG SODIUM

NUTRITION BONUS:
Vitamin C (190% DAILY VALUE), Vitamin A (20% DV).

EXCHANGES
1 VEGETABLE

Quote

"The recipes that work for me are simple ones. Grilled, broiled or roasted meat, salads with a simple oil and vinegar dressing, fresh fruit and unadulterated vegetables. No high fat cream sauces or salty foods either, since I also have hypertension and hyperlipidemia. Try explaining that to the hostess at a dinner party who has her heart set on some elaborate main dish or fancy dessert!"

—Carol W.,
Idaho

Black Bean & Tomato Salsa

Quick ☼ Easy

Adding canned beans to a spicy salsa is an easy way to boost fiber and improve nutritional value. This salsa is also a good accompaniment for burgers or Scrambled Egg Burritos, (*page 59*).

1	cup seeded, diced plum tomatoes (3-4 tomatoes)
1	cup canned black beans, rinsed
2	tablespoons chopped scallions
1	tablespoon chopped fresh cilantro *or* parsley
1	tablespoon lime juice
1½	teaspoons extra-virgin olive oil
½-1	teaspoon minced canned chipotle in adobo sauce (*see Ingredient Note, page 323*)
⅛	teaspoon salt, or to taste

Combine all ingredients in a medium bowl; stir to blend. If not serving immediately, cover and refrigerate for up to 2 days.

Roasted Corn Salsa

High ⬆ Fiber

Toasting corn kernels in a dry skillet brings out their inherent sweetness. This robust salsa is an interesting accompaniment to grilled steak.

4	cups fresh corn (from 6-8 ears; *see box, page 243*) *or* frozen
1	red bell pepper, diced
1	4-ounce can chopped green chiles
¼	cup chopped red onion
2	tablespoons lime juice
2	tablespoons chopped fresh cilantro
1	teaspoon dried oregano
½	teaspoon salt, or to taste
½	teaspoon ground cumin
¼	teaspoon freshly ground pepper

1. Heat a dry cast-iron skillet over medium heat until hot. Add corn and bell pepper; cook, stirring occasionally, until well browned, 12 to 15 minutes.
2. Transfer to a large bowl and mix in remaining ingredients. Let stand for 30 minutes before serving.

1

CARBOHYDRATE
SERVING

MAKES 4 SERVINGS, ½ CUP EACH

PREP TIME: 10 MINUTES
START TO FINISH: 10 MINUTES

PER SERVING
83 CALORIES
2 G FAT (0 G SAT, 1 G MONO)
0 MG CHOLESTEROL
11 G CARBOHYDRATE
4 G PROTEIN
4 G FIBER
283 MG SODIUM

NUTRITION BONUS: Vitamin C
(25% DAILY VALUE), Fiber (16% DV).

EXCHANGES
1 STARCH

For Roasted Corn Salsa:

2

CARBOHYDRATE
SERVINGS

MAKES 4 SERVINGS, 1 CUP EACH

PREP TIME: 20 MINUTES
START TO FINISH: 1 HOUR

TO MAKE AHEAD: Cover and
refrigerate for up to 1 day. Bring to
room temperature before serving.

PER SERVING
161 CALORIES
2 G FAT (0 G SAT, 1 G MONO)
0 MG CHOLESTEROL
35 G CARBOHYDRATE
7 G PROTEIN
6 G FIBER
338 MG SODIUM

EXCHANGES
2 STARCH

Old-Fashioned Desserts

> **"**At first I was worried about how to eat, but soon found out that healthy, whole food choices work for me. Mainly, I count carbs for the day. If we have company or eat out, I save up for a small serving of dessert. Counting has become automatic, but I make myself a daily chart to check off my carb allowances if I feel I'm getting off course.**"**
> —*Garnett A., Michigan*

Plum & Apple Compote with Vanilla Custard

Jennifer Sanders of Cambridge, Ontario, came up with this winning combination of plums and apples, which she stews into a compote and accompanies with a light and comforting custard sauce.

COMPOTE

12	prune plums *or* 8 red *or* black plums, pitted and chopped
1/3	cup apple cider
1/4	cup sugar *or* Splenda Granular (*see page 18*)
1/4	teaspoon ground cinnamon
4	large apples, such as Mutsu (Crispin), Fuji *or* Gala

CUSTARD

1½	cups 1% milk, divided
1/4	cup sugar *or* Splenda Granular
1	tablespoon cornstarch
	Pinch of salt
2	large eggs, lightly beaten
1	teaspoon vanilla extract

1. **To prepare compote:** Combine plums, cider, ¼ cup sugar (or Splenda) and cinnamon in a medium saucepan; bring to a simmer over medium heat. Cook, stirring occasionally, until the plums are soft and falling apart, about 5 minutes. Remove from the heat. Peel and grate apples. Stir the grated apples into the plums. Spoon the compote into a large bowl and chill in the refrigerator.

2. **To prepare custard:** Heat 1 cup milk in a saucepan over medium heat until steaming; do not boil. Mix ¼ cup sugar (or Splenda), cornstarch and salt in a medium bowl. Add eggs and whisk until smooth. Whisk in the remaining ½ cup cold milk. Add the heated milk to the egg mixture, whisking constantly. Return the mixture to the saucepan. Cook over low heat, whisking constantly, until thickened, about 3 minutes. Remove from the heat and whisk in vanilla. Transfer the custard to a clean bowl and let cool slightly or refrigerate until chilled.

3. To serve, spoon custard into dessert dishes and top each with compote.

1¹⁄₂ CARBOHYDRATE SERVINGS

MAKES 12 SERVINGS,
½ CUP EACH

PREP TIME: 20 MINUTES

START TO FINISH: 1 HOUR

TO MAKE AHEAD: Refrigerate compote and custard in separate containers for up to 2 days.

PER SERVING

119 CALORIES
1 G FAT (0 G SAT, 1 G MONO)
37 MG CHOLESTEROL
25 G CARBOHYDRATE
3 G PROTEIN
2 G FIBER
37 MG SODIUM

EXCHANGES

1½ OTHER CARBOHYDRATE

PER SERVING WITH SPLENDA

1 CARBOHYDRATE SERVING
91 CALORIES, 18 G CARBOHYDRATE

Chocolate Velvet Pudding

Quick ☼ Easy

Although instant mixes and premade puddings abound in every supermarket, they just can't compare with homemade. This reduced-fat version is almost as quick as a mix and delivers a rich chocolate flavor.

1	large egg
⅓	cup nonfat sweetened condensed milk
¼	cup unsweetened cocoa powder
2	tablespoons cornstarch
⅛	teaspoon salt
2	cups 1% milk
1	ounce bittersweet *or* semisweet (*not* unsweetened) chocolate, chopped
2	teaspoons vanilla extract

1. Whisk egg, condensed milk, cocoa, cornstarch and salt in a heavy saucepan until smooth. Gradually whisk in milk. Bring to a boil over medium-low heat, whisking constantly, until thickened, 7 to 9 minutes.

2. Remove from heat; add chocolate and vanilla, whisking until the chocolate melts. Transfer to a bowl. Place plastic wrap directly on the surface of the pudding to prevent a skin from forming. Refrigerate until ready to serve. Serve warm or chilled.

2

CARBOHYDRATE
SERVINGS

MAKES 4 SERVINGS,
GENEROUS ½ CUP EACH

PREP TIME: 10 MINUTES
START TO FINISH: 20 MINUTES

PER SERVING

215	CALORIES
5	G FAT (3 G SAT, 1 G MONO)
61	MG CHOLESTEROL
33	G CARBOHYDRATE
10	G PROTEIN
2	G FIBER
172	MG SODIUM

NUTRITION BONUS: Calcium
(23% DAILY VALUE).

EXCHANGES

2 OTHER CARBOHYDRATE

> **"**Nothing but chocolate can fulfill a chocolate craving. One thing that sometimes works is hot cocoa with 1 cup skim milk, 1 rounded teaspoon cocoa, ¼ to ½ teaspoon cinnamon and ¼ teaspoon vanilla extract. Another thing I'll try is a half-ounce of bittersweet chocolate, but no more than once a day.**"**
> —Carol W., Idaho

2

**MAKES 8 SERVINGS,
ABOUT 2/3 CUP EACH**

PREP TIME: 40 MINUTES

START TO FINISH: 2 HOURS 40
MINUTES (including chilling time)

TO MAKE AHEAD: Cover and
refrigerate for up to 2 days.

PER SERVING

172 CALORIES

6 G FAT (3 G SAT, 2 G MONO)

69 MG CHOLESTEROL

28 G CARBOHYDRATE

4 G PROTEIN

0 G FIBER

43 MG SODIUM

NUTRITION BONUS: Vitamin C
(18% DAILY VALUE).

EXCHANGES

2 OTHER CARBOHYDRATE

1 FAT (SATURATED)

PER SERVING WITH SPLENDA

1/2 CARBOHYDRATE SERVING

87 CALORIES, 6 G CARBOHYDRATE

Lemon Mousse

This ethereal citrus dessert is from the magazine's *Rx for Recipes* column, where we trimmed 82 calories and 7 grams of saturated fat from each serving. (To reduce calories even further, substitute no-calorie sweetener for the sugar.) Blackberry sauce (*page 273*) makes a delightful contrast; place a spoonful in each dessert glass before adding the mousse.

¼ cup water
1 envelope unflavored gelatin
2 large eggs
1 cup sugar *or* Splenda Granular (*see page 18*), divided
5 teaspoons freshly grated lemon zest (from 3 large or 4-5 small lemons, preferably organic, scrubbed)
⅔ cup lemon juice
½ cup whipping cream
2 tablespoons dried egg whites, such as Just Whites (*see Ingredient Note, page 323*), reconstituted according to package directions (equivalent to 3 egg whites)
¼ teaspoon cream of tartar

1. Have a large bowl of ice water ready for Step 2. Place a small bowl and beaters or a whisk in the freezer to chill for Step 3.
2. Place ¼ cup water in a small bowl; sprinkle in gelatin and stir to blend. Set aside to soften. Whisk eggs, ½ cup sugar (or Splenda), zest and lemon juice in a medium nonreactive saucepan. Place over low heat and cook, whisking constantly, until the mixture thickens slightly and an instant-read thermometer registers 160°F, 8 to 12 minutes. Remove from heat. Add the softened gelatin; whisk until blended. Transfer to a large bowl. Set the bowl over the bowl of ice water and stir gently with a rubber spatula just until the mixture starts to thicken slightly, 3 to 5 minutes. Remove from the ice bath and set aside, but stir occasionally.
3. Whip cream in the chilled bowl until soft peaks form.
4. Place reconstituted egg whites and cream of tartar in a large bowl. Beat with an electric mixer on low speed until frothy. Increase speed to high and beat until soft peaks form. Gradually add the remaining ½ cup sugar (or Splenda), beating until the meringue is stiff and glossy.
5. Whisk one-fourth of the meringue into the cooled lemon mixture. Using the whisk, fold in the remaining meringue. With a rubber spatula, fold in the whipped cream. Divide the mixture among eight ⅔- to ¾-cup dessert dishes or wineglasses. Cover and refrigerate until set, about 2 hours.

Two Toppings

Vanilla Cream

This versatile dessert topping blends the nutritional virtues of yogurt with the luxury of whipped cream.

> **VARIATION: GINGER CREAM**
> Fold in 2 tablespoons finely chopped candied ginger at the end.

- 1 cup low-fat vanilla yogurt
- ¼ cup whipping cream

Line a sieve or colander with cheesecloth and set over a bowl, leaving at least ½-inch clearance from the bottom. (*Alternatively, use a coffee filter lined with filter paper.*) Spoon in yogurt, cover and let drain in the refrigerator for 1 hour. Discard whey. Beat cream in a small bowl until firm peaks form. Fold in drained yogurt.

Blackberry Sauce

Serve this vibrant sauce with Lemon Mouse (*page 272*), Healthy Pancakes (*page 53*) or sliced peaches.

> **NUTRITION NOTE:**
> Blackberries are a source of fiber and beneficial phytochemicals.

- 3½ cups fresh *or* frozen blackberries (one 16-ounce package)
- ¼ cup sugar *or* Splenda Granular (*see page 18*)
- ¼ cup water
- 1 tablespoon lemon juice

Bring blackberries, sugar (or Splenda) and water to a simmer in a medium saucepan, stirring occasionally. Simmer over low heat for 5 minutes. Strain through a fine sieve into a bowl. Stir in lemon juice. Cover and refrigerate until chilled.

O

CARBOHYDRATE SERVINGS

MAKES ABOUT 1 CUP

PREP TIME: 10 MINUTES
START TO FINISH: 1¼ HOURS (including 1 hour to drain yogurt)

TO MAKE AHEAD: Cover and refrigerate for up to 2 days.

PER TABLESPOON
- 24 CALORIES
- 1 G FAT (1 G SAT, 0 G MONO)
- 5 MG CHOLESTEROL
- 2 G CARBOHYDRATE
- 1 G PROTEIN
- 0 G FIBER
- 11 MG SODIUM

EXCHANGES
FREE FOOD

For Blackberry Sauce:

½

CARBOHYDRATE SERVING

MAKES 1 CUP

PREP TIME: 10 MINUTES
START TO FINISH: 1 HOUR (including cooling time)

PER TABLESPOON
- 33 CALORIES
- 0 G FAT
- 0 MG CHOLESTEROL
- 8 G CARBOHYDRATE
- 0 G PROTEIN
- 2 G FIBER
- 0 MG SODIUM

EXCHANGES
½ FRUIT

PER TABLESPOON WITH SPLENDA
½ CARBOHYDRATE SERVING
23 CALORIES, 6 G CARBOHYDRATE

Roasted Pineapple Shortcakes

Shortcake isn't just for strawberries. Roasted pineapple and macadamia nuts give this version a Hawaiian twist and perfume the kitchen with a tropical fragrance. Leftover shortcakes freeze well and the pineapple is also great on its own. (*Photograph: page 174.*)

1 cup Vanilla Cream (*page 273*) *or* "lite" frozen whipped topping, thawed

SHORTCAKES

1¼	cups all-purpose flour
1	cup whole-wheat pastry flour
⅓	cup packed light brown sugar
2	teaspoons baking powder
¼	teaspoon baking soda
¼	teaspoon salt
⅓	cup chilled butter, cut into small pieces
½	cup buttermilk *or* equivalent buttermilk powder (*see page 323*)
1	tablespoon granulated sugar

ROASTED PINEAPPLE FILLING

½	cup unsalted chopped macadamia nuts *or* unsweetened flaked coconut
1	medium pineapple, peeled (*see box*), cored and cut into bite-size triangles
2	tablespoons pineapple juice
1	tablespoon honey
½	teaspoon ground ginger
⅛	teaspoon ground cloves
	Confectioners' sugar for dusting

TO PEEL A PINEAPPLE:
Using a sharp knife, cut off the skin. To remove eyes, following the spiral pattern, cut grooves along the diagonal on either side of the eyes.

1. Prepare Vanilla Cream, if using.
2. Preheat oven to 450°F. Coat a baking sheet with cooking spray.
3. **To prepare shortcakes:** Whisk all-purpose flour, whole-wheat flour, brown sugar, baking powder, baking soda and salt in a large bowl. Cut in butter with a pastry blender or 2 knives until the mixture resembles coarse meal. Add buttermilk and stir with a fork until the dough just comes together.
4. Turn the dough out onto a lightly floured surface; gather together and knead gently 5 or 6 times. Roll to a ½-inch thickness and cut out rounds with a 3¼-inch cookie cutter (*see Equipment Tip*). Reroll scraps and cut to make 12 shortcakes total. Place the shortcakes on the prepared baking sheet. Sprinkle with granulated sugar.
5. Bake the shortcakes until golden, 10 to 12 minutes. Transfer to a wire rack to cool.
6. **To prepare filling:** Spread nuts (or coconut) in a small baking pan and toast in the oven until light golden, 1 to 3 minutes.
7. Coat a baking sheet with sides with cooking spray. Combine pineapple, pineapple juice, honey, ginger and cloves in a large bowl; toss to coat. Spread on the prepared baking sheet. Roast at 450° until the pineapple is lightly browned around the edges and the juices are syrupy, 30 to 35 minutes. Let cool slightly.
8. **To serve:** Split the shortcakes with a serrated knife and place the bottoms on dessert plates. Top each with the pineapple, nuts (or coconut) and a dollop of Vanilla Cream (or whipped topping) and replace the tops. Dust with confectioners' sugar and serve.

2

CARBOHYDRATE
SERVINGS

MAKES 12 SERVINGS

PREP TIME: 45 MINUTES

START TO FINISH: 1 HOUR

TO MAKE AHEAD: The shortcakes will keep in an airtight container for up to 8 hours.

EQUIPMENT TIP
If you don't have a 3¼-inch cookie cutter, you can use a clean 6-ounce can, such as a tuna fish can.

PER SERVING

249 CALORIES
11 G FAT (5 G SAT, 4 G MONO)
20 MG CHOLESTEROL
34 G CARBOHYDRATE
4 G PROTEIN
2 G FIBER
165 MG SODIUM

NUTRITION BONUS: Vitamin C (25% DAILY VALUE).

EXCHANGES

2 OTHER CARBOHYDRATE
2 FAT (SATURATED)

274

Old-Fashioned Apple-Nut Crisp

High ⬆ Fiber

Apples and nuts are a classic—and healthful—combination, especially when you cut back on the saturated fat that typically tops this sweet treat. Our version is just as delicious, and allows the flavor of the hazelnuts to shine through. A dollop of Vanilla Cream (*page 273*) or scoop of vanilla frozen yogurt finishes this homey dessert beautifully.

2½

CARBOHYDRATE
SERVINGS

MAKES 8 SERVINGS

PREP TIME: 20 MINUTES
START TO FINISH: 1½ HOURS
(including cooling time)

PER SERVING

274 CALORIES
10 G FAT (3 G SAT, 4 G MONO)
8 MG CHOLESTEROL
45 G CARBOHYDRATE
3 G PROTEIN
6 G FIBER
1 MG SODIUM

NUTRITION BONUS: Manganese
(17% DAILY VALUE).

EXCHANGES
2½ OTHER CARBOHYDRATE
2 FAT (SATURATED)

PER SERVING WITH SPLENDA
2½ CARBOHYDRATE SERVINGS
265 CALORIES, 43 G CARBOHYDRATE

5	medium-large crisp, tart apples, such as McIntosh, Empire, Granny Smith *or* Cortland, peeled and thinly sliced (about 6 cups)
3	tablespoons granulated sugar *or* Splenda Granular (*see page 18*)
1	tablespoon lemon juice
1	teaspoon ground cinnamon, divided
⅔	cup whole-wheat flour
½	cup old-fashioned rolled oats (*not* instant)
½	cup packed light brown sugar
2	tablespoons butter, cut into small pieces
2	tablespoons canola oil
2	tablespoons frozen apple juice concentrate, thawed
⅓	cup coarsely chopped hazelnuts *or* walnuts

1. Preheat oven to 375°F. Coat an 8-inch square (or 2-quart) deep baking dish with cooking spray.
2. Combine apples with granulated sugar (or Splenda), lemon juice and ½ teaspoon cinnamon in a large bowl. Toss to mix. Transfer to the prepared baking dish, cover with foil and bake for 30 minutes.
3. Meanwhile, combine whole-wheat flour, oats, brown sugar and the remaining ½ teaspoon cinnamon in a medium bowl. Mix to blend. Using your fingers (or a fork or pastry blender), cut in butter until evenly distributed and there are no chunks. Stir in oil, apple juice concentrate and nuts; toss well until evenly moistened and clumpy.
4. Remove the foil from the baking dish and scatter the topping evenly over the apples. Bake uncovered until the topping has browned and the fruit is soft and bubbling, about 30 minutes more. Let cool for at least 15 minutes before serving.

2¹⁄₂

CARBOHYDRATE
SERVINGS

MAKES 8 SERVINGS, ABOUT
¹⁄₂ CUP EACH

PREP TIME: 20 MINUTES
START TO FINISH: 1 HOUR

PER SERVING

220 CALORIES
7 G FAT (1 G SAT, 3 G MONO)
27 MG CHOLESTEROL
38 G CARBOHYDRATE
4 G PROTEIN
2 G FIBER
237 MG SODIUM

EXCHANGES

2¹⁄₂ OTHER CARBOHYDRATE
1 FAT

PER SERVING WITH SPLENDA

1 CARBOHYDRATE SERVING
157 CALORIES, 20 G CARBOHYDRATE

Chocolate-Fudge Pudding Cake

When you have a craving for a comforting dessert, try this pudding cake, which forms its own rich-tasting sauce as it bakes. The coffee flavor is subtle, but it adds complex depth to the cake's flavor.

¹⁄₂	cup whole-wheat pastry flour (*see Ingredient Note, page 324*)
¹⁄₂	cup all-purpose flour
¹⁄₃	cup sugar *or* 3 tablespoons Splenda Sugar Blend for Baking (*see page 18*)
¹⁄₄	cup unsweetened cocoa powder, sifted
1¹⁄₂	teaspoons baking powder
¹⁄₂	teaspoon salt
1	large egg
¹⁄₂	cup 1% milk
2	tablespoons canola oil
2	teaspoons vanilla extract
³⁄₄	cup semisweet chocolate chips (optional)
1¹⁄₃	cups hot brewed coffee
²⁄₃	cup packed light brown sugar *or* Splenda Granular
¹⁄₄	cup chopped walnuts *or* pecans, toasted
	Confectioners' sugar for dusting

1. Preheat oven to 350°F. Coat a 1¹⁄₂- to 2-quart baking dish with cooking spray. Whisk whole-wheat flour, all-purpose flour, sugar (or Splenda Sugar Blend), cocoa, baking powder and salt in a large bowl. Whisk egg, milk, oil and vanilla in a glass measuring cup. Add to the flour mixture; stir with a rubber spatula until just combined. Fold in chocolate chips, if using. Scrape the batter into the prepared baking dish. Mix hot coffee and brown sugar (or Splenda Granular) in the measuring cup and pour over the batter. Sprinkle with nuts. (It may look strange at this point, but don't worry. During baking, cake forms on top with sauce underneath.)

2. Bake the pudding cake until the top springs back when touched lightly, 30 to 35 minutes. Let cool for at least 10 minutes. Dust with confectioners' sugar and serve hot or warm.

> **"**Occasionally, but only occasionally, have a 'forbidden' treat in a small quantity. Do not eat fake versions of 'forbidden' treats.**"**
>
> —*Marilyn C.,*
> *Minnesota*

Strawberries-and-Cream Parfaits

To celebrate spring's fresh strawberries, our Test Kitchen jazzed up old-fashioned tapioca pudding. Grinding the tapioca in a blender makes the texture creamier, maple syrup adds seasonal sweetness and whipping cream gives these airy parfaits a luxurious finish. (*Photograph: page 176.*)

2½

CARBOHYDRATE
SERVINGS

¼	**cup quick-cooking tapioca**
3	**cups low-fat milk *or* unsweetened plain soymilk**
½	**cup maple syrup**
1	**large egg, lightly beaten**
1½	**teaspoons vanilla extract**
2	**pints strawberries, hulled and sliced**
½	**cup whipping cream**
6	**sprigs fresh mint for garnish**

1. Grind tapioca in a blender or coffee grinder until it is a fine granular powder.
2. Whisk milk (or soymilk), maple syrup, egg and the tapioca in a small heavy saucepan. Cook over medium-high heat, whisking constantly, until the mixture comes to a full boil. Remove from the heat, stir in vanilla and transfer to a medium bowl. Place plastic wrap directly on the surface. Refrigerate until chilled, about 3 hours or overnight.
3. Using an electric mixer or whisk, whip cream in a chilled bowl until soft peaks form. Fold the whipped cream into the tapioca mixture using a rubber spatula.
4. Spoon ¼ cup strawberries into each of six 8-ounce parfait glasses or wineglasses. Top each with ⅓ cup tapioca cream. Repeat with another layer of strawberries and tapioca cream. Garnish with the remaining berries and a sprig of mint.

**MAKES 6 SERVINGS,
ABOUT 1 CUP EACH**

PREP TIME: 25 MINUTES
START TO FINISH: 3½ HOURS
(including chilling time)

TO MAKE AHEAD: Prepare through Step 2 up to 1 day ahead. Once assembled, serve immediately or cover and chill for up to 2 hours.

PER SERVING

256	CALORIES
9	G FAT (5 G SAT, 3 G MONO)
63	MG CHOLESTEROL
40	G CARBOHYDRATE
6	G PROTEIN
2	G FIBER
76	MG SODIUM

NUTRITION BONUS: Vitamin C (110% DAILY VALUE), Calcium (20% DV).

EXCHANGES

2½	OTHER CARBOHYDRATE
1	FAT

Fruity Finales

½
CARBOHYDRATE
SERVING

☀ Strawberries with Vinegar   280

☀ CHOCOLATE-DIPPED STRAWBERRIES   280

1¹/₂
CARBOHYDRATE
SERVINGS

☀ Orange Slices with Warm
Raspberries   282

Plum Fool   283

1
CARBOHYDRATE
SERVING

☀ Almond Cream with Strawberries 280

☀ Blueberries with Lemon Cream   281

☀ TROPICAL FRUITS WITH PISTACHIOS &
COCONUT   281

☀ TEA-SCENTED MANDARINS   282

☀ FROSTED GRAPES   283

2
CARBOHYDRATE
SERVINGS

Almond-Pear Gratins   284

ICED LYCHEES   284

Mixed Berry-Almond Gratin   285

Quick ☀ Easy

"COCOA-NUT" BANANAS

Right after slicing on the bias, roll bananas in cocoa, shake off the excess, then dip in toasted unsweetened coconut.

PER ½ CUP: 1 CARBOHYDRATE SERVING, ABOUT 81 CALORIES

1/2

CARBOHYDRATE

SERVING

MAKES **4** SERVINGS

PREP TIME: 10 MINUTES
START TO FINISH: 40 MINUTES

PER SERVING
31 CALORIES
0 G FAT (0 G SAT, 0 G MONO)
0 MG CHOLESTEROL
8 G CARBOHYDRATE
0 G PROTEIN
1 G FIBER
1 MG SODIUM

NUTRITION BONUS: Vitamin C
(105% DAILY VALUE).

EXCHANGES
1/2 FRUIT

For Almond Cream:

1

CARBOHYDRATE

SERVING

MAKES **4** SERVINGS

PREP TIME: 10 MINUTES
START TO FINISH: 10 MINUTES

PER SERVING
189 CALORIES
9 G FAT (3 G SAT, 4 G MONO)
19 MG CHOLESTEROL
17 G CARBOHYDRATE
9 G PROTEIN
2 G FIBER
79 MG SODIUM

NUTRITION BONUS: Vitamin C
(82% DAILY VALUE), Calcium (19% DV).

EXCHANGES
1 FRUIT
1 MEDIUM-FAT MEAT

PER SERVING WITH SPLENDA
1 CARBOHYDRATE SERVING
168 CALORIES, 12 G CARBOHYDRATE

280

Strawberries with Vinegar

Quick ☼ Easy

This may seem like an unusual combination, but a drizzle of good aged vinegar draws out the juices in the berries, creating a sensational full-flavored syrup.

> 2 cups strawberries, rinsed
> 1 teaspoon red-wine vinegar *or* balsamic vinegar
> 2 teaspoons sugar

Hull strawberries, quarter lengthwise and place in a medium bowl. Drizzle vinegar over them and sprinkle with sugar. Let stand at room temperature until a syrup has formed, about 30 minutes.

Almond Cream with Strawberries

Quick ☼ Easy

A dollop of lightly sweetened ricotta over fresh berries makes a sophisticated, super-simple dessert.

> 1/4 cup slivered almonds
> 2 cups strawberries, rinsed
> 1 cup part-skim ricotta
> 2 tablespoons sugar *or* Splenda Granular (*see page 18*)
> 1/4 teaspoon almond extract

1. Toast almonds in a small dry skillet over medium-low heat, stirring constantly, until golden and fragrant, 2 to 3 minutes. Transfer to a plate to cool.
2. Hull strawberries, slice and divide among 4 dessert plates. Mix ricotta with sugar (or Splenda) and almond extract until smooth. Spoon over the berries and sprinkle with the toasted almonds.

Quick ☼ Easy

CHOCOLATE-DIPPED STRAWBERRIES

Dip strawberries (or other seasonal fruit) in high-quality dark chocolate that you have melted over barely simmering water or in the microwave (*see Cooking Tip, page 325*).

PER STRAWBERRY: 1/2 CARBOHYDRATE SERVING, ABOUT 66 CALORIES

Blueberries with Lemon Cream

Quick ☼ Easy

Blending vanilla yogurt and reduced-fat cream cheese creates a topping that's as virtuous as it is delicious. Any fresh berry can be used in this recipe.

4	ounces reduced-fat cream cheese (Neufchâtel)
¾	cup low-fat vanilla yogurt
1	teaspoon honey
2	teaspoons freshly grated lemon zest
2	cups fresh blueberries

1. Using a fork, break up cream cheese in a medium bowl. Drain off any liquid from the yogurt; add yogurt to the bowl along with honey. Using an electric mixer, beat at high speed until light and creamy. Stir in lemon zest.
2. Layer the lemon cream and blueberries in dessert dishes or wineglasses. If not serving immediately, cover and refrigerate for up to 8 hours.

Quick ☼ Easy

TROPICAL FRUITS WITH PISTACHIOS & COCONUT

Drizzle light coconut milk over ripe mango, pineapple and/or papaya slices and sprinkle with chopped pistachios.

PER ½ CUP: 1 Carbohydrate Serving, about 124 calories

1

CARBOHYDRATE
SERVING

MAKES 4 SERVINGS, ½ CUP EACH

PREP TIME: 10 MINUTES
START TO FINISH: 10 MINUTES

PER SERVING

156 CALORIES
7 G FAT (4 G SAT, 0 G MONO)
22 MG CHOLESTEROL
19 G CARBOHYDRATE
6 G PROTEIN
2 G FIBER
151 MG SODIUM

NUTRITION BONUS: Vitamin C (15% DAILY VALUE).

EXCHANGES

1 FRUIT
1 FAT (SATURATED)

Orange Slices with Warm Raspberries

High ↑ Fiber   Quick ☼ Easy

Warming the berries enhances their flavor and makes a pleasing contrast to the cool orange slices. Fresh pineapple can stand in for the oranges.

4	seedless oranges, such as navel oranges
2	tablespoons sugar *or* Splenda Granular (*see page 18*)
1	tablespoon lemon juice
¼	teaspoon ground cinnamon
2	cups frozen unsweetened raspberries (*not* thawed)

1. With a sharp knife, remove and discard the skin and white pith from oranges; slice the oranges crosswise and arrange on 4 dessert plates.
2. Combine sugar (or Splenda), lemon juice and cinnamon in a small saucepan; stir over low heat until bubbling. Add raspberries and stir gently until the berries are just thawed. Spoon over the orange slices and serve immediately.

Quick ☼ Easy

TEA-SCENTED MANDARINS

Pour hot black tea over mandarin oranges or clementine sections; finish with a pinch of ground cardamom and a drizzle of honey.

PER ½ CUP: 1 CARBOHYDRATE SERVING, ABOUT 63 CALORIES

1½

CARBOHYDRATE
SERVINGS

MAKES 4 SERVINGS

PREP TIME: 10 MINUTES

START TO FINISH: 15 MINUTES

PER SERVING

122 CALORIES

0 G FAT (0 G SAT, 0 G MONO)

0 MG CHOLESTEROL

30 G CARBOHYDRATE

2 G PROTEIN

5 G FIBER

2 MG SODIUM

NUTRITION BONUS: Vitamin C (157% DAILY VALUE), Fiber (20% DV).

EXCHANGES

2 FRUIT

PER SERVING WITH SPLENDA

1 CARBOHYDRATE SERVING

100 CALORIES, 25 G CARBOHYDRATE

Plum Fool

A fool is a traditional British dessert of stewed fruit swirled with whipped cream. Here, low-fat yogurt replaces some of the whipped cream. Since plums vary considerably in sweetness, start with the lower amount of sugar or sweetener and add more after tasting, if desired.

1	pound plums, pitted and sliced (about 2¹⁄₂ cups)
¹⁄₄-¹⁄₂	cup sugar *or* Splenda Granular (*see page 18*)
¹⁄₂	teaspoon grated fresh ginger
¹⁄₂	teaspoon ground cinnamon
1¹⁄₂	cups low-fat vanilla yogurt
¹⁄₃	cup whipping cream

1. Set aside a few plum slices for garnish. Combine the remaining plum slices, ¹⁄₄ cup sugar (or Splenda), ginger and cinnamon in a small heavy saucepan. Bring to a simmer, stirring, over medium heat. Cook until the mixture has softened into a chunky puree, 15 to 20 minutes. Taste and add more sugar (or Splenda), if desired. Transfer to a bowl and chill until cool, about 1 hour.

2. Meanwhile, set a fine-mesh stainless-steel sieve over a bowl. Spoon in yogurt and let drain in the refrigerator until reduced to 1 cup, about 1 hour.

3. Whip cream to soft peaks in a chilled bowl. Gently fold in the drained yogurt with a rubber spatula. Fold this mixture into the fruit puree, leaving distinct swirls. Spoon into 6 dessert dishes and cover with plastic wrap. Refrigerate for at least 1 hour or up to 2 days. Garnish with the reserved plum slices before serving.

MAKES 6 SERVINGS,
GENEROUS ¹⁄₂ CUP EACH

PREP TIME: 20 MINUTES
START TO FINISH: 1 HOUR 20 MINUTES

PER SERVING

156 CALORIES
5 G FAT (3 G SAT, 2 G MONO)
18 MG CHOLESTEROL
25 G CARBOHYDRATE
4 G PROTEIN
1 G FIBER
45 MG SODIUM

NUTRITION BONUS: Calcium (12% DAILY VALUE), Vitamin C (12% DV).

EXCHANGES

1¹⁄₂ FRUIT
1 FAT

PER SERVING WITH SPLENDA

1 CARBOHYDRATE SERVING
128 CALORIES, 18 G CARBOHYDRATE

Quick ☼ Easy

FROSTED GRAPES

Wash red or green seedless grapes and pat dry. Place in the freezer for 45 minutes. Remove from the freezer and let sit for 2 minutes before serving.

PER ¹⁄₂ CUP: 1 CARBOHYDRATE SERVING, ABOUT 55 CALORIES

Almond-Pear Gratins

Pears baked in almond tea take on a flavor reminiscent of amaretto but at a fraction of the calories. The crunch of sugar-crusted almonds against tender fruit reveals an intriguing interplay of textures—a critical component of taste pleasure.

SUGARED ALMONDS

- ¼ cup granulated sugar
- ½ teaspoon freshly grated orange zest
- 1 large egg white
- ½ cup sliced almonds

PEARS

- 1¼ cups water
- 4 almond-flavored herbal tea bags
- 5 teaspoons brown sugar *or* Splenda Granular (*see page 18*)
- 1 tablespoon orange juice
- 4 teaspoons lemon juice, divided
- 2 firm Bosc pears

1. **To prepare almonds:** Preheat oven to 300°F. Coat a baking sheet with cooking spray.
2. Mix together sugar and orange zest in a small bowl. Whisk egg white in another bowl until frothy; add the almonds and toss to coat thoroughly. Drain the almonds in a sieve, then toss with the sugar-zest mixture. Spread the coated almonds on the prepared baking sheet.
3. Bake the almonds for 10 minutes. Stir well, spread out again and bake for 5 minutes more. Stir again and bake until toasted and crisp, about 2 minutes more. Loosen the almonds from the baking sheet with a spatula; set aside.
4. **To prepare pears:** While the almonds are baking, bring water to a boil in a small saucepan. Remove from heat and add tea bags. Let steep for 10 minutes. Squeeze the tea bags over the pan, then discard the bags. Stir brown sugar (or Splenda), orange juice and 1 teaspoon lemon juice into the tea.
5. Increase oven temperature to 450°.
6. Peel pears, halve lengthwise and cut out the cores. Toss with the remaining 3 teaspoons lemon juice. Place the pear halves, cut-side down, in 4 individual gratin dishes and put the dishes on a baking sheet. Spoon the tea mixture over and around the pears.
7. Bake, uncovered, until the pears are tender, basting from time to time, about 35 minutes. Sprinkle the reserved almonds over the pears. Serve immediately.

ICED LYCHEES

Drain canned lychees (found in the Asian section of supermarkets) and freeze on a baking sheet for at least 2 hours before serving.

PER ½ CUP: 2 CARBOHYDRATE SERVINGS, ABOUT 115 CALORIES

2
CARBOHYDRATE
SERVINGS

MAKES 4 SERVINGS

PREP TIME: 25 MINUTES

START TO FINISH: 55 MINUTES

TEST KITCHEN TIP
If you don't have individual gratin dishes, use a 1½-quart gratin dish, pie pan or quiche dish.

PER SERVING
- 221 CALORIES
- 9 G FAT (1 G SAT, 6 G MONO)
- 0 MG CHOLESTEROL
- 33 G CARBOHYDRATE
- 5 G PROTEIN
- 4 G FIBER
- 23 MG SODIUM

NUTRITION BONUS: Fiber (16% DAILY VALUE), Vitamin C (13% DV).

EXCHANGES
- 1 FRUIT
- 1 OTHER CARBOHYDRATE
- 2 FAT (MONO)

PER SERVING WITH SPLENDA
2 CARBOHYDRATE SERVINGS
202 CALORIES, 28 G CARBOHYDRATE

Mixed Berry-Almond Gratin

How simple—and delicious—are berries topped with a rich custard and baked into a crusty dessert (or breakfast) gratin. No one will ever guess that you've replaced much of the butter in traditional almond cream with tofu. (*Photograph: page 175.*)

2

CARBOHYDRATE

SERVINGS

- ⅓ cup slivered almonds (1¼ ounces)
- ½ cup granulated sugar *or* Splenda Granular (*see page 18*)
- 2 tablespoons all-purpose flour
  Pinch of salt
- 1 large egg
- ⅓ cup firm silken low-fat tofu
- 1 tablespoon butter, softened
- ¼ teaspoon pure almond extract
- 3 cups mixed berries, such as raspberries, blackberries and blueberries
  Confectioners' sugar for dusting

1. Preheat oven to 400°F. Coat a 1-quart gratin dish or a 9-inch pie pan with cooking spray.
2. Spread almonds in a shallow baking pan and bake until light golden and fragrant, 4 to 6 minutes. Let cool.
3. Place sugar (or Splenda), flour, salt and almonds in a food processor; process until finely ground. Add egg, tofu, butter and almond extract; process until smooth.
4. Spread berries evenly in the prepared gratin dish. Scrape the almond mixture over the top, spreading evenly.
5. Bake the gratin until light golden and set, 40 to 50 minutes. Let cool for at least 20 minutes. Dust with confectioners' sugar and serve warm.

MAKES 6 SERVINGS

PREP TIME: 10 MINUTES
START TO FINISH: 1 HOUR

TO MAKE AHEAD: Prepare recipe through Step 3. Cover and refrigerate for up to 8 hours.

PER SERVING

195	CALORIES
7	G FAT (2 G SAT, 3 G MONO)
40	MG CHOLESTEROL
30	G CARBOHYDRATE
4	G PROTEIN
4	G FIBER
48	MG SODIUM

NUTRITION BONUS: Vitamin C (22% DAILY VALUE), Fiber (16% DV).

EXCHANGES

1	FRUIT
1	OTHER CARBOHYDRATE
1	FAT

PER SERVING WITH SPLENDA

1 CARBOHYDRATE SERVING
138 CALORIES, 16 G CARBOHYDRATE

NUTRITION NOTE

BERRY BENEFITS

Colorful raspberries, blueberries and blackberries provide a wealth of health benefits. High levels of anthocyanins—antioxidants that give berries their characteristic red, blue and black colors—have been linked to stalling the aging process, protecting the heart and circulatory system, and preventing mental decline. The darker the berry, the higher the concentration of antioxidants.

Cakes & Pies

1¹⁄₂

CARBOHYDRATE
SERVINGS

2¹⁄₂

CARBOHYDRATE
SERVINGS

2

CARBOHYDRATE
SERVINGS

3

CARBOHYDRATE
SERVINGS

One-Bowl Chocolate Cake

While cake mixes may be the easiest option for a home-baked cake, they often contain hydrogenated fats. By making this simple "scratch" cake, you can use healthful canola oil, incorporate whole-wheat flour and opt for a no-calorie sweetener, if you like.

MAKES **12** SERVINGS

PREP TIME: 25 MINUTES

START TO FINISH: 1 HOUR 5 MINUTES

PER SERVING

134 CALORIES

3 G FAT (1 G SAT, 2 G MONO)

18 MG CHOLESTEROL

25 G CARBOHYDRATE

2 G PROTEIN

2 G FIBER

211 MG SODIUM

EXCHANGES

1¹/₂ OTHER CARBOHYDRATE

PER SERVING WITH SPLENDA

1 CARBOHYDRATE SERVING

112 CALORIES, 17 G CARBOHYDRATE

¾	**cup plus 2 tablespoons whole-wheat pastry flour**
½	**cup granulated sugar** *or* ¼ **cup Splenda Sugar Blend for Baking** (*see page 18*)
⅓	**cup unsweetened cocoa powder**
1	**teaspoon baking powder**
1	**teaspoon baking soda**
¼	**teaspoon salt**
½	**cup buttermilk** *or* **equivalent buttermilk powder** (*see page 323*)
½	**cup packed light brown sugar** *or* ¼ **cup Splenda Sugar Blend for Baking** (*see page 18*)
1	**large egg, lightly beaten**
2	**tablespoons canola oil**
1	**teaspoon vanilla extract**
½	**cup hot strong black coffee**
	Confectioners' sugar for dusting

1. Preheat oven to 350°F. Coat a 9-inch round cake pan with cooking spray. Line the pan with a circle of wax paper.
2. Whisk flour, granulated sugar (or Splenda), cocoa powder, baking powder, baking soda and salt in a mixing bowl. Add buttermilk, brown sugar (or Splenda), egg, oil and vanilla. Beat with an electric mixer on medium speed for 2 minutes. Add hot coffee and beat to blend. (The batter will be quite thin.) Pour the batter into the prepared pan.
3. Bake the cake until a skewer inserted in the center comes out clean, 30 to 35 minutes. Cool in the pan on a wire rack for 10 minutes; remove from the pan, peel off the wax paper and let cool completely. Dust the top with confectioners' sugar before slicing.

Squash Pie

Try this custard pie with buttercup squash, a sweet, orange-fleshed variety that bakes up luscious, light and surprisingly creamy. Roasted fresh squash has a vibrant color and full flavor, but to save time you can use frozen or canned squash. The pie is best the day it is baked, but much of the preparation can be done in advance. Serve with Ginger Cream (*page 273*).

CRUST

- ¾ cup whole-wheat pastry flour (*see Ingredient Note, page 324*)
- ¾ cup all-purpose flour
- 1 tablespoon sugar
- ¼ teaspoon salt
- 2 tablespoons unsalted butter
- ⅓ cup almond oil (*see Note*) *or* canola oil
- ¼ teaspoon white vinegar
- 3-4 tablespoons ice water

FILLING

- 2 cups pureed squash (*see Cooking Tip, page 325*)
- 1½ cups evaporated low-fat *or* fat-free milk
- ¼ cup honey
- 2 large egg yolks, lightly beaten
- 1 large egg, lightly beaten
- ⅓ cup sugar
- 1 teaspoon ground cinnamon
- ½ teaspoon freshly grated nutmeg
- ¼ teaspoon salt

1. **To prepare crust:** Mix whole-wheat flour, all-purpose flour, sugar and salt in a medium bowl. Using a pastry cutter or two forks, cut in butter until the pieces are roughly the size of peas. Stir in oil and vinegar with a fork, then stir in just enough water so the dough gathers into a ball.
2. Dust a large piece of wax paper with flour, then turn the dough out onto it. Dust a rolling pin with flour and roll the dough into a 14-inch circle. Invert into a 9-inch pie pan, gently pressing the dough into the bottom of the pan. Trim any uneven edges, leaving ½ inch of dough hanging over the rim. Fold the edges under and crimp into a decorative design. Cover with plastic wrap; refrigerate for at least 30 minutes.
3. Preheat oven to 350°F.
4. Prick the crust with a fork several times; line with parchment paper and add enough pie weights or dried beans to cover the bottom. Set the pie pan on a baking sheet. Bake until the crust is firm but not colored, about 20 minutes.
5. **Meanwhile, to prepare filling & bake pie:** Whisk squash, evaporated milk, honey, egg yolks and egg in a large bowl until smooth. Stir in sugar, cinnamon, nutmeg and salt. Pour the filling into the crust (it will be very full). Place the pie pan on the baking sheet.
6. Bake the pie until the crust edges are nicely browned, about 40 minutes. Cover the edges with foil and continue to bake until a knife inserted into the center comes out clean, 25 to 40 minutes more. Cool the pie on a wire rack before slicing, at least 2 hours.

2

CARBOHYDRATE
SERVINGS

MAKES 12 SERVINGS

PREP TIME: 45 MINUTES

START TO FINISH: 2 HOURS

TO MAKE AHEAD: Prepare crust through Step 2; wrap in plastic wrap and refrigerate for up to 2 days or freeze for up to 2 months (do not thaw before baking).

INGREDIENT NOTE: Almond oil is an unrefined oil pressed from almonds. You can find it in many supermarkets and health-food stores. Store in the refrigerator.

PER SERVING

- 225 CALORIES
- 9 G FAT (2 G SAT, 5 G MONO)
- 58 MG CHOLESTEROL
- 31 G CARBOHYDRATE
- 5 G PROTEIN
- 2 G FIBER
- 142 MG SODIUM

NUTRITION BONUS: Vitamin A (30% DAILY VALUE), Calcium (10% DV).

EXCHANGES

- 2 OTHER CARBOHYDRATE
- 2 FAT

Rustic Berry Tart

The secret to this free-form tart is the layer of ground almonds under the berries: it thickens the juices, prevents a soggy crust and delivers an exquisite background flavor for the intense berries.

Sidebar

MAKES 12 SERVINGS

PREP TIME: 1 HOUR

START TO FINISH: 3 HOURS

TO MAKE AHEAD: Prepare crust through Step 1; wrap in plastic wrap and refrigerate for up to 2 days or freeze for up to 3 months.

PER SERVING

200	CALORIES
7	G FAT (3 G SAT, 2 G MONO)
28	MG CHOLESTEROL
31	G CARBOHYDRATE
3	G PROTEIN
4	G FIBER
55	MG SODIUM

NUTRITION BONUS: Fiber (16% DAILY VALUE), Vitamin C (15% DV).

EXCHANGES

2 OTHER CARBOHYDRATE

1 FAT

PER SERVING WITH SPLENDA

1½ CARBOHYDRATE SERVINGS

175 CALORIES, 25 G CARBOHYDRATE

CRUST

- ¾ cup whole-wheat pastry flour (*see Ingredient Note, page 324*)
- ¾ cup all-purpose flour
- 2 tablespoons sugar, plus 1 teaspoon for sprinkling
- ¼ teaspoon salt
- 4 tablespoons cold butter (½ stick), cut into small pieces
- 1 tablespoon canola oil
- ¼ cup ice water, plus more as needed
- 1 large egg, separated (*see Cooking Tip, page 325*; save the white to glaze the pastry)
- 1 teaspoon lemon juice *or* white vinegar

FILLING & GLAZE

- ¼ cup slivered almonds (1 ounce)
- ¼ cup whole-wheat flour (regular *or* pastry flour)
- ¼ cup plus 3 tablespoons sugar *or* Splenda Granular (*see page 18*)
- 4 cups mixed berries, such as blackberries, raspberries and blueberries
- 2 teaspoons lemon juice
- 1 tablespoon water
- 2 tablespoons raspberry, blueberry *or* blackberry jam

1. **To prepare crust:** Whisk whole-wheat flour, all-purpose flour, 2 tablespoons sugar and salt in a medium bowl. Cut in butter with a pastry blender or your fingers until the mixture resembles coarse crumbs with a few larger pieces. Add oil and stir with a fork to blend. Mix ¼ cup water, egg yolk and 1 teaspoon lemon juice (or vinegar) in a measuring cup. Add just enough of the egg yolk mixture to the flour mixture, stirring with a fork, until the dough clumps together. (Add a little water if the dough seems too dry.) Turn the dough out onto a lightly floured surface and knead several times. Form the dough into a ball, then flatten into a disk. Wrap in plastic wrap and refrigerate for at least 1 hour.

2. Preheat oven to 425°F. Line a baking sheet with parchment paper or foil and coat with cooking spray.

3. **To prepare filling & assemble tart:** Spread almonds in a small baking pan. Bake until light golden and fragrant, about 5 minutes. Let cool. Combine whole-wheat flour, ¼ cup sugar (or Splenda) and the toasted almonds in a food processor or blender; process until the almonds are ground.

4. On a lightly floured surface, roll the dough into a rough 13- to 14-inch circle, about ¼ inch thick. Roll it back over the rolling pin, brush off excess flour, and transfer to the prepared baking sheet. Spread the almond mixture over the pastry, leaving a 2-inch border all around. Toss berries with the remaining 3 tablespoons sugar (or Splenda) and 2 teaspoons lemon juice in a large bowl; spoon over the almond mixture. Fold the border up

and over the filling, pleating as necessary. Blend the reserved egg white and 1 tablespoon water with a fork; brush lightly over the tart rim. Sprinkle with the remaining 1 teaspoon sugar.

5. Bake the tart for 15 minutes. Reduce oven temperature to 350° and bake until the crust is golden and the juices are bubbling, 30 to 40 minutes. Leaving the tart on the parchment (or foil), carefully slide it onto a wire rack. Let cool.

6. Shortly before serving, melt jam in a small saucepan over low heat; brush over the berries. Cut the tart into wedges.

> **"**I don't use artificial sweeteners. If I have a dessert, it means a small portion or more exercise (walking) to counteract the blood sugar rise. I feel that trying to choose a lot of altered sweets is just self-defeating, and misses the point that sweet flavors don't work for me.**"**
>
> —*Paul M., Oregon*

2

CARBOHYDRATE
SERVINGS

- - - - - - - - - - - - - - - -

MAKES 16 SERVINGS

- - - - - - - - - - - - - - - -

PREP TIME: 30 MINUTES

START TO FINISH: 4½ HOURS

- - - - - - - - - - - - - - - -

TO MAKE AHEAD: Prepare
through Step 5. Cover and
refrigerate for up to 2 days.

- - - - - - - - - - - - - - - -

PER SERVING

199 CALORIES

7 G FAT (3 G SAT, 1 G MONO)

30 MG CHOLESTEROL

26 G CARBOHYDRATE

9 G PROTEIN

1 G FIBER

293 MG SODIUM

- - - - - - - - - - - - - - - -

EXCHANGES

2 OTHER CARBOHYDRATE

1 FAT (SATURATED)

- - - - - - - - - - - - - - - -

PER SERVING WITH SPLENDA

1 CARBOHYDRATE SERVING

171 CALORIES, 19 G CARBOHYDRATE

Marmalade-Glazed Orange Cheesecake

Our Test Kitchen created this showpiece cheesecake to celebrate one of winter's brightest gifts: the orange. It is exceptionally rich and creamy-tasting, but lower in saturated fat than a traditional cheesecake. The secret is to replace most of the cream cheese with pureed cottage cheese. Be sure to let the food processor do its job and process the cottage cheese until it has a silky texture.

CRUST

20	vanilla snaps *or* wafers (*see Ingredient Note, page 323*)
1	tablespoon canola oil

FILLING

2½	cups low-fat (1%) cottage cheese
12	ounces reduced-fat cream cheese (*not* nonfat), cut into pieces
⅔	cup granulated sugar *or* Splenda Granular (*see page 18*)
⅓	cup packed light brown sugar
¼	cup cornstarch
1	large egg
2	large egg whites
1	cup nonfat *or* low-fat plain yogurt
4	teaspoons freshly grated orange zest, preferably organic
2	tablespoons orange juice
1	teaspoon vanilla extract

GLAZE & GARNISH

2	tablespoons orange marmalade
2	tablespoons orange liqueur *or* orange juice
1	seedless orange, scrubbed and thinly sliced
	Mint sprigs

1. Preheat oven to 325°F. Coat a 9-inch springform pan with cooking spray. Put a kettle of water on to boil for the water bath. Wrap the outside of the pan with a double thickness of foil.

2. **To prepare crust:** Grind vanilla snaps in a food processor. Add oil and process until the crumbs are moistened. Press crumbs evenly into the bottom of the prepared pan.

3. **To prepare filling:** Puree cottage cheese in a food processor (use a clean workbowl) until smooth, scraping down the sides once or twice. Add cream cheese, granulated sugar (or Splenda), brown sugar and cornstarch. Process until *very* smooth. Add egg, egg whites, yogurt, orange zest, orange juice and vanilla; process until smooth. Pour over the crust.

4. Place the cheesecake in a shallow roasting pan and pour in enough boiling water to come ½ inch up the outside of the springform pan. Bake until the edges are set but the center still jiggles when the pan is tapped, 50 to 60 minutes.

5. Turn off the oven. Spray a knife with cooking spray and run it around the inside edge of the pan. Let the cheesecake stand in the oven, with the door ajar, for 1 hour. Remove the cheesecake from the water bath and remove the foil. Refrigerate, uncovered, until chilled, about 2 hours.

6. **To glaze & garnish cheesecake:** Shortly before serving, combine marmalade and orange liqueur (or juice) in a small saucepan. Heat over low heat, stirring, until melted and smooth. Place cheesecake on a serving platter and remove pan sides. Brush glaze over the top of the cheesecake. Make a slit in each orange slice, then twist and wrap it into a rosette. Garnish cheesecake with the orange rosettes and mint.

Berry-Ricotta Cheesecake

This light Italian-inspired ricotta cheesecake is the perfect platform for summer's bountiful berries.

CRUST

    4   hazelnut *or* almond biscotti (4 ounces)

    1   tablespoon canola oil

FILLING

    4   ounces reduced-fat cream cheese, softened

    1   cup sugar *or* Splenda Granular (*see page 18*)

    2   cups part-skim ricotta cheese

   ½   cup nonfat plain yogurt

   ⅓   cup cornstarch

    2   large eggs

    3   large egg whites

    2   teaspoons freshly grated lemon zest

    2   tablespoons lemon juice

   ¼   teaspoon salt

TOPPING & GLAZE

    2   cups fresh berries, such as strawberries, blueberries, raspberries and blackberries

   ¼   cup red currant jelly

1. Preheat oven to 300°F. Coat a 9-inch springform pan with cooking spray.
2. **To prepare crust:** Break biscotti into several pieces and pulse in a food processor until finely ground. Add oil and pulse until incorporated. Press the crumbs evenly into the bottom of the prepared pan.
3. **To prepare filling:** Beat cream cheese in a large mixing bowl with an electric mixer until smooth. Add sugar (or Splenda) and beat until smooth. Add ricotta, yogurt, cornstarch, eggs, egg whites, lemon zest, lemon juice and salt. Beat until well blended. (*Alternatively, mix ingredients in a food processor.*) Scrape the batter into the prepared pan and smooth the top.
4. Bake the cheesecake until the edges are puffed but the center still jiggles when the pan is tapped, 50 to 55 minutes. Turn off the oven and let the cheesecake stand, with the door ajar, for 1 hour. Transfer to a wire rack and let cool completely. (The top may crack.)
5. **To glaze & garnish cheesecake:** Place cheesecake on a platter and remove pan sides. Arrange berries on top. Warm jelly in a small saucepan over low heat, stirring, until melted. With a pastry brush, coat the berries with the jelly glaze. Serve at room temperature or refrigerate until cold.

2½ CARBOHYDRATE SERVINGS

MAKES 12 SERVINGS

PREP TIME: 30 MINUTES
START TO FINISH: 3½ HOURS

TO MAKE AHEAD: Cover and refrigerate for up to 1 day.

PER SERVING

259 CALORIES
9 G FAT (4 G SAT, 2 G MONO)
62 MG CHOLESTEROL
37 G CARBOHYDRATE
9 G PROTEIN
1 G FIBER
176 MG SODIUM

NUTRITION BONUS: Vitamin C (16% DAILY VALUE), Calcium (15% DV).

EXCHANGES

2½ OTHER CARBOHYDRATE
1½ FAT (SATURATED)

PER SERVING WITH SPLENDA

2 CARBOHYDRATE SERVINGS
234 CALORIES, 28 G CARBOHYDRATE

Strawberry-Rhubarb Tart

Ground toasted oats not only boost fiber, they help give this low-fat crust a tender texture and contribute a yummy nutty taste.

FILLING

- 2 cups diced fresh *or* frozen rhubarb
- 3 cups fresh strawberries, sliced, divided
- ¼ cup sugar *or* Splenda Granular (*see page 18*)
- ½ teaspoon freshly grated lemon zest
- 1½ tablespoons cornstarch
- 1 tablespoon cold water
- 3 tablespoons red currant jelly

CRUST

- ½ cup old-fashioned rolled oats
- 3 tablespoons 1% milk
- ½ teaspoon vanilla extract
- ⅔ cup all-purpose flour
- ¼ cup sugar
- 1 teaspoon freshly grated lemon zest
- ¾ teaspoon baking powder
- ¼ teaspoon salt
- 2 tablespoons canola oil

1. **To prepare filling:** Combine rhubarb, 1 cup of the strawberries, sugar (or Splenda) and lemon zest in a large nonreactive saucepan. Let sit for 20 minutes (35 minutes if rhubarb is frozen). Bring to a simmer over medium-low heat. Cook, stirring often, until the rhubarb is tender but still holds its shape, 5 to 8 minutes.

2. Meanwhile, stir cornstarch and water in a small bowl until smooth. Stir into the simmering fruit. Cook, stirring constantly, until the mixture is clear and very thick, about 1 minute. Transfer to a bowl. Place a piece of plastic wrap directly on the surface and refrigerate until chilled.

3. **To prepare crust & assemble tart:** Preheat oven to 350°F. Coat a 9-inch tart pan with a removable bottom with cooking spray.

4. Spread oats in a small baking dish and bake, stirring occasionally, until toasted, 10 to 15 minutes. Let cool. Place the oats in a food processor and process until finely ground.

5. Combine milk and vanilla in a small bowl. Whisk the ground oats, flour, sugar, lemon zest, baking powder and salt in a large bowl. Drizzle oil onto the dry ingredients and stir with a fork or your fingers until crumbly. Use a fork to stir in the milk mixture, 1 tablespoon at a time, until the dough just comes together.

6. Turn the dough out onto a floured work surface and knead 7 to 8 times. Roll the dough out to an 11-inch circle, dusting with flour if necessary. Transfer to the prepared pan, pressing to fit. Trim the edges.

7. Line the tart shell with a piece of foil or parchment paper and fill with pie weights or dried beans. Bake the tart shell until set, 10 to 12 minutes. Remove weights and foil or paper and bake until lightly browned, 8 to 12 minutes more. Cool in the pan on a wire rack.

8. Shortly before serving, spread the reserved strawberry-rhubarb filling evenly into the tart shell. Arrange the remaining 2 cups strawberries decoratively over the filling.

9. Heat jelly in a small saucepan over low heat, stirring constantly. With a pastry brush, glaze the strawberries with the jelly.

Nanan's Gingerbread

This homey gingerbread is sweetened and moistened with dark honey instead of molasses. Lemon zest and crystallized ginger complement the traditional spices, delivering a complex, well-rounded flavor.

1½	**cups all-purpose flour**
1	**cup whole-wheat pastry flour (*see Ingredient Note, page 324*)**
2	**teaspoons baking powder**
½	**teaspoon baking soda**
2	**teaspoons ground ginger**
1½	**teaspoons ground cinnamon**
½	**teaspoon ground cloves**
½	**teaspoon ground nutmeg**
½	**teaspoon salt**
2	**large eggs**
⅔	**cup packed brown sugar *or* ⅓ cup Splenda Sugar Blend for Baking (*see page 18*)**
⅔	**cup dark honey, such as buckwheat *or* chestnut**
½	**cup canola oil**
2	**teaspoons freshly grated lemon zest**
1	**cup boiling water**
½	**cup finely chopped crystallized ginger (optional)**
	Confectioners' sugar for dusting

1. Preheat oven to 350°F. Coat a 9-by-13-inch baking dish with cooking spray.

2. Whisk all-purpose flour, whole-wheat flour, baking powder, baking soda, ground ginger, cinnamon, cloves, nutmeg and salt together in a large bowl.

3. Whisk eggs, brown sugar (or Splenda), honey and oil in a medium bowl. Make a well in the center of the flour mixture and add the egg mixture and lemon zest. Using a whisk, begin blending dry and wet ingredients together, adding boiling water as you go. Mix until the ingredients are fully incorporated, but do not overmix. Stir in crystallized ginger, if using.

4. Pour the batter into the prepared dish and bake the gingerbread until the top springs back when pressed lightly, 30 to 35 minutes. Let cool in the pan on a wire rack. Just before serving, dust with confectioners' sugar.

2½ CARBOHYDRATE SERVINGS

MAKES **15** SERVINGS

PREP TIME: 30 MINUTES
START TO FINISH: 1 HOUR

TO MAKE AHEAD: Wrap well and store at room temperature for up to 4 days.

PER SERVING
230 CALORIES
8 G FAT (1 G SAT, 5 G MONO)
28 MG CHOLESTEROL
37 G CARBOHYDRATE
3 G PROTEIN
1 G FIBER
199 MG SODIUM

EXCHANGES
2½ OTHER CARBOHYDRATE
1 FAT (MONO)

PER SERVING WITH SPLENDA
2 CARBOHYDRATE SERVINGS
215 CALORIES, 31 G CARBOHYDRATE

Double Lemon-Poppy Seed Bundt Cake

The central cone in a Bundt cake pan ensures that a dense cake batter—like the luscious buttermilk and lemon-flecked one here—cooks evenly and thoroughly. We love that Bundt cakes don't demand frosting—just let a sweet lemon glaze run over the warm cake and you've got perfection.

2½

CARBOHYDRATE
SERVINGS

MAKES 16 SERVINGS

PREP TIME: 30 MINUTES
START TO FINISH: 1¼ HOURS

PER SERVING

211 CALORIES
5 G FAT (1 G SAT, 2 G MONO)
27 MG CHOLESTEROL
37 G CARBOHYDRATE
4 G PROTEIN
2 G FIBER
144 MG SODIUM

EXCHANGES

2½ OTHER CARBOHYDRATE
1 FAT

PER SERVING WITH SPLENDA

2 CARBOHYDRATE SERVINGS
188 CALORIES, 28 G CARBOHYDRATE

¼	cup poppy seeds
1½	cups whole-wheat pastry flour (*see Ingredient Note, page 324*)
1	cup all-purpose flour
1½	teaspoons baking powder
½	teaspoon baking soda
¼	teaspoon salt
1	cup buttermilk *or* equivalent buttermilk powder (*see page 323*)
¼	cup canola oil
1	teaspoon vanilla extract
2	tablespoons freshly grated lemon zest
2	tablespoons lemon juice
2	large eggs, at room temperature (*see Cooking Tip, page 325*)
2	large egg whites, at room temperature
1¼	cups sugar *or* ½ cup plus 2 tablespoons Splenda Sugar Blend for Baking (*see page 18*)

LEMON GLAZE

¾	cup confectioners' sugar, plus more for dusting
3	tablespoons lemon juice
1	tablespoon water

1. Preheat oven to 350°F. Coat a 10-inch (12-cup) Bundt pan, preferably nonstick, with cooking spray and dust with flour (or use cooking spray with flour).

2. Toast poppy seeds in a small dry skillet over medium heat, stirring constantly, until fragrant, 3 to 4 minutes. Transfer to a plate to cool.

3. Whisk whole-wheat flour, all-purpose flour, baking powder, baking soda, salt and the poppy seeds in a medium bowl. Combine buttermilk, oil, vanilla, lemon zest and lemon juice in a glass measuring cup.

4. Beat eggs, egg whites and sugar (or Splenda) in a large bowl with an electric mixer on high speed until thickened and pale, about 5 minutes.

5. With a rubber spatula, fold the dry ingredients into the egg mixture a third at a time, alternating with 2 additions of the buttermilk mixture. Scrape the batter into the prepared pan, spreading evenly.

6. Bake the cake until the top springs back when touched lightly and a toothpick inserted in the center comes out clean, 35 to 40 minutes. Let cool in the pan on a wire rack for 5 minutes. Loosen the edges and turn the cake out onto the rack.

7. **Meanwhile, prepare glaze:** Sift ¾ cup confectioners' sugar into a small bowl; mix with lemon juice and water to create a thin glaze. Using a skewer, poke 1-inch-deep holes all over the cake. Using a pastry brush, coat the warm cake with the glaze. Let cool completely. To serve, set the cake on a serving plate and dust with confectioners' sugar.

Carrot Cake

Despite its wholesome name, this classic celebration cake is typically overloaded with empty calories. We cut them back by reducing the oil, sugar and nuts, and boosted fiber by switching to whole-wheat pastry flour.

CAKE

½	cup chopped walnuts
1	20-ounce can crushed pineapple
2	cups whole-wheat pastry flour (*see Ingredient Note, page 324*)
2	teaspoons baking soda
½	teaspoon salt
2	teaspoons ground cinnamon
3	large eggs
1½	cups sugar *or* ¾ cup Splenda Sugar Blend for Baking (*see page 18*)
¾	cup nonfat buttermilk *or* equivalent buttermilk powder (*see page 323*)
½	cup canola oil
1	teaspoon vanilla extract
2	cups grated carrots (4-6 medium)
¼	cup unsweetened flaked coconut

FROSTING

2	tablespoons coconut chips (*see Ingredient Note, page 323*) *or* flaked coconut
12	ounces reduced-fat cream cheese, softened
½	cup confectioners' sugar, sifted, *or* Splenda Granular (*see page 18*)
1½	teaspoons vanilla extract

1. **To prepare cake:** Preheat oven to 350°F. Coat a 9-by-13-inch baking dish with cooking spray.
2. Toast walnuts in a small baking pan in the oven until fragrant, 5 to 10 minutes. Drain pineapple in a sieve set over a bowl, pressing on the solids. Reserve the drained pineapple and ¼ cup of the juice.
3. Whisk flour, baking soda, salt and cinnamon in a medium bowl. Whisk eggs, sugar (or Splenda), buttermilk, oil, vanilla and ¼ cup of the reserved pineapple juice in a large bowl until blended. Stir in pineapple, carrots and ¼ cup coconut. Add the dry ingredients and mix with a rubber spatula just until blended. Stir in the nuts. Scrape the batter into the prepared pan, spreading evenly.
4. Bake the cake until the top springs back when touched lightly and a toothpick inserted in the center comes out clean, 40 to 45 minutes. Let cool completely on a wire rack.
5. **To prepare frosting & finish cake:** Place 2 tablespoons coconut in a small baking pan and toast in the oven at 300°F, stirring several times, until light golden, 5 to 10 minutes.
6. Beat cream cheese, confectioners' sugar (or Splenda) and vanilla in a mixing bowl with an electric mixer until smooth and creamy. Spread the frosting over the cooled cake. Sprinkle with the coconut.

3
CARBOHYDRATE
SERVINGS

MAKES 16 SERVINGS

PREP TIME: 30 MINUTES
START TO FINISH: 1 HOUR 10 MINUTES

PER SERVING

344	CALORIES
17	G FAT (5 G SAT, 6 G MONO)
56	MG CHOLESTEROL
43	G CARBOHYDRATE
6	G PROTEIN
3	G FIBER
349	MG SODIUM

NUTRITION BONUS: Vitamin A (40% DAILY VALUE), Fiber (12% DV).

EXCHANGES

3	OTHER CARBOHYDRATE
2½	FAT

PER SERVING WITH SPLENDA (CAKE ONLY):
2 CARBOHYDRATE SERVINGS
242 CALORIES, 29 G CARBOHYDRATE

PER SERVING WITH SPLENDA (FROSTING ONLY):
0 CARBOHYDRATE SERVINGS
63 CALORIES, 2 G CARBOHYDRATE

Cookies & Bars

"I love to cook and bake—especially breads and desserts. I seldom use recipes with sugar substitutes. I'd rather use regular sweeteners and cut the amount by one-third or even one-half—testing to see what will work. Low-fat, low-sugar biscotti cookies are my standby."

—*Garnett A., Michigan*

Chocolate Cappuccino Wafers

Crisp, chewy and chocolaty, one of these cookies makes a delightfully satisfying treat. To ward off the temptation to eat more than one at a time, store them in the freezer.

¾	**cup whole-wheat pastry flour**
½	**cup all-purpose flour**
⅔	**cup unsweetened cocoa powder**
¼	**teaspoon salt**
1	**large egg white**
¾	**cup sugar** *or* ⅓ **cup Splenda Sugar Blend for Baking** (*see page 18*), **plus 3 tablespoons sugar for dipping**
¼	**cup canola oil**
2	**tablespoons light corn syrup**
1	**tablespoon instant coffee granules dissolved in 1 tablespoon hot water**
2	**teaspoons vanilla extract**

1. Whisk whole-wheat flour, all-purpose flour, cocoa and salt in a medium bowl.
2. Combine egg white, ¾ cup sugar (or ⅓ cup Splenda), oil, corn syrup, dissolved coffee granules and vanilla in a mixing bowl. Beat with an electric mixer at medium speed until well blended. Reduce mixer speed to low and gradually beat in the dry ingredients until smooth.
3. Wrap the dough in plastic wrap and refrigerate until firm, at least 1½ hours.
4. Position oven rack in the upper third of the oven; preheat to 350°F. Coat several large baking sheets and the bottom of a drinking glass with cooking spray.
5. Put the remaining 3 tablespoons sugar in a small shallow bowl. With lightly oiled hands, roll the dough into ¾ -inch balls. Place about 3 inches apart on prepared baking sheets. Dip the glass into the sugar and use it to flatten the balls into 2-inch circles, dipping in the sugar between each one.
6. Bake cookies, 1 sheet at a time, in upper third of oven until just becoming firm in the center, 5 to 7 minutes. (Do not overbake.) With a metal spatula, immediately transfer cookies to wire racks. Let cool completely.

1/2 CARBOHYDRATE SERVING

MAKES ABOUT 48 COOKIES

PREP TIME: 30 MINUTES

START TO FINISH: 2½ HOURS (including chilling time)

TO MAKE AHEAD: Prepare the dough through Step 3; wrap well and refrigerate for up to 2 days or freeze for up to 1 month. (If frozen, return to room temperature before using.) Store the cookies in an airtight container for up to 10 days or freeze for longer storage.

PER COOKIE

42 CALORIES
1 G FAT (0 G SAT, 1 G MONO)
0 MG CHOLESTEROL
7 G CARBOHYDRATE
1 G PROTEIN
1 G FIBER
15 MG SODIUM

EXCHANGES

½ OTHER CARBOHYDRATE

PER COOKIE WITH SPLENDA

½ CARBOHYDRATE SERVING
37 CALORIES, 6 G CARBOHYDRATE

Rolled Sugar Cookies

These make great holiday cookies when cut into shapes and decorated, but they're also a fine addition to your everyday cookie jar. We've cut the butter from an entire stick to just 2 tablespoons, cooking it until it turns a nutty brown to maximize the rich flavor.

½

CARBOHYDRATE
SERVING

¾	cup whole-wheat flour
¾	cup unsifted cake flour
1	teaspoon baking powder
¼	teaspoon salt
2	tablespoons butter
½	cup sugar *or* ¼ cup Splenda Sugar Blend for Baking (*see page 18*)
2	tablespoons canola oil
1	large egg
1½	teaspoons vanilla extract

1. Set a rack in the upper third of the oven; preheat to 350°F. Coat 2 baking sheets with cooking spray.
2. Whisk whole-wheat flour, cake flour, baking powder and salt in a medium bowl.
3. Melt butter in a small saucepan over low heat. Cook, swirling the pan, until the butter turns a nutty brown, about 1 minute, and pour into a mixing bowl. Add sugar (or Splenda) and oil; beat with an electric mixer until smooth. Mix in egg and vanilla; beat until smooth. Add the flour mixture and mix on low speed until just combined. Divide the dough in half and press each piece into a disk.
4. Working with one disk at a time, roll dough on a lightly floured surface to a thickness of ⅛ inch. Cut out cookies with small (about 2- to 2½-inch) cookie cutters. Place the cookies about ½ inch apart on the prepared baking sheets.
5. Bake the cookies in the upper third of the oven, 1 sheet at a time, until slightly golden on the edges, 5 to 7 minutes. Do not overbake. Transfer to wire racks to cool.

MAKES ABOUT 30 COOKIES

PREP TIME: 30 MINUTES
START TO FINISH: 50 MINUTES

TO MAKE AHEAD: Prepare the dough through Step 3; wrap well and refrigerate for up to 2 days or freeze for up to 1 month. (If frozen, return to room temperature before rolling out.) Store the cookies in an airtight container for up to 3 days or freeze for longer storage.

PER COOKIE

53	CALORIES
2	G FAT (1 G SAT, 1 G MONO)
9	MG CHOLESTEROL
8	G CARBOHYDRATE
1	G PROTEIN
0	G FIBER
35	MG SODIUM

EXCHANGES

½ OTHER CARBOHYDRATE

PER COOKIE WITH SPLENDA

½ CARBOHYDRATE SERVING
49 CALORIES, 6 G CARBOHYDRATE

Ginger-Orange Biscotti

Authentic biscotti are low in fat and easy to make. To achieve the characteristic crisp texture, they are "twice-cooked," first as a log, then again as slices. These fragrant spiced biscotti are excellent dipped in a steaming cup of tea or coffee.

MAKES ABOUT 54 BISCOTTI

PREP TIME: 30 MINUTES

START TO FINISH: 1 HOUR 10 MINUTES

TO MAKE AHEAD: Store in an airtight container for up to 2 weeks.

PER BISCOTTI

34 CALORIES

0 G FAT (0 G SAT, 0 G MONO)

8 MG CHOLESTEROL

7 G CARBOHYDRATE

1 G PROTEIN

0 G FIBER

35 MG SODIUM

EXCHANGES

1/2 OTHER CARBOHYDRATE

PER BISCOTTI WITH SPLENDA

0 CARBOHYDRATE SERVINGS

28 CALORIES, 5 G CARBOHYDRATE

- ¾ **cup whole-wheat pastry flour**
- ¾ **cup all-purpose flour**
- 1 **cup sugar** *or* ½ **cup Splenda Sugar Blend for Baking** (*see page 18*)
- ½ **cup cornmeal**
- 2 **teaspoons ground ginger**
- 1 **teaspoon baking powder**
- ½ **teaspoon baking soda**
- ¼ **teaspoon salt**
- 2 **large eggs**
- 2 **large egg whites**
- 2 **teaspoons freshly grated orange zest**
- 1 **tablespoon fresh orange juice**

1. Preheat oven to 325°F. Line a baking sheet with parchment paper or a silicone baking mat.
2. Whisk whole-wheat flour, all-purpose flour, sugar (or Splenda), cornmeal, ginger, baking powder, baking soda and salt in a medium bowl. Whisk eggs, egg whites, orange zest and orange juice in a large bowl until blended. Stir in the dry ingredients with a wooden spoon until just combined.
3. Divide the dough in half. With dampened hands, form each piece into a 14-by-1½-inch log. Place the logs side by side on the prepared baking sheet
4. Bake until firm, 20 to 25 minutes. Cool on the pan on a wire rack. Reduce oven temperature to 300°.
5. Slice the logs on the diagonal into cookies ½ inch thick. Arrange, cut-side down, on 2 ungreased baking sheets. Bake until golden brown and crisp, 15 to 20 minutes. (Rotate the baking sheets if necessary to ensure even browning.) Transfer the biscotti to a wire rack to cool.

Double-Chocolate Biscotti

Dense and crunchy, these are the classic Italian dunking cookies. Although they are traditionally dipped in Vin Santo, a sweet Italian dessert wine, these chocolaty biscotti are ultra-satisfying with a cup of coffee or a glass of milk.

1½ cups whole-wheat pastry flour
1½ cups all-purpose flour
⅓ cup plus 1 tablespoon unsweetened cocoa powder
1¼ teaspoons baking powder
½ teaspoon baking soda
½ teaspoon salt
3 large eggs
1 large egg yolk
1 cup sugar *or* ½ cup Splenda Sugar Blend for Baking (*see page 18*)
1 tablespoon vanilla extract
5 ounces semisweet chocolate, chopped, *or* chocolate chips, melted (*see Cooking Tip, page 325*)

VARIATION: For Triple-Chocolate Biscotti, stir 1 cup mini chocolate chips into the batter with the flour mixture. Or add 1 cup whole hazelnuts, skinned, or 1 cup dried cherries.

1. Position rack in the center of the oven; preheat to 325°F. Line 2 large baking sheets with parchment paper or a silicone baking mat.
2. Whisk whole-wheat flour, all-purpose flour, cocoa powder, baking powder, baking soda and salt in a large bowl. In another large bowl, beat eggs, egg yolk and sugar (or Splenda) with an electric mixer until thick and pale yellow, about 2 minutes. Beat in vanilla and melted chocolate. Stir in the dry ingredients with a wooden spoon until just moistened.
3. Turn the dough out onto a lightly floured surface; knead for 1 minute, then divide in half. Roll each piece into an 8-inch log; flatten slightly to about ¾ inch high and 3½ inches wide. Place the logs side by side on one of the prepared baking sheets.
4. Bake until lightly browned and firm, about 20 minutes. Cool on the pan on a wire rack for 20 minutes. Keep the oven on; switch the oven racks to the upper and lower thirds of the oven.
5. Slice the logs on the diagonal into cookies ½ inch thick. Arrange, cut-side down, on the 2 baking sheets. Bake for 10 minutes. Turn the biscotti over and rotate the pans from top to bottom; bake until dry, 15 to 20 minutes more. Transfer to a wire rack to cool.

1

CARBOHYDRATE
SERVING

MAKES ABOUT 32 BISCOTTI

PREP TIME: 20 MINUTES
START TO FINISH: 1¾ HOURS

TO MAKE AHEAD: Store in an airtight container for up to 2 weeks.

PER BISCOTTI
97 CALORIES
2 G FAT (1 G SAT, 1 G MONO)
26 MG CHOLESTEROL
18 G CARBOHYDRATE
2 G PROTEIN
1 G FIBER
78 MG SODIUM

EXCHANGES
1 STARCH

PER BISCOTTI WITH SPLENDA
1 CARBOHYDRATE SERVING
88 CALORIES, 15 G CARBOHYDRATE

1

CARBOHYDRATE

SERVING

MAKES ABOUT 45 COOKIES

PREP TIME: 15 MINUTES

START TO FINISH: 1 HOUR

TO MAKE AHEAD: Store in an airtight container for up to 2 days or freeze for longer storage.

PER COOKIE

101 CALORIES

5 G FAT (2 G SAT, 1 G MONO)

7 MG CHOLESTEROL

13 G CARBOHYDRATE

2 G PROTEIN

1 G FIBER

45 MG SODIUM

EXCHANGES

1 OTHER CARBOHYDRATE

1 FAT

PER COOKIE WITH SPLENDA

1 CARBOHYDRATE SERVING

97 CALORIES, 12 G CARBOHYDRATE

Oatmeal Chocolate Chip Cookies

Here's a new take on an American classic. Tahini (sesame paste) makes the cookies sophisticated for adults and lower in saturated fat, while brown sugar and chocolate keeps them ever so delicious for the whole family.

2   cups rolled oats (*not* quick-cooking)

½   cup all-purpose flour

½   cup whole-wheat pastry flour

1   teaspoon ground cinnamon

½   teaspoon baking soda

½   teaspoon salt

½   cup tahini (*see Ingredient Note, page 324*)

4   tablespoons cold unsalted butter, cut into pieces

⅔   cup granulated sugar *or* ⅓ cup Splenda Sugar Blend for Baking (*see page 18*)

⅔   cup packed light brown sugar

1   large egg

1   large egg white

1   tablespoon vanilla extract

1   cup semisweet *or* bittersweet chocolate chips

½   cup chopped walnuts

1. Position racks in the upper and lower thirds of the oven; preheat to 350°F. Line 2 baking sheets with parchment paper.
2. Whisk oats, all-purpose flour, whole-wheat flour, cinnamon, baking soda and salt in a medium bowl. Beat tahini and butter in a large bowl with an electric mixer until blended into a paste. Add granulated sugar (or Splenda) and brown sugar; continue beating until well combined—the mixture will still be a little grainy. Beat in egg, then egg white, then vanilla. Stir in the oat mixture with a wooden spoon until just moistened. Stir in chocolate chips and walnuts.
3. With damp hands, roll 1 tablespoon of the batter into a ball, place it on a prepared baking sheet and flatten it until squat, but don't let the sides crack. Continue with the remaining batter, spacing the flattened balls 2 inches apart.
4. Bake the cookies until golden brown, about 16 minutes, switching the pans back to front and top to bottom halfway through. Cool on the pans for 2 minutes, then transfer the cookies to a wire rack to cool completely. Let the pans cool for a few minutes before baking another batch.

Spiced Pumpkin Cookies

The deep flavors of molasses, pumpkin and spices make these wholesome cookies delicious without the addition of butter—and they lend themselves beautifully to the inclusion of whole-wheat flour.

- ⅔ cup whole-wheat pastry flour
- ⅔ cup all-purpose flour
- 1 teaspoon baking powder
- ½ teaspoon baking soda
- ½ teaspoon salt
- 1 teaspoon ground cinnamon
- ½ teaspoon ground ginger
- ¼ teaspoon ground allspice
- ¼ teaspoon freshly grated nutmeg
- ¾ cup canned plain pumpkin puree
- ¾ cup packed light brown sugar *or* ⅓ cup Splenda Sugar Blend for Baking (*see page 18*)
- 2 large eggs
- ¼ cup canola oil
- ¼ cup dark molasses
- 1 cup raisins

1. Preheat oven to 350°F. Coat 3 baking sheets with cooking spray.
2. Whisk whole-wheat flour, all-purpose flour, baking powder, baking soda, salt, cinnamon, ginger, allspice and nutmeg in a large bowl.
3. Whisk pumpkin, brown sugar (or Splenda), eggs, oil and molasses in a second bowl until well combined. Stir the wet ingredients and raisins into the dry ingredients until no traces of dry ingredients remain. Drop the batter by level tablespoonfuls onto the prepared baking sheets, spacing the cookies 1½ inches apart.
4. Bake the cookies until firm to the touch and lightly golden on top, 10 to 12 minutes, switching the pans back to front and top to bottom halfway through. Transfer to a wire rack and let cool.

1

CARBOHYDRATE
SERVING

MAKES ABOUT 36 COOKIES

PREP TIME: 15 MINUTES
START TO FINISH: 1 HOUR

TO MAKE AHEAD: Store in an airtight container, with wax paper between the layers, for up to 2 days or freeze for longer storage.

PER COOKIE

68 CALORIES
2 G FAT (0 G SAT, 1 G MONO)
12 MG CHOLESTEROL
12 G CARBOHYDRATE
1 G PROTEIN
1 G FIBER
67 MG SODIUM

NUTRITION BONUS: Vitamin A (15% DAILY VALUE).

EXCHANGES

1 OTHER CARBOHYDRATE

PER COOKIE WITH SPLENDA

½ CARBOHYDRATE SERVING
62 CALORIES, 10 G CARBOHYDRATE

Apricot-Almond Bars with Chocolate

Pureed dried apricots form the base of these irresistible bars, providing both moisture and sweetness. (A touch of honey is all the additional sweetening needed.) Chunks of dark chocolate are an exquisite contrast to the tangy apricots.

1	cup dried apricots, divided
½	cup water
¾	cup whole-wheat pastry flour
½	teaspoon baking powder
¼	teaspoon baking soda
¼	teaspoon salt
1	large egg
1	large egg white
¼	cup canola oil
2	tablespoons honey
1	teaspoon vanilla extract
¾	cup chopped bittersweet chocolate (6 ounces) *or* semisweet chocolate chips, divided
¼	cup sliced almonds

1. Preheat oven to 350°F. Coat a 7-by-11-inch baking pan with cooking spray.
2. Combine ½ cup dried apricots and water in a small saucepan; bring to a simmer over medium heat. Cover and cook for 2 minutes. Remove from heat and set aside to cool. Coarsely chop the remaining ½ cup apricots.
3. Whisk flour, baking powder, baking soda and salt in a medium bowl.
4. Puree the cooked apricots and any remaining cooking liquid in a food processor. Add egg, egg white, oil, honey and vanilla; process until smooth. Add the flour mixture, ½ cup chocolate and the chopped apricots; pulse just until combined. Scrape the batter into the prepared pan, spreading evenly. Sprinkle with almonds.
5. Bake the bars until lightly browned and a toothpick inserted in the center comes out clean, 20 to 25 minutes. Let them cool in the pan on a wire rack.
6. Melt the remaining ¼ cup chocolate in a double boiler over barely simmering water or in the microwave on Medium for 30 to 60 seconds. Spoon the chocolate into a ziplock bag, cut off the tip of one corner and drizzle the melted chocolate over the cooled bars. Let stand for about 10 minutes before cutting into bars.

1

CARBOHYDRATE
SERVING

MAKES ABOUT **24** BARS

PREP TIME: 30 MINUTES

START TO FINISH: 1 HOUR 10 MINUTES

TO MAKE AHEAD: Store in an airtight container for up to 2 days or freeze for longer storage.

PER BAR

96 CALORIES

5 G FAT (1 G SAT, 2 G MONO)

9 MG CHOLESTEROL

12 G CARBOHYDRATE

2 G PROTEIN

2 G FIBER

51 MG SODIUM

EXCHANGES

1 OTHER CARBOHYDRATE

½ FAT

Chewy Chocolate Brownies

These brownies are a high-energy treat you can pack in your lunch bag or tuck into your fanny pack when you are out walking.

- 16 whole chocolate graham crackers (8 ounces) (*see Ingredient Note, page 323*)
- 2 tablespoons unsweetened cocoa powder
- ¼ teaspoon salt
- 2 large eggs
- 1 large egg white
- ⅓ cup packed light brown sugar *or* 3 tablespoons Splenda Sugar Blend for Baking (*see page 18*)
- ⅓ cup granulated sugar *or* 3 tablespoons Splenda Sugar Blend for Baking
- 2 teaspoons instant coffee granules
- 2 teaspoons vanilla extract
- ⅔ cup chopped pitted dates
- ¼ cup semisweet chocolate chips

1. Preheat oven to 300°F. Coat an 8-by-11½-inch baking dish with cooking spray.
2. Pulse graham crackers into crumbs in a food processor or place in a large plastic bag and crush with a rolling pin. You should have about 2 cups crumbs. Transfer to a small bowl; add cocoa and salt and mix well.
3. Combine eggs, egg white, brown sugar (or Splenda) and granulated sugar (or Splenda) in a large bowl. Beat with an electric mixer at high speed until thickened, about 2 minutes. Blend in coffee granules and vanilla. Gently fold in dates, chocolate chips and the reserved crumb mixture. Scrape the batter into the prepared baking dish, spreading evenly.
4. Bake the brownies until the top springs back when lightly touched, 25 to 30 minutes. Let cool completely in the pan on a wire rack before cutting.

1

CARBOHYDRATE
SERVING

MAKES ABOUT 24 BROWNIES

PREP TIME: 20 MINUTES
START TO FINISH: 50 MINUTES

TO MAKE AHEAD: Store in an airtight container for up to 3 days or freeze for longer storage.

PER BROWNIE

93 CALORIES
2 G FAT (0 G SAT, 0 G MONO)
18 MG CHOLESTEROL
18 G CARBOHYDRATE
2 G PROTEIN
1 G FIBER
72 MG SODIUM

EXCHANGES

1 OTHER CARBOHYDRATE

PER BROWNIE WITH SPLENDA

1 CARBOHYDRATE SERVING
87 CALORIES, 15 G CARBOHYDRATE

Pecan & Toasted Oat Nuggets

Quick ☼ Easy

Pecans are ground into a nut butter, which forms the base of these wholesome treats. Baking these scaled-down snacks in mini muffin pans is a good way to control portion size. If you do not have a mini muffin pan, spread the batter in a 9-by-13-inch baking dish (coated with cooking spray) and bake at 350°F for 15 to 20 minutes. Let cool in the pan, then cut into 24 squares.

½ **cup water**
½ **cup dried figs, finely chopped**
1 **cup old-fashioned rolled oats**
¾ **cup whole-wheat flour**
1 **teaspoon baking powder**
¼ **teaspoon baking soda**
¼ **teaspoon salt**
1 **cup pecans** *or* **walnuts**
1 **large egg**
½ **cup packed light brown sugar** *or* ¼ **cup Splenda Sugar Blend for Baking** (*see page 18*)
2 **tablespoons canola oil**
1 **teaspoon vanilla extract**

1. Preheat oven to 350°F. Coat 24 mini (2-inch) muffin cups with cooking spray.
2. Bring water to a boil in a small saucepan. Remove from heat, stir in figs and set aside to plump.
3. Spread oats in a small baking pan and bake, stirring twice, until light golden and fragrant, 10 to 15 minutes. Let cool.
4. Whisk flour, baking powder, baking soda and salt in a large bowl.
5. Grind pecans (or walnuts) in a food processor until they form a paste. Add egg, brown sugar (or Splenda), oil and vanilla; process until smooth, stopping to scrape down the sides. Add to the dry ingredients. Add the figs (with liquid) and oats; stir just until combined. Scoop the batter into the prepared muffin cups.
6. Bake the muffins until the tops spring back when touched lightly, 12 to 15 minutes. Let them cool in the pan on a wire rack for 5 minutes, then loosen the edges and turn out onto the rack to cool slightly before serving.

1

CARBOHYDRATE SERVING

MAKES 24 MINI-MUFFINS

PREP TIME: 20 MINUTES

START TO FINISH: 40 MINUTES

TO MAKE AHEAD: These taste best the day they are baked. For longer storage, wrap and freeze for up to 2 months.

PER MUFFIN

102 CALORIES
5 G FAT (1 G SAT, 1 G MONO)
9 MG CHOLESTEROL
12 G CARBOHYDRATE
2 G PROTEIN
2 G FIBER
57 MG SODIUM

EXCHANGES

1 STARCH
1 FAT

PER MUFFIN WITH SPLENDA

½ CARBOHYDRATE SERVING
97 CALORIES, 10 G CARBOHYDRATE

Apricot-Walnut Cereal Bars

By harnessing health benefits from oats, dried apricots, nuts and tofu, this bar is a nutritious alternative to store-bought cereal bars. The recipe also works with other fruit and nut combinations, such as dried cherries and almonds.

- 3 cups old-fashioned rolled oats
- ½ cup chopped walnuts (about 2 ounces)
- 3 cups unsweetened puffed-grain cereal, such as Kashi
- 2 cups chopped dried apricots
- ¼ cup all-purpose flour
- ½ teaspoon salt
- 12 ounces silken tofu, drained (about 1⅓ cups)
- 1 large egg
- ½ cup canola oil
- 1 cup honey
- 1 tablespoon vanilla extract
- 2 tablespoons freshly grated lemon zest, preferably organic

1. Preheat oven to 350°F. Coat a jellyroll-style pan (15¼-by-10¼-inch) with cooking spray.
2. Spread oats and walnuts on a baking sheet with sides. Bake until fragrant and light golden, 8 to 10 minutes. Transfer to a large bowl and add puffed cereal, dried apricots, flour and salt; stir to combine.
3. Meanwhile, puree tofu, egg, oil, honey, vanilla and lemon zest in a food processor or blender until smooth, scraping down the sides as needed. Make a well in the center of the dry ingredients; fold in the tofu mixture until combined. Spread evenly in the prepared pan.
4. Bake until firm in the center and golden brown, 35 to 40 minutes. Let cool completely in the pan on a wire rack before cutting into bars with a sharp knife.

3

CARBOHYDRATE

SERVINGS

MAKES 16 BARS

PREP TIME: 30 MINUTES

START TO FINISH: 1 HOUR 10 MINUTES

TO MAKE AHEAD: Store in an airtight container for up to 3 days or freeze for longer storage.

PER BAR

- 306 CALORIES
- 12 G FAT (1 G SAT, 5 G MONO)
- 13 MG CHOLESTEROL
- 46 G CARBOHYDRATE
- 6 G PROTEIN
- 4 G FIBER
- 87 MG SODIUM

NUTRITION BONUS: Fiber (14% DAILY VALUE).

EXCHANGES

- 2 STARCH
- 1 FRUIT
- 2 FAT

Frozen Desserts

1

CARBOHYDRATE
SERVING

1¹⁄₂

CARBOHYDRATE
SERVINGS

2

CARBOHYDRATE
SERVINGS

FAQ

FROZEN SPLENDA

Q: Can I substitute no-calorie sweetener for sugar in frozen desserts?

A: In addition to sweetening, sugar plays many roles in cooking. In the case of frozen desserts, sugar helps soften and improve the texture. When our Test Kitchen experimented with Splenda in the Zingy Tea Granita (*page 314*), the tea mixture froze solidly to the walls of the ice cream maker. Other frozen desserts, such as Frozen Raspberry Mousse (*page 316*), developed an icy texture. Therefore, we recommend that you stick with sugar in frozen desserts. Even when made with sugar, all of the recipes presented here are low in calories and carbohydrates.

1

CARBOHYDRATE

SERVING

MAKES 6 SERVINGS, 1/2 CUP EACH

PREP TIME: 15 MINUTES

START TO FINISH: 1 1/2 HOURS
(including 1 hour chilling time)

EQUIPMENT: Ice cream maker

TO MAKE AHEAD: Store in an airtight container in the freezer for up to 1 week. Let soften in the refrigerator for 1/2 hour before serving.

VARIATION
Spoon Strawberry Frozen Yogurt between layers of ginger snaps for a great ice cream sandwich.

PER SERVING

82 CALORIES

0 G FAT (0 G SAT, 0 G MONO)

0 MG CHOLESTEROL

20 G CARBOHYDRATE

1 G PROTEIN

2 G FIBER

12 MG SODIUM

NUTRITION BONUS: Vitamin C (100% DAILY VALUE).

EXCHANGES

1 FRUIT

Strawberry Frozen Yogurt

An ice cream maker allows you to create your own frozen desserts with wholesome ingredients like fruit and yogurt. This one is a terrific alternative to commercial ice cream. It is fat-free and, even though it contains some sugar, it is very low in calories. When strawberries are not in season, frozen are a fine alternative.

> 4 **cups strawberries, rinsed and hulled**
> 1/3 **cup sugar**
> 2 **tablespoons orange juice**
> 1/2 **cup nonfat *or* low-fat plain yogurt**

1. Place berries in a food processor and process until smooth, scraping down the sides as necessary. Add sugar and orange juice; process for a few seconds. Add yogurt and pulse several times until blended. Transfer to a bowl. Cover and refrigerate until chilled, about 1 hour or overnight.

2. Pour the strawberry mixture into an ice cream maker and freeze according to manufacturer's directions. Serve immediately or transfer to a storage container and let harden in the freezer for 1 to 1 1/2 hours. Serve in chilled dishes.

Tropical Fruit Ice

Quick ☼ Easy

This super-simple recipe makes an exotic ice with intense flavor. To turn it into a showstopper dessert, garnish with sliced fresh tropical fruit and toasted coconut. Welch's frozen passion fruit concentrate can be found in supermarkets. Substitute the same size can of other frozen juice concentrates for endless variations.

- 1 11½-ounce can frozen passion fruit concentrate
- 2 cups water
- 2 tablespoons lime juice

1. Combine all ingredients in a medium bowl.
2. Pour the juice mixture into an ice cream maker and freeze according to manufacturer's directions. (*Alternatively, freeze the mixture in a shallow metal pan until solid, about 6 hours. Break into chunks and process in a food processor until smooth.*) Serve immediately or transfer to a storage container and let harden in the freezer for 1 to 1½ hours. Serve in chilled dishes.

> **❝**When I was diagnosed in August 2004 with type 2 diabetes, the news sent me reeling … but now that the dust has settled somewhat, I'm putting the joy of cooking and eating back into my life.**❞**
> *—Nina C., New York*

1
CARBOHYDRATE SERVING

MAKES 8 SERVINGS, ½ CUP EACH

PREP TIME: 5 MINUTES
START TO FINISH: 30 MINUTES

EQUIPMENT: Ice cream maker or food processor

TO MAKE AHEAD: Store in an airtight container in the freezer for up to 2 days. Let soften in the refrigerator for ½ hour before serving.

PER SERVING
84 CALORIES
1 G FAT (0 G SAT, 0 G MONO)
0 MG CHOLESTEROL
15 G CARBOHYDRATE
2 G PROTEIN
0 G FIBER
31 MG SODIUM

NUTRITION BONUS:
Vitamin A (35% DAILY VALUE), Vitamin C (25% DV).

EXCHANGES
1 FRUIT

1

MAKES 8 SERVINGS, ½ CUP EACH

PREP TIME: 5 MINUTES

START TO FINISH: 2½ HOURS
(including 2 hours steeping and
chilling time)

EQUIPMENT: Ice cream maker or
food processor

TO MAKE AHEAD: Store in an
airtight container in the freezer for
up to 2 days. Let soften in the
refrigerator for ½ hour before
serving.

PER SERVING

65 CALORIES

0 G FAT (0 G SAT, 0 G MONO)

0 MG CHOLESTEROL

17 G CARBOHYDRATE

0 G PROTEIN

0 G FIBER

0 MG SODIUM

EXCHANGES

1 OTHER CARBOHYDRATE

Zingy Tea Granita

Granita, a sweet Italian ice, is characterized by its grainy texture. Lemon Zinger tea, which gets its distinctive flavor from hibiscus flowers, gives this one an exquisite garnet hue and refreshing taste.

⅔ cup sugar

4 Lemon Zinger tea bags

3 cups boiling water

2 tablespoons lemon juice

1. Place sugar and tea bags in a heatproof bowl. Pour in boiling water; stir until sugar has dissolved. Let steep until cooled to room temperature, about 1 hour.

2. Remove tea bags, squeezing out liquid. Stir in lemon juice. Cover and refrigerate until chilled, about 1 hour or overnight.

3. Pour the tea mixture into an ice cream maker and freeze according to manufacturer's directions. (*Alternatively, freeze the mixture in a shallow metal pan until solid, about 6 hours. Break into chunks and process in a food processor until smooth and creamy.*) Serve immediately or transfer to a storage container and let harden in the freezer for 1 to 1½ hours. Serve in chilled dishes.

314

Berry Frozen Yogurt

Quick ☼ Easy

Somewhere between a fruity sorbet and a creamy ice cream lies this richly flavored low-fat dessert.

1¹/₂

CARBOHYDRATE

SERVINGS

3 cups fresh *or* frozen and partially thawed blackberries *or* raspberries *or* a mixture of blackberries, raspberries and blueberries

6 tablespoons sugar

1 tablespoon lemon juice

¾ cup low-fat plain yogurt

1. Combine berries, sugar and lemon juice in a food processor; process until smooth. Add yogurt and pulse until mixed in. If using fresh berries, transfer the mixture to a medium bowl, cover and refrigerate until chilled, about 1 hour.

2. Transfer the berry mixture to an ice cream maker and freeze according to manufacturer's directions. (*Alternatively, freeze the mixture in a shallow metal pan until solid, about 6 hours. Break into chunks and process in a food processor until smooth and creamy.*) Serve immediately or transfer to a storage container and let harden in the freezer for 1 to 1½ hours. Serve in chilled dishes.

VARIATION:

FROZEN BERRY TRUFFLES

Use a melon baller to scoop frozen yogurt and roll the balls in granola.

MAKES 6 SERVINGS, ½ CUP EACH

PREP TIME: 10 MINUTES

START TO FINISH: 35 MINUTES

EQUIPMENT: Ice cream maker or food processor

TO MAKE AHEAD: Store in an airtight container in the freezer for up to 1 week. Let soften in the refrigerator for ½ hour before serving.

PER SERVING

106 CALORIES

1 G FAT (0 G SAT, 0 G MONO)

2 MG CHOLESTEROL

24 G CARBOHYDRATE

2 G PROTEIN

4 G FIBER

21 MG SODIUM

NUTRITION BONUS: Vitamin C (28% DAILY VALUE), Fiber (16% DV).

EXCHANGES

1½ FRUIT

Frozen Raspberry Mousse

High ⬆ Fiber

Pamper your guests with this pretty, elegant dessert—no one will ever guess that it easily conforms to any healthy weight-loss regime. A fluffy meringue creates a sublime texture, while just a little real whipped cream delivers velvety richness. Straining the raspberries is a labor of love (consider delegating this task), but all the work is done well ahead and the results are absolutely worth the effort, guaranteed.

<table>
<tr><td>6</td><td>cups fresh raspberries or two 12-ounce packages unsweetened frozen raspberries, thawed</td></tr>
<tr><td>¼</td><td>cup confectioners' sugar or Splenda Granular (see page 18)</td></tr>
<tr><td>2</td><td>tablespoons orange juice</td></tr>
<tr><td>1</td><td>teaspoon unflavored gelatin</td></tr>
<tr><td>8</td><td>teaspoons dried egg whites (see Ingredient Note, page 323), reconstituted in ½ cup warm water according to package directions (equivalent to 4 egg whites)</td></tr>
<tr><td>⅔</td><td>cup sugar</td></tr>
<tr><td>⅓</td><td>cup whipping cream</td></tr>
</table>

2 cups fresh raspberries, blueberries, blackberries *and/or* strawberries for garnish
Mint sprigs for garnish

1. Place a small mixing bowl in the freezer to chill for Step 5.
2. Puree raspberries in a food processor until smooth. Pass through a fine sieve set over a large bowl; discard seeds. Measure out 1 cup raspberry puree, whisk in confectioners' sugar (or Splenda), cover and set aside in the refrigerator for sauce.
3. Place orange juice in a small saucepan. Sprinkle in gelatin. Let soften for 1 minute. Place over low heat and stir until the gelatin has completely dissolved. Let stand for 5 minutes.
4. Meanwhile, beat reconstituted egg whites in a large mixing bowl with an electric mixer until soft peaks form. Gradually add sugar, beating until the meringue is stiff and glossy.
5. Beat cream in the chilled bowl until soft peaks form.
6. Add the melted gelatin to the remaining raspberry puree and whisk until blended. Set the bowl over a bowl of ice water and stir just until the mixture starts to thicken slightly, 5 to 10 minutes. Add one-fourth of the meringue to the raspberry puree and whisk until blended. Using a whisk, fold in the remaining meringue. With a rubber spatula, fold in the whipped cream. Scrape the mousse into a 6-cup metal bowl (or other decorative mold) or a 9-by-5-inch metal loaf pan. Cover with plastic wrap and foil and freeze until firm, at least 6 hours.
7. To serve, fill a bowl or basin (large enough to hold the mold comfortably) with very hot water. Run a knife around the edges of the mold. Quickly dip the mold in hot water, then invert a serving platter over the top. Grasping the mold and platter, jerk downward several times. If the mousse does not release, dip in hot water again and repeat. Cut the mousse into wedges or slices. Serve with the reserved raspberry sauce and garnish each serving with a scattering of berries and a mint sprig.

2

CARBOHYDRATE
SERVINGS

MAKES 8 SERVINGS

PREP TIME: 1 HOUR

START TO FINISH: 7 HOURS
(including 6 hours freezing time)

TO MAKE AHEAD: Cover and freeze for up to 4 days.

TEST KITCHEN TIP
A stand-up mixer makes beating egg whites easier, but a hand-held electric mixer will work fine.

SERVING TIP
If you prefer to skip the unmolding step, you can divide the mousse among eight 6-ounce ramekins and serve the dessert directly from them (it is difficult to unmold the mousse from a glass container).

PER SERVING

168 CALORIES
4 G FAT (2 G SAT, 1 G MONO)
11 MG CHOLESTEROL
32 G CARBOHYDRATE
3 G PROTEIN
6 G FIBER
33 MG SODIUM

NUTRITION BONUS: Vitamin C (45% DAILY VALUE), Fiber (24% DV).

EXCHANGES

2 FRUIT
1 FAT

PER SERVING WITH SPLENDA

1½ CARBOHYDRATE SERVINGS
156 CALORIES, 29 G CARBOHYDRATE

Roasted Mango Sorbet

Switching from ice cream to sorbet is an excellent way to reduce saturated fat. This recipe, contributed by Diana Dalsass of Teaneck, New Jersey, has an exceptionally creamy texture, thanks to the banana and roasted mango.

    3 ripe mangoes
    ½ cup sugar
    ½ cup water
    ⅓ cup coarsely mashed banana (1 small)
    2 tablespoons lime juice

1. Preheat oven to 350°F. Place whole mangoes in a shallow baking pan and roast until very soft, 70 to 90 minutes. Refrigerate until cool, about 1 hour.
2. Meanwhile, combine sugar and water in a small saucepan. Bring to a boil, stirring to dissolve sugar. Remove from heat and refrigerate until cold, about 1 hour.
3. When the mangoes are cool enough to handle, remove skin and coarsely chop pulp, discarding pit. Place the mango pulp and accumulated juices in a food processor. Add banana and lime juice; process until very smooth. Transfer to a large bowl and stir in the sugar syrup. Cover and refrigerate until cold, 40 minutes or overnight.
4. Freeze the mixture in an ice cream maker according to manufacturer's directions. (*Alternatively, freeze the mixture in a shallow metal pan until solid, about 6 hours. Break into chunks and process in a food processor until smooth.*) Serve immediately or transfer to a storage container and let harden in the freezer for 1 to 1½ hours. Serve in chilled dishes.

2

CARBOHYDRATE
SERVINGS

MAKES 8 SERVINGS, ABOUT ½ CUP EACH

PREP TIME: 20 MINUTES

START TO FINISH: 4½ HOURS (including chilling time)

EQUIPMENT: Ice cream maker or food processor

TO MAKE AHEAD: Store in an airtight container in the freezer for up to 1 week. Let soften in the refrigerator for ½ hour before serving.

PER SERVING

108 CALORIES
  0 G FAT (0 G SAT, 0 G MONO)
  0 MG CHOLESTEROL
 28 G CARBOHYDRATE
  1 G PROTEIN
  2 G FIBER
  2 MG SODIUM

NUTRITION BONUS: Vitamin C (40% DAILY VALUE).

EXCHANGES

  2 FRUIT

Glossary

ACESULFAME POTASSIUM (ACESULFAME-K): a crystalline sweetener discovered in 1967 and marketed under the brand names Sunett and Sweet One, among others. It is about 200 times sweeter than table sugar. (*More information, page 18.*)

ASPARTAME: about 200 times sweeter than table sugar, this artificial sweetener is widely marketed under the brand names NutraSweet and Equal. Discovered in 1965, it is largely a synthesis of two amino acids (aspartic acid and phenylalanine). It is not heat-stable so it is used in foods that do not require cooking. (*More information, page 18.*)

BODY MASS INDEX (BMI): the number most health-care providers and obesity researchers prefer to use to determine a healthy body weight. A person's BMI is calculated by using a formula that takes into account both height (in meters) and weight (in kilograms). In general, the higher your BMI, the higher your risks of health problems, including heart disease and diabetes. These risks are increased if your waist size is greater than 40 inches for men or 35 inches for women. To calculate your BMI, take your height in meters, square that number, then divide that into your weight in kilograms ($BMI=kg/m^2$). Sound difficult? Let others do the calculating at websites like www.consumer.gov/weightloss.

CHOLESTEROL: a fatlike, waxy substance found in the bloodstream and in cells. It is used for producing cell membranes and some hormones, and serves other important bodily functions. However, too high a level of cholesterol in the blood (hypercholesterolemia) is a major risk for coronary heart disease, which leads to heart attack. It's also a risk factor for stroke. Your body makes some cholesterol; the rest comes from animal products, such as meats, poultry, fish, eggs, butter, cheese and whole milk. Food from plants—like fruits, vegetables and cereals—doesn't have cholesterol. Some foods that don't contain animal products may contain trans fats, which cause your body to make more cholesterol. Foods with saturated fats also cause the body to make more cholesterol. Cholesterol is transported to and from cells by lipoproteins. Low-density lipoprotein, or LDL, is known as "bad" cholesterol. Too much LDL cholesterol can clog your arteries, increasing your risk of heart attack and stroke. High-density lipoprotein, or HDL, is known as "good" cholesterol. It carries cholesterol away from your arteries. Studies suggest that high levels of HDL cholesterol reduce your risk of heart attack.

CHROMIUM PICOLINATE: chromium is an essential trace mineral found in a variety of foods like whole grains, nuts, seafood, green beans, broccoli and potatoes. It helps insulin make blood glucose available to cells. Chromium picolinate is the form of the mineral commonly sold as a supplement, but the best avenue for chromium intake is food.

DAILY VALUE (DV): the amount of a nutrient that the FDA has set as a benchmark for adults eating 2,000 calories per day. These values are identical to those found on food labels.

FRUCTOSE: (sometimes called "levulose") a simple sugar that occurs naturally in foods, including fruits and honey, and a key component in table sugar (which is sucrose, a blend of half fructose and half glucose). While it has the same amount of calories and carbohydrates as sugar, fructose produces a lower and slower rise in blood glucose, and requires less insulin for the body to process. But fructose can raise triglycerides and LDL cholesterol, potentially raising heart-disease risks. Some scientists and nutritionists are concerned about the rapidly growing presence of fructose in the food supply, largely through the increasing use of high-fructose corn syrup. (*More information, page 19.*)

GLUCOSE (BLOOD GLUCOSE, BLOOD SUGAR): the form of sugar that your body needs for fuel. Delivered to cells by means of insulin.

GLYCEMIC INDEX (GI): a system of ranking foods containing equal amounts of carbohydrate according to how much they raise blood-glucose levels. A food with a GI under 55 is considered low, while anything more than 70 is high. (*More information, page 16.*)

GLYCEMIC LOAD (GL): a measure of the carbohydrate "impact" of a portion of food, calculated by taking the glycemic index (GI) of a given food and multiplying it by the grams of carbohydrate in a serving. A GL of 20 or more is considered high, a GL of 11 to 19 inclusive is considered medium, and a GL of 10 or less is considered low. (*More information, page 16.*)

HDL (HIGH-DENSITY LIPOPROTEIN): *see cholesterol*

HEMOGLOBIN A1c: a blood test that reflects your average blood-glucose control over three months by measuring the amount of attached (glycated) hemoglobin in your red blood cells. When a red blood cell first forms, it has no glucose attached to it. But with diabetes, there is extra glucose in the bloodstream, which enters the red blood cells and attaches to the molecules of hemoglobin in the cell. The more glucose in the blood, the more hemoglobin gets attached. The A1c test uses a small sample of your blood to measures the percentage of that attached hemoglobin. Because red blood cells live about three months before they die off and are replaced by new ones, the percentage offers a snapshot of how much glucose has been in your bloodstream over that period. People without diabetes have levels of about 6. The American Diabetes Association recommends keeping levels below 7.

HYDROGENATED STARCH HYDROLYSATES (HSH): *see sugar alcohols*

INSULIN: a hormone produced by beta cells in the pancreas that is vital to the transport of glucose from the bloodstream into the cells where it can be used as fuel. Insulin is the "key" that unlocks the door to your cells to allow glucose inside.

INSULIN RESISTANCE: a condition in which cells become less able to process insulin's signals. As long as the body can make enough insulin to overcome the resistance, blood-glucose levels will remain normal. Eventually, however, the pancreas can't produce enough insulin to overcome the resistance, and the problem becomes an insulin deficiency. Even though insulin levels may be higher than normal, the amount isn't enough to keep blood-glucose levels within a normal range.

LACTITOL: *see sugar alcohols*

LDL (LOW-DENSITY LIPOPROTEIN): *see cholesterol*

MALTITOL: *see sugar alcohols*

MANNITOL: *see sugar alcohols*

OBESE: according to the National Institute of Health, having a body mass index (BMI) of 30 or over. (A BMI of 40+ is considered "extremely obese," one of the fastest-growing categories of obesity in the U.S.)

OBESIGENIC: contributing to obesity. It is often said that the combination of a pervasive fast-food culture, sedentary lifestyle and ubiquitous food advertising has created an obesigenic environment in America.

OVERWEIGHT: according to the National Institute of Health, having a body mass index (BMI) between 25 and 29.9.

SACCHARIN: a sugar substitute discovered in the 1800s and said to be about 300 times sweeter than sugar. The FDA called its safety into question in 1977 because of reported possible carcinogenic effects in animal studies. In 1991, the FDA reversed its position because no human studies had confirmed the findings. Saccharin is widely used to sweeten commercial foods and beverages and is sold as Sweet'n Low, SugarTwin and other brands.

SODIUM: one of the two elements in table salt (40% sodium; 60% chloride). Sodium occurs naturally in foods and is essential to normal body functions, such as maintaining fluid balance and regulating blood pressure. Too much sodium, however, can be problematic. Studies show that, on average, as sodium intake rises, so does the incidence of high blood pressure—and, when people make a conscious effort to reduce their salt intake, their high blood pressure tends to drop. The Institute of Medicine of the National Academies (IOM) recommends that people with diabetes try to stay under 2,300 milligrams (mg) of sodium daily, which is slightly less than the amount in a teaspoon of salt (2,400 mg).

SORBITOL: *see sugar alcohols*

STEVIA (STEVIOSIDE): a natural sweetener extracted from the leaves of the stevia plant. Not currently approved by the FDA for use as a sweetener, but widely available as a "dietary supplement." The Center for Science in the Public Interest concurs with the FDA that more testing is needed to determine stevia's safety before it gains widespread use, for example in soft drinks. (*More information, page 19.*)

SUCRALOSE: a sweetener made from sugar but altered so that the body does not recognize it as a carbohydrate. About 600 times sweeter than sugar, it is used in low-calorie foods and drinks and as a tabletop sugar substitute. Sold as Splenda and, in combination with sugar, as Splenda Sugar Blend for Baking. (*More information, page 18.*)

SUCROSE: common table sugar, made up of an equal blend of glucose and fructose. Sucrose occurs naturally in plants, such as sugar beets and cane sugar, from which it is extracted for commercial purposes.

SUGAR ALCOHOLS: sugar substitutes that are called "alcohols" because of their chemical structure (not because they are "alcoholic"). These sweeteners, such as sorbitol, mannitol, xylitol, lactitol and hydrogenated starch isolates, are used by food manufacturers to add sweetness without as many calories as sugar. Because sugar alcohols are only partially digested, they cause a lower rise in blood glucose, but this lack of digestibility can cause stomach upset, gas or diarrhea in some people, especially if eaten in large amounts. Sugar alcohols still contribute some carbohydrate to foods. (*More information, page 19.*)

TRIGLYCERIDES: the chemical form in which most fat exists in food and in the body. The triglycerides measured in the bloodstream are part of the "lipid profile" that make up part of a cholesterol test. Excess triglycerides are linked to coronary artery disease. The American Diabetes Association triglyceride goal for adults with diabetes is less than 150 milligrams per deciliter.

TYPE 1 DIABETES: a condition in which the beta cells of the pancreas no longer produce insulin. This form of diabetes often begins in childhood (it is often called "juvenile diabetes") although it can occur at any age. People with type 1 diabetes must receive insulin by injection or a pump to control excess blood glucose. (*More information, page 12.*)

TYPE 2 DIABETES: the most common kind of diabetes, accounting for nine out of ten American cases. Usually begins as body cells become insulin resistant. The excess blood glucose in type 2 diabetes can often be controlled or minimized by making and maintaining changes in eating and physical activity. (*More information, page 12.*)

XYLITOL: *see sugar alcohols*

Resources

General Diabetes Information

THE AMERICAN DIABETES ASSOCIATION, with affiliates in every state, is a one-stop source of comprehensive information and services for people with diabetes. It funds research, publishes guides and cookbooks and advocates for the rights of people with diabetes.
www.diabetes.org
1-800-DIABETES (1-800-342-2383)

INTERNATIONAL DIABETES CENTER provides diabetes care, education and clinical research to meet the needs of people with diabetes, their families and the health professionals who care for them. Their website is a good source of basic information about managing diabetes.
www.internationaldiabetescenter.com
1-888-825-6315

THE NATIONAL DIABETES INFORMATION CLEARING-HOUSE, part of the National Institutes of Health (NIH), is the site for several important government documents on diabetes—as well as the basic information put out by the National Diabetes Education Program.
diabetes.niddk.nih.gov
1-800-860-8747

HEALTHFINDER offers links to the many government Web resources on diabetes.
www.healthfinder.gov

JOSLIN DIABETES CENTER, a diabetes treatment, research and education institution affiliated with Harvard Medical School, has reports on the latest clinical research related to diabetes causes and treatment, along with basic diabetes information and education, discussion boards and an online library.
www.joslin.org

THE JUVENILE DIABETES RESEARCH FOUNDATION is the leading charitable funder and advocate of juvenile (type 1) diabetes research worldwide. The JDRF website features "JDRF Kids Online," where kids can find pen pals and share stories. Includes a special section for newly diagnosed kids.
www.jdrf.org
1-800-533-CURE (2873)

CHILDREN WITH DIABETES is an online community for kids, families and adults with diabetes. It provides hands-on information on living with diabetes, including the latest news from clinical studies and users' reports on their experiences with diabetes drugs, insulin pumps and more. Features forums for kids with diabetes, parent-support forums and even a lively humor section with entries like "You know you're a parent of a child with diabetes when …"
www.childrenwithdiabetes.com

Educational Tools/Nutrition Information

NUTRITIONDATA.COM has nutrition label information for just about any food, including up-to-date offerings from fast-food restaurants.
www.nutritiondata.com

MEAL PLANNING EXCHANGE LISTS, which include carbohydrate counts, are produced by the American Diabetes Association and are available through dietitians and certified diabetes educators.
www.diabetes.org
1-800-342-2383

TYPE 1 TOOLS is an online catalog of educational tools designed to simplify everyday tasks and build knowledge and confidence in children with type 1 diabetes, but their graphically striking materials are useful for all ages, including "Flashcarbs"—cards with photos of common foods that include carbohydrate information and meal-planning tips.
www.type1tools.com

Healthy Pantry Essentials

If you have these healthy staples at the ready, you'll always be able to put together a simple, soul-satisfying meal.

Canned/shelf-stable goods

Beans (cannellini, kidney, great northern, chickpeas, black, pinto, black-eyed peas)
Chunk light tuna and salmon
Diced tomatoes
Tomato paste
Reduced-sodium chicken broth, beef broth and/or vegetable broth (*see Note, page 324*)
Lentil soup
Roasted red peppers
Low-fat or fat-free bean dip
Lite coconut milk
Marinara sauce
Silken tofu (in aseptic packages)

Condiments & flavorings

Oils: extra-virgin olive oil, canola, sesame
Vinegars: balsamic, red-wine, cider, rice
Reduced-sodium soy sauce
Chile-garlic sauce
Hot sauce
Reduced-fat mayonnaise
Kalamata olives and green olives
Dijon mustard and dry mustard
Capers
Canned chopped green chiles
Salsa
Reduced-sodium ketchup
Worcestershire sauce
Onions
Garlic
Fresh ginger
Dried herbs: bay leaves, oregano, rosemary, tarragon, thyme

Spices: allspice, cayenne pepper, cinnamon, chili powder, crushed red pepper, cumin, curry powder, paprika, nutmeg, ground ginger
Salt: table and kosher
Black peppercorns

Grains & legumes

Whole-wheat pasta (assorted shapes)
Brown rice or instant brown rice
Pearl barley or quick-cooking barley
Old-fashioned rolled oats
Whole-wheat couscous
Bulgur
Dried lentils
Dried beans
Cornmeal
Plain dry breadcrumbs

Nuts & seeds

Walnuts
Pecans
Almonds
Pine nuts
Dry-roasted unsalted peanuts
Natural peanut butter
Sesame seeds
Flaxseeds (*see Note, page 324*)

Baking & dessert basics

Whole-wheat flour, regular and pastry flour (*see Note, page 324*)
All-purpose flour
Cornstarch

Wheat bran or oat bran
Granulated sugar
Brown sugar
Honey
Maple syrup
No-calorie sweeteners, such as Splenda Granular and Splenda Sugar Blend for Baking (*see page 18*)
Baking powder
Baking soda
Active dry yeast or bread-machine yeast (*see Note, page 74*)
Dried egg whites (*see Note, page 323*)
Buttermilk powder (*see Note, page 323*)
Vanilla extract
Dried fruit: apricots, prunes, dates, cranberries, raisin
Unsweetened cocoa powder
Cooking spray

Refrigerator basics

Low-fat milk or soymilk
Low-fat plain or vanilla yogurt
Reduced-fat sour cream
Parmesan cheese or Romano cheese
Sharp Cheddar cheese
Eggs
Lemons, limes and oranges

Freezer basics

Frozen juice concentrates
Frozen vegetables
Frozen berries

Ingredient Notes

BASMATI RICE is a nutty-flavored, light-textured aromatic variety of rice imported from India and Pakistan. Brown basmati rice is available in the natural-foods section of the supermarket. For cooking directions, refer to the Grain-Cooking Guide, page 237.

BREAD FLOUR, which is milled from high-protein wheats, develops strong gluten when kneaded, resulting in well-risen loaves. It is generally recommended for bread machines and is valuable when making breads with a high percentage of whole-wheat flour.

BULGUR Fiber-rich bulgur is made from whole-wheat kernels that are precooked, dried and cracked. You can find it in natural-foods stores and large markets.

BUTTERMILK POWDER is the buttermilk version of powdered milk. Shelf-stable, it is a convenient alternative to fresh buttermilk in pancakes and baked goods, especially if you hesitate to buy a one-quart carton just to make a recipe. Substitute according to package directions, but for added calcium and protein, replace liquid with low-fat milk instead of water. You can find it in the baking section of most supermarkets.

CHILE-GARLIC SAUCE (or chili-garlic sauce, or paste) is a spicy blend of chiles, garlic and other seasonings; it is found in the Asian section of the market.

CHIPOTLE PEPPERS are smoked jalapeños with a fiery taste that are canned in adobo sauce. Look for them in the Hispanic section of large supermarkets and in specialty stores.

COCONUT CHIPS—large thin flakes of dried coconut— make attractive garnishes. Find them in the produce section of large supermarkets or by mail (*see box*).

COCONUT MILK We use unsweetened reduced-fat coconut milk, usually identified on the label as "lite."

COOKIES, GRAHAM CRACKERS & WAFERS, FOR CRUMBS Many commercial cookies and wafers contain partially hydrogenated oil, a source of trans-fatty acids. Fortunately, you can find tasty alternatives without these oils. Look for brands like My-Del and Newman's Own Organics in natural-foods stores and the natural-foods section of large supermarkets.

DRIED EGG WHITES are pasteurized so this product is a wise choice in mousses and dishes that call for an uncooked meringue. They are also convenient in recipes calling for egg whites because there is no waste. Look for brands like Just Whites in the baking section or the natural-foods section of most supermarkets.

SHOPPING

INGREDIENT SOURCES

We strive to feature recipes with easily accessible ingredients, but some ingredients are worth going out of your way to find. Even if you live in a remote area, the Internet and overnight shipping mean that specialty and ethnic ingredients are just a click away. Here are some mail-order purveyors we like.

◆ **Bob's Red Mill**, www.bobsredmill.com, (800) 349-2173. A great resource for a vast array of whole-grain products, including whole-wheat pastry flour.

◆ **Dean & DeLuca**, www.deandeluca.com, (800) 781-9246. The wonders of this Manhattan food shop can be delivered to your kitchen.

◆ **EthnicGrocer.com**: An incredible selection of ingredients from all corners of the world.

◆ **Frieda's**, www.friedas.com, (800) 241-1771. Specialty produce, exotic fruits and more.

◆ **Kalustyan's**, www.kalustyans.com, (800) 352-3451. A good place to look for Middle Eastern and Indian ingredients.

◆ **King Arthur Flour**, www.kingarthurflour.com, (800) 827-6836. Wonderful source of whole grains, specialty flours, flaxseeds, baking supplies and more.

◆ **Melissa's**, www.melissas.com, (800) 588-0151. Specialty produce, coconut chips and more.

◆ **Penzeys Spices**, www.penzeys.com, (800) 741-7787. Specializing in premium spices, herbs and seasonings.

EDAMAME are fresh soybeans (also called "sweet beans"), picked in their fuzzy pods just before they reach full maturity. They look like bright green lima beans and have a flavor that is sweet and mild, with a touch of "beaniness." You can find frozen, partially cooked edamame, either in pods or shelled, in natural-foods stores and large supermarkets. In season, fresh ones sometimes turn up at farmers' markets. Use them in bean salads, toss into stir-fries or soups.

FISH SAUCE is a pungent Southeast Asian sauce made from salted, fermented fish. You can find it in large supermarkets and Asian markets.

FLAXSEEDS are one of the best plant sources of omega-3 fatty acids. They provide both soluble fiber, linked to reduced risk of heart disease, and insoluble fiber, which provides valuable roughage. Flaxseeds must be ground for your body to absorb the benefits. Whole flaxseeds have a longer shelf life (grind them in a clean coffee grinder or dry blender). Once ground, flaxseeds are highly perishable, so store them in a tightly covered container in the refrigerator or freezer. You can purchase whole seeds and ground flaxmeal in natural-foods markets or by mail-order (*see box, page 323*).

MIRIN is a low-alcohol rice wine essential to Japanese cooking. Look for it in your supermarket with the Asian or gourmet ingredients. An equal portion of sherry or white wine with a pinch of sugar may be substituted for mirin.

MISO, made from fermented soybeans, is a common ingredient in Japanese cooking. There are different types of miso, in shades ranging from white and yellow to reddish brown and dark brown. Available at health-food stores and Japanese markets.

NAPA CABBAGE has an elongated head and is pale green in color with tender, tapered white ribs. Its tightly packed, crinkled leaves have a crisp texture. Discard the cone-shaped core. One small head yields about 8 cups shredded.

RED CURRY PASTE is a blend of chile peppers, garlic, lemongrass and galanga (a root with a flavor similar to ginger). Look for it in jars or cans in the Asian section of the supermarket or specialty stores.

RED LENTILS, which can be found in natural-foods stores and Middle Eastern markets, cook in less than 20 minutes.

RICE VINEGAR is a mild vinegar made from glutinous rice; it is found in the Asian section of the supermarket. Substitute cider vinegar in a pinch.

SOY FLOUR is made from roasted soybeans that have been ground into a fine powder. Its high protein content makes it a valuable ingredient in baked goods. Look for it in the natural-foods section of your supermarket or mail-order it (*see box, page 323*).

TAHINI is a paste made from ground sesame seeds. It is often used in Middle Eastern cooking and found in popular dishes, such as hummus. High in monounsaturated fats, tahini is a good choice for enriching salad dressings and dips. It is even useful in baking (*see Oatmeal Chocolate Chip Cookies, page 304*). Look for it near the peanut butter in large supermarkets or in natural-foods stores.

TOFU is made by heating soymilk with a curdling agent in a process similar to dairy cheesemaking. To make silken tofu, the curds are allowed to stand and thicken. When stirred and separated from the whey, the pressed curds, with their spongier texture, are known as water-packed or "regular" tofu. Silken tofu is delicate and custardlike, perfect for pureeing and using in dressings and smoothies. Extra-firm water-packed tofu is ideal for stir-fries, sautés and grilling.

TOMATILLOS look like small green tomatoes covered by a parchment-like husk. Often found in salsas and salads, they can be used raw but cooking enhances the flavor and softens the tough outer skin. Look for them near the tomatoes in markets.

VEGETABLE BROTH Commercial vegetable broth is readily available in natural-foods stores and many supermarkets. We like the Imagine and Pacific brands, sold in convenient aseptic packages that allow you to use small amounts and keep the rest refrigerated.

WHOLE-WHEAT PASTRY FLOUR, lower in protein than regular whole-wheat, has less gluten-forming potential (needed for bread) but is a better choice for tender baked goods. You can find it in large supermarkets and natural-foods stores. Store in the freezer.

Cooking Tips

BERRIES, TO FREEZE: Wash berries and pat dry. Spread in a single layer on a tray, cover with plastic wrap and freeze until solid. Pack frozen fruit into ziplock bags, taking care to remove air from the bags. Freeze for up to 1 year.

CHOCOLATE, TO MELT (STOVETOP): Bring 1 inch of water to a simmer in a double boiler set over medium-high heat, then place chocolate in the top pan. (*Alternatively, to improvise a double boiler, place chocolate in a heat-safe mixing bowl that fits snugly over a pan with 1 inch of simmering water.*) Stir until half the chocolate has melted. Remove the bowl and continue stirring until the chocolate has fully melted. Cool for 5 minutes at room temperature.

(MICROWAVE): Place the chocolate in a microwave-safe bowl and microwave on High for 1 minute. Stir well, then continue microwaving in 30-second increments on High until two-thirds of the chocolate has melted, stirring well after each heating. Remove the bowl and continue stirring until all the chocolate has melted. Cool for 5 minutes at room temperature.

EGGS, EGG WHITES AT ROOM TEMPERATURE: To bring cold eggs to room temperature quickly, place in a mixing bowl and set it in a larger bowl of warm water for a few minutes; the eggs will beat to a greater volume.

EGGS, TO SEPARATE: Use an egg separator, an inexpensive gadget found in cookware stores; separating eggs by passing the yolk back and forth between pieces of eggshell or your hands can expose the eggs to bacteria.

MANGO, TO PEEL & CUT: Slice both ends off the mango, revealing the long, slender seed inside. Set the fruit upright on a work surface and remove the skin with a sharp knife. With the seed perpendicular to you, slice the fruit from both sides of the seed, yielding two large pieces. Turn the seed parallel to you and slice the two smaller pieces of fruit from each side. Cut the fruit into the desired shape.

SQUASH, TO PEEL: Fresh winter squash can be difficult to peel and cut. To soften the skin slightly, pierce squash in several places with a fork. Microwave on high for 45 to 60 seconds, heating it just long enough to slightly steam the skin, not actually cook the flesh. Easier still, buy ready-peeled squash in season or cubed frozen squash.

SQUASH, TO ROAST & PUREE: Preheat oven to 400°F. Cut squash (butternut, buttercup, acorn) in half and scrape out seeds and membranes. Oil a baking sheet with sides and place squash on it, cut-side down. Bake until soft, 35 to 45 minutes for buttercup or acorn squash, 40 to 50 minutes for butternut. Let cool slightly, then scoop flesh into a food processor. Pulse until smooth. For a chunkier texture, mash squash with a potato masher. A 2-pound butternut squash yields about 2 cups puree. A 2-pound buttercup or acorn squash yields about 1½ cups puree.

Index

Page numbers in italics indicate photographs.

Contributors

Our thanks to the fine food writers whose work was previously published in EATINGWELL *Magazine.*

Allen, Darina: Whole-Wheat Irish Soda Bread, 72

Baggett, Nancy: Chocolate Cappuccino Wafers, 300

Bittman, Mark: Broiled Halibut with Miso Glaze, 192

Blanchard, Nanette: Jícama & Orange Salad, 115; Southwestern Corn & Zucchini Sauté, 243

Brennan, Georgeanne: Spicy Mushroom & Rice Soup, 103

Calta, Marialisa: Spinach Salad with Goat Cheese & Pine Nuts, 112; Asian Chicken Salad, 153

Chesman, Andrea: Low-Sugar Plum Spread, 60

Compestine, Ying Chang: Curried Chicken Wraps, 178

Danford, Natalie: Spicy Cornmeal-Crusted Catfish, 196

Evans, Mary Ellen: Fragrant Bulgur Pilaf, 236

Farrell-Kingsley, Kathy: Roasted Apple Butter, 61; Roasted Corn, Black Bean & Mango Salad, 118; Chicken Breasts with Roasted Lemons, 148; Curry-Roasted Shrimp with Oranges, 202; Curried Corn & Crab Cakes, 206; Pork Tenderloin with Roasted Plums & Rosemary, 227; Herbed Corn & Edamame Succotash, 242; Spiced Corn & Rice Pilaf, 247; Roasted Pineapple Shortcakes, 274

Fletcher, Janet: Whole-Wheat Spaghetti with Roasted Onions & Chard, 143

Fritschner, Sarah: Curried Corn Bisque, 102; Mediterranean Lima Beans, 245

Goldman, Marcy: Lamb Chops with a Mustard Crust, 210

Haedrich, Ken: Spiced Apple Butter Bran Muffins, 69

Hendley, Joyce: Ingrid's Muesli, 58; Nil & Tonic, 90; Mango-Tea Cooler, 90; Sparkling Mary, 90; Cranberry Sunrise, 90; Iced Cinnamocha, 90; Baja-Style Shrimp, 193; Shrimp with Artichokes & Lemon, 201; Black Beans & Barley, 255

Herr, Susan: Baked Curried Brown Rice & Lentil Pilaf, 249

Jamieson, Patsy: Pear Butter, 61; Maple Nut & Pear Scones, 71; Triple-Rich Whole-Wheat Bread, 74; Asian Peanut Dip, 80; Carrot Cake, 297

Kalen, Wendy: Indian Vegetable Stew, 141

Madison, Deborah: Open-Face Spinach, Mushroom & Pine Nut Sandwiches, 129; Brussels Sprouts with Shallots & Walnuts, 240; Peppers Stuffed with Zucchini & Corn, 246

Meyers, Perla: Salmon with Cucumbers & Dill, 195

Niall, Mani: Nanan's Gingerbread (adapted from *Covered in Honey*; Rodale, 2003), 295

Piraino, Marie: Berry-Ricotta Cheesecake, 293

Raichlen, Steven: Shrimp Spedini with Basil & Peppers (adapted from *Steven Raichlen's Big Flavor Cookbook*; Black Dog & Leventhal Publishers, 2003), 189; Coconut-Curry Salmon Kebabs, 190

Riccardi, Victoria Abbott: Chickpea-Spinach Salad with Spiced Yogurt Dressing, 114; Chicken Fricassee with Tarragon, 154; Wild Rice with Shiitakes & Toasted Almonds, 248; Old-Fashioned Apple-Nut Crisp, 275

Romagnoli, Franco: Italian Seafood Stew, 194

Sands, Brinna: Whole-Wheat Flax Bread, 75

Schrambling, Regina: Bulgur-Chickpea Pilaf, 251; Quinoa with Sun-Dried Tomatoes, 253

Scicolone, Michele: Lentil & Escarole Soup, 98; Broccoli Rabe with Chickpeas, 238

Simmons, Marie: Zucchini Frittata, 48; Scrambled Egg Burritos, 59; Parmesan Crisps, 85; Tamari Walnuts, 87; Salmon Roasted with Tomatoes & Olives, 203; Rosemary & Garlic Crusted Pork Loin with Butternut Squash & Potatoes, 225; Black Bean & Tomato Salsa, 267

Sterling, Richard: Green Mango Salad, 115

Weinstein, Bruce & Mark Scarbrough: Chili Pecans, 88; Asian Slaw with Tofu & Shiitake Mushrooms, 108; Honey-Mustard Vinaigrette, 120; Squash Pie, 289; Double-Chocolate Biscotti, 303; Oatmeal Chocolate Chip Cookies, 304